NEXT MOVE

TEACHER'S BOOK
WITH MULTI-ROM

1

TIMOTHY JOHN FOSTER

Contents

Introduction

Welcome to *Next Move*! This four-level course allows students to use twenty-first century skills to expand their knowledge across the curriculum and positions the learning of English within a framework of culture and citizenship. It provides students and their teachers with a range of dynamic, new digital and print materials for use in class and at home. The rich combination of online, offline and digital content creates an environment that is fun, fast-moving and familiar for students who are *digital natives*. And for their less digitally native teachers, or *digital tourists*, it provides a user-friendly tool which enhances the teaching experience.

Next Move embraces a holistic approach to the education of today's students. It provides them with a solid grounding in core knowledge of the English language combined with crucial twenty-first century skills. Within the context of contemporary themes, students develop the essential skills for success in today's world, such as creativity and innovation, critical thinking, problem solving, communication and collaboration. Because we now live in a technology and media-driven environment, with access to an abundance of information, students need to be skilled not just in manipulating the technological tools with which to do the research but also in analysing and evaluating the information they discover.

The clear, classroom-based methodology incorporates the concept of multiple intelligences as outlined by Howard Gardner in 1983 thereby encouraging every child, whatever their learning style, to develop both their cognitive and language skills, to be educated in the round (see page 8).

Please go to www.pearsonelt.com/NextMove for a full description of the course and further resources.

About the methodology

Motivation

Next Move captures students' attention by setting the content and approach of the course firmly within the world of the modern teenager. The core subjects and twenty-first century themes such as global awareness and citizenship engage students' curiosity. The topics promote social and cross-cultural awareness while the approach helps them to develop initiative and self-direction.

In this way students benefit not just in terms of improvement in their language competence but also in terms of their life and career skills.

Digital look and feel

There is one key difference that makes students today different from students a decade ago. That is that students today are *digital natives*, to use the term coined by author Marc Prensky in 2001. In simple terms, the students using this course have never known a life before digital technologies were commonplace, while their teachers most definitely have. Teenagers today have grown up with technology all around them, and life without the internet, mobile phones, games consoles, touch-sensitive tablet computers, MP3 players, social networking sites and the like seems unimaginable to them. They do not necessarily see the digital world as 'unreal' and the rest of the world as 'real' in the same way as previous generations, they are used to receiving and evaluating large quantities of information at great speed, they multitask and they are comfortable jumping rapidly from one topic or area to another.

This type of student will feel comfortable with the various modes of delivery employed in *Next Move*, whether via downloadable, interactive digital or online platforms, and so be empowered to achieve more than ever before.

So what does this mean for teachers today? Obviously we need to update our vocabulary to be able to talk fluently about the world that these digital natives come from, we need to find points of reference and comparison between our world and theirs, and we need to update our teaching materials and techniques. The *Next Move* course aims to motivate digital natives through the modern design, regular changes of pace and focus, and references to and examples of familiar digital media such as email, social networking and webpages. The user-friendly format enables less digitally-native teachers (*digital tourists*) to manage the materials with ease.

Inductive grammar

Next Move uses an inductive approach to grammar presentation. Rather than merely presenting grammar rules for students to memorise, students are asked to examine the grammatical forms, think about their use in context and complete for themselves some of the key rules relating to each grammar point. This student-centred approach, in which students learn by doing rather than learn by being told, involves students more deeply in the process of learning and understanding and helps assimilation of the rules.

Visual approach to vocabulary

Extensive use is made of illustration to present new vocabulary, twice in each Students' Book unit to introduce the topic as well as in the additional, extension vocabulary reference section at the back of the Workbook.

Mixed ability

Next Move is designed to address each student of whatever profile or level as an individual so that even those in large, mixed-ability classes will thrive. Wherever possible, suggestions have been made to help teachers working with mixed-ability groups. Workbook activities are provided at three levels of difficulty while the tests and photocopiable materials are available at two levels. With this range of materials, a wide range of levels within the same class can be catered for as well as different learning styles. See pages 8–9 for information about Multiple Intelligences and Learning Styles.

Course components

Students' Book	Workbook (+ audio CD)	Class Audio
Starter Unit	Starter unit	Students' Book audio
Nine units of one lesson per page	Units 1–9	
Three Review units	Three Check your Progress	**ActiveTeach (for whiteboards)**
Nine Brain Trainer pages	Language Reference and Practice	Students' Book pages
Six Culture pages		Class audio and audioscripts
	Teacher's Book	DVD and audioscripts
MyEnglishLab	Introduction	DVD worksheets
Digital practice:	Unit-by-unit Teaching Notes	Photocopiable worksheets
Starter Unit	Interleaved Students' Book pages	Tests
Units 1–9	Workbook Answer Key	Tests audio and audioscripts
Three Progress Tests	Audioscripts (SB and WB)	Writing page from Workbook as PDF
Language Reference		Mini dictionary
Grammar and Punctuation Tips	**Teacher's Resource Multi-ROM**	WB audio and audioscripts
Word list, Irregular Verb List,	Tests	Grammar Reference from Workbook
Phonetics Chart, Grammar Reference	Tests audio	Irregular verb list
Workbook audio	Photocopiable worksheets	Phonetic chart
		Games (two per unit)
		Access to *MyEnglishLab*

About the Students' Book

At the centre of the course is the Students' Book itself, which contains a host of innovative and motivating features to make your classes a real success.

The Students' Book begins with a *Starter unit*, which introduces some of the key points in *Next Move* and helps students refresh their studies from previous courses.

There are nine main Students' Book units, each of which contains ten pages:

Page 1 *Vocabulary* – Students are introduced to the topic of the unit through motivating work on an extended lexical set. The lexis is presented and practised systematically and extensive use is made of illustration to help students understand and assimilate the vocabulary.

Page 3 *Grammar* – The first grammar point of the unit, which has been indirectly introduced in the preceding reading text, is presented. Deductive concept questions help students reach a deeper understanding of the grammar before they move on to a series of carefully organised controlled and freer-practice activities.

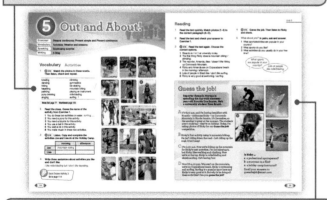

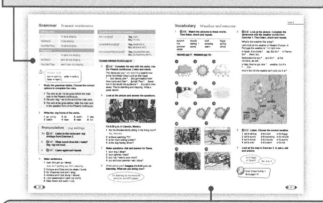

Page 2 *Reading* – The topic is developed further and the vocabulary recycled through an extended reading text related to the theme of the unit. Comprehension is fully checked through a variety of activities, including sentence completion, traditional questions and *True or False?* questions.

Page 4 *Vocabulary* – The second vocabulary page of the unit covers another lexical set related to the topic of the unit. The total number of lexical items introduced per unit is around thirty, approximately half on each vocabulary page.

Page 5–6 *Chatroom* – This double-page feature in each unit follows a group of teenagers of a similar age to the students through a variety of situations. Through an extended conversation, students focus on an area of functional language in context and are given controlled and freer practice. The feature also includes a second grammar focus, indirectly introduced in the conversation and followed by a variety of practice activities. Teenage idiomatic language is highlighted in the 'Say it in your language …' box.

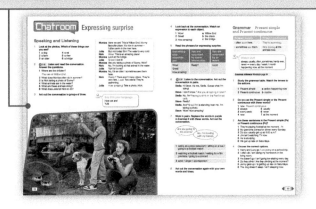

Page 7 *Reading* and *Listening* – This page further develops the topic of the unit and gives extended work on these key skills. Students work first on an extended reading text before moving on to the listening section. The comprehension of both sections is checked through a wide range of activities.

Page 8 *Writing* – This page works intensively on a specific text type. Students work with a model text, reading it for meaning before moving on to analyse the structure and features of the text type. The final task is to write a text of their own, using the model to support them.

Page 9 *Refresh Your Memory!* – Each unit concludes with a page of review exercises, covering grammar, vocabulary, speaking and dictation. At the end of each page, students are referred to their *Assessment Profile* which relates their work to the 'Can do …' statements of the Common European Framework and is designed to help students become more autonomous learners.

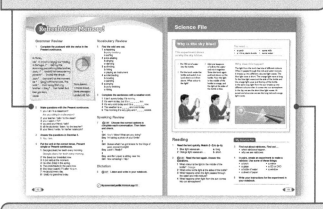

Page 10 *… File* – Odd-numbered units include a *… File*, essentially a *CLIL* page working on a cross-curricular area, loosely related to the theme of the unit. There is a reading text which presents the topic and appropriate activities to check comprehension before students work on a related project themselves.

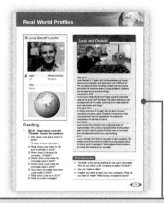

Even-numbered units include a *Real World Profile*, which works extensively on citizenship. These pages present a teenager of a similar age to the students who has made an important contribution to society as a whole and give opportunities for extended discussion on the topic.

Each unit also contains a *Pronunciation* focus, related either to individual sounds or to features of connected speech. The exact location of this section varies depending on the area being covered.

After every three units there are extended *Review* sections to identify any areas which are causing your students particular problems and to provide them with timely revision.

The Students' Book also includes an innovative *Brain Trainer* section designed to appeal to multiple intelligences and learner types.

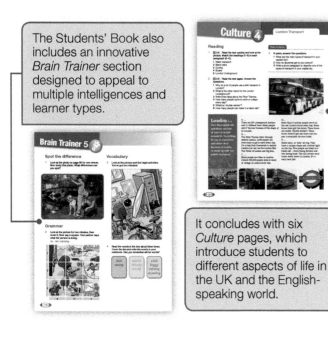

It concludes with six *Culture* pages, which introduce students to different aspects of life in the UK and the English-speaking world.

Other components

MyEnglishLab

The digital workbook for *Next Move* is a complete and comprehensive set of practice materials for the student to use independently at home or in the digital classroom. It provides students with reinforcement and extra practice of grammar, vocabulary and skills through a wide range of exercises and varied activity types. While in structure it mirrors the Students' Book, MyEnglishLab also provides students with an extensive full-colour reference section covering Grammar, Speaking and Listening and Pronunciation. It is ideal for mixed-ability groups as activities are classified with stars according to their level of difficulty. It should be possible for all students to complete the one-star activities, while two-star activities are aimed at the average students.

Work is assigned digitally and student scores are recorded in the Gradebook to be monitored by the teacher. Feedback is given by grammar tips at relevant points.

Workbook

The *Next Move* Workbook provides students with reinforcement and extra practice of the grammar, vocabulary and skills at each level through a wide range of exercises and varied activity types. While in structure it mirrors the Students' Book, the Workbook also provides students with an extensive full-colour reference section covering Grammar, Vocabulary, Speaking and Listening, Pronunciation and Self Assessment.

The Workbook can be used either in class, to keep fast-finishers or stronger students busy, or as homework. It is ideal for mixed-ability groups as activities are classified with one, two or three stars according to their level of difficulty. It should be possible for all students to complete the one-star activities, while two-star activities are aimed at the average students and three-star activities should be reserved for those students who need an additional challenge.

Teacher's Resource and Tests Multi-ROM

The wide range of photocopiable material contained on the Teacher's Resource Multi-ROM supplements and practises further the language presented in the Students' Book itself. Much of this material is offered at two levels of difficulty. One-star activities are for students who need extra help and support; two-star activities are for students who require an additional challenge. As this material is photocopiable, a teacher can grade the activities to the level of the group or to particular students in the case of a group with a spread of levels.

The *Teacher's Resource Multi-ROM* contains:
- *Grammar and Vocabulary worksheets* at two levels of difficulty;
- *Reading and Listening worksheets* at two levels of difficulty;
- *Writing worksheets* offering guided writing practice and model texts;
- *Speaking worksheets* designed for use individually or in pairs.

The final section of the *Teacher's Resource* material is a comprehensive collection of Tests which consist of:
- an initial *Diagnostic Test* to allow teachers to assess how familiar students are with the grammar and vocabulary presented in the Starter Unit;
- nine *Language Tests* to check the grammar, vocabulary and speaking items within each of the nine core units;
- three *Skills Tests* for use after each three units to test general progress, language proficiency and fluency;
- an *End Of Year Test* for use at the end of the course covering items from the whole level;
- a full answer key.

Apart from the Diagnostic Test all the tests are at two levels of difficulty so teachers can test more appropriately and offer the correct level of challenge. All the tests are provided in A and B versions which are different in content as well as in order of presentation.

The *Teacher's Resource Multi-ROM* also contains the Workbook audio.

ActiveTeach

For teachers working with digital natives, the ActiveTeach software for Interactive Whiteboards will really help bring classes alive. This interactive version of the class materials will allow you to:

- focus students' attention on the task in hand and keep their heads up and out of their books in class;
- clarify instructions and the mechanics of activities quickly and efficiently;
- complete exercises and check answers in a fun and motivating way;
- make sure that weaker students do not fall behind or get lost during the class;
- access all the multimedia resources with a few simple clicks;
- select and print worksheets from the Teacher's Resource File;
- plan work and keep track of individual students' progress.

This powerful and flexible tool provides everything needed for the fully digital classroom and in such a way that even the most peripatetic *digital tourist* teacher will be able to use it with ease.

About the Teacher's Book

This Teacher's Book contains unit objectives, cross references to other course components, full teacher's notes, answer keys and extra activities interleaved with the pages of the Students' Book itself for quick and easy reference. At the end of the Teacher's Book are the audioscripts for the listening activities in the Students' Book and a full answer key and audioscripts for the Workbook. In short, everything you need to prepare and teach your classes in one easy reference guide.

Extra activities

There are a range of 'no-preparation' extra activities in the Teacher's Book notes which extend or revise points from the Students' Book itself. The majority of these are self-explanatory, but the following five are worthy of some further comment.

Mixed ability

Wherever possible, suggestions have been made to help teachers working with mixed-ability groups. As you get to know your students, you will come to learn which students work faster and which more slowly, and can therefore start to use the suggested activities to occupy the stronger students and fast finishers thereby giving weaker students time to complete the tasks in the Students' Book without feeling that all eyes are on them. Before using these activities do check though that fast finishers have also been accurate in their work. Should you find that they have completed a task quickly but with a lot of errors then, before giving them an additional task, have them review their work, check it thoroughly and self-correct.

Live listening

Extended teacher talk time is often regarded in the modern classroom very negatively. However the students' inherent interest in their teacher and his or her world can be exploited most effectively through live-listening activities and such activities can also provide a much needed change of focus and pace in the classroom.

The key to a live-listening activity is that the teacher should provide a natural and realistic model of spoken language while students complete a relatively simple task. Language can of course be graded, taking into account the level of the students, and grammar and vocabulary can be recycled. However over-preparing or reading aloud a written text destroys the spontaneity in these activities. When talking to your group, make sure you make eye contact as much as possible and use natural pronunciation and rhythm. Bear in mind that what you tell your class does not have to be true, in fact, in order to maximise recycling of grammar and vocabulary, it is often more useful if it is fictional.

When a model text has been provided, this should be taken as an example only. Take the basic ideas and the basic structure but make it your own and bring it to life for your students. Due to space limitations, a model text cannot always be included. When activities contain questions for the students to answer, do make sure that you cover all those areas when speaking.

Dictation

There are a variety of additional dictation activities in the Teacher's Book notes which can be used to help students develop their understanding of sound-spelling relationships. When using these dictation activities, make sure that you provide a realistic pronunciation model at all times. Repeat the sentences as many times as necessary, with natural pronunciation and intonation and at a natural speed. Use the audio recording if you are not confident of your own spoken English as a model. If students are not completely successful in writing down what you are saying, this is not a problem. What is essential is that students hear a realistic model of the pronunciation at various times, which, during the checking stage, they can relate to the written form. At the end of each dictation activity, write the sentences on the board for students to check their answers and then highlight for them particular features of the pronunciation of each sentence (assimilation, intrusion, consonant clusters, etc.) which may have caused them problems.

Drilling

Throughout the Teacher's Book suggestions are made for drilling. There are numerous variations on drilling, the value of which should never be underestimated. Experiment with drilling techniques, for example:

forward drilling – drill phonetically, starting at the beginning of the sentence and adding one more syllable each time, e.g.

/maɪ/ ('My …')
/maɪ neɪm/ ('My name …')
/maɪ neɪm ɪz/ ('My name is …')
/maɪ neɪm ɪz dʒəʊ/ ('My name is Joe.')

or *backward* drilling – drill phonetically, starting at the end of the sentence, e.g.

/tə/ ('… tor.')
/dɒktə/ ('… doctor.')
/ə dɒktə/ ('… a doctor.')
/ʃiːz ə dɒktə/ ('She's a doctor.')

When working on a conversation, either take one role yourself or divide the class in half or into three groups and work in sequence on each line of the conversation building towards a final 'performance'.

Consider also telling students to cover the text while you are working on pronunciation. The complex sound-spelling relationships in English confuse many students and there can be serious L1 interference when students look at the written form. Removing the visual reference often results in a notable improvement in students' pronunciation.

Pronunciation

As well as drills there are many other suggestions for revision and extension of pronunciation work in the Teacher's Book. For successful communication it is very important that students can understand a wide variety of native and non-native speakers. Students usually have considerably more problems understanding native speakers of English than understanding people who are using English as a second language so regular pronunciation work in class really helps students understand how native speakers use the language. Students will reap many benefits from this in the long term, most notably an improvement in listening comprehension resulting from a deeper knowledge of sounds and how these relate to spelling.

Multiple Intelligences

In 1983 Howard Gardner, an American developmental psychologist, outlined the concept of multiple intelligences as an alternative to traditional definitions of intelligence as expressed by IQ. The debate about how many intelligences exist and their precise classification continues today but it is generally agreed that there are a minimum of seven:

Visual/Spatial Intelligence

Profile: sees things with the mind's eye; thinks in pictures and creates mental images to help memory; enjoys looking at visually intricate materials

Typical skills: understanding charts, graphs and plans; good sense of direction; drawing, sketching and painting; designing practical objects; interpreting and creating visual images; good at solving puzzles

Typical careers: architect, artist, sculptor, designer, inventor, mechanic, engineer

Verbal/Linguistic Intelligence

Profile: adept at using words and language; highly developed listening skills; generally thinks in words rather than images; enjoys reading and writing and story telling

Typical skills: good at discussing, debating and arguing points; note reading, writing and note taking; memorising information and dates; able to learn and analyse both their own and foreign languages

Typical careers: lawyer, journalist, writer, teacher, politician, translator, poet

Logical/Mathematical Intelligence

Profile: connects pieces of information by looking for patterns; asks lots of questions; likes to experiment; reasons logically; often has a high IQ

Typical skills: excellent with numerical, mathematical activities and computer programming; able to handle long, complicated sequences of information; good at geometry

Typical careers: scientist, IT programmer, accountant, mathematician, doctor, economist

Bodily/Kinaesthetic Intelligence

Profile: uses physical interaction with objects or space to process information; responds to getting up and moving around; may become restless if not given a chance to move

Typical skills: good muscle control leading to capacity to minutely control body movements and handle delicate objects; good at making things; advanced muscle memory; good hand-eye coordination

Typical careers: athlete, dancer, actor, firefighter, surgeon, soldier, pilot

Musical/Rhythmic Intelligence

Profile: highly sensitised to sounds, rhythms and tones; well developed language skills; sensitive to background sounds; responds to music and can talk about it critically

Typical skills: singing and playing musical instruments; memory for complex rhythmic and melodic patterns; understands music, rhythm and structure; perfect musical pitch

Typical careers: musician, singer, conductor, composer, writer, public speaker

Interpersonal Intelligence

Profile: relates to others and able to see things from their point of view; extremely sensitive to other people's emotions and moods; enjoys discussion or debate; extroverted

Typical skills: good organisation; is cooperative in groups and acts as peace-maker; good at communicating verbally and non verbally using body language and eye contact

Typical careers: social worker, manager, businessperson, sales representative

Intrapersonal Intelligence

Profile: tends towards self-reflection and analysis of strengths and weaknesses; introverted; often intuitive; has a profound understanding of self; prefers to work alone

Typical skills: good at understanding and recognising feelings and emotions; well-developed awareness of strengths and weaknesses; realistic about their role in the world

Typical careers: researcher, philosopher, writer, lawyer

Naturally, developing an awareness of intelligence type can help teachers support students in their studies and in their future career decisions.

Learning Styles

Additional studies by Neil Fleming establish a model, usually referred to as VAK, which specifically deals with the way learners interact with information. This model focuses on three basic learning styles which should also be considered in any classroom situation:

Visual Learners

… like to see information expressed as maps, charts, graphs, diagrams and mind maps. Clear and logical use of pictures, colour, font, layout and graphics keep them focused. They learn well with activities which involve drawing lines, arrows and circles, and underlining, highlighting and crossing out.

Auditory Learners

… like to hear information and learn best from listening and pronunciation activities, teacher talk time and group and pair discussion work. They tend to deal with language as they speak rather than before which means they may make mistakes but these are a key part of their learning process.

Kinaesthetic/Tactile Learners

… respond best to 'reality' be it through demonstration, simulations or video of the physical world. They may have difficulty learning by reading or listening and will retain information better when they are free to move. They will respond well to activities with micro-movement in class such as games and card matching activities.

Catering for diversity in the classroom is a key objective in *Next Move* which has been written to include the widest possible range of material for students of all intelligences and learner types. All the activities in *Next Move* have been designed to ensure maximum variety in order to ensure that all students get the most out of the course.

The *Brain Trainer* material at the end of the Students' Book allows you to focus a little more consciously on multiple intelligences and learning styles in the classroom. Raise awareness after completing each activity by asking students how easy or difficult they found the activity and gradually helping them understand what type of learner they are.

Learning Styles Test

At the beginning of the course, use the following test to get a general idea about your students' preferences. This also serves as an introduction for them to the basic idea of learning styles and helps them understand that the *Brain Trainer* section is not merely another collection of grammar and vocabulary activities, but rather a way to find out about themselves and learn how to learn more effectively.

Tell the students to write the numbers 1–30 on a piece of paper and tell them that you are going to ask them 30 simple questions to which they must answer simply *yes* or *no*. Read the following questions in students' L1, repeating them as necessary.

Ask students to divide their answers into three groups, 1–10, 11–20, 21–30. They count up how many times they wrote *yes* in each group. Tell students who have the majority of *yes* answers in the first block (1–10) to stand up and explain that they are predominantly *visual* learners. Repeat the procedure with the second block (11–20) for the *auditory* learners and finally with the third block for the *kinaesthetic/tactile* learners. Point out that within the class there are a range of learner types and that the Students' Book has material for all of them.

1 Are you good at using maps?
2 Do you remember people's faces even if you've only seen them once or twice?
3 Are you good at spelling?
4 Do you like clothes and fashion?
5 Can you understand charts and diagrams quickly?
6 Is it difficult for you to study when it is noisy?
7 Do you like using different colour pens?
8 Do you dream in colour?
9 Do you read a lot outside class?
10 Do you often write letters or emails?
11 Do you like studying with other people?
12 Are you good at explaining things?
13 Do you spend a long time talking on the phone?
14 Do you like discussing things in class?
15 Do you often hum or sing to yourself?
16 Do you like listening to the radio?
17 Are you good at remembering people's names?
18 Do you like hearing people telling stories?
19 Do you like acting?
20 Are you happy talking in front of groups of people?
21 Do you like making things?
22 Are you good at sports and physical activities?
23 Is your handwriting a bit messy?
24 Do you like making models and building things?
25 Are you a good dancer?
26 Do you like Science classes?
27 Do you do activities like martial arts?
28 If you buy something new, do you ignore the instructions and start to use it immediately?
29 Is it difficult for you to sit still for long?
30 Has anybody ever told you you're hyperactive?

Contents

■ Curriculum File   ■ Real World Profiles

◀ 3 ▶

Starter Unit

Vocabulary

Countries and Nationalities

1 Match the countries (1–8) to the nationalities (a–h).

Country	Nationality
1 Spain	a Greek
2 England	b Mexican
3 Brazil	c French
4 France	d Portuguese
5 Italy	e English
6 Portugal	f Spanish
7 Mexico	g Brazilian
8 Greece	h Italian

2 Match the countries from Exercise 1 to the letters (a–h) on the map. Do you know any other countries?

a *England*

Numbers

3 Do the sums. Write the answer.
1 fifteen + twenty-six *forty-one*
2 one hundred and twelve – nineteen
3 eighty-five + seventy-nine
4 one thousand and six – eleven
5 sixty-one + six hundred and two

```
  15
+ 26
―――
  41
```

4 1.2   Listen. Write the numbers you hear in your notebook.

Spelling

5 1.3   Say the letters to spell these words. Listen and check.
1 B-R-A-Z-I-L-I-A-N
2 E-L-E-V-E-N
3 B-A-C-K-P-A-C-K
4 M-P-3 P-L-A-Y-E-R
5 S-E-C-O-N-D-A-R-Y

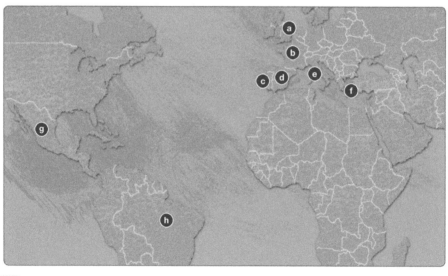

Exercise 6
2 dictionary/book
3 shelf
4 backpack
5 chair
6 notebooks
7 rulers
8 pens
9 pencil
10 rubber
11 calculators

Classroom Objects

6 Look for one minute. Remember and write the objects in your notebook.
1 *interactive whiteboard*

Exercise 7
Point out to students that days of the week have capital letters in English.

Tuesday, Wednesday, Thursday, Friday, Saturday, Sunday

Exercise 9
2 S **3** S/T **4** T
5 S **6** T **7** T
8 S/T **9** S

Days of the Week and Months of the Year

7 Put the days in the correct order. Which is your favourite day?
- Wednesday
- Saturday
- Friday
- Sunday
- Monday *1*
- Tuesday
- Thursday

8 Find four months in each line.
1 cow*november*armarchapplejanuarybreaddecember
2 daycookjuneolyaprilgremondayoctoberpencilljuly
3 februarygreenmayaugustairportcarseptember

Classroom Language

9 🔊 1.4 Match the sentences to the speaker. Is it student (S) or teacher (T)? Listen and repeat.
1 Open your books! *T*
2 Can you repeat …, please?
3 How do you spell …?
4 Listen carefully.
5 I'm sorry, I don't understand.
6 Please be quiet!
7 Check your answers.
8 How do you say … in English?
9 What's the homework?

5

Exercise 8
Point out to students that months of the year have capital letters in English.
1 *November*, March, January, December
2 June, April, October, July
3 February, May, August, September

Grammar

To be

1   **Study the grammar table.**

Affirmative	Negative
I'm (am)	I'm not
You're (are)	You aren't (are not)
He's (is)	He isn't (is not)
She's (is)	She isn't (is not)
It's (is)	It isn't (is not)
We're (are)	We aren't (are not)
They're (are)	They aren't (are not)
Questions and short answers	
Am I ...?	Yes, I am / No, I'm not.
Is he/she/it ...?	Yes, he/she/it is. No, he/she/it isn't.
Are you/we/they...?	Yes, you/we/they are. No, you/we/they aren't.

Watch Out!
Subject pronouns
- I
- You
- He
- She
- It
- We
- They

Exercise 2
2 aren't
3 am
4 Are
5 are

2   **Choose the correct options.**
1 My friend Leo *is / are* American.
2 We *aren't / isn't* from London. We are Spanish.
3 I *are / am* in a new class.
4 *Is / Are* they at the park?
5 You *is / are* in the classroom!

3   **Complete the sentences.**
1 He *is* a boy but she .... a boy, she .... a girl!
2 .... he a doctor?
3 I .... French, I'm Italian. I come from Milan.
4 .... you twelve years old? You are very tall!
5 .... it a cat? No, I think it's a dog.
6 You .... in Class 6 with Miss Taylor.

Exercise 3
1 *is*; isn't/is not; 's/is
2 Is
3 'm not/am not
4 Are
5 Is
6 're/are

Wh- questions

4   **Study the grammar table.**

wh- questions
What's your name?
Where are you from?
How old are you?
When is your birthday?
Why are you happy?
Who is your sister?

5   **Complete the questions.**
1 *Where* is Paris?
   It's in France. Paris is the capital of France.
2 .... is your brother?
   He's fifteen. And my little sister is two.
3 .... is that?
   It's a bicycle.
4 .... are you happy?
   I am happy because it's my birthday today.
5 .... is your best friend?
   My best friend is Pedro.
6 .... is Halloween?
   In October.

Exercise 5
2 How old
3 What
4 Why
5 Who
6 When

6   **Make questions.**
1 name / What's / your ?
   What's your name?
2 you / from / Where / are ?
3 How / are / you / old ?
4 is / your / birthday / When ?
5 you / happy / Why / are ?
6 Who / best friend / your / is ?

7   **In pairs, ask and answer the questions in Exercise 6.**

Exercise 6
2 Where are you from?
3 How old are you?
4 When is your birthday?
5 Why are you happy?
6 Who is your best friend?

This/That/These/Those

8 Study the grammar table.

Singular		Plural	
This is a pen.		These are rubbers.	
That is a desk.		Those are chairs.	

9 Look at the picture below. Say *this*, *that*, *these* or *those*.

1 *That* is an interactive whiteboard.
2 .... are backpacks.
3 .... are chairs.
4 .... are pens.
5 .... is a pencil.
6 .... are rubbers.
7 .... are rulers.
8 .... is a calculator.

Watch Out!

This is a pen. NOT ~~This is pen.~~
These are chairs. NOT ~~These are a chairs.~~

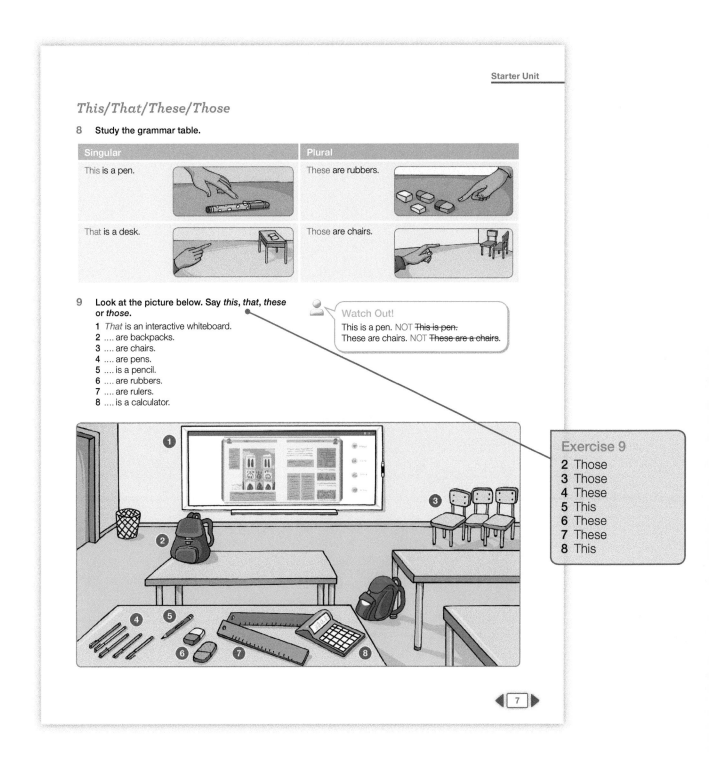

Exercise 9

2 Those
3 Those
4 These
5 This
6 These
7 These
8 This

7

Exercise 1
Three people – Nick, Julia and Leo

Reading

1 Look at the text. How many people are in the Wildlife Club?

Welcome to ....
The Wildlife Club!

- The Wildlife Club ... **what** is it?
  It's a great nature club at our school.
- The Wildlife Club ... **when** is it?
  It's on Thursday afternoons, from 3.30 to 4.30.
- The Wildlife Club ... **who** is in it?
  Say hello to our Wildlife Club members!

I'm Nick. I'm in Year 9 and I'm 13 years old. My favourite animal is my dog, Sunny. The Wildlife Club is cool! Wildlife and nature are very important for me.

I'm Julia and this is my brother, Leo. I'm 12 and Leo is 8. He is in the Wildlife Club because animals and nature are his favourite things.

2 🔊 1.5 Read the text again. Are the sentences true (T) or false (F)?
1 The Wildlife Club is an arts club. *F*
2 The Wildlife Club is on Friday afternoons.
3 Nick is 13 years old.
4 Sunny is a rabbit.
5 Leo and Julia are friends.

Exercise 2
1 *False* (The Wildlife Club is a nature club.)
2 False (The Wildlife Club is on Thursday afternoons, from 3.30–4.30.)
3 True
4 False (Sunny is Nick's dog.)
5 False (Leo is Julia's brother.)

Exercises 3 and 4
Monica is the new member of the Wildlife Club.

Exercise 6
1 True
2 False (Nick is in Year 9.)
3 True

Starter Unit

Listening and Speaking

3 Look at the photo. Find the new member of the Wildlife Club.

4))) 1.6 Listen to the conversation. Who is the new member?

5))) 1.6 Listen to the conversation again and complete the form.

6))) 1.6 Listen to the conversation again. Are these sentences true (T) or false (F)?
1 Monica is in Year 8.
2 Nick is in Year 8.
3 Sunny is in the Wildlife Club.

7 In pairs, ask and answer to complete your profile.

Exercise 5
Age 12
Class Year 8 (Note: in this case 'Year 8' is the same as 'Class 8')
Favourite animal otters

Exercise 7
Students' own answers

Wildlife Club
New Member Form

Name [Monica]
Age [....]
Class [....]

What's your favourite animal?

[....]

Wildlife Club
New Member Form

Name [....]
Age [....]
Class [....]

What's your favourite animal?

[....]

My assessment profile: Workbook page 126

1 My World

Grammar — *Have got*; Possessive adjectives; Possessive *'s*
Vocabulary — Objects; Adjectives
Speaking — Talking about position
Writing — A personal profile

Vocabulary Objects

1 🔊 1.7 **Match the photos to these words. Then listen, check and repeat.**

camera	comics *1*	DVD
games console	guitar	ice skates
laptop	magazine	mobile phone
MP3 player	poster	skateboard
wallet	watch	

Word list page 43 **Workbook** page 104

2 **Match the definitions to seven objects from Exercise 1.**

1 It's a musical instrument. *guitar*
2 It's a film.
3 It's a computer.
4 It's a small clock.
5 They're stories with superheroes.
6 It's a board with wheels.
7 It's a big picture.

3 🔊 1.8 **Listen and spot the missing letter.**

1 wallet /   3 camera
2 comics   4 skateboard

4 **Think of three words with missing letters. In pairs, ask and answer.**

What letter is missing? W - A - C - H.

It's T.

Good.

⚙ Brain Trainer Activity 3
Go to page 112

Unit contents

Vocabulary
→ Objects – *camera, comics, DVD, games console, guitar, ice skates, laptop, magazine, mobile phone, MP3 player, poster, skateboard, wallet, watch*
→ Adjectives – *bad, big, boring, cheap, difficult, easy, expensive, good, interesting, new, old, popular, small, unpopular*

Grammar
→ *Have got* – affirmative, negative, questions and short answers
→ Possessive adjectives – *my, your, his, her, its, our, their*
→ Possessive apostrophe – *'s* and *s'*

Communication
→ Talking about position
→ Writing – A personal profile; Punctuation – capital letters, full stops, apostrophes

Pronunciation
→ Short forms

Key competences
→ Linguistic competence
→ Interpersonal, social and civic competence
→ Cultural and artistic competences
→ Learning-to-learn
→ Autonomy and personal initiative

Vocabulary　Objects

Exercise 1 (Track 1.7)
- Individually, students match the words and the pictures.
- Play the recording for students to listen and check.
- Repeat the recording. Pause after each word to check students' pronunciation.

Answers
2 camera		9 ice skates	
3 games console		10 magazine	
4 laptop		11 guitar	
5 skateboard		12 mobile phone	
6 wallet		13 MP3 player	
7 watch		14 DVD	
8 poster			

Exercise 2
- In pairs, students match the definitions with the objects.
- Check answers as a class.

Answers
2 DVD	5 comics
3 laptop	6 skateboard
4 watch	7 poster

Extra activity
Stronger groups or fast finishers can write simple definitions for some of the other objects. Monitor and help with grammar and vocabulary if necessary, and encourage students to keep their language simple. They can then read their definitions to the class for the other students to identify the objects.

Exercise 3 (Track 1.8)
- Play the recording once for gist, asking students to identify what it is that they are listening to (Answer: *a radio game show*).
- Revise the alphabet with students.
- Focus on letters which cause students particular difficulty.
- Repeat the recording for students to listen and spot the missing letters.
- Check answers by asking individual students to write the missing letters on the board.

Answers
2 i　3 e　4 a

Exercise 4
- Students write three words with missing letters.
- Monitor and check students' spelling.
- Students work in pairs, asking and answering their missing letter questions.
- When answering questions, students should keep their books closed.
- Encourage them to make appropriate sound effects for correct and incorrect answers.
- Monitor but do not interrupt fluency unless they make mistakes with the spelling.

Extra activity
Write the following as a word snake on the board:
walletskateboardgamesconsoledvdmagazinewatch mp3player
Ask students to find the words in the snake.
(Answers: *wallet, skateboard, games console, DVD, magazine, watch, MP3 player*)
Note that both this activity and the missing letter activity in Exercises 3 and 4 can be re-used at any point during the course when you want students to focus on the spelling of new vocabulary.

Further practice:
Workbook pages 8 and 104

Brain Trainer Activity 3
See Teacher's Book page 210 and Students' Book page 112

Reading

Revision

First – Revise with students the 14 objects covered on the previous Vocabulary page.

Second – Read the following definitions and ask students to identify the objects.

1 It's for carrying money.
2 It's for checking the time.
3 It's for playing games.
4 It plays music.
5 It's for taking photos.
6 It's got photos and stories.

Third – Check answers and spelling by asking individual students to write words on the board.
(Answers: *wallet*, *watch*, *games console*, *MP3 player*, *camera*, *magazine*)

Cultural notes

- *The Simpsons* is an animated comedy series, first broadcast in 1989, featuring the adventures of a distinctive yellow family in a fictional American town. It has been a global success and nearly 500 episodes have been broadcast. The franchise includes video games, comics, merchandising of all types and even a ride at Universal Studios.
- *Lionel 'Leo' Messi* (Argentina, born 1987) is considered one of the best football players of his generation. He has played for Argentina in the FIFA World Cup. The colour of the Argentinian national team is blue, hence Emilio's father's blue laptop, mobile phone and car.

Exercise 1

- Draw attention to the photos and ask students what they can see.
- Students work in pairs, talking about who has got each of the things.

Exercise 2

- Make sure students understand not to read in detail at this point.
- Students scan the text quickly and check their answers to Exercise 1.
- Ask students why Emilio's father has a blue laptop, mobile phone and car. (Answer: *Because it is the colour of the Argentinian national team.*)

Answers

1 Lisa   2 Emilio   3 Lisa   4 Emilio

Exercise 3 (Track 1.9)

- Individually, students answer the question.
- If you wish, play the recording for students to listen and read.
- Students check in pairs before checking answers as a class.
- Elicit from stronger students or explain yourself the meaning of any new vocabulary.

Answers

Lisa mentions six objects
Emilio mentions nine objects

Exercise 4 (Track 1.9)

- Students read the text again and answer the questions.
- They then check in pairs before you check answers as a class.

Answers

2 He's from Mar del Plata in Argentina.
3 Lisa is a fan of *The Simpsons*.
4 Emilio is a football fan.
5 They are comics, a computer game, a DVD, a watch, a skateboard and a guitar.
6 They are a shirt, a scarf, a wallet, a backpack, (lots of) posters, a laptop, a mobile phone, a car and photos of players

Exercise 5

- Check the pronunciation of the questions before students work in pairs.
- In pairs, students ask and answer the questions.
- Monitor but do not interrupt fluency unless they make mistakes with the question forms.
- Discuss the questions as a class and find out how much consensus there is among the group.

Extra activity

Allow students to interview you, using the questions in Exercise 5. Remember to grade your language appropriately.

Further practice:
Workbook page 9

Reading

1 Look at the photos. Who has got these things: Lisa (L) or Emilio (E)?

1 a skateboard
2 a camera
3 comics
4 posters

2 Read and check your answers to Exercise 1.

3 🔊 1.9 Read the text. How many objects do Lisa and Emilio mention?

4 🔊 1.9 Read the text again. Answer the questions.

1 Where is Lisa from? *She's from Canada.*
2 Where is Emilio from?
3 What is Lisa a fan of?
4 What is Emilio a fan of?
5 Name *The Simpsons* objects.
6 Name the football objects.

5 What about you? In pairs, ask and answer.

1 What programme / team / sport are you a fan of?
2 Who is your favourite TV character / sports person?

> *I'm a fan of Glee.*

> *I'm a Manchester United fan.*

Fans of the month

Simpsons fan!

My brother and I are *Simpsons* fans. We've got about two hundred comics and they've got very funny stories and pictures. Have you got a *Simpsons* comic?

The Simpsons computer game is fantastic, but we haven't got a *Simpsons* DVD. I've got a *Simpsons* watch and a big skateboard with Bart Simpson on it. My brother hasn't got a skateboard, but he's got a guitar with a picture of Homer on it. It's awesome!

Oh, and guess what? My name is Lisa ... but my brother's name isn't Bart!

Lisa, Canada

Football fan!

I'm from Mar del Plata in Argentina. We've got a great football team here. I've got a football shirt, a scarf, a wallet and a backpack ... and lots of posters on my bedroom wall! Mum and Dad are big football fans, too. Dad's got a blue laptop, a blue mobile phone and a blue car!

I've also got photos of some players on my camera. Messi is my favourite player. He is a top goal scorer!

Emilio, Argentina

11

Grammar   *Have got*

Affirmative		
I/You/We/They	've got (have got)	a new DVD.
He/She/It	's got (has got)	

Negative		
I/You/We/They	haven't got (have not got)	a new DVD.
He/She/It	hasn't got (has not got)	

Questions		
Have I/you/we/they	got	a new DVD?
Has he/she/it	got	

Short answers
Yes, I/you/we/they have. / No, I/you/we/they haven't.
Yes, he/she/it has. / No, he/she/it hasn't.

Grammar reference Workbook page 86

> **Watch Out!**
> have got → 've got
> have not got → haven't got
> has got → 's got
> has not got → hasn't got

1   Study the grammar tables. Complete the rules.

> **1** We say *I* / .... / .... / .... *have got* or *haven't got*.
> **2** We say *he* / .... / .... *has got* or *hasn't got*.
> **3** The question form of *they have got* is .... ?
> **4** The short form of *have got* is ' .... .
> **5** The short form of *has got* is ' .... .

2   Choose the correct options.

1 Carla and Luisa *has got / have got* posters of Lady Gaga.
2 Elena *hasn't got / haven't got* a *Twilight* DVD.
3 *Have / Has* your parents got a laptop?
4 I *has got / have got* a camera in my backpack.
5 Harry *hasn't got / haven't got* a Superman comic.
6 *Have / Has* Angela got a new watch?

3   Find the subject + verb. Write the full form in your notebook.

1 He's got a new games console.
He has got
2 They haven't got a laptop.
3 We've got posters for the classroom.
4 I've got a camera on my mobile phone.
5 The teacher's got an MP3 player.
6 You haven't got a watch.

4   Complete the text with the full form of *have got*.

My Dad is a DJ. He ¹*has* got a radio show. He gets famous people on his show. We ².... got autographs from the famous people. We ³.... got autographs from Will Smith and Angelina Jolie. We ⁴.... (not) got an autograph from a sports person. My favourite singer is Katy Perry but I ⁵.... (not) got her autograph. ⁶.... you got an autograph from a famous person?

> **Pronunciation**   *Short forms*
>
> **5a**)) 1.10   Look at the verbs. Find the short forms and listen.
>
> **1** I've got a mobile phone.
> **2** She's got a magazine.
> **3** They've got my ice skates.
> **4** He hasn't got a camera.
> **5** We haven't got watches.
>
> **b**)) 1.10   Listen again and repeat.

6   What about you? In pairs, ask and answer about these objects.

DVD	guitar	magazine
MP3 player	skateboard	watch

Have you got a camera?
Yes, I have.

Grammar *Have got*

Language notes

- The use of *have got* is taught here for possession before any other work on the Present simple. Generally students do not have a problem with this structure in isolation but later on they may have problems when they see the use of the auxiliaries *do/don't* and *does/doesn't* with the Present simple. At that point you may need to clarify that *have got* is not grammatically the same as the Present simple.
- *Have got* is a very common construction in British English but, depending on your teaching context, you may find students are more influenced by American English where the verb *have* (*I have, he has, it doesn't have, we don't have, do you have, does he have,* etc.) is more commonly used.

Exercise 1

- Read the grammar tables with students.
- Students work individually, completing the sentences and referring back to the grammar tables where necessary.
- Check answers as a class.

Answers

1 *I / you / we / they*   2 *he / she / it*   3 Have they got
4 've got   5 's got

Exercise 2

- Students choose the correct options.
- Check answers by asking individual students to read the sentences.

Answers

2 hasn't got   3 Have   4 have got   5 hasn't got   6 Has

Exercise 3

- Check students understand the task before they start.
- Individually, students change the contracted forms to the full forms.

Answers

2 They haven't got	They have not got
3 We've got	We have got
4 I've got	I have got
5 The teacher's got	The teacher has got
6 You haven't got	You have not got

Exercise 4

- Remind students to use full forms not contractions in this exercise.
- Check answers by asking individual students to read sentences from the text.

Answers

2 have   3 have   4 have not   5 have not   6 Have

Pronunciation   Short forms

Language notes

- Speakers of many languages have major problems with the eccentricities of English pronunciation. This can affect their ability to understand spoken English. Many students have a tendency to over-emphasise the auxiliaries *have/has*. The aim of this exercise is to show how the auxiliaries are actually pronounced in connected speech.

Exercise 5a (Track 1.10)

- Play the recording for students to listen, read and find the short form.

Answers

1 've   2 's   3 've   4 hasn't   5 haven't

Exercise 5b (Track 1.10)

- Play the recording again for students to listen and repeat. Pause as appropriate to check students' pronunciation.

Extra activity

Extend the work on short forms to cover the verb *to be*. Write the following sentences on the board:
1 I'm a teacher.
2 You're a student.
3 What's the missing letter?
4 It isn't a big picture.
5 He's a fan of *The Simpsons*.
6 We aren't from Argentina.
Students look at the sentences and find the short form. Model and drill the sentences for students to practise the short form. Ask students to give you the full form of the verbs.

Further practice:
Workbook page 123

Exercise 6

- Ask two students to read aloud the example question and answer.
- Students work in pairs, asking and answering questions about the objects.
- Monitor but do not interrupt fluency unless they make mistakes with *have got*.

Further practice:
Workbook pages 10 and 86–87

Brain Trainer Activity 2
See Teacher's Book page 210 and Students' Book page 112

Vocabulary   Adjectives

Revision

First – Tell students you are a big fan of someone or something. Elicit suggestions from the class for your obsession and write them on the board (e.g. Robert Pattinson, Lady Gaga, etc.).

Second – Demonstrate the activity by choosing one of the people/items on the board, for example Robert Pattinson, and saying 'I've got a Robert Pattinson backpack.' Choose a stronger student and explain that they now have to repeat and add an item to the list, e.g. 'I've got a Robert Pattinson backpack and a "Twilight" DVD.' Another student continues the list ('I've got a Robert Pattinson backpack, a "Twilight" DVD and the new "Eclipse" computer game.'). Make sure students understand that they have to keep adding items and expanding the list.

Third – Divide the class into groups of three. Students take turns to see how long a list they can make without writing anything down. Encourage them to use vocabulary from the first page of the unit and to ask you for any other vocabulary they need.

Exercise 1 (Track 1.11)

- Students work individually, matching the opposite adjectives.
- Play the recording for students to listen, check and repeat.

Answers

2 a   **3** f   **4** b   **5** c   **6** g   **7** e

Exercise 2 (Track 1.12)

- Individually, students choose the correct options.
- They then check in pairs before checking answers with the recording.

Answers

2	old	**5**	big
3	popular	**6**	good
4	expensive	**7**	interesting

Exercise 3 (Track 1.13)

- Play the recording. Pause after each item to give students time to suggest adjectives.

Answers

1	*good*	**5**	expensive
2	bad	**6**	cheap
3	boring	**7**	popular
4	interesting/good	**8**	unpopular

Exercise 4

- Make sure students understand that there are various possible answers, depending on their opinions. They then work individually.
- Check answers by asking individual students to read the sentences.
- Ask students if they agree or disagree with their classmates' sentences.

Answers

Students' own answers

Exercise 5

- Individually, students write three sentences.
- Monitor and help with vocabulary and feed in ideas if necessary.

Answers

Students' own answers

Exercise 6

- Ask two students to read aloud the example question and answer.
- Students work in pairs, asking about the objects in Exercise 2.
- Monitor but do not interrupt fluency unless they make mistakes with *have got* or the adjectives.

Extra activity

Help students memorise the vocabulary by playing 'opposites tennis'. Demonstrate with a stronger student, explaining that you are going to say an adjective and they must respond with the opposite. The student then says a new adjective and you respond with the opposite, e.g.
Teacher old
Student new – cheap
Teacher expensive – popular
Student unpopular, etc.
Explain that, like real tennis, the rhythm is very important. The speed is not important but the person who breaks the rhythm loses and the other player wins a point.

Further practice:
Workbook pages 11 and 104

Brain Trainer Activity 4
See Teacher's Book page 210 and Students' Book page 112

Vocabulary Adjectives

1 🔊 1.11 **Match the adjectives (1–7) to the opposite adjectives (a–g). Then listen, check and repeat.**

1 bad
2 cheap
3 difficult
4 popular
5 boring
6 new
7 small

a expensive
b unpopular
c interesting
d good
e big
f easy
g old

Word list page 43 **Workbook** page 104

2 🔊 1.12 **Choose the correct options. Then listen, check and repeat.**

1 Help! I've got this game. It's really *easy / difficult*.

2 We've got a sports game for your console. It's from 2007, so it's *new / old*.

3 I've got two Rihanna posters. She's great – she's very *popular / unpopular*.

4 Look at this camera. It's £500 so it's *cheap / expensive*.

5 I've got about fifteen school books! I've got a *big / small* backpack.

6 I've got these fantastic DVDs. They're very *good / bad*.

7 Have you got *New Moon*? It's an *interesting / boring* novel. Read it now!

3 🔊 1.13 **Listen and guess the adjective. More than one answer may be possible.**

Well done! Excellent work!

Is it 'good'?

4 **Complete the sentences with adjectives from Exercise 1.**

1 The film *The Pirates of the Caribbean* is *good*.
2 A Ferrari is .... .
3 Keira Knightley is .... .
4 The Harry Potter books are .... .
5 Brazil is .... .
6 I think English is .... .
7 Usher's songs are .... .

5 **Choose one thing from each group. Use an adjective and write a sentence in your notebook.**

- computer game / book / film / song
- sports star / actor / singer
- object in your school / home

The computer game is difficult.

6 **Look at the objects in Exercise 2. In pairs, ask and answer.**

Is the camera expensive?

Yes, it is.

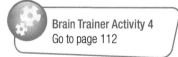

Brain Trainer Activity 4
Go to page 112

 13

Chatroom Talking about position

Speaking and Listening

1 Look at the photo and answer the questions.
1 Who is in Nick's room?
2 Name three objects in Nick's room.

2   1.14 Listen and read the conversation. Answer the questions.
1 Is Nick's room big or small? *It's small.*
2 Has Nick got a games console?
3 Has Nick got a football game?
4 Are Nick's ice skates on the bed?
5 What is under the desk?

3 Act out the conversation in groups of three.

Julia	This is a nIce room!
Nick	Thanks. It's small, but it's OK.
Julia	Oh look, Sunny's in your room.
Nick	Sit, Sunny. Good dog.
Leo	Is this your games console, Nick?
Nick	Yes, it is.
Leo	Cool! What games have you got?
Nick	I've got a new football game – it's really difficult!
Leo	Where is it?
Nick	It's next to the games console. Oh, my ice skates are on the desk! Sorry.
Leo	Hey Nick, what's that under the desk?
Nick	Oh, it's my skateboard.
Leo	Great. I've got one too.

Say it in your language …
Cool!
Great.

14

Chatroom   Talking about position

Revision

First – Write the following words on the board randomly:
bad, *big*, *boring*, *cheap*, *difficult*, *easy*, *expensive*, *good*, *interesting*, *new*, *old*, *popular*, *small*, *unpopular*

Second – Tell students to match the words to form pairs of opposites.

Third – Check answers by asking individual students to say pairs of words.
(Answers: *bad–good*; *big–small*; *boring–interesting*; *cheap–expensive*; *difficult–easy*; *new–old*; *popular–unpopular*)

Speaking and Listening

Exercise 1

* Check students are clear about the names of the characters before they complete the exercises.

Answers

1 Nick, Julia, Leo and Sunny the dog.
2 Students' own answers

Extra activity

Use the photo to elicit basic information about the characters, e.g. how old they are, what they are wearing, what hobbies they might enjoy and what sports they might like playing. Remember to grade your language appropriately.

Brain Trainer Activity 1

See Teacher's Book page 210 and Students' Book page 112

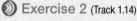 **Exercise 2** (Track 1.14)

* Play the recording for students to listen and read.
* Individually, students answer the questions.
* They then check in pairs before you check answers as a class.

Answers

2 Yes, he has.
3 Yes, he has.
4 No, they aren't. They are on the desk.
5 Nick's backpack and skateboard are under the desk.

Exercise 3

* Divide the class into groups of three.
* Groups act out the conversation.
* Monitor and correct students' pronunciation as appropriate.
* Nominate one group to perform the conversation for the class.

Extra activity

Stronger, more fluent students will complete this task before weaker ones. Suggest stronger students repeat the conversation three times, assuming different roles each time. Alternatively, give them one minute to try to memorise their part. They then cover the conversation and try to perform it from memory. After they have tried to reproduce the conversation they look at the version in the book and see where theirs differs.

Note that this activity can be re-used at any point during the course when you want to extend work on a conversation.

Say it in your language ...

 Ask students to find the phrases in the conversations and look at them in context to try to deduce the meaning.

Cool! – exclamation which can be used to indicate that something is *good* or *great* as in this case. Depending on the context and intonation it can also imply something is seen as stylish or fashionable.

Great. – exclamation used to show that we are happy about something that has happened. Students, for example, could use this expression if you give them a homework holiday, or if you are going to use a song or video in class. Or you might use it yourself if all the students hand their homework in on time.

Extra activity

Drill the conversation for correct pronunciation. Divide the class in half down the centre. Tell the half on the left that they are going to be Nick and the half on the right that they are going to be Leo. Explain that you will be Julia. Build up the conversation step by step until students can perform it unprompted.

Exercise 4

- Students read the conversation again and find the phrases.
- Check answers as a class.

Answers

2 Julia   3 Leo   4 Nick

Exercise 5

- Read through the phrases with the class.
- Ask students to identify which words and phrases in the sentences talk about where things are.
- Elicit further sentences using the words and phrases, and objects in the classroom (e.g. *'The book is on the desk.'*; *'The backpack is under the chair.'*; *'The pencil is in the backpack.'*).

Exercise 6

- Individually, students match the words and the pictures.
- Check answers as a class.

Answers

1 on
2 in
3 under
4 in front of
5 behind
6 next to

Exercise 7 (Track 1.15)

- Play the recording for students to listen to the conversation.
- Repeat the recording, pausing after each line to check students' pronunciation.
- In pairs, students act out the conversations.

Exercise 8

- Read the examples in the speech bubbles with the class. Then elicit a second conversation from the class using *DVD*.
- Students then make their own conversations by replacing the words in purple.
- Monitor but do not interrupt fluency unless students make mistakes with the use of the words and position phrases.

Further practice:
Workbook pages 12 and 113

Grammar   Possessive adjectives and Possessive 's

Language notes

The possessive *'s* is an item which many students find hard to assimilate. Common errors from low level learners include:

- inverting the items and adding the *'s* to the wrong word (e.g. *'It's dog's Nick'*);
- transferring the article which may be used in students' L1 to the English construction (e.g. *'It's the Nick's dog'*);
- avoiding the construction altogether (e.g. *'The dog of Nick'*).

It's therefore important to monitor students' work continuously and point out errors in this area for them to self-correct.

Exercise 1

- Read the grammar table with students.
- Elicit further examples of possessive adjectives from the conversation on page 14 of the Students' Book (e.g. *'Sunny's in your room.'*; *'Is this your games console, Nick?'*; *'Oh, my ice skates …'*).

Exercise 2

- Individually, students change the underlined words for possessive adjectives.
- They then check in pairs before you check answers as a class.

Answers

2 That's their room.
3 Those are our DVDs.
4 It's his laptop.
5 Are these her books?
6 This is his ball.

Exercise 3

- Make sure students are clear about the two positions of the apostrophe *'s*.
- Check answers by asking individual students to write answers on the board.

Answers

2 Have you got Andy's mobile phone?
3 Here is my grandparents' house.
4 This is the teacher's MP3 player.
5 Where is Marina's dad's camera?
6 My sisters' names are Olivia and Lina.

Exercise 4

- Demonstrate the activity by holding up a pen and asking a student *'Is this your pen?'*.
- Repeat the process with two other items before students work in pairs asking and answering questions.

Further practice:
Workbook pages 13 and 86–87

4 Look back at the conversation. Who says what?

1 It's next to the games console. *Nick*
2 Sunny's in your room.
3 What's that under the desk?
4 My ice skates are on the desk.

5 Read the phrases for talking about position.

Talking about position
Sunny's in your room.
Where is it?
It's next to the games console.
My ice skates are on the desk!
What's that under the desk?

6 Match the pictures to these words.

behind	in	in front of	next to	on	under

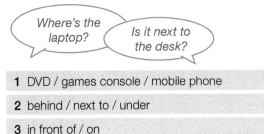

7))) 1.15 Listen to the conversation. Act out the conversation in pairs.

Ryan Where's the ¹ magazine?
Tania Is it ² on the desk?
Ryan No.
Tania Look. It's ³ under the desk.

8 Work in pairs. Replace the words in purple in Exercise 7. Use these words and/or your own ideas. Act out the conversation.

> Where's the laptop?
> Is it next to the desk?

1 DVD / games console / mobile phone
2 behind / next to / under
3 in front of / on

Grammar Possessive adjectives and Possessive 's

Possessive adjectives		Possessive 's
I	my	**One person**
you	your	Monica's bag.
he	his	Nick's dog.
she	her	
it	its	**Two or more people**
we	our	My parents' car.
they	their	John and Tom's room.

Grammar reference Workbook page 86

1 Study the grammar table and learn.

2 Make sentences. Change the underlined words.

1 It's Julia's watch.
   It's her watch.
2 That's my parents' room.
3 Those are my brother's and my DVDs.
4 It's Mr Green's laptop.
5 Are these Anna's books?
6 This is the boy's ball.

3 Copy the sentences. Put the apostrophe in the correct place.

1 I've got my mums wallet.
   I've got my mum's wallet.
2 Have you got Andys mobile phone?
3 Here is my grandparents house.
4 This is the teachers MP3 player.
5 Where is Marinas dads camera?
6 My sisters names are Olivia and Lina.

4 What about you? In pairs, ask and answer questions about five objects in the classroom.

> Is this your pen?
> No, it's Rafa's pen.

15

Reading

1 **Look quickly at the text and the photos. Answer the questions.**

1 What type of text is it?
a a quiz
b a competition
c an interview

2 Who are the characters in the photo?
a They're from a film.
b They're from a book.
c They're from a play.

My dad in his *Star Wars* costume.

Help!

Dad's got an embarrassing hobby!

This week's problem page interview is with Nicole from Montreal, Canada.

■ **Have you got a special collection, Nicole?**

No, I haven't got a collection, but my dad's got a *Star Wars* collection. It's his favourite film, but it's an old film now and I'm not a big *Star Wars* fan. Here's a photo of Dad with his friends at a *Star Wars* convention. Look at their costumes – it's really embarrassing!

■ **Is it a big collection?**

Yes, it is. Dad's got hundreds of props and costumes from the *Star Wars* films. He's got DVDs and posters in the living room. He's got Luke Skywalker's 'light sabre' in the dining room and *Star Wars* books and magazines in his bedroom, too. I've got a *Star Wars* bed in my room with Darth Vader on it. Yuk! Our house is full!

■ **Is this a problem?**

Well, it's OK because we've got a big shed in the garden, but guess what? That's full of *Star Wars* things too. Dad is happy with his collection, but Mum isn't happy because *Star Wars* things are very expensive.

My dad's collection.

> **Key Words**
>
> embarrassing   convention   costume
> props   shed

2 **Read and check your answers to Exercise 1.**

3 🔊 1.16 **Read the interview again. Are the sentences true (T) or false (F)?**
1 Nicole is a fan of *Star Wars* films. *F*
2 Nicole's dad has got a *Stars Wars* costume.
3 Her dad has got thousands of *Star Wars* things.
4 Nicole has got a *Star Wars* bed.
5 Her parents have got a small shed in the garden.
6 *Star Wars* things aren't cheap.

Listening

1 🔊 1.17 **Listen to three interviews. Match the speaker to the interview.**

Interview 1   a Peter's mum
Interview 2   b Peter's brother
Interview 3   c Peter

2 🔊 1.17 **Listen again. Answer the questions.**
1 Who's got a *Karate Kid* collection?
a Peter's brother   b Peter's mum   c Peter
2 What is Peter's mum's opinion?
a The collection is big.
b The collection is small.
c The collection is cheap.
3 What is Peter's brother's opinion of *Karate Kid*?
a It's cool.   b It's great.   c It's boring.

Reading

Cultural notes

- *Star Wars* is a science-fiction fantasy film and was first released in 1977. It was followed by two more instalments in 1980 and 1983 and three prequels from 1999 to 2005. The characters in the Reading text come from the original trilogy (1977–83). It was one of the highest grossing film series in cinema history.

Exercise 1

- Draw attention to the photos and the text and ask students what they can see.
- In pairs, students answer the questions.

Exercise 2

- Make sure students understand not to read in detail at this point.
- Students scan the text quickly and check their answers to Exercise 1.
- Ask students what else they know about *Star Wars*.

Answers

1 c　2 a

Key Words

Be prepared to focus on the Key Words, either by pre-teaching them, eliciting their meaning after students have read the text, or through dictionary or definition writing work.

convention – a special organised event where people with similar interests meet, usually for two or three days

costume – the clothes worn by actors in a film

embarrassing – something that makes you feel shy, ashamed or uncomfortable

props – the small objects used in films by actors e.g. guns, 'light sabres', keys

shed – a simple building in the garden, usually made of wood, to keep things in

Exercise 3 (Track 1.16)

- Students read the text again and decide if the sentences are true or false.
- If you wish, play the recording for students to listen and read.
- Elicit from stronger students or explain yourself the meaning of any new vocabulary.
- When checking answers, ask students to correct the false sentences.

Answers

1 *False* (Nicole is not a big *Star Wars* fan.)
2 True
3 False (Her dad has got hundreds of *Star Wars* things.)
4 True
5 False (Her parents have got a big shed in the garden.)
6 True

Listening

Cultural notes

- *Karate Kid* is a martial arts film and was first released in 1984. It was well received by the critics and was a commercial success. It was remade in 2010 starring Jackie Chan and Will Smith's son, Jaden Smith. It has also been adapted as both an animated TV series and a computer game.

Exercise 1 (Track 1.17)

- Play the recording for students to listen and match the speakers and the interviews.
- Check answers as a class.

Answers

Interview 1　c　Peter
Interview 2　a　Peter's mum
Interview 3　b　Peter's brother

Audioscript:
See Teacher's Book page 225

Exercise 2 (Track 1.17)

- Repeat the recording for students to answer the questions.
- They then check in pairs before you check answers as a class.

Answers

1 c　2 b　3 c

Extra activity

Students answer additional comprehension questions. Write the following questions on the board:
1 Who is Peter's favourite character in *Karate Kid*? (*Dre*)
2 Who is Jaden Smith's father? (*Will Smith*)
3 How many objects has Peter got? (*about 20*)
4 What adjectives describe objects in Peter's collection? (*big, not cheap, popular*)
5 What's Peter's brother's favourite film? (*Toy Story*)
6 Who's Peter's brother's favourite film character? (*Buzz*)
Repeat the recording for students to answer the questions.

Further practice:
Workbook page 14

Writing   A personal profile

Revision

First – Books closed. Quickly review the pronunciation of the alphabet with the class, paying particular attention to any letters which habitually cause problems to your learners. Then write the following word skeleton on the board:

s _ _ _ e _ _ _ _ d

Second – Pick individual students, asking them to say a letter. If the letter they choose is in the word, write it in the correct position. If it is not, write it in a column on one side of the board. When students think they know what the word is, they put their hands up. (Answer: *skateboard*)

Third – Continue with other vocabulary from the unit, leaving out all the vowels when you write it up on the board. If you have a stronger group, allow individual students to come to the board and take your place, or continue the activity in pairs.

Cultural notes

- *Guitar Hero* is a multi-platform music game. Players use a guitar-like control to play along with a wide range of pop and rock songs.
- *Kaiser Chiefs* are an English indie rock group who formed in 1997. The single *Ruby* was from their third album and was number one in the UK.

Exercise 1

- Read the Writing File with students.
- Ask students if the punctuation rules are the same in their L1 or different.

Exercise 2

- In pairs, students match the words in blue to the rules.
- When checking answers, ask students to say the full form of the contractions and check if the missing letter in the short form with *'s* corresponds to *is* or *has*.

Answers

1 Janek – capital letter for a name
2 I'm – first person, missing letters (= I am)
3 Kraków – capital letter for a name
4 Poland – capital letter for a name
5 haven't – missing letters (= have not)
6 they're – missing letters (= they are)
7 *Guitar Hero* – capital letter for a name
8 It's – missing letters (= It is)
9 game's – possession
10 *Ruby* – capital letter for a name
11 The Kaiser Chiefs – capital letter for a name

Exercise 3

- Individually, students rewrite the sentences with appropriate punctuation.
- Monitor and point out errors for students to self-correct.
- Check answers by asking individual students to write answers on the board.

Answers

2 She's my sister.
3 I'm thirteen years old.
4 Our teacher's name is Mr Day.
5 We've got fifty posters of Lady Gaga.
6 They haven't got a games console.

Exercise 4

- Individually, students answer the questions.
- They then compare their answers in pairs.
- Check answers by asking pairs of students to read questions and answers.

Answers

2 He's from Kraków in Poland.
3 His two favourite things are his new games console and *Guitar Hero*.
4 Because they're expensive.
5 Because he's got an electric guitar for *Guitar Hero*.
6 His favourite song is *Ruby* by The Kaiser Chiefs.

Exercise 5

- Explain that students should only make notes at this point or write short sentences.
- Encourage students to ask you for any vocabulary they need.

Answers

Students' own answers.

Exercise 6

- Show students how the text guide is divided into two paragraphs and tell them that they should now organise their notes in the same way.
- Read through the 'My favourite things' writing guide. Make sure students understand that they should answer questions 1 and 2 in Exercise 5 in the first paragraph and questions 3 and 4 in the second paragraph.
- Draw students' attention to the 'Remember!' checklist.

Answers

Students' own answers.

Extra activity

At the end of each unit make a set of Word Cards with 10–15 vocabulary items from the unit for students to memorise. Prepare some blank cards in advance and an envelope or bag to keep them in. On the front of the card, write the lexical item in large clear letters. Have fast finishers decorate the front of the card with a picture or design to help students remember the word. On the back they write the following: a definition of the word in English or in their L1 and an example sentence in English containing a blank where the word appears.

Further practice:
Workbook page 15

Writing   A personal profile

1   Read the Writing File.

Writing File   Punctuation 1

We use punctuation to make our writing clear.
- We use capital letters (*A*, *B*, *C* ...) for the names of people, places, songs, games and groups.
- We also use capital letters for the first person *I*.
- We use full stops (.) at the end of sentences.
- Apostrophes (') can show missing letters, e.g. in short forms.
- Apostrophes can also show possession.

2   Read the profile. Match the words in blue to the rules in the Writing File.

My favourite things

My name's ¹ Janek and ² I'm eleven years old. I'm from ³ Kraków. It's a big city in ⁴ Poland.
My favourite thing is my new games console. I ⁵ haven't got a lot of games because ⁶ they're expensive. I've got about five. My favourite is ⁷ *Guitar Hero* because I've got an electric guitar for this game. ⁸ It's a great game and the ⁹ game's songs are good. My favourite song is ¹⁰ *Ruby* by ¹¹ The Kaiser Chiefs.

3   Rewrite the sentences. Use capital letters, full stops and apostrophes.

1 his names luke   *His name's Luke.*
2 shes my sister
3 im thirteen years old
4 our teachers name is mr day
5 weve got fifty posters of lady gaga
6 they havent got a games console

4   Read the profile again. Answer the questions.

1 How old is Janek?   *He's eleven years old.*
2 Where is he from?
3 What are his two favourite things?
4 Why hasn't he got a lot of games?
5 Why is *Guitar Hero* his favourite game?
6 What is his favourite song?

5   Answer the questions.

1 What's your name and how old are you?
2 Where are you from?
3 What are your favourite things?
4 Give extra information about your favourite things.

6   Write a description about you and your favourite things. Use 'My favourite things' and your answers from Exercise 5.

My favourite things

Paragraph 1
- Your personal information
  My name is ... and I'm ... . (age)
  I'm from ... .

Paragraph 2
- Your favourite things
  My favourite thing is ... / My favourite things are ... and ... .
- Extra information
  I've got ... . (number)
  I haven't got ... .
  My favourite ... is ... because ... .

Remember!
- Use capital letters, apostrophes and full stops in the correct places.
- Use the vocabulary in this unit.
- Check your grammar and spelling.

17

Refresh Your Memory!

Grammar Review

1 Make affirmative and negative sentences with *have got*.

	Felipe	Adriana and Damon
1 a guitar	✓	✗
2 a skateboard	✗	✓
3 a games console	✗	✗
4 an MP3 player	✓	✓

1 *Felipe has got a guitar.*

2 Make questions and short answers about the things in Exercise 1.

1 *Has Felipe got a guitar? / Yes, he has.*

3 Complete the sentences with the correct possessive adjective.

1 I've got *my* lunch in this bag.
2 Have you got .... MP3 player?
3 Mr Smith has got .... watch.
4 Mrs Jones hasn't got .... laptop.
5 We've got .... magazines.
6 They've got .... cameras.

4 Rewrite the sentences. Use possessive *'s* or *s'*.

1 Kasia / laptop / is new

   Kasia's laptop is new.

2 My brother / camera / is expensive
3 Jessica and Oscar / dog / is small
4 My teacher / book / is interesting
5 Fabio / favourite football player / is Ronaldo
6 My cousins / DVD / is old

Vocabulary Review

5 Complete the sentences with these words.

~~comics~~	laptops	mobile phone
MP3 player	skateboard	watch

1 The teacher hasn't got any *comics* in her classroom.
2 My .... is in my bag.
3 I've got some new songs on my .... .
4 I haven't got a .... but I've got a bike.
5 What's the time? I haven't got my .... .
6 The school has got .... for the students.

6 Find seven adjectives.

from **small** the got **unpopular**
fan name easy **cheap** **look**
expensive **room** **bad** **boring**

Speaking Review

7 🔊 1.18 Look at the picture and complete the conversation. Then listen and check.

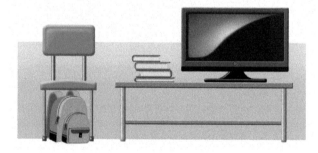

A Where's my backpack?
B It's there, ¹ .... the chair.
A Are my school books ² .... my bag?
B No, they aren't.
A Where are they?
B They're ³ .... the table, ⁴ .... the TV – here!

Dictation

8 🔊 1.19 Listen and write in your notebook.

✓ **My assessment profile:** Workbook page 127

Refresh Your Memory!

Exercise 1

Answers

1 Adriana and Damon haven't got a guitar.
2 Felipe hasn't got a skateboard.
  Adriana and Damon have got a skateboard.
3 Felipe hasn't got a games console.
  Adriana and Damon haven't got a games console.
4 Felipe has got an MP3 player.
  Adriana and Damon have got an MP3 player.

Exercise 2

Answers

1 Have Adriana and Damon got a guitar? /
  No, they haven't.
2 Has Felipe got a skateboard? / No, he hasn't.
  Have Adriana and Damon got a skateboard? /
  Yes, they have.
3 Has Felipe got a games console? / No, he hasn't.
  Have Adriana and Damon got a games console? /
  No, they haven't.
4 Has Felipe got an MP3 player? / Yes, he has.
  Have Adriana and Damon got an MP3 player? /
  Yes, they have.

Exercise 3

Answers

2 your   3 his   4 her   5 our   6 their

Exercise 4

Answers

2 My brother's camera is expensive.
3 Jessica and Oscar's dog is small.
4 My teacher's book is interesting.
5 Fabio's favourite football player is Ronaldo.
6 My cousins' DVD is old.

Exercise 5

Answers

2 mobile phone   3 MP3 player   4 skateboard
5 watch   6 laptops

Exercise 6

Answers

small, unpopular, easy, cheap, expensive, bad, boring

Exercise 7 (Track 1.18)

Answers

1 under   2 in   3 on   4 next to

Exercise 8 (Track 1.19)

Answers and Audioscript

1 I've got a camera and a wallet in my backpack.
2 Her brother hasn't got a skateboard.
3 This poster is nice but it's very expensive.
4 Ben's favourite game is *Guitar Hero*.
5 Their names are Lisa and Bart.

My assessment profile:
Workbook page 127

Extra activity

Revise *have got*, objects and adjectives from this unit:
– Write *My friend* in a cloud in the centre of the board and copy the figure underneath it.
– Elicit suggestions of names for the character based on the letter on her shirt (e.g. *Susan*).
– Divide the board in half and on the left of the board draw a tick and write *She's got …* and on the right of the board draw a cross and write *She hasn't got … .*
– Draw one of the items that Susan has got, and elicit a sentence from the class. Encourage students to use an adjective to describe the object (e.g. *'She's got an expensive watch.'*).
– Continue until you have drawn all six items, eliciting a sentence with an adjective for each. Allow students to draw additional items on the board using the vocabulary from the unit.
– Delete the phrases, cloud and the drawing of your friend and replace them with two speech bubbles, one containing *'Have you got …?'* and the other *'Yes, I have.'* / *'No, I haven't'*.
– Students work in pairs, asking each other about the items on the board. Monitor but do not interrupt students' fluency.

35

Art File   20th Century painting

Cultural notes

- *Cubism* as an artistic movement first appeared in the first decade of the twentieth century. Painting, sculpture and even architecture were part of the movement. The three leading Cubist painters were Picasso, Braque and Gris.
- *Juan Gris* (Spain, 1887–1927) was a Spanish painter and sculptor. He studied in Madrid then moved to Paris in 1906 where he became friends with Matisse, amongst others. An early Cubist, he stood out from many of his contemporaries with his use of bright colours as opposed to monochrome.
- *Pointillism* was an artistic movement developed in 1886 by Georges Seurat. It uses tiny dots of colour which blend in the eyes of the viewer when seen from a distance, giving Pointillist works a unique 'shimmering' quality. The most famous work in this style is probably *A Sunday Afternoon on the Island of La Grande Jatte* by Seurat.
- *Giuseppe Pellizza da Volpedo* (Italy, 1868–1907) lived and died in Volpedo in Piedmont. He used the theories of pointillism in his work and is considered a neo-impressionist. His most famous painting, *The Fourth Estate*, has an almost photographic realism when seen from a distance.

Language notes

Be prepared to elicit from stronger students or explain yourself the meaning of the following lexical items which appear in the Reading text: *style, vase, bowl, mug, geometrical shape, bright colour, typical, artist, basket, washing, shadow, dot*

Exercise 1

- Students match the artists to the paintings.
- They then scan the text quickly to check their answers.

Answers

1 *Washing in the Sun*
2 *Guitar and Fruit Bowl*

Exercise 2 (Track 1.20)

- Students read the text and answer the questions.
- If you wish, play the recording for students to listen and read.
- Students check in pairs before checking answers as a class.
- Check answers by asking pairs of students to read questions and answers.

Answers

1 Cubism and Pointillism
2 Juan Gris, Pablo Picasso and Georges Braque
3 *Washing in the Sun* is a landscape and *Guitar and Fruit Bowl* is a still life.
4 Pointillism

My Art File

Exercise 3

- In pairs, students choose another famous twentieth-century painting.
- Remind students that further information about artists and artistic movements is available by searching the internet.

Exercise 4

- Monitor and help with grammar and vocabulary and feed in ideas if necessary.
- Give students time to practise their presentation.
- Make a note of any mistakes related to the content of this unit in students' presentations to go over with the class afterwards.

In this unit have you …

… used Grammar and Vocabulary worksheet?
… used Reading and Listening worksheet?
… used Writing worksheet?
… used Speaking worksheet?
… used Unit test?

With the exception of the Writing worksheets, all the Teacher's Resources are at two levels of difficulty:
*   For students who need extra help and support
** For students who require an additional challenge

Art File

20th Century Painting

On this page there are examples of two different styles of early 20th Century painting: Cubism and Pointillism. One painting is a still life - a painting of objects, for example, vases, bowls or mugs. The other painting is a landscape – this is a painting of the countryside.

Guitar and Fruit Bowl

This picture has got a guitar, a fruit bowl, a bottle and a book in it. Juan Gris's style of painting is Cubism. The picture has got lots of geometrical shapes and the colours are not very bright. This is typical of Cubist paintings. Other famous Cubist artists are Pablo Picasso and Georges Braque.

Washing in the Sun

This painting is from 1905. There is a basket with some washing in it. The trees are blue and there are long shadows. Pellizza da Volpedo's style of painting is called Pointillism. Pointillist paintings have got very small dots of colour. Georges Seurat and Paul Signac are other famous Pointillist artists.

Reading

1   **Match the artists to the pictures.**
    1 Pellizza da Volpedo
    2 Juan Gris

2   ◗) 1.20   **Read about the two paintings. Answer the questions.**
    1 Which two styles of painting can you see on this page?
    2 Name three Cubist artists.
    3 Which of these paintings is a landscape? Which is a still life?
    4 Which style of painting uses bright colours?

My Art File

3   **In pairs, find out about another famous 20th century painting. Think about:**
    • the artist
    • the style of painting
    • other artists in the same style
    • the objects/people in the painting
    • why you like it

4   **Design a poster about your painting. Use your notes from Exercise 3 to help you. Then present your poster to your class.**

19

2 Around Town

Grammar	*There is/There are; some/any; Can/Can't* for ability
Vocabulary	Places in town; Action verbs
Speaking	Orders and warnings
Writing	A description of a town

Vocabulary Places in town

1))) 1.21 **Match the places in the picture to these words. Then listen, check and repeat.**

bank	bus station	café
cinema	hospital *1*	library
museum	park	police station
post office	shopping centre	sports centre
town square	train station	

Word list page 43   **Workbook** page 105

2 **Where can you find these things? Match the things to the places in Exercise 1.**
   1 ticket *cinema*
   2 book
   3 ball
   4 tree
   5 money
   6 coffee

3 **Read the clues and find the places in the picture.**
   1 It's behind the shopping centre.
      train station
   2 It's behind the park.
   3 It's next to the post office.
   4 It's in front of the cinema.
   5 It's next to the shopping centre.
   6 It's in front of the police station.

4 **In pairs, make a list of other places in a town.**
   supermarket, playground

Brain Trainer Activity 3
Go to page 113

20

Unit contents

Vocabulary
→ Places in town – *bank, bus station, café, cinema, hospital, library, museum, park, police station, post office, shopping centre, sports centre, town square, train station*
→ Action verbs – *climb, cycle, dance, fly, juggle, jump, play, run, sing, skate, swim, walk*

Grammar
→ *There is/There are* – affirmative, negative, questions and short answers
→ *Some/Any*
→ *Can/Can't* for ability – affirmative, negative, questions and short answers

Communication
→ Orders and warnings
→ Writing a description of a town – My home town; Linking words – *and, but, or*

Pronunciation
→ Silent letters

Key competences
→ Linguistic competence
→ Competence in knowledge and interaction with the physical world
→ Interpersonal, social and civic competence
→ Learning-to-learn
→ Autonomy and personal initiative

Vocabulary   Places in town

Exercise 1 (Track 1.21)
• Individually, students match the words and places in the picture.
• Play the recording for students to listen and check.
• Repeat the recording. Pause after each word to check students' pronunciation.

Answers
2 train station	9 bus station
3 sports centre	10 police station
4 bank	11 town square
5 post office	12 café
6 shopping centre	13 museum
7 park	14 library
8 cinema	

Extra activity
Stronger groups or individual students cover the words in the box and complete Exercise 1 'blind'. They then uncover the box and see if they used the same words or different ones. This type of activity is very valuable as it helps students notice the gap between their knowledge and the target language.

Exercise 2
• In pairs, students match the things with the places.
• Check answers by asking individual students to say pairs of words (e.g. *ticket–cinema*).

Answers
2 book–library
3 ball–sports centre
4 tree–park/town square
5 money–bank
6 coffee–café

Exercise 3
• Students look at the picture and identify the places.
• Check answers as a class.

Answers
2 sports centre
3 bank
4 town square
5 post office
6 museum

Exercise 4
• Students brainstorm vocabulary which they already know for places in a town.
• They then change partners and peer teach the vocabulary they have thought of.
• Collate all suggestions on the board.

Possible Answers
supermarket, playground, theatre, bookshop, music shop, swimming pool, art gallery, football stadium, restaurant

Further practice:
Workbook pages 16 and 105

Brain Trainer Activity 3
See Teacher's Book page 211 and Students' Book page 113

Reading

Revision

First – Revise with students four of the prepositions of place (*in, in front of, behind, next to*) covered in Unit 1.

Second – Students look at the picture of the virtual town on page 20 of the Students' Book. Read the following sentences and ask students to identify the places in the town.
1 It's in the town square behind the museum. (police station)
2 It's next to the post office. (bank)
3 It's behind the bus station. (shopping centre)
4 It's in the town square next to the park. (cinema)
5 It's in the town square in front of the bus station. (café)

Third – Check answers and spelling by asking individual students to write words on the board.

Cultural notes

- *Cybertown* is one of various online city simulation games. In such games users can create online homes and communities, interact with other users, and even earn money with 'jobs' in order to purchase home and leisure items.
- Further information is available by searching the internet.

Exercise 1

- Draw attention to the pictures and the text and ask students what they can see.
- Individually, students answer the question.

Exercise 2

- Make sure students understand not to read in detail at this point.
- Students scan the text quickly to check their answer.

Answer

1 b

Exercise 3 (Track 1.22)

- Students work individually, deciding if the sentences are true or false.
- If you wish, play the recording for students to listen and read.
- When checking answers, ask students to correct the false sentences.
- Elicit from stronger students or explain yourself the meaning of any new vocabulary.

Answers

1 *False* (TanyaCity has got a museum.)
2 True
3 False (Fabville has got houses.)
4 False (Fabville hasn't got a school.)
5 True
6 True

Extra activity

Individually, students write three more *true/false* sentences, one about each town, using *has/hasn't got*. Monitor and point out errors for students to self-correct. They then work with a partner, reading their sentences and answering *true* or *false*.

Exercise 4

- Ask two students to read aloud the example question and answer.
- Check the pronunciation of the questions before students work in pairs.
- In pairs, students ask and answer the questions.
- Monitor and help with vocabulary but do not interrupt fluency.

Extra activity

Use the texts as a model for a dictation of your own. Ask students the following gist questions:
What's the name of my Cybertown? (Answer: *Teacherville*)
Is it a good town? (Students' own answers)
Then read the following text:
My Cybertown is called Teacherville. It's got two big schools and a new library. It's got a great museum and a hospital but it hasn't got a shopping centre or a café. It's got a police station and a very good transport system. It's really beautiful.
Check answers to the gist questions as a class. Then repeat as necessary for students to write down the full text.

Further practice:
Workbook page 17

Reading

1 Look at the text. What do you think it is about?

a sports centres
b virtual towns
c shopping centres

2 Read the text and check your answer to Exercise 1.

3)) 1.22 Read the text again. Are the sentences true (T) or false (F)?

1 TanyaCity hasn't got any museums. *F*
2 TanyaCity has got a library.
3 Fabville hasn't got any houses.
4 Fabville has got a school.
5 Garboton has got some shops.
6 Garboton has got a train station.

4 What about you? Invent your Cybertown. In pairs, ask and answer.

1 What's the name of the town?
2 Where is it?
3 What places has it got? Where are they?

What's the name of the town?

It's MusicTown.

Cybertown

it's our town, it's your town

Tanya

My Cybertown is TanyaCity. I've got a big house and lots of friends. There are two shopping centres next to my house with lots of great shops. There's a museum and a park in front of the library and there are some big houses behind my school. TanyaCity is a beautiful town.

Ben

My Cybertown is Fabville. It's really cool. I ♥ sport, and Fabville has got two sports centres and three parks. My house is next to a big library. In the town square there is a bank and a small post office and there's a very big hospital. Next to the hospital there's a great café. In Fabville there aren't any schools!

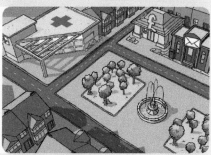

Sanjay

Garboton is my Cybertown. It's got very good connections - there's a train station and a bus station. There's a town square in Garboton and there are some shops but there isn't a shopping centre. There isn't a museum or a library, but there's a big police station. It's my police station! I'm the Chief of Police in Garboton!

21

Grammar   *There is/There are; some/any*

Affirmative
There's (There is) **a** museum.
There are **some** houses/**two** shopping centres.

Negative
There isn't (is not) **a** library.
There aren't (are not) **any** schools.

Watch Out!
There are → **some** cafés.
There aren't → **any** restaurants.
Are there → **any** restaurants?

1 Study the grammar tables. Complete the rules with *there is, there are, there isn't* and *there aren't*.

> **1** We use .... and .... with singular nouns, e.g. *a museum, a cat, a house.*
> **2** We use .... and .... with plural nouns, e.g. *some/any shops, a lot of schools.*

2 Choose *There is* or *There are* to complete the sentences.

1 *There is* a big shopping centre in our town.
2 .... three French girls in my school.
3 .... some books under your bed.
4 .... a big party on Saturday. It's my birthday!
5 .... a new interactive whiteboard in my class.
6 .... two swimming pools in this sports centre.

3))) 1.23 **Complete the conversation. Then listen and check.**

Tom   What's in your town, Emma?
Emma ¹ *There's* a big cinema and an international school. ² .... any parks. ³ .... any parks in your town?
Tom   Yes, ⁴ ..... . ⁵ .... some beautiful parks and ⁶ .... a shopping centre called GoShop. ⁷ .... a sports centre in your town?
Emma No, ⁸ ..... . But ⁹ .... a modern art museum.

Questions and short answers	
Is there **a** hospital?	Yes, there **is.** No, there **isn't.**
Are there **any** houses?	Yes, there **are.** No, there **aren't.**

Grammar reference Workbook page 88

4 **Make questions and answers.**

1 any good films / on TV? (✗)
Are there any good films on TV?
No, there aren't.

2 a mobile phone / in your bag? (✓)
3 a swimming pool / in your house? (✗)
4 any English students / in your class? (✓)
5 any libraries / in your town? (✗)

5 **Look at the information about Sandra's backpack. Find and correct five mistakes in the text.**
There isn't a wallet.

My backpack

pen	✓
wallet	✗
DVDs	✗
apple	✗
MP3 player	✗
laptop	✓
book	✗
magazine	✓

There's a pen in my backpack and there's a wallet. There are some DVDs and there's an apple and an MP3 player. There isn't a laptop. There aren't any books in my bag but there's a magazine.

6 **What about you? Imagine you have got a new backpack. What have you got in it? Write six sentences.**
In my backpack, there's ... .

Grammar *There is/There are; some/any*

- *There is/There are* does not usually pose a major problem for learners. However, do be aware that not all languages make the distinction between the singular and plural verb form, so some nationalities may find this a little more complicated.
- The basic use of *some* and *any* is not usually problematic either but make sure students understand clearly the information in the grammar table before starting the practice exercises.

Exercise 1

- Read the grammar tables with students.
- Students work individually, completing the rules and referring back to the grammar tables where necessary.
- Make sure students understand that *some* is used in affirmative sentences, and *any* in negatives and questions.
- Check answers as a class.

Answers

1 there is, there isn't
2 there are, there aren't

Exercise 2

- Students complete the sentences with *There is* or *There are*.
- Check answers by asking individual students to read the sentences.

Answers

2 There are   3 There are   4 There is   5 There is
6 There are

Exercise 3 (Track 1.23)

- Individually, students complete the conversation.
- Play the recording for students to listen and check.

Answers

2 There aren't   3 Are there   4 there are   5 There are
6 there is   7 Is there   8 there isn't   9 there is

Extra activity

Drill the conversation for correct pronunciation. Divide the class in half down the centre. Tell the half on the left that they are going to be Tom and the half on the right that they are going to be Emma. Build up the conversation step by step until students can perform it unprompted.

Exercise 4

- Students work in pairs, making the questions and answers.
- Check answers by asking pairs of students to read questions and answers aloud.
- Correct students' pronunciation as appropriate.

Answers

2 Is there a mobile phone in your bag? Yes, there is.
3 Is there a swimming pool in your house? No, there isn't.
4 Are there any English students in your class? Yes, there are.
5 Are there any libraries in your town? No, there aren't.

Exercise 5

- Draw attention to the photo and ask students what they can see.
- Students read the text, identifying and correcting the five mistakes.
- Check answers by reading the text yourself and telling students to shout *Stop!* whenever you reach a mistake.

Answers

There isn't a wallet.   There isn't an MP3 player.
There aren't any DVDs.   There's a laptop.
There isn't an apple.

Exercise 6

- Monitor and point out errors for students to self-correct.
- Encourage students to ask you for any vocabulary they need.

Answers

Students' own answers

Extra activity

Plan a *Live Listening* about the town where you live or a fictional town. Remember to grade your language appropriately and include examples of both *has got*, *there is/are* and prepositions of place. Use the following text as an example:
My town is beautiful. It's got a big park and lots of cafés in the town square. It's got a bus station and a train station and in front of the train station there's a great shopping centre. Next to the shopping centre there's a cinema and there's a post office. Behind the post office there's a police station. My town hasn't got a museum, but it has got a small library and a new sports centre.
Students make a list of eight of the places in town from the vocabulary page in their notebooks. Students listen to your *Live Listening* and tick or cross the items on their lists. If you do not specify some of the places, they leave them blank. Students compare their answers in pairs. As their lists of places will be different, they can collate their answers. Take feedback as a class. Elicit from students '*Your town has/hasn't got …*' and allow students to ask you '*Has your town got …?*' for any places you didn't mention. Avoid using the structure *There is/There are* at this stage.

Further practice:
Workbook pages 18 and 88–89

Brain Trainer Activity 2
See Teacher's Book page 211 and Students' Book page 113

Vocabulary Action verbs

Revision

First – Plan to use the contents of your own bag to revise objects from Unit 1 and *Is/Are there …?* questions. Try to have at least three or four items in your bag which students know the vocabulary for (e.g. *camera, laptop, MP3 player, magazine, mobile phone, wallet*).

Second – In pairs, ask students to predict what you could have in your bag and make a list. Monitor and help with vocabulary and spelling if necessary but don't tell students if you have those items or not.

Third – Pairs take turns to ask you questions (e.g. *'Is there a mobile phone in your bag?'*). If they are correct, take out the item to show it to them. Students can then repeat the activity in pairs and guess the contents of each other's bags.

Exercise 1 (Track 1.24)

- Individually, students match the words and the pictures.
- Play the recording for students to listen and check.
- Repeat the recording. Pause after each word to check students' pronunciation.

Answers

2	jump	8	skate
3	cycle	9	play
4	run	10	swim
5	juggle	11	fly
6	dance	12	walk
7	sing		

Extra activity

Books closed. Students try to remember and spell all the action verbs. When they have finished, students self-correct by looking back at the book.

Exercise 2

- Students match the verbs to the phrases.
- They then check in pairs before you check answers as a class.
- Check answers by asking individual students to say complete collocations.
- Correct students' pronunciation as appropriate.

Answers

2 f 3 a 4 c 5 g 6 e 7 b 8 h

Extra activity

Stronger groups or fast finishers memorise the vocabulary for one minute. Students then test themselves or their partner by covering first the column of verbs and then the column of phrases and seeing how many collocations they can remember.

Exercise 3

- Individually, students make sentences with the collocations from Exercise 2.
- Monitor and point out errors for students to self-correct.

Possible Answers

2 I swim 100 metres/in the pool.
3 I juggle six balls.
4 I climb a tree/a mountain.
5 I jump very high.
6 I cycle to school.
7 I sing a song.
8 I run a marathon.

Further practice:
Workbook pages 19 and 105

Pronunciation Silent letters

Exercise 4a (Track 1.25)

- Explain that in English many words have letters which are written but not pronounced.
- Write *walk* on the board and play the recording for students to identify the silent letter.
- Play the recording for students to identify the other silent letters.

Answers

1 wal*k* 2 clim*b* 3 *g*uitar 4 tal*k* 5 *k*no*w*

Exercise 4b (Track 1.25)

- Play the recording for students to listen and repeat. Pause as appropriate to check students' pronunciation.

Extra activity

Give students some extra practice with silent letters. Write the following words on the board and model the pronunciation for students to identify the silent letters.
*w*heels, Sim*p*sons, cam*e*ra, inter*v*iew, shopping cent*r*e
(Answers: *underlined*)

Further practice:
Workbook page 123

Brain Trainer Activity 4
See Teacher's Book page 211 and Students' Book page 113

Vocabulary   Action verbs

1 🔊 1.24 **Match the pictures to these words. Then listen, check and repeat.**

climb *1*	cycle	dance	fly	juggle	jump
play	run	sing	skate	swim	walk

Word list page 43   **Workbook** page 105

2 **Match the verbs (1–8) to the phrases (a–h).**

1 play *d*
2 swim
3 juggle
4 climb
5 jump
6 cycle
7 sing
8 run

a six balls
b a song
c a tree, a mountain
d a game, football, the guitar
e to school
f 100 metres, in the pool
g very high
h a marathon

3 **Make complete sentences with the information in Exercise 2.**

1 *I play football.*

Pronunciation
Silent letters

4a 🔊 1.25 **Listen and find the silent letter in each word.**

1 walk
2 climb
3 guitar
4 talk
5 know

b 🔊 1.25 **Listen again and repeat.**

 Brain Trainer Activity 4
Go to page 113

Chatroom — Orders and warnings

Speaking and Listening

1 Look at the photo. Are these things in the photo?

1 backpack ✓	5 food	8 mobile phone
2 book	6 laptop	9 ice skates
3 canoes	7 map	10 wallet
4 dog		

2 1.26 Listen and read the conversation. Are the sentences true (T) or false (F)?

1 There is a lake in the park. *T*
2 The park isn't a good place for a picnic.
3 Monica's got the map.
4 The food is in Nick's bag.
5 Leo is very careful.
6 Julia isn't very happy.
7 At the end, the picnic is in the lake.

3 Act out the conversation in groups of four.

Monica	Where are we now? Look at the map, Nick.
Nick	OK, we're at the lake. The park's a really good place for our picnic.
Leo	A picnic! Great! Oh, and it's in my backpack. Apples! Watch me! I can juggle!
Julia	Leo, be careful!
Monica	Leo! Don't play with our food!
Nick	Come on everyone. Let's go!
Leo	Hang on, guys. Wait for us!
Julia	Don't shout, Leo!
Leo	OK. Look! I can dance in the canoe.
Julia	Leo! Please, don't do that. Stop!
Leo	Oh no! Help!
Monica	Are you OK, Leo? Can you swim?
Leo	Yes, I can, but there's a small problem.
Nick	What?
Leo	Our picnic's in the lake.
M, N & J	Oh Leo!

Say it in your language …
Let's go!
Hang on.

24

Chatroom Orders and warnings

Revision

First – Write the following verbs on the board randomly:
climb, cycle, juggle, jump, play, run, sing, swim
Tell students you are going to read eight sentences about
yourself. Students must put the eight verbs in the order they
hear them. Read the following sentences.

1 I run a kilometre.
2 I cycle to school.
3 I swim in the pool.
4 I play the guitar.
5 I sing a song.
6 I climb a mountain.
7 I juggle six balls.
8 I jump very high.

Second – Repeat the sentences. Tell students to note
down more information. In pairs, students reconstruct the
sentences. Monitor and point out errors for students to
self-correct.

Third – Check answers and spelling by asking individual
students to write sentences on the board.

Speaking and Listening

Exercise 1

- Draw attention to the photo and ask students what they
  can see.
- Students look in more detail and find what things are in
  the photo.
- Check answers as a class.

Answers

2 ✗ **3** ✓ **4** ✗ **5** ✓ **6** ✗ **7** ✓ **8** ✗ **9** ✗ **10** ✗

Brain Trainer Activity 1
See Teacher's Book page 211 and Students' Book page 113

 ## Exercise 2 (Track 1.26)

- Elicit the names of the characters before students
  complete the exercise.
- Play the recording for students to decide if the
  sentences are true or false.
- They then check in pairs before checking answers as a
  class.

Answers

2 False (The park's a really good place for a picnic.)
3 False (Nick's got the map.)
4 False (The food is in Leo's backpack.)
5 False (Leo isn't careful/plays with their food.)
6 True
7 True

Extra activity

Stronger groups or fast finishers rewrite the false
sentences in Exercise 2 so that they are correct.

Exercise 3

- Divide the class into groups of four.
- Groups act out the conversation.
- Monitor and correct students' pronunciation as
  appropriate.
- Nominate one group to perform the conversation for the
  class.

Say it in your language …

Ask students to find the phrases in the conversation
and look at them in context to try to deduce the
meaning.

Let's go! – is used here to mean *time to start*. The
phrase *Let's* can be used before many verbs to make
a suggestion. You might use it in class in phrases
such as *'Let's practise some pronunciation!'* or *'Let's
have some quiet!'* although these, of course, are in
fact orders disguised as suggestions.

Hang on. – is a colloquial expression meaning *wait
a short time*. It is often used when another person is
impatient to do something or is being unreasonable.
Students, for example, could use this expression
if they need another moment to finish an exercise
before you check the answers.

Exercise 4

- Students read the conversation again and complete the instructions.
- Check answers as a class.
- Drill the phrases for pronunciation and intonation.

Answers

2 Be careful!   5 Don't shout!
3 Don't play with our food!   6 Stop!
4 Wait for us!

Exercise 5

- Read through the phrases for giving orders and warnings with the class.
- Make sure students understand that this type of phrase does not have a subject pronoun.

Exercise 6 (Track 1.27)

- Play the recording for students to listen and repeat. Pause as appropriate to check students' pronunciation.
- In pairs, students act out the conversations.

Exercise 7

- Elicit a second conversation from the class using the first set of prompts.
- Students then make their own conversations by replacing the words in purple.
- Stronger groups or fast finishers can use their own ideas and their own names.

Further practice:
Workbook pages 20 and 114

Grammar *Can/Can't for ability*

Language notes

- Students are introduced here to *can* and *can't* for ability. As with *have got,* generally students do not have a problem with this structure in isolation but later on may have problems when they see the use of the auxiliaries *do/don't* and *does/doesn't* with the Present simple.
- The most common problem for students is differentiating the weak, unstressed pronunciation of *can* in affirmative sentences and the strong, stressed pronunciation of *can't* in negative sentences. Distinguishing the affirmative from the negative can become a serious impediment to communication in some cases. It's therefore important to monitor students' work continuously and point out errors in pronunciation for them to self-correct.

Exercise 1

- Read the grammar table with students.

Answer

Correct rule: 2

Exercise 2

- Individually, students decide who the sentences are about.
- They then check in pairs before checking answers as a class.

Answers

2 Jon   3 Dan

Exercise 3

- Students look at the chart again and write sentences for Anna and Meg.
- Make sure students understand that there are various possible ways to write the sentences.

Possible Answers

Anna can dance and juggle but she can't sing.
Meg can sing and dance but she can't juggle.

Extra activity

Work on the pronunciation of *can* and *can't* in affirmative and negative sentences. Tell students you are going to read six sentences. Students must write down if they are affirmative (+) or negative (−). Read the following sentences, making sure that you use the weak form of *can* in affirmative sentences.

1 You can't juggle.   4 They can skate.
2 I can't swim.   5 He can't sing.
3 She can run a kilometre.   6 I can climb a tree.

Check answers as a class. Tell students to listen carefully to how *can* and *can't* are pronounced. Repeat the sentences. Elicit that in the affirmative *can* is pronounced /kən/ and is unstressed and in the negative *can't* is pronounced /kɑːnt/ and is stressed. Drill the six sentences. Correct students' pronunciation as appropriate.

Exercise 4

- Students work individually, making the questions and referring back to the grammar table where necessary.

Answers

2 Can you juggle?
3 Can you sing?
4 Can you play tennis?
5 Can you play the piano?
6 Can you climb trees?

Further practice:
Workbook pages 21 and 88–89

4 Look back at the conversation. Complete the instructions.
1 W _a t c h_ me!
2 B_ careful!
3 Don't p _ _ _ with our food!
4 W _ _ _ for us!
5 Don't s _ _ _ _!
6 S_ _ p!

5 Read the phrases for giving orders and warnings.

Orders
Watch me!
Don't play … !
Wait for us!
Don't shout!
Please, don't do that.

Warnings
Be careful!
Stop!
Help!

6))) 1.27 Listen to the conversation. Act out the conversation in pairs.

Julia Leo, don't play with [1] our food.
Leo OK, Julia. But don't shout!

Julia Leo, don't [2] swim in the lake.
Leo OK, Julia. But don't shout!

7 Work in pairs. Replace the words in purple in Exercise 6 with these words. Act out the conversations.

Leo, don't play with my camera.
OK, Julia. But don't shout!

1 my mobile phone / my laptop / my book

2 run / climb trees / dance in the canoe

8 Act out the conversation again with your own words and ideas.

Grammar _Can/Can't_ for ability

Affirmative
I/You/He/She/It/We/They can juggle.

Negative
I/You/He/She/It/We/They can't dance.

Questions and short answers
Can I/you/he/she/it/we/they play the guitar?
Yes, I/you/he/she/it/we/they can.
No, I/you/he/she/it/we/they can't.

> Grammar reference Workbook page 88

1 Study the grammar table. Choose the correct rule, _1_ or _2_.

1 We say _can / can't_ + _to_ + verb.
2 We say _can / can't_ + verb.

2 Look at the table. Then read the sentences and say _Jon_, _Dan_ or _Matt_.

	sing	dance	juggle
Jon	✓	✗	✗
Dan	✗	✗	✓
Matt	✓	✓	✗
Anna	✗	✓	✓
Meg	✓	✓	✗

1 This boy can sing and he can dance but he can't juggle. _Matt_
2 This boy can't dance and he can't juggle but he can sing.
3 This boy can juggle but he can't sing and he can't dance.

3 Complete the sentences for Anna and Meg.
Anna can … .
Meg can … .

4 Make questions with _can_.
1 ride a bike? _Can you ride a bike?_
2 juggle?
3 sing?
4 play tennis?
5 play the piano?
6 climb trees?

25

Reading

1 Look at the photos. What animals can you see?

Great Parks in London

Richmond Park

This is a very big park in the south of London – it's 10 square kilometres. You can walk around the park and look at the trees, plants and lakes. You can also see lots of deer in this park. There are more than 650 deer here! You can hire bikes and cycle around the park. There are amazing views of London from King Henry's Mound. You can see St Paul's Cathedral in the centre of London. You can play golf and go fishing in the lake or have a picnic in the park. You can also go to the Pembroke Lodge café. The food is great.

Roof Gardens

These are secret gardens in the middle of London. Find a door with the sign: '99 Kensington High Street'. Open the door and walk up to the roof. There's an amazing garden here, 30 metres above the street. It's 6,000 square metres and it's got 70 trees, tropical plants and four pink flamingos called Bill, Ben, Splosh and Pecks! There's a famous (and expensive!) restaurant here. You can eat lunch and look at the flamingos in the garden. It's a fantastic experience.

Key Words		
to hire	view	to play golf
to go fishing	roof	experience

2 Read the text and check your answer to Exercise 1.

3 🔊 1.28 Read the text. Answer the questions.
1. Where is Richmond Park?
   It is in the south of London.
2. What animals can you see in Richmond Park?
3. What famous building can you see from King Henry's Mound?
4. What is the address of the Roof Gardens?
5. How big are the Roof Gardens?
6. What animals can you see in the Roof Gardens?

4 🔊 1.28 Read the text again. Choose *Richmond Park* (RP) or *Roof Gardens* (RG).
1. It's in the centre of London. *RG*
2. You can eat at an expensive restaurant here.
3. You can have a picnic here.
4. This place is behind a door on Kensington High Street.
5. You can play golf.
6. You can ride a bike in this place.

Listening

1 🔊 1.29 Listen to the audition. Say Latika, Kate, or Latika and Kate.

TALENT WANTED!

Tuesday, 7th November
Auditions at the Regal Cinema,
3 p.m.

1. She can climb trees.
2. She can swim.
3. She can't sing.
4. She can dance.
5. She can jump up high.
6. She can run very fast.

Reading

Cultural notes

- *Richmond Park*, one of London's nine Royal Parks, has existed for nearly 4,000 years. It is a conservation area for various forms of wildlife. The view of St Paul's Cathedral is actually a 'protected' view, meaning nothing can be built to obscure it.
- *Kensington Roof Gardens*, designed in the 1930s, are the largest roof gardens in Europe. There are actually three gardens (one is based on the Alhambra in Spain, one is like a sixteenth-century Tudor garden, and one is woodland, where the flamingos live). It has been the property of Richard Branson's *Virgin* group since 1981.

Exercise 1

- Draw attention to the photos and the text and ask students what they can see.
- In pairs, students identify the animals.

Exercise 2

- Students scan the text quickly and find the words for the animals in the pictures.

Answers

deer, flamingos

Key Words

Be prepared to focus on the Key Words, either by pre-teaching them, eliciting their meaning after students have read the text, or through dictionary or definition writing work.

to hire – to pay money in order to use something like a car or a bicycle for a specific period of time

view – what you can see from a specific place

to play golf – a popular game with special metal sticks and a small, hard, white ball

to go fishing – to catch fish in a lake, river or the sea using a special stick and a line

roof – the exterior part of a building at the top

experience – something that you do that is memorable

Exercise 3 (Track 1.28)

- Students read the text again and answer the questions.
- If you wish, play the recording for students to listen and read.
- Check answers by asking pairs of students to read questions and answers.
- Elicit from stronger students or explain yourself the meaning of any new vocabulary.

Answers

2 You can see lots of deer.
3 You can see St Paul's Cathedral.
4 It's 99 Kensington High Street.
5 They are/It's 6,000 square metres.
6 You can see four pink flamingos.

Exercise 4 (Track 1.28)

- Students read the text again and decide which place the sentences refer to.
- Check answers as a class.

Answers

2 RG   3 RP   4 RG   5 RP   6 RP

Extra activity

Stronger groups or individual students prepare a short text about a park in their city or country. Encourage them to recycle and adapt phrases from the Reading text as far as possible and to include a photo.
When checking students' work, focus on the positive use of the grammar and vocabulary taught so far. After correcting the texts you could display them on the classroom walls or use them as the basis for further comprehension work with your class.

Listening

Extra activity

Books closed. Remind students that they have seen 12 different action verbs in this unit. In pairs, students try to remember all the action verbs. When they have finished, students self-correct by looking back at page 23 of the Students' Book.

Exercise 1 (Track 1.29)

- Ask students if they have ever been to an audition.
- Play the recording for students to listen and match the sentences to the people.
- They then check in pairs before you check answers as a class.

Answers

1 Latika   2 Kate   3 Kate   4 Latika and Kate
5 Latika   6 Kate

Audioscript:
See Teacher's Book page 225

Further practice:
Workbook page 22

Writing   A description of a town

Revision

First – Write the following verbs from the unit on the left of the board and ask students to unscramble them (answers in brackets):

yalp (play), *wims* (swim), *gujgel* (juggle), *blimc* (climb), *leccy* (cycle), *urn* (run)

Second – Write the following items from the unit on the right of the board and ask students to unscramble them (answers in brackets).

xsi lalbs (six balls), *a tunomain* (a mountain), *het ratigu* (the guitar), *ni teh loop* (in the pool), *ot holocs* (to school), *a rthanamo* (a marathon)

Third – Students match the words on the left and the right of the board to make 6 collocations from the unit. Students compare their ideas in pairs before checking answers as a class.

(Answers: *climb a mountain*, *cycle to school*, *juggle six balls*, *play the guitar*, *run a marathon*, *swim in the pool*)

Exercise 1

- Read the Writing File with students.
- Make sure students understand that *and* is used to link two positive items, *but* is used to link a positive and a negative item, and *or* is used to link two negative items.

Exercise 2

- Students read the description and find examples of *and*, *or* and *but*.
- Point out that we can use more than one of the words in a single sentence (e.g. *'There is a swimming pool and there's a library* but *there isn't a sports centre or a museum.'*).

Answers

In my home town there is a swimming pool and there's a library, but there isn't a sports centre or a museum. There are lots of houses and shops, but there aren't any cinemas. There are two restaurants and there are four cafés. There are some parks and there's a shopping centre, but there isn't a bus station or a train station. There is a post office, but there isn't a bank. My home town is small, but it's great.

Exercise 3

- Individually, students choose the correct options.
- Check answers by asking individual students to read the sentences.

Answers

2 and   **3** or   **4** but   **5** and

Exercise 4

- Students refer back to the description and complete the list.
- They then check in pairs before checking answers as a class.

Answers

2 a library ✓	**7** some parks ✓
3 two sports centres ✗	**8** a shopping centre ✓
4 a museum ✗	**9** a bus station ✗
5 some houses ✓	**10** a train station ✗
6 some shops ✓	**11** a post office ✓

Exercise 5

- Explain that students should only make notes at this point or write short sentences.
- Encourage students to ask you for any vocabulary they need.

Answers

Students' own answers

Exercise 6

- Read through the 'My town' writing guide. Make sure students understand that there are various possible ways to organise their information but they must now present it as a complete text, not as notes or unconnected sentences. Point out that they can model their answer on the description in Exercise 2.
- Draw students' attention to the 'Remember!' checklist.

Answers

Students' own answers

Extra activity

Add an extra 10–15 vocabulary items from this unit to the collection of Word Cards.

Revise all the vocabulary by playing a drawing game. Tell students that they are going to have an informal vocabulary 'test'. Ask one student to come up to the board, secretly show them one of the Word Cards and explain that they have to draw a picture on the board to illustrate that word. They can't use words as part of their drawing.

The rest of the class look at the drawing and write down what they think the word is. On the count of three, everybody calls out the word they have written down. Those who guess correctly give themselves one point. To resolve any disputes about the awarding of points, students show the teacher the words they have written down. Repeat the procedure with a different student each time until you have revised all the vocabulary. The winner is the student with the most points.

Further practice:
Workbook page 23

Writing
A description of a town

1 Read the Writing File.

> **Writing File** **Linking words**
>
> - There's a cinema **and** a library in my town.
> - There's a swimming pool, **but** there isn't a sports centre.
> - Jess can't dance, **but** she can sing.
> - I can't swim **or** ride a bike.
> - There isn't a shopping centre **or** a park.

2 Read Emma's description of her home town. Find examples of *and*, *or* and *but*.

My Home Town

In my home town there is a swimming pool (and) there's a library, but there isn't a sports centre or a museum. There are lots of houses and shops, but there aren't any cinemas. There are two restaurants and there are four cafés. There are some parks and there's a shopping centre, but there isn't a bus station or a train station. There is a post office, but there isn't a bank. my home town is small, but it's great.

3 Choose the correct options.
1 I can play football *and / but* I can't play tennis.
2 In Paris there are lots of restaurants *and / but* cafés.
3 There isn't a police station *but / or* a bank.
4 There aren't any new students in my class *and / but* there are two new teachers.
5 We can have a picnic *and / but* ride our bikes.

4 Read Emma's description again. What has she got in her home town?
1 a swimming pool ✓
2 a library
3 two sports centres
4 a museum
5 some houses
6 some shops
7 some parks
8 a shopping centre
9 a bus station
10 a train station
11 a post office

5 Imagine a town or think about your home town. What is in your town? Make notes. Use the list from Exercise 4.

6 Write a description of your town. Use 'My town' and your notes from Exercise 5.

> **My town**
>
> **1** Name
> *My town is called ... .*
> **2** Description
> *In ... there is a/are some ... .*
> *In ... there isn't a/aren't any ... .*
> **3** Conclusion
> *My town is ... .*

 Remember!
- Use *and*, *or* and *but*.
- Use the vocabulary in this unit.
- Check your grammar, spelling, and punctuation.

Refresh Your Memory!

Grammar Review

1 **Choose the correct options.**

1 There *is / are* two parks behind my school.
2 There *is / are* a calculator on my desk.
3 There *isn't / aren't* a train station in my town but there *is / are* a bus station.
4 There *isn't / aren't* any comics in my bag.
5 **A** *Is / Are* there a post office next to the shopping centre?
   B No, there *isn't / aren't*.
6 **A** *Is / Are* there any posters in your classroom?
   B Yes, there *is / are* five posters in our classroom.

2 **Look at the list. Make sentences.**

There is one Spanish student in Class 5b.

International School	Class 5b
Spanish students	1
Greek students	0
French students	5
English students	2
Brazilian students	1
Portuguese students	0
Mexican students	4

3 **Complete the text with *can* or *can't* and the verbs.**

My brother, James, ¹ *can climb* (✓ climb) and he ² .... (✓ juggle) but he ³ .... (✗ run) fast. My sister, Hatty, ⁴ .... (✓ dance) but she ⁵ .... (✗ sing). I ⁶ .... (✗ dance) and I ⁷ .... (✗ juggle) but I ⁸ .... (✓ swim).

4 **Make questions and answers.**

1 you / speak English?   ✓
   Can you speak English? Yes, I can.
2 your friends / skate?   ✗
3 your teacher / swim?   ✗
4 Fred / play chess?   ✓
5 Fred's dog / dance?   ✗
6 your dad / fly a plane?   ✗

Vocabulary Review

5 **Look at the pictures and complete the places.**

1 *library*   **2** t .... s ....   **3** h ....   **4** c ....

5 p ....   **6** s .... c ....   **7** p .... o ....   **8** b .... s ....

6 **Complete the sentences with these verbs.**

cycle	sing	juggle	run
~~jump~~	dance	climb	play

1 Trev can *jump* very high.
2 Dave and Sarah can .... beautiful songs.
3 I can't .... the guitar.
4 My dad can .... six balls.
5 I can't .... up that tree!
6 My sister can .... the tango.
7 I can't .... to school because I haven't got a bike.
8 Can you .... fast?

Speaking Review

7 🔊 **1.30** **Complete the sentences with these words. Then listen and check.**

Be	cycle	jump	Open	shout	~~swim~~

1 Don't *swim* in the lake!
2 .... quiet!
3 .... your book.
4 Don't .... at school.
5 Don't .... on the desks!
6 Don't .... in the library.

Dictation

8 🔊 **1.31** **Listen and write in your notebook.**

✓ **My assessment profile:** Workbook page 128

◄ 28 ►

Refresh Your Memory!

Exercise 1

Answers

2 is   **3** isn't, is   **4** aren't   **5** Is, isn't   **6** Are, are

Exercise 2

Answers

There aren't any Greek students in Class 5b.
There are five French students in Class 5b.
There are two English students in Class 5b.
There is one Brazilian student in Class 5b.
There aren't any Portuguese students in Class 5b.
There are four Mexican students in Class 5b.

Exercise 3

Answers

2 can juggle   **6** can't dance
3 can't run   **7** can't juggle
4 can dance   **8** can swim
5 can't sing

Exercise 4

Answers

2 Can your friends skate?
No, they can't.
3 Can your teacher swim?
No, he/she can't.
4 Can Fred play chess?
Yes, he can.
5 Can Fred's dog dance?
No, it/he/she can't.
6 Can your dad fly a plane?
No, he can't.

Exercise 5

Answers

2 train station   **6** sports centre
3 hospital   **7** post office
4 café   **8** bus station
5 park

Exercise 6

Answers

2 sing   **3** play   **4** juggle   **5** climb   **6** dance   **7** cycle
8 run

Exercise 7 (Track 1.30)

Answers

2 Be   **3** Open   **4** cycle   **5** jump   **6** shout

Exercise 8 (Track 1.31)

Answers and Audioscript

1 I can't dance but I can play the piano.
2 Can we skate on the lake?
3 Is there a library in your school?
4 There aren't any parks in my town but there is a big sports centre.
5 Don't sing that song!
6 Watch me! I can climb this tree!

My assessment profile:
Workbook page 128

Extra activity

Revise describing places in town and action verbs:
– Draw speech bubble 1 at the top of the board and write *What's in your town?* in it.
– Elicit some of the places in towns covered in this unit. Write them down the left hand side of the board. Elicit suggestions of things you can do in the places. Write these down the right hand side of the board.
– Ask for possible responses to question 1. Draw and complete speech bubble 2. Elicit a phrase with *There is/are* and a preposition of place (e.g. *'There's a lake. It's in the park.'*).
– Elicit a question with *Can …?* related to the previous bubble (e.g. *'Can you go fishing?'*) and draw and complete speech bubble 3. Then complete speech bubble 4 having elicited the short answer.
– Make sure students understand that this is only an example and that their conversations will not necessarily be the same.
– Allow students to copy the example from the board if they wish.
– Students work in pairs, making similar conversations. Monitor but do not interrupt students' fluency.
– Make a note of any mistakes related to the content of this unit to go over with the class afterwards but make sure these mistakes remain anonymous during the correction stage.

Real World Profiles

Cultural notes

- *Kabul* is the capital city of Afghanistan. The area has been inhabited and fought over for over 5,000 years because of its strategic location on the Asian trade routes. The city suffered due to the wars in the last years of the twentieth century but the situation has improved in the last few years. Still in the process of being redeveloped thanks to foreign investment, the population has increased from 500,000 to just under 4 million since 2001.
- *Skateistan*™ is a new initiative based in Kabul promoting cross-cultural interaction through skateboarding and education. It aims to empower students from all over Afghanistan and from all economic and ethnic backgrounds and to help them develop healthy habits and a sense of social responsibility. It also teaches them about ICT, the arts and language.
- *Fazila Shirindel* is a real person and more information about her is available on the Skateistan website.

Exercise 1

- Draw students' attention to the photo and ask students what they can see.
- Students read the profile and answer the questions.
- Check answers as a class.
- If you have a world map available, ask students where Afghanistan and Kabul are.

Answers

1 She is 14.
2 She comes from Afghanistan.

Exercise 2 (Track 1.32)

- Students read the text and decide if the sentences are true or false.
- If you wish, play the recording for students to listen and read.
- Students check in pairs before you check answers as a class.
- When checking answers, ask students to correct the false sentences.
- Elicit from stronger students or explain yourself the meaning of any new vocabulary.

Answers

2 False (Skateistan has got some classrooms with computers.)
3 True
4 False (Girls and boys don't do activities together in Afghanistan.)
5 False (Fazila hasn't got a skateboard but she can borrow one from the school.)
6 True

Extra activity

Extend the work on Skateistan and ask students to prepare a profile of one of the other workers there. There is information on the current staff on the Skateistan website and contact email addresses for many of them. Students can use their imagination if necessary or even email the person they are writing about.
Alternatively, students can choose another charity they are familiar with and investigate one of the people who works there.

Class discussion

- Read through the questions with students.
- They then work in pairs or small groups talking about the questions.
- Monitor but do not interrupt fluency.
- Take feedback as a class.
- Ideally the class discussion activity should be completed in English but you may want to support weaker students with some L1.

Extra activity

Ask students additional questions related to the topic of the text, e.g.
1 What other things do you know about Afghanistan?
2 Do you think it's a good part of the world to live in? Why/Why not?
3 What countries are near Afghanistan?
4 Do you think it's a good idea for boys and girls not to do activities together?
5 Do you think you are lucky to live where you live? Why/Why not?

In this unit have you …
… used Grammar and Vocabulary worksheet?
… used Reading and Listening worksheet?
… used Writing worksheet?
… used Speaking worksheet?
… used Unit test?

With the exception of the Writing worksheets, all the Teacher's Resources are at two levels of difficulty:
* For students who need extra help and support
** For students who require an additional challenge

Real World Profiles

⊗ Fazila Shirindel's Profile

Age:
14 years old

Home country:
Afghanistan

City:
Kabul

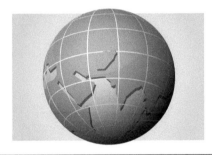

Fazila and Skateistan

Fazila is a 14-year-old girl from Qalai Zaman Khan in Kabul, Afghanistan. Her family is very poor and Fazila's life is difficult, but she is happy because she is a student at a school in Kabul. The school is called 'Skateistan' and it's the first skateboarding school in Kabul. Skateistan has got a big indoor skate park and some classrooms with computers. Children can study English, ICT, Journalism, Art and Music there. There's a special 'Back to school' programme for children who aren't at school. There are separate school days for boys and for girls because girls and boys don't do activities together in Afghanistan, and there are also special classes for disabled children.

After the lessons, there is a 50-minute skateboarding lesson for all the girls in Fazila's class. Fazila hasn't got a skateboard, but she can borrow one from the school. Now Fazila is very good at skateboarding and she is also a teacher at Skateistan. 'Life is hard for me because my family is poor,' says Fazila. 'But when I'm at Skateistan, I'm in a nice place.'

Reading

1 **Read Fazila's profile. Answer the questions.**

   1 How old is Fazila?
   2 Where does she come from?

2 🔊 **1.32 Read about Fazila. Are the sentences true (T) or false (F)?**

   1 Fazila lives in Afghanistan. *T*
   2 There aren't any classrooms in Skateistan.
   3 Children can study English at Skateistan.
   4 Boys and girls work together in schools in Afghanistan.
   5 Fazila has got a skateboard.
   6 Fazila is happy at school.

Class discussion

- Can you skateboard?
- Do you think Skateistan is a good idea? Why/Why not?
- Would you like a skateboarding school in your town?
- What special schools are there in your country?

3 School Days

Grammar	Present simple: affirmative and negative; Present simple: questions
Vocabulary	Daily routines; School subjects
Speaking	Time
Writing	An email

Vocabulary Daily routines

1 🔊 1.33 **Match the pictures to these words. Then listen, check and repeat.**

clean my teeth	do homework	get dressed
get up *1*	go home	go to bed
have a shower	have breakfast	have dinner
have lunch	meet friends	start school
tidy my room	watch TV	

> **Word list** page 43   **Workbook** page 106

2 **Complete the sentences with words from Exercise 1.**

1 I *get up* in the morning and I *have a shower*.
2 I .... breakfast, then I .... my teeth.
3 I .... my friends on the bus.
4 I start .... at 9.00 a.m. My favourite lesson is Maths.
5 We .... lunch at 1.00 p.m.
6 I .... my homework after school. I study in my bedroom.
7 In the evening, I .... TV with my family.
8 We .... to bed at 10.30 p.m. on school days.
9 I .... my room on Saturdays.

3 **What words can follow these verbs?**
1 clean *my teeth*   2 have   3 get   4 go

4 **In pairs, say a sentence about your day. Your partner guesses true or false.**

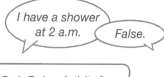

I have a shower at 2 a.m.   *False.*

Brain Trainer Activity 3
Go to page 114

Unit contents

Vocabulary
→ Daily routines – *clean my teeth, do homework, get dressed, get up, go home, go to bed, have a shower, have breakfast, have dinner, have lunch, meet friends, start school, tidy my room, watch TV*
→ School subjects – *Art, English, French, Geography, History, ICT, Literature, Maths, Music, PE, Science, Social Science*

Grammar
→ Present simple – affirmative, negative, questions and short answers

Communication
→ Time
→ Writing an email – My email; Time phrases

Pronunciation
→ *-s* endings

Culture 1 – The United Kingdom: facts and figures

Key competences
→ Linguistic competence
→ Mathematical competence
→ Competence in knowledge and interaction with the physical world
→ Data processing and digital competence
→ Interpersonal, social and civic competence
→ Learning-to-learn
→ Autonomy and personal initiative

Vocabulary   Daily routines

Extra activity

Stronger groups can brainstorm vocabulary they already know for daily routines before looking at the vocabulary in the book. Books closed. In pairs or small groups, students list all the words and expressions they can think of connected with daily routines. Students change partners or groups and peer teach the vocabulary they have thought of. Collate suggestions on the board and correct students' spelling and pronunciation as appropriate.

Exercise 1 (Track 1.33)
• Individually, students match the words and the pictures.
• Play the recording for students to listen and check.
• Repeat the recording. Pause after each word to check students' pronunciation.

Answers

2	have a shower	9	do homework
3	get dressed	10	have dinner
4	have breakfast	11	watch TV
5	meet friends	12	tidy my room
6	start school	13	clean my teeth
7	have lunch	14	go to bed
8	go home		

Exercise 2
• Students work individually and then compare their answers in pairs.
• Check answers by asking individual students to read the sentences.
• Drill the sentences for pronunciation and intonation.

Answers

2	have, clean	6	do
3	meet	7	watch
4	school	8	go
5	have	9	tidy

Exercise 3
• Make sure students understand that there are various possible answers for each verb.
• Collate answers on the board.

Answers
2 have – a shower, breakfast, lunch, dinner
3 get – up, dressed
4 go – to school, home, to bed

Exercise 4
• Students work in pairs, making sentences about their day and deciding if they are true or false.
• Monitor but do not interrupt fluency unless they make mistakes with the daily routine verbs.
• Ask some students to say their sentences for the class to hear.

Extra activity

Reinforce vocabulary and spelling by doing a group mime activity at this point. Ask one student to come to the front of the class and turn his or her back to the board. Write one of the daily routine verbs on the board. On the count of three, everybody else in the class mimes the action for the student to guess. After the student has guessed the action, ask him or her to spell it for you. Repeat the process until you have revised all 14 items.

Further practice:
Workbook pages 24 and 106

Brain Trainer Activity 3
See Teacher's Book page 212 and Students' Book page 114

Reading

Revision

First – Write the following word snake on the board:
meetcleandohavegogetstartwatchtidy

Second – Write a second word snake on the board:
homeworkhometvdressedfriendsmyteethbreakfastupmy roomschool

Third – Students match the verbs from the first word snake with the words from the second to make daily routines. Check answers by asking individual students to write the actions on the board in the most logical order.
(Answers: *get up, clean my teeth, have breakfast, start school, meet friends, go home, watch TV, do homework, tidy my room*)

Extra activity

Use a mill-drill to find out who in the class has the biggest family. Write on the board:
How many brothers have you got?
I've got X brothers./I haven't got any brothers.
How many sisters have you got?
I've got X sisters./I haven't got any sisters.
Students move around the classroom and ask the questions, noting the answers. When they have spoken to all their classmates, they form a line from the biggest to the smallest family.

Exercise 1

- Draw attention to the photo and the text and ask students if they think the small child in the mother's arms is a boy or a girl (he's a boy).
- Individually, students answer the questions.

Exercise 2

- They read the blog quickly to check their answers.

Answers

1 She's got three brothers.
2 She's got two sisters.
3 There are eight people (Maisie, plus five brothers and sisters, and her parents).

Exercise 3 (Track 1.34)

- Individually, students put Maisie's daily routine in order.
- If you wish, play the recording for students to listen and read.
- Elicit from stronger students or explain yourself the meaning of any new vocabulary.

Answers

a 5 **b** 2 **c** 1 **d** 6 **e** 3 **f** 4

Exercise 4 (Track 1.34)

- Students read the text again and complete the sentences.
- They compare their ideas in pairs before you check answers as a class.
- Check answers by asking individual students to write sentences on the board.

Possible Answers

2 (very) big
3 five/5 minutes
4 a minibus
5 6.00 p.m.
6 can do her homework, read a book or watch TV

Extra activity

Stronger groups or fast finishers rewrite the sentences in Exercise 4 to make them true about themselves. They change *Maisie* for the first person, make the necessary grammatical changes and then adjust the other information accordingly. Monitor and point out errors for students to self-correct.

Exercise 5

- Ask two students to read aloud the example question and answer.
- Check the pronunciation of the questions before students work in pairs.
- In pairs, students ask and answer the questions.
- Monitor and help with vocabulary but do not interrupt fluency.
- Make a note of any mistakes relating to the use of *have got* or *can* to go over with the class afterwards.

Extra activity

Use the Reading text as a model to plan a *Live Listening* about your family. This can be real or fictional. Remember to grade your language appropriately and only talk about immediate family members, i.e. parents, brothers and sisters and children.
Write the following questions on the board:
Has your teacher got a big family?
How many brothers and sisters has your teacher got?
How many children has your teacher got?
Has your teacher got a car?
Students listen and individually answer the questions. They then quickly compare their answers in pairs before you check answers as a class. Elicit answers as full sentences, e.g. *'You've got a very big family.'*

Further practice:
Workbook page 25

Reading

1 Look at Maisie's family photo. Answer the questions.

   1 How many brothers has she got?
   2 How many sisters has she got?
   3 How many people are in her family?

2 Read and check your answers to Exercise 1.

3))) 1.34 Read Maisie's blog again. Put these things in the order Maisie does them.

   a play with brothers and sisters
   b have a shower
   c have breakfast *1*
   d do homework
   e go to school
   f tidy the living room

4))) 1.34 Read Maisie's blog again. Complete the sentences.

   1 Life in Maisie's house *is fun but it's difficult, too.*
   2 Maisie's family is …. .
   3 Every morning, Maisie is in the bathroom for …. .
   4 Maisie's parents haven't got a car, they've got …. .
   5 Maisie has dinner at …. .
   6 After 8.00 p.m., Maisie …. .

5 What about you? In pairs, ask and answer.

   1 Have you got a big family?
   2 How many brothers and sisters have you got?
   3 Can you watch TV on school days?
   4 Can you meet your friends after school?

> How many brothers and sisters have you got?

> I've got two sisters.

A day with … my big family

My name is Maisie Hall and I've got five brothers and sisters! Life in our house is fun, but it's difficult, too.

On school days I get up very early at 6.00 a.m. but I don't have a shower straight away. I have my breakfast first. Our family is big so we don't have breakfast together. After breakfast I have a shower and get dressed. I only have five minutes in the bathroom before my sister knocks on the door!

At 8.00 a.m. we go to school in our minibus. It's got ten seats, it's big and it's fun!

School starts at 8.30 a.m. and we go home at 3.00 p.m. After school I don't watch TV. I tidy the living room for my mum and I play with my brothers and sisters.

We have dinner all together at 6.00 p.m. My baby brother goes to bed at 7.00 p.m. and my other brothers and sisters go to bed at 8.00 p.m. Then I can work!

From 8.00 p.m. to 9.00 p.m. I do my homework, read a book or watch TV with my parents. After that I clean my teeth and go to bed.

Me and my family

Me

31

Grammar Present simple: affirmative and negative

Affirmative		
I/You/We/They	get up	at 7.00 a.m.
He/She/It	gets up	

Negative		
I/You/We/They	don't (do not) get up	at 7.00 a.m.
He/She/It	doesn't (does not) get up	

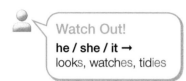

Watch Out!

he / she / it →
looks, watches, tidies

1 **Study the grammar tables. Choose the correct options to complete the rules.**

1 We add -s to the verb after *I, you, we, they / he, she, it.*
2 The words *don't* and *doesn't* make the *affirmative / negative* of the Present simple.

Pronunciation   -s endings

2a 🔊 1.35 **Listen to the -s endings.**

likes → /s/
plays → /z/
watches → /ɪz/

b 🔊 1.36 **Listen and say /-s/, /-z/ or /-ɪz/.**

1 gets up	5 eats
2 has	6 dances
3 cleans	7 does
4 watches	8 goes

c 🔊 1.36 **Listen again and repeat.**

3 **Choose the correct options.**

1 I *get / gets* up early and have breakfast before 7.30 a.m.
2 My teachers *has / have* lunch at school.
3 They *has / have* dinner at 9.00 p.m.
4 We *goes / go* to the cinema on Wednesdays.
5 Tom *meet / meets* his friends after school.
6 My father *has / have* got a red car.
7 Sue *go / goes* to school by bike.
8 You *does / do* your homework before dinner.

Grammar reference Workbook page 90

4 **Make negative sentences.**

1 Josh has breakfast at 9.00 a.m.
Josh doesn't have breakfast at 9.00 a.m.
2 Adam goes to school by train.
3 I do Sudokus.
4 Lorenzo and Tina have lunch at one o'clock.
5 Anita plays football on Saturdays.
6 Ella goes to bed at 9.30 p.m.
7 We have dinner together.
8 You speak Chinese.

5 **Complete the descriptions. Then guess the person.**

get dressed	~~get up~~	get up	go
have	not have	not get up	

1 Every Saturday I ¹ *get up* at 7.00 a.m. and I ² .... in my old clothes. First, I clean out the animals on our farm and then, the animals ³ .... breakfast. My parents and I ⁴ .... breakfast early. We eat eggs and toast at about 10.00 a.m.
2 I ⁵ .... early on Saturday. I watch TV in bed and I ⁶ .... at 11.00 a.m. In the afternoon my friends and I ⁷ .... to the park and play football. My dog Sunny likes football too!

6 **What about you? Write affirmative and negative sentences about your weekend.**

I watch TV on Saturday.

Grammar   Present simple: affirmative and negative

Language notes

The spelling rules relating to the formation of the Present simple for *he/she/it* are as follows:
- Verb + *s*: Most verbs simply add an *-s* to make the third person form.
- Verb + *es*: Some verbs take *-es* at the end, generally verbs which end in *-s*, *-sh*, *-ch* and *-x*, but also the verbs *do* and *go*.
- Verb + *ies*: Verbs which end in a consonant followed by *-y* form the third person by changing *-y* to *-i* and adding *-es* (e.g. *study–studies*, *try–tries*, *copy–copies*).

Exercise 1
- Read the grammar tables with students.
- Students work individually, choosing the correct options and referring back to the grammar tables where necessary.
- Read the 'Watch Out!' section with students.
- If you have a stronger group, elicit from the class the spelling rules for the Present simple.
- Alternatively, be prepared to explain for weaker groups the spelling changes for the third person.

Answers
1 *he, she, it*   2 negative

Pronunciation   *-s* endings

Language notes
- Third person singular verbs are pronounced with /s/ at the end when the infinitive ends with an unvoiced consonant sound and with /z/ at the end when the infinitive ends with a voiced consonant sound. Only when the infinitive ends with the sounds /ʃ/, /tʃ/, /ʒ/ or /dʒ/ do we add the complete syllable /ɪz/.
- Note that the pronunciation of *do/does* in the following exercise is irregular in that the vowel sound changes from the infinitive /duː/ to the third person /dʌz/.

Exercise 2a (Track 1.35)
- Play the recording for students to listen to the *-s* endings.

Exercise 2b (Track 1.36)
- Students classify the verbs according to the endings.
- They then check in pairs before you check answers as a class.

Answers
1 /s/   2 /z/   3 /z/   4 /ɪz/   5 /s/   6 /ɪz/
7 /z/   8 /z/

Exercise 2c (Track 1.36)
- Repeat the recording for students to listen and repeat. Pause after each word to check students' pronunciation.

Further practice:
Workbook page 123

Exercise 3
- Individually, students choose the correct options.
- Check the pronunciation of the third person forms used in sentences 5, 6 and 7.

Answers
2 have   3 have   4 go   5 meets   6 has   7 goes
8 do

Exercise 4
- Remind students of the use of the auxiliaries *don't* and *doesn't* in the negative.
- Individually, students change the sentences from affirmative to negative.

Answers
2 Adam doesn't go to school by train.
3 I don't do Sudokus.
4 Lorenzo and Tina don't have lunch at one o'clock.
5 Anita doesn't play football on Saturdays.
6 Ella doesn't go to bed at 9.30 p.m.
7 We don't have dinner together.
8 You don't speak Chinese.

Exercise 5
- Students complete the descriptions. Check students remember the names of the two people before they start the exercise.
- Check answers by asking individual students to write answers on the board.

Answers
2 get dressed   3 have   4 don't have   5 don't get up
6 get up   7 go
Text 1 Monica   **Text 2** Nick

Exercise 6
- Monitor and point out errors for students to self-correct.
- Ask some students to say their sentences for the class to hear.

Answers
Students' own answers

Further practice:
Workbook pages 26 and 90–91

Brain Trainer Activity 2
See Teacher's Book page 212 and Students' Book page 114

Vocabulary   School subjects

Revision
First – Write the following infinitives on the board:
climb, dance, eat, juggle, play, sit, study, swim, tidy, walk

Second – Students write the third person form of the verbs
and decide if the endings are pronounced with /s/, /z/ or /ɪz/.

Third – Check spelling and pronunciation by asking individual
students to write answers on the board and say them
correctly.
(Answers: /s/ – *eats, sits, walks*; /z/ – *climbs, juggles, plays,
swims*; /ɪz/ – *dances, studies, tidies*)

Exercise 1 (Track 1.37)
- In pairs, students match the words in the box with the pictures.
- Play the recording for students to listen and check. Pause as appropriate to check students' pronunciation.

Answers
2 Science
3 English
4 French
5 Music
6 PE (Physical Education)
7 History
8 Geography
9 Art
10 Literature
11 Social Science
12 ICT (Information and Communication Technology)

Extra activity
Stronger groups or individual students can prepare a
copy of their school timetable for you in English. They
prepare a grid and add the times, days of the week,
classrooms, subjects and teachers. Monitor and help
with vocabulary, particularly any subjects which are not
covered in the Students' Book.

Exercise 2 (Track 1.38)
- Explain that Jimmy is a new student in the school.
- Play the recording for students to write the lesson.
- Repeat the recording, pausing after each section to check students' answers.

Answers
2 Classroom 2   French
3 Classroom 3   Art
4 Classroom 4   Science
5 Classroom 5   Music
6 Classroom 6   PE/Physical Education

Exercise 3
- Make sure students understand that there are various possible subjects for some of the activities.
- Students compare their ideas in pairs before you check answers as a class.
- Collate answers on the board.

Possible Answers
1 *Literature*, *History*, English, Geography, Social Science
2 English, French, Social Science
3 ICT
4 PE
5 Maths, Science
6 Music
7 English, French, History, Literature, Social Science
8 Art
9 Geography
10 Science
11 Social Science
12 Literature

Exercise 4
- Students answer the questions.
- Monitor and point out errors for students to self-correct.

Extra activity
If you are familiar with your students' timetable, prepare
a quiz based around their normal school week. Prepare
eight to ten items, for example:
1 You've got this subject on Monday at 10:00 a.m.
2 You've got this subject on Monday, Tuesday and Thursday.
3 You haven't got this subject on Wednesday or Thursday.
4 You've got this subject in classroom X on Thursday.
5 You've got this subject on Tuesday with Mr Y.
Limit the questions so that the answers are only subjects
which are covered in the Students' Book and grade your
language appropriately. Students compare their answers
in pairs. Repeat sentences as necessary then check
answers as a class.

Further practice:
Workbook pages 27 and 106

Brain Trainer Activity 4
See Teacher's Book page 212 and Students' Book page 114

Vocabulary School subjects

1 🔊 1.37 **Match the pictures to these words. Then listen, check and repeat.**

Art	English	French	Geography
History	ICT	Literature	Maths *1*
Music	PE	Science	Social Science

Word list page 43   **Workbook** page 106

  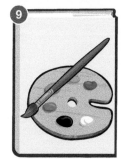

2 🔊 1.38 **Jimmy can't find the right classroom. Listen and say the lessons.**

1 Classroom 1 *Maths*
2 Classroom 2
3 Classroom 3
4 Classroom 4
5 Classroom 5
6 Classroom 6

3 Match these activities to subjects from Exercise 1.

1 write essays
   Literature, History…
2 speak in pairs
3 use a computer
4 move your body
5 work with numbers
6 sing
7 read books
8 draw or paint
9 work with maps
10 do experiments
11 talk about society
12 write stories

4 What about you? In pairs, ask and answer.

1 What lessons have you got on Monday?
2 Who is your Art teacher?
3 What days are your French lessons?
4 Are you good at Maths?
5 Have you got PE today?
6 What is your favourite lesson?

What lessons have you got on Monday?

I've got History, Maths, English and PE.

 Brain Trainer Activity 4 Go to page 114

33

Chatroom Time

Speaking and Listening

1 Look at the photo.

1 Where are they?
2 What objects can you see in the photo?

2 **1.39 Listen and read the conversation. Match the phrases to make sentences.**

1 Monica meets Nick *b*
2 Monica gets up early
3 Monica lives
4 Nick has got a
5 Nick's lesson starts

a on a farm.
b at quarter past eight.
c at nine o'clock.
d because the bus leaves at seven fifteen.
e History lesson.

3 Act out the conversation in pairs.

Monica	Hi Nick! You're early.
Nick	Really? What's the time?
Monica	It's quarter past eight.
Nick	Why are you early?
Monica	Because the bus from our village leaves at seven fifteen.
Nick	You're lucky to live on a farm. I love farms.
Monica	Yes, I know. Do you want to come over on Saturday?
Nick	Yes, great idea. Thanks.
Monica	Great! What subject have you got now?
Nick	I've got History first.
Monica	What time does it start?
Nick	It starts at nine o'clock. What time is it?
Monica	It's eight twenty. See you later!

Say it in your language …
I know.
See you later!

34

Chatroom   Time

Revision

First – Before the class, write the days of the week from Monday to Friday across the top of the board. Underneath, draw a series of small clock faces that correspond to the starting times of classes in your school. Below that, write the names of the teachers who teach your students the different subjects covered on the previous Vocabulary page.

Second – Use a 'silent approach' for this activity. Mime 'zipping' your mouth closed to make it clear that you are not going to speak. Point at one of the days of the week, one of the times and the teacher who is teaching the students at that time. Elicit the subject students have at that time. Nod your approval and continue eliciting other subjects.

Third – Allow some students to take a turn, again in complete silence. Students who have been particularly silent during the teacher-led stage of the activity come forward and repeat the process, eliciting subjects from their classmates.

Speaking and Listening

Exercise 1

- Draw attention to the photo and ask students who they can see.
- Check answers as a class.

> **Answers**
>
> 1 They are at school.
> 2 You can see a backpack, ice skates, a magazine and a watch.

Brain Trainer Activity 1
See Teacher's Book page 212 and Students' Book page 114

 ### Exercise 2 (Track 1.39)

- Play the recording for students to match the phrases.
- Check answers by asking individual students to read the sentences.

> **Answers**
>
> 2 d   3 a   4 e   5 c

> **Extra activity**
>
> Stronger groups or fast finishers memorise the sentences in Exercise 2 for one minute. Students then test themselves or their partner by covering first the beginnings of the sentences and then the ends and seeing how many complete sentences they can remember.

Exercise 3

- Divide the class into pairs.
- Pairs act out the conversation.
- Monitor and correct students' pronunciation as appropriate.
- Nominate one pair to perform the conversation for the class.

> **Extra activity**
>
> Drill the conversation for correct pronunciation. Tell the class that they are going to be Monica and that you are going to be Nick. Build up the conversation step by step until students can perform it unprompted.

Say it in your language ...

 Ask students to find the phrases in the conversation and look at them in context to try to deduce the meaning.

I know. – used in this context to indicate that you understand what someone is saying to you, possibly in a slightly odd situation. Care must be taken with the intonation which should fall gently in order not to appear irritated.

See you later! – an informal way to say goodbye, usually when you are expecting to see the person again later in the same day. Students, for example, could use this expression after a class in the morning if they expect to see you around the school again during the day.

Exercise 4
- Students refer back to the conversation and find the times.
- When checking answers, draw small clocks on the board to make sure students are clear about the times.

Answers

quarter past eight   seven fifteen   nine o'clock
eight twenty

Exercise 5
- Read through the phrases for asking and answering about time with the class.
- Drill the phrases for word stress and intonation.

Exercise 6
- Individually, students write sentences.
- Tell them that they should write each time in two ways as in the example question.
- Check answers as a class then drill the sentences for pronunciation.

Answers

2 It's twenty-five past eleven. / It's eleven twenty-five.
3 It's five past eight. / It's eight oh five.
4 It's ten to three. / It's two fifty.
5 It's half past three. / It's three thirty.

Exercise 7 (Track 1.40)
- Play the recording for students to listen to the conversation.
- In pairs, students act out the conversation.
- Monitor and correct students' pronunciation as appropriate.

Exercise 8
- Students make their own conversations by replacing the words in purple.
- Monitor but do not interrupt fluency unless students make mistakes with the times or school subjects.

Exercise 9
- Choose some pairs to act out their conversation to the class.

Further practice:
Workbook pages 28 and 115

Grammar   Present simple: questions and short answers

Language notes

- Students are introduced here to the use of the auxiliaries *Do* and *Does* to form questions with the Present simple. They have already seen question forms with *be*, *have got* and *can* but as the different question forms are not mixed at this point this should not prove problematic.

- Be prepared to explain to students that these auxiliaries have no meaning, their function is simply to indicate that we are asking a question rather than making an affirmative sentence.

Exercise 1
- Read the grammar table with students.
- Students work individually, completing the rules and referring back to the grammar table where necessary.

Answers

1 Does   **2** does   **3** doesn't

Exercise 2
- Elicit the second question before students work individually.
- Remind students to refer to the conversation in Speaking and Listening Exercise 2 to answer the questions.
- Check answers as a class.

Answers

2 Do; Yes, they do.
3 Does; No, she doesn't.
4 Does; Yes, she does.
5 Does; Yes, he does.

Exercise 3
- Monitor and help with grammar if necessary.
- Students compare their answers in pairs.
- Check answers by asking pairs of students to read questions and answers.

Answers

2 Do you live in Poland?
3 Does she go to school by bus?
4 Do you write essays in English?
5 Do you have lunch at 1 p.m.?
6 Does he study French?

Exercise 4
- Check the questions before students work in pairs.

Answers

2 Do you go to school at 7.15?
3 Does your friend like Maths?
4 Does your teacher watch TV after school?
5 Do you and your family have dinner together?
6 Do you go to bed at half past ten?
7 Do your friends cycle to school?

Further practice:
Workbook pages 29 and 90–91 Teacher's Book Page 71

4 Look back at the conversation. Find the times Nick and Monica talk about.

1 *quarter past eight...*

5 Read the phrases for asking and answering about time.

Asking about time	Answering about time
What's the time?	It's quarter past eight.
What time is it?	It's eight twenty.
What time does it start?	At seven fifteen.
	It starts at nine o'clock.
What time does it finish?	It finishes at half past one.

6 What time is it?

1 7.15 *It's quarter past seven. / It's seven fifteen.*
2 11.25
3 8.05
4 2.50
5 3.30

7 🔊 1.40 Listen to the conversation. Act out the conversation in pairs.

Girl What's the time?
Boy It's [1] quarter past eleven.
Girl What time is our [2] French lesson?
Boy It starts at [3] twenty past eleven. We're early.
Girl What time does it finish?
Boy It finishes at [4] ten past twelve.

8 Work in pairs. Replace the words in purple in Exercise 7 with these words. Act out the conversation.

What's the time? *It's quarter past eight.*

1 eleven o'clock / five past eleven / half past eleven

2 English / Geography / Science / Maths

3 twelve o'clock / twenty-five past twelve / twelve forty-five

4 twelve forty-five / one o'clock / half past one

9 Act out the conversation again with your own words and ideas.

Grammar   Present simple: questions and short answers

Questions		
Do I/you/we/they	get up	at seven o'clock?
Does he/she/it	get up	

Short answers
Yes, I/you/we/they do.
No, I/you/we/they don't.
Yes, he/she/it does.
No, he/she/it doesn't.

Grammar reference Workbook page 90

1 Study the grammar table. Complete the rules.

1 Present simple questions start with *Do* or ..... .
2 Short answers with *Yes* end with *do* or ..... .
3 Short answers with *No* end with *don't* or ..... .

2 Choose the correct options to make questions. Then write answers.

1 *Do / Does* Nick and Monica get up early?
Do Nick and Monica get up early? Yes, they do.
2 *Do / Does* they go to the same school?
3 *Do / Does* Monica walk to school?
4 *Do / Does* Monica live on a farm?
5 *Do / Does* Nick have History first?

3 Make questions for these answers.

1 No, I don't speak German.
Do you speak German?
2 No, we don't live in Poland.
3 Yes, she goes to school by bus.
4 Yes, we write essays in English.
5 No, I don't. I have lunch at 2 p.m.
6 Yes, he studies French.

4 Make questions. In pairs, ask and answer.

1 you / get up / at half past six?
Do you get up at half past six? No, I don't.
2 you / go to school / at 7.15?
3 your friend / like / Maths?
4 your teacher / watch TV / after school?
5 you and your family / have dinner together?
6 you / go to bed / at half past ten?
7 your friends / cycle to school?

35

Reading

1 **Look quickly at the quiz. Can you find this information?**

   1 Eight countries.
   2 The names of two schools.

The big school quiz

Do you know about schools in other countries?
Do this quiz and find out!

1 The City Montessori School in Lucknow, India, is very, very big. How many pupils study there?
   a 12,000
   b 22,000
   c 39,500

2 In France, some pupils never go to school on …
   a Saturdays and Sundays.
   b Wednesdays and Sundays.
   c Sundays and Mondays.

3 In Sweden, Switzerland and Denmark, some children start school at …
   a 7 years old.
   b 8 years old.
   c 9 years old.

4 In South Korea, some pupils stay at school after lessons finish at 4.00 p.m. Do they …
   a do their homework?
   b clean their classrooms?
   c watch TV?

5 Australian children go to school 200 days a year. How many days a year do Chinese children go to school?
   a 211 days a year.
   b 231 days a year.
   c 251 days a year.

6 Shishi Middle School in China is about …
   a one thousand years old.
   b three thousand years old.
   c two thousand years old.

7 In China, some children finish school at …
   a 12 years old.
   b 15 years old.
   c 16 years old.

Answer key

1 c 2 b 3 a 4 a 5 c 6 c 7 b

Key Words

find out   to stay
thousand

2 🔊 1.41 **Do the quiz. Then listen and check your answers.**

3 **Now read about your score.**

   0 – 2 Oh dear! Find out about other countries.
   3 – 5 Well done. You know some interesting facts.
   6 – 7 Fantastic!

4 🔊 1.41 **Read the quiz again. Name the countries.**

   1 There is a 2,000-year-old school in this country.
      China
   2 The school day finishes at 4.00 p.m. in this country.
   3 The City Montessori School is in this country.
   4 Children go to school for 200 days a year in this country.
   5 Pupils can finish school when they are 15 in this country.
   6 Some children start school at 7 years old in these three countries.

Listening

1 🔊 1.42 **Listen to an interview. Put the topics in order 1–3.**
   a summer
   b clothes
   c break

2 🔊 1.42 **Listen again. Correct the sentences.**
   1 Jin goes to school in Japan.
   2 His school day finishes at 4.00 p.m.
   3 He has one hour for his lunch break.
   4 He wears a blue shirt and blue trousers.
   5 He does exercise on Monday and Thursday.
   6 He doesn't study in summer.

3 🔊 1.42 **Listen again. Swap books and check your partner's answers.**

Reading

Cultural notes

- The information contained in the quiz and the recording is all true. Further information is available by searching the internet.

Exercise 1

- Students scan the quiz quickly and find the information.
- Check answers as a class.
- If you have a world map available, ask students where the countries are.

Answers

1 India, France, Sweden, Switzerland, Denmark, South Korea, Australia, China
2 City Montessori School, Shishi Middle School

Exercise 2 (Track 1.41)

- Students read the quiz again and answer the questions.
- Play the recording for students to listen and check.

Answers

1 c **2** b **3** a **4** a **5** c **6** c **7** b

Key Words

Be prepared to focus on the Key Words, either by pre-teaching them, eliciting their meaning after students have read the text, or through dictionary or definition writing work.

find out – to get specific information about something

to stay – to remain or continue to be in a place

thousand – the number, 1,000

Exercise 3

- Students read about their score.
- Take feedback as a class. Ask them if they think it is a fair assessment and find out who scored the highest.

Exercise 4 (Track 1.41)

- Students refer back to the quiz and name the countries.
- Check the pronunciation of the countries.

Answers

2 South Korea
3 India
4 Australia
5 China
6 Sweden, Switzerland, Denmark

Extra activity

Write the word *COUNTRIES* vertically down the centre of the board. Following on from the C horizontally write five dashes to indicate letters. Pick individual students, asking them to say a letter. If the letter they choose is in the word, write it in the correct position. If it is not, write it in a column on one side of the board. When students think they know what the word is, they put their hands up. (Answer: *Canada*)
Continue working down the puzzle until students have completed all the words and the board looks as follows.

```
        C A N A D A
        B O L I V I A
          U K R A I N E
      H U N G A R Y
      V I E T N A M
    N I G E R I A
      M E X I C O
  G R E E C E
M A D A G A S C A R
```

Drill the countries for pronunciation and word stress.

Listening

Exercise 1 (Track 1.42)

- Play the recording for students to listen and order the topics.
- Check answers as a class.

Answers

a 3 **b** 2 **c** 1

Audioscript:
See Teacher's Book page 225

Exercise 2 (Track 1.42)

- Make sure students understand that all the sentences have mistakes.
- Repeat the recording for students to correct the sentences.

Answers

1 Jin goes to school in China.
2 His school day finishes at 5.00 p.m.
3 He has two hours for his lunch break.
4 He wears a white shirt and blue trousers.
5 He does exercise every day.
6 He studies in summer.

Exercise 3 (Track 1.42)

- Play the recording again for students to peer-correct each other's work.
- Check answers by asking individual students to write answers on the board.

Further practice:
Workbook page 30

Writing   An email

Revision

First – Revise the countries from the previous Reading and Listening page (*Australia, China, Denmark, France, India, Japan, South Korea, Sweden, Switzerland*). Drill for pronunciation and word stress.

Second – Read the following clues and ask students to identify the countries.

1 The food in this country is great. The Eiffel Tower is in this country. (Answer: *France)*
2 This country is very expensive. It's got great chocolate and big banks! (Answer: *Switzerland)*
3 This is a big country. There are kangaroos and koalas there. (Answer: *Australia)*
4 This country's got four big islands and many small islands and it's very expensive. (Answer: *Japan)*
5 In this country there's a very, very big school. It's a cheap country. (Answer: *India)*
6 This country's got lots of people and it's very big. There's a big wall there. (Answer: *China)*

Third – Check answers and spelling by asking individual students to write answers on the board.

Language notes

- Students are introduced to the time phrases *on, in* and *at* in this unit in a very controlled way. Preposition use in other languages often seems random. It is however no more random in English than in any other language, it will merely seem so to students who are learning it as a second language.
- Here students see three basic uses of the prepositions. Avoid the temptation to go into more detail than is necessary at this point as there are many irregularities (e.g. *in the morning/afternoon/ evening* but *at night; on Christmas Day* but *at Christmas time,* etc.). The material here has been carefully selected to avoid these problems.

Exercise 1

- Read the Writing File with students.

Exercise 2

- Students read the email and find examples of *on, in* and *at.*
- Check answers with the class by eliciting some examples from the students.

Answers

on Monday, in the class, in the morning, at quarter past two, in his lessons

Exercise 3

- Individually, students answer the questions.
- They then check in pairs before you check answers as a class.
- Check answers by asking pairs of students to read questions and answers.

Answers

2 It's at 9.05/five past nine.
3 Yes, he does.
4 Yes, he is.
5 Mr Singer.
6 He sings (all the time) in his lessons.

Exercise 4

- Individually, students choose the correct options.
- Check answers by asking individual students to read the sentences.

Answers

2 on   3 at   4 in

Exercise 5

- Explain that students should only make notes at this point or write short sentences.
- Encourage students to ask you for any vocabulary they need.

Answers

Students' own answers

Exercise 6

- Show students how the example email is sequenced.
- Read through the 'My email' writing guide. Tell students they must now present their information as a complete text, not as notes or unconnected sentences.
- Draw students' attention to the 'Remember!' checklist.

Answers

Students' own answers

Extra activity

Add an extra 10–15 vocabulary items from this unit to the collection of Word Cards.

Revise all the vocabulary by playing a mime game. Divide students into small groups and divide the vocabulary cards between the groups. If you have a few cards left over, give these to the stronger groups or fast finishers. Tell students to take turns to communicate the meaning of the vocabulary using only gestures. They can't use sounds or words. The rest of the group have to guess what the word is.

When a group finish with their vocabulary cards, change them with another group until all the groups have revised all the cards.

Further practice:
Workbook page 31

Writing   An email

1   **Read the Writing File.**

> **Writing File**   **Time phrases**
>
> We use these words to make time phrases.
> * **on** + day
> * **in** + *the morning / the afternoon*
> * **at** + time

2   **Read the email. Find time phrases with *on*, *in* and *at*.**

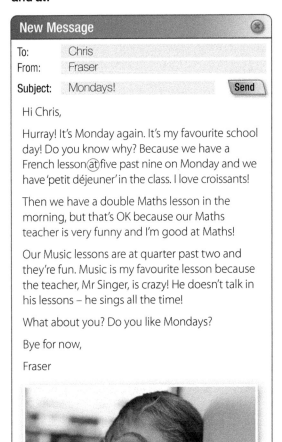

> **New Message**   ⊗
>
> To: Chris
> From: Fraser
>
> Subject: Mondays!   **Send**
>
> Hi Chris,
>
> Hurray! It's Monday again. It's my favourite school day! Do you know why? Because we have a French lesson at five past nine on Monday and we have 'petit déjeuner' in the class. I love croissants!
>
> Then we have a double Maths lesson in the morning, but that's OK because our Maths teacher is very funny and I'm good at Maths!
>
> Our Music lessons are at quarter past two and they're fun. Music is my favourite lesson because the teacher, Mr Singer, is crazy! He doesn't talk in his lessons – he sings all the time!
>
> What about you? Do you like Mondays?
>
> Bye for now,
>
> Fraser

3   **Read the email again. Answer the questions.**

1 Does Fraser like Mondays? *Yes, he does.*
2 What time is Fraser's French lesson?
3 Does Fraser have Maths on Mondays?
4 Is Fraser good at Maths?
5 Who is Fraser's Music teacher?
6 What does the Music teacher do?

4   **Choose the correct options.**

1 I have English *in / at* the morning.
2 Our Art lesson is *at / on* Friday.
3 My school day starts *in / at* eight o'clock.
4 We have PE *in / on* the afternoon.

5   **Think about your favourite school day. Answer the questions.**

1 What is your favourite day?
2 What lessons do you have on your favourite day?
3 Who are your teachers? What subjects do they teach?
4 What time are your lessons?
5 What is your favourite lesson?

6   **Write a short email about your favourite school day. Use 'My email' and your answers from Exercise 5.**

> **My email**   ⊗
>
> 1   Start your email.
>   *Dear / Hi … ,*
> 2   Say what your favourite day is.
>   *My favourite day is … .*
> 3   Say what lessons you have.
>   *We have … on … .*
> 4   Say who your teachers are and what subjects they teach.
> 5   Say what time your lessons are.
> 6   Say what your favourite lesson is and why.
>   *… is my favourite lesson because … .*
> 7   Finish your email.
>   *See you soon! / Bye for now!*

> **Remember!**
> * Use time phrases to describe when things happen.
> * Use the Present simple.
> * Use the vocabulary in this unit.
> * Check your grammar, spelling and punctuation.

◀ 37 ▶

Refresh Your Memory!

Grammar Review

1 **Make sentences. Use the Present simple affirmative.**

   1 Linda / watch / TV before school.
     Linda watches TV before school.

   2 Max / study / French / at university.
   3 Eva and Sara / study / Maths.
   4 My dad / tidy / the house every evening.
   5 My brother / play / football in the garden.
   6 You / get up / before me.

2 **Complete the sentences with the Present simple negative.**

   1 I get up early, but Adam .... .
     I get up early but Adam *doesn't get up early.*

   2 You like History, but Nadia .... .
   3 I have lunch at school, but Mum and Dad .... .
   4 We walk to school, but Maria and Anna .... .
   5 I go to bed at 10.00 p.m., but my sister .... .
   6 I do my homework in front of the TV, but you .... .

3 **Complete the email with *do*, *don't*, *does* or *doesn't*.**

   Hi Marta,

   What subjects [1] *do* you study at school? We can choose subjects now because we are 14. I [2] .... have History lessons now, but I study Geography. I [3] .... study Art because I can't paint. My friend Matt [4] .... like French, so his language lesson is German. [5] .... your school give you a choice? At what age [6] .... you choose?

   Write and tell me!

   Veronica

4 **Match the questions to the correct answer.**

   1 Does Alan like dogs? *b*
   2 Do you walk to school?
   3 Do I start school before you?
   4 Do Pepe and Nina read books in English?
   5 Does Angela meet her friends before school?

   a Yes, they do.
   b No, he doesn't.
   c Yes, she does.
   d Yes, I do.
   e No, you don't.

Vocabulary Review

5 **Complete the routine verbs.**

   Dan gets [1] *up* at 6.00 a.m. every morning. He doesn't [2] .... dressed or [3] .... his teeth and he doesn't [4] .... a shower. He [5] .... breakfast, but he doesn't [6] .... TV and he doesn't [7] .... homework. He [8] .... to bed when he wants to. Why? Because Dan is my dog!

6 **Match the definitions to these words.**

Art	English	~~French~~	Geography
ICT	Literature	Music	PE

   1 They speak this language in France. *French*
   2 We learn about the world and other countries in this lesson.
   3 We play football and basketball in this lesson.
   4 This lesson teaches us about books, stories and poems.
   5 We paint pictures in this lesson.
   6 We learn about computers in this lesson.
   7 They speak this language in the UK.
   8 We play instruments in this lesson.

Speaking Review

7))) 1.43 **Put the sentences in the correct order. Then listen and check.**

   a It starts at quarter past eleven. We're early.
   b What's the time? *1*
   c What time does it finish?
   d Oh. What time is our French lesson?
   e It finishes at twenty past twelve.
   f It's ten past ten.

Dictation

8))) 1.44 **Listen and write in your notebook.**

9 **Swap books and check your partner's work.**

✓ **My assessment profile:** Workbook page 129

Refresh Your Memory!

Exercise 1

Answers

2 Max studies French at university.
3 Eva and Sara study Maths.
4 My dad tidies the house every evening.
5 My brother plays football in the garden.
6 You get up before me.

Exercise 2

Answers

2 doesn't like History
3 don't have lunch at school
4 don't walk to school
5 doesn't go to bed at 10.00 p.m.
6 don't do your homework in front of the TV

Exercise 3

Answers

2 don't   3 don't   4 doesn't   5 Does   6 do

Exercise 4

Answers

2 d   3 e   4 a   5 c

Exercise 5

Answers

2 get   3 clean   4 have   5 has   6 watch   7 do
8 goes

Exercise 6

Answers

2 Geography   3 PE   4 Literature   5 Art   6 ICT
7 English   8 Music

Exercise 7 (Track 1.43)

Answers

a 4   b 1   c 5   d 3   e 6   f 2

Exercise 8 (Track 1.44)

Answers and Audioscript

1 My sister gets up at 8 a.m.
2 I meet my friends at the weekend.
3 Have you got Maths this afternoon?
  No, I haven't.
4 What time is your French lesson?
  It's at ten past twelve.
5 I start school at 9 a.m.

My assessment profile:
Workbook page 129

Extra activity

Revise question forms which have appeared in the first three units:
– Write *A typical student* in a cloud in the centre of the board and copy the figure. Include the flag of the country you are teaching in.
– Elicit suggestions for names for the character based on the letter on his shirt. The name should be typical of the country.
– Tell students they are going to interview this 'typical' student. In pairs, students brainstorm questions they might ask. They make questions with *you*.
– Draw 12 speech bubbles around the board and fill in the prompts one at a time, eliciting in each case the full question and drilling for pronunciation and intonation. Ask students if they thought of any other questions.
– Divide the class into pairs. One student asks the questions and the other answers in the character of a typical student from the country.
– Discuss the questions as a class using the third person and find out how much consensus there is among the group about what is typical.

Culture 1 – The United Kingdom, facts and figures
See Teacher's Book page 219 and Students' Book page 121 (for extra reading, discussion and writing work).

Technology File   How to make a Camera Obscura

Cultural notes

- The *Camera Obscura* takes its name from Latin where 'camera' means 'room' and 'obscura' means 'dark'. The first camera obscuras were indeed darkened rooms although the principle was actually discovered in Ancient Greece. Over the centuries the camera obscura became smaller and the principles involved led in part to the invention of photography. Camera obscura of the type demonstrated are also frequently referred to as 'pinhole cameras'.
- Essential to the success of a camera obscura is a precise, small pinhole; effective light-proofing and a well-illuminated subject. The characteristic upside-down image is best seen when the camera is pointed at a scene in direct sunlight or bright artificial light.
- Further information on the camera obscura and the scientific principles involved is available on the internet.

Language notes

- Be prepared to elicit from stronger students or explain yourself the meaning of the following lexical items which appear in the Reading text: *tube, scissors, aluminium foil, needle, sticky tape, tracing paper, elastic band, inside, draw, bottom, cut, hole, middle, outside, hold, hand, sky, point, image, strange*
- Students will almost certainly not know the term *upside-down* to describe the image produced by the camera obscura. Do not pre-teach this term but rather let students discover for themselves that the image is upside-down before teaching the correct term.

Exercise 1

- Make sure students understand not to read in detail at this point.
- Students compare their answers in pairs before checking answers as a class.

Answers

2 f   3 g   4 c   5 d   6 a   7 e

Exercise 2 (Track 1.45)

- Use the images to clarify the meaning of any new vocabulary.
- Students read the text and answer the questions.
- If you wish, play the recording for students to listen and read.
- Check answers as a class.
- Ask students to cover the instructions and in pairs try to describe the process using imperatives.

Answers

2 the bottom
3 with a needle
4 aluminium foil
5 Close one eye and put the tube over the other eye.
6 You see the image on the tracing paper inside the tube.

My Technology File

Exercise 3

- Divide the class into pairs, wherever possible grouping stronger students with weaker ones.
- Monitor the practical stage closely and offer help where necessary. Make sure students take care with both the scissors and the needle.
- For the camera obscura to work it is essential that the hole is small and neat and that the tube is fully light-proofed.
- When students discover that the image is projected upside-down, tell them to keep it a secret to allow the other students to discover this for themselves.

Exercise 4

- Students write their sentences.
- Ask students to read their sentences aloud.

In this unit have you ...

... used Grammar and Vocabulary worksheet?
... used Reading and Listening worksheet?
... used Writing worksheet?
... used Speaking worksheet?
... used Unit test?

With the exception of the Writing worksheets, all the Teacher's Resources are at two levels of difficulty:
*   For students who need extra help and support
** For students who require an additional challenge

Technology File

How to make a Camera Obscura

What you need ...

- a tube – for example, an old crisps tube
- a ruler
- scissors
- some aluminium foil
- a needle
- some sticky tape
- some black paint and a paintbrush
- tracing paper
- two big elastic bands

1 Eat the crisps! Then, clean the inside of the tube and paint it black.
2 Draw a line around the tube 5cm from the bottom. Then, cut along the line. You now have two tubes – one short tube and one long tube.
3 Make a hole at the bottom of the short tube with the needle.
4 Tape some tracing paper on the top of the short tube. Then, tape the short tube and the long tube together again. The tracing paper is now in the middle of the tube.
5 Put the aluminium foil all around the tube and attach with elastic bands.
6 Go outside. Close one eye. Put the tube over the other eye. Hold your hand up to the sky and point the tube at it.
7 The light comes through the pinhole and makes a colour image on the tracing paper. What is strange about the image?

Reading

1 Read the text quickly. Put the pictures in the correct order.

    1 *b*

2 ◖◗ 1.45 Read the text again. Answer the questions.

    1 What colour do you paint the inside of the tube? *black*
    2 Do you cut round the top or the bottom of the tube?
    3 How do you make the hole in the tube?
    4 What do you put around the tube?
    5 How do you look through the camera?
    6 Where do you see the image when you use a Camera Obscura?

My Technology File

3 In pairs, make a Camera Obscura.

4 Write two sentences about the image on the tracing paper.

◀ 39 ▶

Review

Grammar
Have got

1 Complete the sentences with the correct form of *have got*. Use short forms when possible.
1 He's got seven brothers.
2 They .... a black and white dog.
3 It .... big teeth.
4 I .... my mobile phone.
5 You .... a big house.
6 We .... a good French teacher.

2 Put the sentences in Exercise 1 in the negative.
1 He hasn't got seven brothers.

3 Complete the conversation.
A ¹ Have you ² .... a TV in your bedroom?
B No, I ³ .... but I ⁴ .... got a laptop. I watch my sister's DVDs on it.
A ⁵ .... your sister got lots of DVDs?
B Yes, she ⁶ .... but she hasn't ⁷ .... the new Robert Pattinson film.
A ⁸ .... they got it in the shops now?
B Yes, they ⁹ ..... I love Robert Pattinson!

Possessive 's

4 Copy the sentences. Add an apostrophe in the correct place.
1 My dad's shoes are horrible.
2 Her sisters names are Kate and Lianne.
3 This towns shopping centre is boring.
4 I like Sams parents.
5 They're Stan and Sophies friends.
6 All the teachers cars are in front of the school.

Possessive adjectives

5 Complete the second sentence so it has a similar meaning to the first sentence.
1 I've got a green bag.
My bag is green.
2 She's got an interesting book.
.... book is interesting.
3 It's got fantastic pictures.
.... pictures are fantastic.
4 They've got a good camera.
.... camera is good.

40

There is/There are; some and any

6 Complete the questions about Winford. Then answer them with information from the table.
1 Are there any houses? Yes, there are.
2 .... a post office? .... .
3 .... any banks? .... .
4 .... a cinema? .... .
5 .... a park? .... .
6 .... any schools? .... .

WHAT'S IN WINFORD?			
houses	800	shops	4
schools	2	lakes	✗
banks	✗	a museum	✓
a park	✓	cafés	6
a post office	✓	a sports centre	✗
a cinema	✗	a library	✗

7 The information in this paragraph is not correct. Rewrite the paragraph correctly.
There aren't any shops in Winford but there are some lakes. There are some museums and there's a café. There's a sports centre and there's a library.
There are some shops in Winford but .... .

Can/Can't for ability

8 Make sentences with *can/can't*.
1 I / climb / trees / ✓
I can climb trees.
2 My dad / dance / ✗
3 My friends / juggle / ✓
4 You / skate / ✗
5 We / cycle / to school / ✓
6 The baby / walk / ✗

9 Make questions. Then answer.
1 Lady Gaga / sing / Can / ?
Can Lady Gaga sing? Yes, she can.
2 dogs / fly / Can / ?
3 you / Can / in English / write / ?
4 Can / run / good football players / ?

Exercise 10
2 don't go/do not go
3 have
4 doesn't live/does not live
5 stays
6 see
7 studies

Exercise 1
2 next to
3 behind
4 in
5 under
6 in front of

Present simple

10 Complete the text with the Present simple of the verbs.

I ¹ *live* (live) in Australia. My home is 200 km from a town, so I ² .... (not go) to school every day. I ³ .... (have) lessons on the internet. My brother ⁴ .... (not live) at home from Monday to Friday. He ⁵ .... (stay) at his school and we only ⁶ .... (see) him at the weekend. After his lessons, he ⁷ .... (study) with his friends.

11 Look at the information. Then complete the sentences.

On Fridays at ...	4 o'clock	5 o'clock	6 o'clock
Maria and Dan	play football	do homework	meet friends
Jacob	tidy the classroom	go to the park	have dinner

1 Maria and Dan *don't meet* friends at 4 o'clock.
2 Jacob .... the classroom at 4 o'clock.
3 Maria and Dan .... homework at 5 o'clock.
4 Jacob .... to the park at 6 o'clock.
5 Jacob .... dinner at 6 o'clock.
6 Maria and Dan .... football at 6 o'clock.

Exercise 11
tidies
do
doesn't go/does not go
has
don't play/do not play

12 Make questions. Then answer using the information from Exercise 11.

1 Jacob / have dinner / at 5 o'clock / ?
   Does Jacob have dinner at 5 o'clock?
   No, he doesn't.

2 he / tidy the classroom / at 4 o'clock / ?
3 Maria and Dan / play football / at 6 o'clock / ?
4 they / go to the park / at 5 o'clock / ?
5 Maria and Dan / meet friends / at 6 o'clock / ?
6 Jacob / do homework / at 6 o'clock / ?

13 Make questions.

1 No, I don't. (have breakfast at school)
   Do you have breakfast at school?

2 Yes, we do. (walk to school)
3 No, she doesn't. (read lots of books)
4 Yes, it does. (start at half past nine)
5 No, I don't. (get up at six o'clock)

Exercise 12
2 Does he tidy the classroom at 4 o'clock?
   Yes, he does.
3 Do Maria and Dan play football at 6 o'clock?
   No, they don't.
4 Do they go to the park at 5 o'clock?
   No, they don't.
5 Do Maria and Dan meet friends at 6 o'clock?
   Yes, they do.
6 Does Jacob do homework at 6 o'clock?
   No, he doesn't.

Speaking
Talking about position

1 Look at the picture and complete the sentences with these words.

behind   in   in front of   next to   ~~on~~   under

1 The laptop is *on* the desk.
2 The mobile phone is .... the laptop.
3 The backpack is .... the laptop.
4 The guitar is .... the backpack.
5 The ball is .... the desk.
6 The skateboard is .... the ball.

Orders and warnings

2 Match the beginnings (1–5) and endings (a–e) of the teacher's instructions.

1 Open — a down!
2 Stand   b your books.
3 Be   c quiet!
4 Sit   d up!
5 Don't   e shout in class.

Exercise 2
2 d 3 c 4 a 5 e

Time

3 Make questions. Then look at the clocks and write the answers.

1 does / What time / start / it / ?
   What time does it start?
   It starts at quarter to four.

2 time / the / What's / ?
3 is / time / What / it / ?
4 finish / time / What / it / does / ?

41

Exercise 3
2 What's the time?
   It's ten past seven/7.10.
3 What time is it?
   It's twenty to two/1.40.
4 What time does it finish?
   It finishes at half past nine/9.30.

Exercise 13
2 Do you walk to school?
3 Does she read lots of books?
4 Does it start at half past nine?
5 Do you get up at six o'clock?

Review

Vocabulary

Objects

1 Complete the sentences with these words.

DVD	~~guitar~~	games console
laptop	MP3 player	magazines
posters	wallet	watch

1 My brother can play the *guitar*. He's very good!
2 I read lots of .... .
3 I haven't got a ..... What's the time?
4 Do you do your homework on a .... ?
5 Have you got any good music on your .... ?
6 I've only got one euro in my .... .
7 Can you play *MotorMania* on that .... ?
8 I've got ten .... in my bedroom.
9 Can we watch a .... ?

Exercise 1

2 magazines
3 watch
4 laptop
5 MP3 player
6 wallet
7 games console
8 posters
9 DVD

Adjectives

2 Complete the words.

1 He's a g o o d actor but I don't like his films.
2 Lots of people play football. It's very p_ _ _ _ar.
3 You can do today's homework in 15 minutes. It's e_ _ _ .
4 £20 for a pen?! That's very e_ _ _ns_ _ _.
5 Our car's very o_ _ but we like it.
6 She's got a sm_ _ _ dog in her bag. Look!
7 I play tennis but I'm a very b_ _ player.
8 That watch is very ch _ _ _, only £3.
9 Don't watch that DVD. It's b_ _ i _ _.
10 Her lessons are very in_ _ _ _ _ _ng.

Exercise 2

2 popular
3 easy
4 expensive
5 old
6 small
7 bad
8 cheap
9 boring
10 interesting

Places in town

3 Match the beginnings (1–8) and endings (a–h) of the sentences.

1 Send a letter
2 You can see old things at
3 You can find new clothes at
4 There are a lot of euros at
5 You can eat at
6 Dogs and people walk in
7 There are a lot of books at
8 You can watch films at

a the bank.
b the cinema.
c the shopping centre.
d at the post office.
e the museum.
f the café.
g the park.
h the library.

Exercise 3

2 e **3** c **4** a **5** f
6 g **7** h **8** b

Action verbs

4 Complete the sentences with these words.

climb	cycle	fly	juggle
jump	play	run	~~walk~~

1 My friends *walk* to school.
2 I .... to school on my mountain bike.
3 My gran can .... ten kilometres.
4 My grandad can .... with six balls.
5 Lots of people .... to Greece in August.
6 I can't .... football.
7 She can .... very high.
8 Can you .... this tree?

Exercise 4

2 cycle
3 run
4 juggle
5 fly
6 play
7 jump
8 climb

Daily routines

5 Complete the sentences with these words.

bed	breakfast	clean	dinner
dressed	~~get~~	go	homework
lunch	meet	shower	start
tidy	watch		

I [1] *get* up at seven o'clock. Then I get [2] .... in my school uniform, have [3] .... (eggs and toast!) and [4] .... my teeth. I [5] .... school at nine o'clock. I have [6] .... at school. After school, I [7] .... my friends in the park. Then I [8] .... home, do my [9] .... and [10] .... TV. Then I have [11] .... . My favourite is pizza! I have a [12] .... after that. Then I [13] .... my room and go to [14] .... .

Exercise 5

2 dressed
3 breakfast
4 clean
5 start
6 lunch
7 meet
8 go
9 homework
10 watch
11 dinner
12 shower
13 tidy
14 bed

School subjects

6 Complete the school subjects.

1 M a t h s
2 M u _ _ _
3 F _ _ _ c h
4 E _ _ _ _ s h
5 H _ s t _ _ _
6 S c _ _ n _ _
7 L i t _ _ _ t u r e
8 G _ _ g r _ _ _ y
9 I _ _

Exercise 6

2 Music
3 French
4 English
5 History
6 Science
7 Literature
8 Geography
9 ICT

42

Word list

Unit 1 My World

Objects

camera	/'kæmərə/
comics	/'kɒmɪks/
DVD	/di:vi:'di:/
games console	/'geɪmz 'kɒnsəʊl/
guitar	/gɪ'tɑ:/
ice skates	/'aɪs skeɪts/
laptop	/'læptɒp/
magazine	/mægə'zi:n/
mobile phone	/'məʊbi:l 'fəʊn/
MP3 player	/empi: θri: 'pleɪə/
poster	/'pəʊstə/
skateboard	/'skeɪtbɔ:d/
wallet	/'wɒlɪt/
watch	/wɒtʃ/

Adjectives

bad	/bæd/
big	/bɪg/
boring	/'bɔ:rɪŋ/
cheap	/tʃi:p/
difficult	/'dɪfɪkəlt/
easy	/'i:zi/
expensive	/ɪk'spensɪv/
good	/gʊd/
interesting	/'ɪntrəstɪŋ/
new	/nju:/
old	/əʊld/
popular	/'pɒpjʊlə/
small	/smɔ:l/
unpopular	/ʌn'pɒpjʊlə/

Unit 2 Around Town

Places in town

bank	/bæŋk/
bus station	/'bʌs 'steɪʃən/
café	/'kæfeɪ/
cinema	/'sɪnəmə/
hospital	/'hɒspɪtəl/
library	/'laɪbrəri/
museum	/mju:'zi:əm/
park	/pɑ:k/
police station	/pə'li:s 'steɪʃən/
post office	/'pəʊst 'ɒfɪs/
shopping centre	/'ʃɒpɪŋ 'sentə/
sports centre	/'spɔ:ts 'sentə/
town square	/'taʊn 'skweə/
train station	/'treɪn 'steɪʃən/

Action verbs

climb	/klaɪm/
cycle	/'saɪkəl/
dance	/dɑ:ns/
fly	/flaɪ/
juggle	/'dʒʌgəl/
jump	/dʒʌmp/
play	/pleɪ/
run	/rʌn/
sing	/sɪŋ/
skate	/skeɪt/
swim	/swɪm/
walk	/wɔ:k/

Unit 3 School Days

Daily routines

clean my teeth	/'kli:n maɪ ti:θ/
do homework	/'du: maɪ 'həʊmwɜ:k/
get dressed	/'get drest/
get up	/'get ʌp/
go home	/'gəʊ həʊm/
go to bed	/'gəʊ tə bed/
have a shower	/'hæv ə 'ʃaʊə/
have breakfast	/'hæv 'brekfəst/
have dinner	/'hæv 'dɪnə/
have lunch	/'hæv lʌntʃ/
meet friends	/'mi:t frendz/
start school	/'stɑ:t sku:l/
tidy my room	/'taɪdi maɪ ru:m/
watch TV	/'wɒtʃ ˌti:'vi:/

School subjects

Art	/ɑ:t/
English	/'ɪŋglɪʃ/
French	/frentʃ/
Geography	/dʒi'ɒgrəfi/
History	/'hɪstəri/
ICT	/aɪsi:'ti:/
Literature	/'lɪtərɪtʃə/
Maths	/'mæθs/
Music	/'mju:zɪk/
PE	/pi:'i:/
Science	/'saɪəns/
Social Science	/'səʊʃəl 'saɪəns/

 43

4 Animal Magic

Grammar	Adverbs of frequency; Present simple with *wh-* questions; *Must/Mustn't*
Vocabulary	Unusual animals; Parts of the body
Speaking	Likes and dislikes
Writing	An animal fact sheet

Vocabulary   Unusual animals

1))) 2.1 **Match the pictures to these words. Then listen, check and repeat.**

frog	giant rabbit	hissing cockroach	lizard
parrot *1*	piranha	pygmy goat	python
stick insect	tarantula		

Word list page 77   **Workbook** page 107

2 **Find one animal in Exercise 1 for each of these categories. Then think of two more.**

1 fish *piranha*, ... ,
2 spider   5 reptile
3 bird   6 mammal
4 amphibian   7 insect

3 **In pairs, read the clues and guess the animal.**

1 It can fly. *A bird*
2 It's green. It lives in water. It eats insects.
3 It can swim but it can't walk.
4 It lives under the ground. It eats vegetables. It's a popular pet.
5 It makes a loud noise. It's an insect.
6 It can't walk and it can't fly but it can climb trees.
7 People drink its milk.
8 It can say words.

4 **Think of an animal. In pairs, ask and answer.**

Can it fly?   *Yes, it can.*

Is it a parrot?   *Yes, it is.*

Brain Trainer Activity 4
Go to page 115

44

Unit contents

Vocabulary
→ Unusual animals – *frog, giant rabbit, hissing cockroach, lizard, parrot, piranha, pygmy goat, python, stick insect, tarantula*
→ Parts of the body – *arm, beak, fin, finger, foot, hand, head, leg, neck, paw, tail, toe, wing*

Grammar
→ Adverbs of frequency – *never, hardly ever, sometimes, often, usually, always*
→ Present simple with *wh-* questions – *Where, When, What, Who, Why, How often*
→ *Must/Mustn't*

Communication
→ Likes and dislikes – verbs with *-ing*
→ Writing – My unusual animal; Making notes

Pronunciation
→ Contrastive sentence stress

Culture 2 – Education in the UK

Key competences
→ Linguistic competence
→ Competence in knowledge and interaction with the physical world
→ Interpersonal, social and civic competence
→ Learning-to-learn
→ Autonomy and personal initiative

Vocabulary   Unusual animals

> **Extra activity**
>
> Books closed. Copy the following onto the board:
>
> Ask students to do the same with the word *snake*, writing the name of the animal inside the shape. Students work in pairs. Give each pair the name of a different animal which they already know (e.g. *cat, dog, mouse*) or an animal similar in English and in their L1. They write the name of the animal inside the shape. Students show their drawings to the class.

Exercise 1 (Track 2.1)
- Individually, students match the words and the pictures.
- Play the recording for students to listen and check.
- Repeat the recording. Pause after each word to check students' pronunciation.
- Ask students if they have any of these pets or if they know somebody else who does.

> **Answers**
>
> | | | |
> |---|---|---|
> | 2 lizard | 5 frog | 8 tarantula |
> | 3 giant rabbit | 6 piranha | 9 python |
> | 4 hissing cockroach | 7 stick insect | 10 pygmy goat |

Exercise 2
- Make sure students understand that they have more animals than they need for some of the categories.
- Students brainstorm vocabulary for animals which they already know and classify it (possible answers in brackets).
- Collate suggestions on the board.
- Feed in vocabulary for any animals typical of the country you are teaching in.

> **Answers**
>
> 1 fish – *piranha* (goldfish, salmon)
> 2 spider – tarantula (black widow, money spider)
> 3 bird – parrot (blackbird, eagle)
> 4 amphibian – frog (toad, newt)
> 5 reptile – lizard/python (crocodile, tortoise)
> 6 mammal – giant rabbit/pygmy goat (dog, sheep)
> 7 insect – hissing cockroach, stick insect (ant, fly)

Exercise 3
- Tell students only to use vocabulary from this section.
- Students read the clues and identify the animals.
- Monitor and help with vocabulary.
- Students compare their ideas in pairs before checking answers as a class.

> **Answers**
>
> | | |
> |---|---|
> | 2 A frog | 6 A snake/python |
> | 3 A fish/piranha | 7 A pygmy goat |
> | 4 A giant rabbit | 8 A parrot |
> | 5 A hissing cockroach | |

> **Extra activity**
>
> Stronger groups or fast finishers work in pairs and write similar sentences about other animals. Monitor and point out errors for students to self-correct. They then work with another pair, reading their clues and identifying the animals.

Exercise 4
- Ask two students to read aloud the example questions and answers.
- Demonstrate the activity by choosing another animal yourself and letting the class ask you questions until they guess.
- Make sure students understand that they can only ask *yes/no* questions and use short *yes/no* answers.
- Monitor but do not interrupt fluency.

Further practice:
Workbook pages 34 and 107

Brain Trainer Activity 4
See Teacher's Book page 213 and Students' Book page 115

Reading

Revision

First – Books closed. Write *teachroom* and *classer* on the board. Show students how the words have been mixed up and the parts can be reshuffled to make *teacher* and *classroom*.

Second – Write the following groups of words on the board:
1 pazard, lirrot
2 pimysect, pyginnha, stick ragoat
3 giran cockla, tassing raroach, hiant tubbit
Tell students that these are all animals but that the parts have been mixed up. They then work in pairs, separating the parts and rearranging them as animals.

Third – Ask individual students to write answers on the board to check spelling.
(Answers: *1 lizard, parrot; 2 piranha, pygmy goat, stick insect; 3 giant rabbit, hissing cockroach, tarantula*)

Exercise 1

- Draw attention to the photos and the text and ask students what they can see.
- Individually, students answer the question.

Exercise 2

- Make sure students understand not to read in detail at this point.
- Students scan the text quickly to check their answer.

Answer

b

Exercise 3 (Track 2.2)

- Individually, students answer the questions.
- If you wish, play the recording for students to listen and read.
- Check answers as a class.
- Elicit from stronger students or explain yourself the meaning of any new vocabulary.

Answers

2 Tom gets up at 6.30.
3 He starts work at 8.00.
4 The hissing cockroaches come from Madagascar.
5 The tarantula comes from Mexico.
6 He's scared of spiders.
7 It's always interesting.

Exercise 4 (Track 2.2)

- Students read the text again and decide if the sentences are true or false.
- They then check in pairs before you check answers as a class. When checking answers, ask students to correct the false sentences.

Answers

1 *False* (Tom feeds the animals in the afternoon.)
2 True
3 False (Tiny is twenty-five years old.)
4 False (Visitors to the zoo love the red-knee tarantula.)
5 True
6 False (Tom is often very tired.)

Exercise 5

- Ask two students to read aloud the example question and answer.
- Check the pronunciation of the questions before students work in pairs.
- In pairs, students ask and answer the questions.
- Monitor and help with vocabulary but do not interrupt fluency.
- Discuss the questions briefly as a class.

Extra activity

Use the questions in Exercise 5 for a class survey. Students use a mill-drill to find out their classmates' answers to the questions and make a note of all the answers.
In pairs, they then collate this data and prepare a poster to present to the class as follows:
For *Do you like animals?* – Prepare a pie-chart showing how many people answered *Yes* and *No*.
For *Which animals do you like/dislike?* – Create a 'top-ten' with pictures and the names of the animals.
For *What unusual animals do you know?* – Make a collage with pictures and the names of the animals.
For *Are you scared of spiders or insects?* – Prepare a bar-chart with four columns for *Both – Neither – Spiders – Insects*.

Further practice

Workbook page 35

Reading

1 **Look at the photos. What do you think the text is about?**

a An article about tarantulas.
b A text about life in a zoo.
c A blog about animals.

2 **Read the text and check your answers to Exercise 1.**

3 🔊 2.2 **Read the text. Answer the questions.**

1 What's Tom's job? *He's a zoo keeper.*
2 When does Tom get up?
3 When does he start work?
4 Where do the hissing cockroaches come from?
5 Where does the tarantula come from?
6 What animal is Tom scared of?
7 What does Tom think about his job?

4 🔊 2.2 **Read the text again. Are the sentences true (T) or false (F)?**

1 Tom feeds the animals in the morning. *F*
2 Tom sometimes hides the hissing cockroaches' food in different places.
3 Tiny is only ten years old.
4 Visitors to the zoo are scared of the red-knee tarantula.
5 Tom enjoys his job because he can learn more about the animals.
6 Tom isn't tired at the end of the day.

5 **What about you?** **In pairs, ask and answer.**

1 Do you like animals? Which animals do you like/dislike?
2 What unusual animals do you know?
3 Are you scared of spiders or insects?

> Do you like animals?

> I love animals but I'm scared of reptiles.

A Day in the Life ...

Tom works at the Unusual Pets section of Hardy's Animal Park. He is a zoo keeper. We talk to him about a typical day.

Describe a typical day at the zoo.

I get up at 6.30 and I start work at 8.00. I usually put on my boots because it's often very dirty in the animal enclosures. I clean the animal enclosures every day and in the afternoon I feed the animals. I'm always busy! I never finish work before 5.30.

What animals do you like and what animals do you dislike?

I love the hissing cockroaches! They come from Madagascar and they're very noisy. I sometimes hide their food in different places. It's a game for them! But I don't like the tarantulas. We have a red-knee tarantula from Mexico. Her name's Tiny and she's twenty-five years old. Visitors to the zoo love her, but I'm scared of spiders. I hardly ever work with them.

Why do you like your job?

I work with great people and I learn new things about animals every day. At the end of the day, I'm often very tired, but my job is always interesting.

45

Grammar Adverbs of frequency

0%	10%	25%	50%	80%	100%
never / hardly ever		sometimes / often		usually / always	
I hardly ever work with them.		I'm often very tired.		My job is always interesting.	

1 Study the grammar table. Choose the correct options to complete the rule.

Adverbs come *before / after* the verb *to be* and *before / after* most other verbs.

2 Put the adverbs in the correct place.

1 We go to the zoo at the weekend. (sometimes)
We sometimes go to the zoo at the weekend.

2 My English class is interesting. (usually)
3 My parrot watches TV in the morning. (often)
4 My dad is happy on Friday evening. (always)
5 I cycle to school. (never)
6 You take our dog for a walk. (hardly ever)

3 Put the words in order to make sentences.

1 often / Tom / very / is / tired / work / After
After work Tom is often very tired.

2 trees / sometimes / Goats / climb
3 eighteen / Cats / sleep / often / hours / for
4 after / feed / rabbit / my / usually / I / school
5 ever / Sarah / her / hardly / parrot / talks / to

4 Look at the chart and complete the sentences.

At the weekend	Peter	Betty
1 play football	100%	50%
2 play computer games	90%	10%
3 do homework	80%	100%
4 listen to music	0%	80%

1 Peter *always* plays football at the weekend.
Betty *often plays football at the weekend.*

2 Peter .... plays computer games at the weekend.
Betty .... .
3 Peter .... does his homework at the weekend.
Betty .... .
4 Peter .... listens to music at the weekend.
Betty .... .

Present simple with *wh-* questions

wh- questions	
Where do you live?	In Manchester.
When do you finish school?	At four o'clock.
What does she eat for breakfast?	Cereal.
Who does Mrs West teach?	Class 8c.
Why do you walk to school?	Because we don't have a car.
How often do you play football?	Every day!

Grammar reference Workbook page 92

5 Study the grammar table. Choose the correct options to complete the rules.

1 We use *who* to ask about *people / things*.
2 We use *what* to ask about *people / things*.
3 We use *when* to ask about *place / time*.
4 We use *where* to ask about *place / time*.

6 Match the questions to the answers.

1 How often do elephants eat?
2 Who is your favourite singer?
3 When is your birthday?
4 What is in your bag?
5 Why do you take the bus?
6 Where do piranhas live?

a Alicia Keys.
b It's on 17th June.
c Because we don't have a car.
d They live in South American rivers.
e They eat every three hours.
f Two pens, a ruler and a book about spiders.

7 What about you? Make questions. In pairs, ask and answer.

Where do you live? (I live) in Alicante.

1 Where / you / live?
2 Who / your / best friend?
3 How often / you / play sport?
4 What / your / favourite animal?
5 What / you / usually / do / at the weekend?
6 How often / you / go / to the zoo?

Grammar   Adverbs of frequency

Language notes

Make sure students understand that, in English, these adverbs of frequency always come *before* the verb, except in the case of the verb *to be* where they come after. From 0% to 100% the order of the adverbs of frequency is *never, hardly ever, sometimes, often, usually, always*.

Exercise 1

- Read the grammar table with students.
- Students work individually, completing the rule and referring back to the grammar table where necessary.

Answer

Adverbs come *after* the verb *to be* and *before* most other verbs.

Exercise 2

- Individually, students put the adverbs in the correct place.
- Check answers by asking individual students to read the sentences.

Answers

2 My English class is usually interesting.
3 My parrot often watches TV in the morning.
4 My dad is always happy on Friday evening.
5 I never cycle to school.
6 You hardly ever take our dog for a walk.

Exercise 3

- Monitor and point out errors for students to self-correct.
- Students compare their answers in pairs.
- Check answers by asking individual students to write answers on the board.

Answers

2 Goats sometimes climb trees.
3 Cats often sleep for eighteen hours.
4 I usually feed my rabbit after school.
5 Sarah hardly ever talks to her parrot.

Exercise 4

- Draw attention to the chart and the examples.

Answers

2 Peter usually plays computer games at the weekend.
  Betty hardly ever plays computer games at the weekend.
3 Peter usually does his homework at the weekend.
  Betty always does her homework at the weekend.
4 Peter never listens to music at the weekend.
  Betty usually listens to music at the weekend.

Further practice:
Workbook pages 36 and 92–93

Brain Trainer Activity 3
See Teacher's Book page 213, Students' Book page 115

Present simple with *wh-* questions

Exercise 5

- Read the grammar table with students.
- Check answers by asking individual students to read the sentences.

Answers

1 people 2 things 3 time 4 place

Exercise 6

- Individually, students match the questions and answers.
- Drill the questions and answers for pronunciation and intonation.

Answers

1 e 2 a 3 b 4 f 5 c 6 d

Extra activity

Stronger groups or fast finishers memorise the questions and answers in Exercise 6 for one minute. Students then test themselves or their partner by covering first the answers and then the questions and seeing how many they can remember.

Exercise 7

- Ask two students to read aloud the example question and answer.
- Check the questions before students work in pairs.
- Monitor but do not interrupt fluency unless they make mistakes with the question forms. Encourage students to use contractions in their answers where appropriate.

Answers

2 Who is your best friend?
3 How often do you play sport?
4 What is your favourite animal?
5 What do you usually do at the weekend?
6 How often do you go to the zoo?

Further practice:
Workbook pages 37 and 92–93

Brain Trainer Activity 2
See Teacher's Book page 213, Students' Book page 115

Vocabulary   Parts of the body

Revision

First – Revise with students the six adverbs of frequency and their position in relation to the verb in sentences.

Second – Write the following sentences on the board and ask students to put adverbs of frequency in the sentences to make them true for them.
1 I get up at 6.30 on Sundays.
2 I cycle to school.
3 I play a computer game in the morning.
4 My Literature class is interesting.
5 I have a picnic in the park in summer.
6 I'm on time for school.

Third – Check answers by asking individual students to read complete sentences. The position of the adverb should be the same for the whole class although the adverb will change according to the student.

Extra activity

Stronger groups or individual students cover the picture in Exercise 1 and identify which of the things in the box humans do not have. When they have finished, students self-correct by looking at the book and labelling the picture.

Exercise 1 (Track 2.3)

- In pairs, students use the words in the box to label the picture.
- Play the recording for students to listen, check and repeat.
- Correct students' pronunciation as appropriate.

Answers

2 wing	6 neck	10 leg
3 head	7 finger	11 toe
4 hand	8 paw	12 foot
5 arm	9 tail	13 fin

Exercise 2

- Make sure that students understand that they have to complete the sentences about humans.
- When checking answers, be prepared to correct mistakes with the irregular plural *foot – feet*.

Answers

1 We've got zero *tails*, paws, wings, beaks and fins.
2 We've got one head and neck.
3 We've got two legs, arms, hands and feet
4 We've got ten fingers and toes.

Exercise 3

- Students read the clues and identify the animals.
- Check answers as a class.

Answers

2 It's a hissing cockroach.
3 It's a spider.
4 It's a bird.
5 It's a pygmy goat.

Exercise 4 (Track 2.4)

- Individually, students complete the descriptions.
- Play the recording for students to listen and check.

Answers

2 eyes   3 head   4 insects   5 bird   6 beak   7 wings
8 tail

Extra activity

Extend the work on clues and descriptions of people, animals and birds. Students work in pairs either to prepare more clues like those in Exercise 3, or to prepare a longer, more cohesive description similar to the ones in Exercise 4 but leaving a blank in place of the name. Monitor and help with vocabulary and feed in ideas if necessary and point out errors for students to self-correct.

Students exchange their clues/descriptions with another pair and identify the animal described. Alternatively, ask students to read aloud their clues/descriptions for the whole class to guess.

Further practice:
Workbook pages 37 and 107

Brain Trainer Activity 5
See Teacher's Book page 213, Students' Book page 115

Vocabulary Parts of the body

1 🔊 **2.3** **Label the picture with these words. Then listen, check and repeat.**

arm	beak *1*	fin	finger	foot	hand	head
leg	neck	paw	tail	toe	wing	

Word list page 77   Workbook page 107

2 **What have we got? Complete the sentences with words from Exercise 1.**

1 We've got **zero** *tails.*
2 We've got **one** .... .
3 We've got **two** .... .
4 We've got **ten** .... .

3 **What animal is it? Read the clues and guess.**

bird   ~~fish~~   pygmy goat   hissing cockroach   spider

1 It hasn't got legs. It's got a head. It hasn't got arms. It's got fins. *It's a fish.*
2 It's got six legs. It's got a head. It hasn't got a neck.
3 It's got eight legs. It hasn't got a tail.
4 It's got two legs. It's got a tail. It hasn't got arms. It's got wings and a beak.
5 It's got four legs and a tail. It hasn't got fins.

4 🔊 **2.4** **Complete the descriptions with these words. Then listen and check.**

beak	bird	eyes	head
insects	~~legs~~	tail	wings

The wolf spider is an unusual pet. It has got eight ¹ *legs* and it can run and jump. It has also got eight ² .... , and it can see in the dark. The wolf spider's ³ .... is small, but its body is large. It eats ⁴ .... .

A cockatiel is a ⁵ .... . It's got a yellow, grey or white head, with a small ⁶ .... . Its ⁷ .... are usually grey and white and it's got a long black or grey ⁸ .... . Cockatiels are from Australia but they are popular pets around the world.

Brain Trainer Activity 5
Go to page 115

47

Chatroom Likes and dislikes

Speaking and Listening

1 Look at the photos. Answer the questions.

1 Where are the children?
2 What animals can you see?
3 Do you think Nick is angry or happy?

2 ◁)) 2.5 Listen and read the conversation. Are the sentences true (T) or false (F)?

1 Sunny mustn't be on a lead in the farm. *F*
2 Sunny doesn't like running around the farm.
3 Monica likes living on a farm.
4 Monica likes getting up early.
5 Leo doesn't like getting up early.
6 Leo wants to feed the animals.
7 Monica's goats don't like eating Sunny's lead.

3 Act out the conversation in groups of four.

Monica	Hi guys! Nick, you must put Sunny on a lead, please.
Nick	Sorry, Monica. Sunny loves running around the farm.
Julia	Do you like living on a farm, Monica?
Monica	Yes, I do, but I don't like getting up early in the morning.
Leo	Me too! I hate getting up early.
Julia	That's true! At the weekend, you don't get up before 11!
Leo	I love feeding the animals. Look! I've got some sweets for them.
Monica	No, don't give them unhealthy food, Leo.
Leo	Sorry!
Nick	Sunny! Come here. You mustn't run away.
Monica	That's strange. Where's Sunny's lead?
Nick	I don't know.
Julia	Monica, what do your goats like eating?
Monica	They like eating everything!
Leo	Look! They love eating Sunny's lead!

Say it in your language …
Hi guys!
Me too!

48

90

Chatroom   Likes and dislikes

Revision

First – Prepare a *Live Listening* about your daily routine and including the six adverbs of frequency. This can be real or fictional. Remember to grade your language appropriately and include all six adverbs of frequency at least once. Use the following text as an example:

My life is very boring! I <u>always</u> get up at 7.00 and I start work at 8.45 but on Saturday and Sunday I <u>sometimes</u> get up late. On Monday morning at 10.00 I <u>always</u> teach you and the English class is <u>always</u> interesting! I <u>usually</u> have lunch at school and I <u>hardly ever</u> go to a restaurant. Restaurants are expensive. I <u>often</u> walk home and I <u>usually</u> take Charlie the dog for a walk. In the evening I <u>never</u> do homework – I'm a teacher not a student!

Second – Draw students' attention to the chart in Exercise 4 on page 46. Read your text to the class. Students note down the activities you mention and the corresponding percentage relating to the adverbs of frequency in the same way as in the chart about Peter and Betty.

Third – Students compare their answers in pairs. Check answers as a class, e.g. *get up – 100%*; *get up late Saturday/Sunday – 40%*.

Speaking and Listening

Exercise 1

- Elicit the names of the characters before students complete the exercise.
- Students look at the photos and answer the questions.
- They compare their ideas in pairs before you check answers as a class.

Answers

1 The children are at Monica's farm.
2 There's a sheep, a goat and Sunny the dog.
3 In the big photo he's happy, but in the small photo he's angry.

Brain Trainer Activity 1
See Teacher's Book page 213, Students' Book page 115

 ### Exercise 2 (Track 2.5)

- Play the recording for students to decide if the sentences are true or false.
- They then check in pairs before you check answers as a class.

Answers

1 *False* (Sunny must be on a lead in the farm.)
2 False (Sunny loves running around the farm.)
3 True
4 False (Monica doesn't like getting up early.)
5 True
6 True
7 False (Monica's goats like eating everything.)

Extra activity

Stronger groups or fast finishers rewrite the false sentences in Exercise 2 so that they are correct.

Exercise 3

- Divide the class into groups of four.
- Groups act out the conversation.
- Monitor and correct students' pronunciation as appropriate.
- Nominate one group to perform the conversation for the class.

Say it in your language …

Ask students to find the phrases in the conversation and look at them in context to try to deduce the meaning.

Hi guys! – guy is commonly used colloquially to refer to a man, but here it's part of an informal greeting for a group of boys and girls. Can also be used in 'Bye guys!' You or your students could use these at the beginning or the end of the class.

Me too! – exclamation to express agreement with something someone else has just said. Useful at this level for students to use rather than the grammatically more complex 'So/Neither do I' type of construction.

Exercise 4

- Students refer back to the conversation and find the synonyms.
- Check answers as a class.

Answers

1 love (e.g. *'I love feeding the animals.'*)
2 hate (e.g. *'I hate getting up early.'*)

Language notes

In some languages verbs of preference are followed by the infinitive form and this can cause L1 interference for some learners. Although in British English the use of the infinitive is in fact possible after these verbs in certain circumstances, it is a complicated area usually taught only at higher levels. Throughout *Next Move* the form taught after verbs of preference is *-ing*.

Exercise 5

- Read through the phrases for expressing likes and dislikes with the class.
- Point out that the verbs *love* and *hate* express a more intense feeling than *like* and *not like*.

Further practice:
Workbook pages 38 and 116

Pronunciation   Contrastive stress

Language notes

In this exercise students are indirectly introduced to the concept of contrastive stress in sentences. A common feature of spoken English is to shift the stress in a sentence based on our response to what another person says. In the first conversation the second speaker emphasises *computer games* in response to the first speaker's emphasis on *football*. In the second conversation the second speaker contrasts both the verb of preference (*loves*) and the person who does the action (*Emma*) with what the first speaker has said.

Exercise 6a (Track 2.6)

- Play the recording.
- Individually, students identify the stress in the sentences.
- Check answers by writing the sentences on the board and asking students to underline the stresses.

Answers

1 football, computer games   2 hates, loves, Emma

Exercise 6b (Track 2.6)

- Play the recording for students to listen and repeat.
- Drill the sentences for stress and intonation.

Further practice:
Workbook page 123

Exercise 7 (Track 2.7)

- Play the recording for students to listen and repeat. Pause as appropriate to check students' pronunciation.
- In pairs, students act out the conversations.

Exercise 8

- Students make their own conversations by replacing the words in purple.
- Monitor but do not interrupt fluency unless students make mistakes with the expressions for likes and dislikes.

Grammar   *Must/Mustn't*

Language notes

Presented too rapidly, modal verbs can often cause students real problems, so in *Next Move* they are introduced over a number of units and always in very clear contexts. Students have already seen *can/can't* for ability in Unit 2 and here they are introduced to *must/mustn't* in affirmative and negative sentences for rules. Note that students are not taught any question forms to ask about rules at this point.

Exercise 1

- Read the grammar table with students.
- Check the answer as a class.

Answer

Correct rule – 2

Exercise 2

- Students choose the correct options.
- Check answers by asking individual students to read the sentences.

Answers

2 mustn't   3 must   4 must   5 mustn't

Exercise 3

- Use the pictures or mime to pre-teach the words *shut* and *hurt*.
- Individually, students make the sentences.
- They then check in pairs before you check answers as a class.

Answers

2 You must shut the gates.
3 You must keep your dog on a lead.
4 You mustn't hurt the animals.
5 You mustn't give sweets to the animals.
6 You mustn't climb the trees.

Further practice:
Workbook pages 39 and 92–93

4 Look back at the conversation. Find another way of saying …
1 *like* doing something
2 *don't like* doing something

5 Read the phrases for expressing likes and dislikes.

Likes	Dislikes
Sunny loves running around the farm.	I don't like getting up early.
They like eating everything.	I hate getting up early.

Pronunciation Contrastive stress

6a 🔊 2.6 **Listen. Which words are stressed?**

1 A I love playing football.
  B Do you? I don't. I love playing computer games.

2 A Joe hates getting up early.
  B No, Joe loves getting up early. Emma hates getting up early.

b 🔊 2.6 **Listen again and repeat.**

---

7 🔊 2.7 **Listen to the conversations. Act out the conversations in pairs.**

Nick I love [1] watching animal programmes on TV.
Julia I don't.

Nick I hate [2] getting up early!
Julia Me, too.

Julia I like [3] cooking!
Leo I don't.

8 Work in pairs. Replace the words in purple in Exercise 7. Use these words and/or your own ideas. Act out the conversations.

1 go to the cinema / go to the theatre
2 go to bed early / stay up late
3 sing / juggle

Grammar *Must/Mustn't*

Affirmative
I/You/He/She/It/We/They must get up early.

Negative
I/You/He/She/It/We/They mustn't get up late.

Grammar reference Workbook page 92

1 Study the grammar table. Choose the correct option, 1 or 2, to complete the rule.

We use *must* and *mustn't* to talk about …
1 likes and dislikes.   2 important rules.

2 Choose *must* or *mustn't* for these school rules.
1 Students *must / mustn't* be late for school.
2 Students *must / mustn't* eat food in class.
3 Students *must / mustn't* listen to the teacher.
4 Students *must / mustn't* do their homework.
5 Students *must / mustn't* use mobile phones in class.

3 Look at the farm notice. Make sentences with *you must* and *you mustn't*.
1 *You must be kind to the animals.*

Visitors to the Farm

✓	✗
1 Be kind to the animals	**4** Hurt the animals
2 Shut the gates	**5** Give sweets to the animals
3 Keep your dog on a lead	**6** Climb the trees

Reading

1 **Look at the text. Match the animals to their homes.**

1	parrot	**a**	tank
2	tarantula	**b**	hutch
3	rabbit	**c**	cage

My pet is a red and blue parrot. She's 25 – but she isn't old. Parrots often live for 70 years! She's from Africa, and she's called Miki. She lives in a cage in my bedroom. Miki likes talking and singing songs. Parrots are very friendly birds and Miki loves being with people. When she sees my friends, she always says, 'Hi guys!'
Rashid

Unusual Pets

This week three readers tell us about their unusual pets.

Boris has got eight legs. His body is black and his legs are black and white. He's a Costa Rican Zebra tarantula from South America. Boris eats small insects and he lives in a tank with some twigs and pieces of wood. There's also a small box in his tank because Boris loves hiding. Spiders like hot, humid temperatures, so Boris's tank is 22–30° C and there's always a bowl of water there.
Lacey

Clarence is a British giant rabbit. He weighs 7.5 kilos and he eats a lot! He sleeps in a hutch in my bedroom. He loves playing under my bed, but sometimes he eats my socks. When he's in the garden he likes digging. His favourite food is grass, but he also loves eating carrots!
Katie

Key Words

twig	to hide	humid
to weigh	to dig	grass

2 **Read the text and check your answers to Exercise 1.**

3 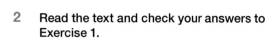 **2.8** **Read the text. Write *Boris*, *Miki* or *Clarence*.**

1 This pet likes hiding. *Boris*
2 This pet is red and blue.
3 This pet likes eating socks and carrots.
4 This pet eats insects.
5 This pet is sometimes outside.
6 This pet likes singing songs.

4 **2.8** **Read the text again. Answer the questions.**

1 Where is Boris from?
   Boris is from South America.
2 Is Boris's tank hot or cold?
3 Is Miki old?
4 What does Miki say when she sees Rashid's friends?
5 How much does Clarence weigh?
6 Where does Clarence sleep?

Listening

1 **2.9** **Listen to the interview with Anna. Why is Dickens a special dog?**

2 **2.9** **Listen again. Answer the questions.**
1 Name four things that Dickens does in the film.
   a He .... a tree.
   b He .... out of a car.
   c He .... in the sea.
   d He .... with a cat.
2 Who teaches Dickens?
3 What does he love doing?

3 **2.9** **Listen again. Swap books and check your partner's answers.**

 50

Reading

Exercise 1

- Draw attention to the photos and the text and ask students what they can see.
- Students match the animals to their homes.

Exercise 2

- Students scan the text quickly and check their answers.

Answers

1 c 2 a 3 b

Extra activity

Use the three texts as a running dictation. Books closed. Divide the class into groups of three. Open your book on your desk at the front of the class. One student from each group runs up to your desk, memorises a short phrase from the first text and then runs back and dictates it to the other two students in their group. The student continues until his/her group completes the first text. Groups then change runner and repeat the activity with the remaining two texts. Each student will be the runner for one of the texts. They then compare their versions with the originals in the Students' Book. Make sure students spell out any difficult words using the English alphabet.

Key Words

Be prepared to focus on the Key Words, either by pre-teaching them, eliciting their meaning after students have read the text, or through dictionary or definition writing work.

twig – a small piece of wood from a tree

to hide – to move to a position where people can't see you

humid – when there is a lot of water in the air

to dig – to make a hole in the ground

to weigh – to find out how heavy something is

grass – a very common green plant which you walk on and which grows in gardens and parks

Exercise 3 (Track 2.8)

- Individually, students match the pets to the sentences.
- If you wish, play the recording for students to listen and read.
- Students compare their ideas in pairs before you check answers as a class.
- Elicit from stronger students or explain yourself the meaning of any new vocabulary.

Answers

2 Miki 3 Clarence 4 Boris 5 Clarence 6 Miki

Exercise 4 (Track 2.8)

- Students read the text again and answer the questions.
- Check answers as a class.

Answers

2 Boris's tank is hot.
3 No, she isn't.
4 Miki says 'Hi guys!'
5 Clarence weighs 7.5 kilos.
6 Clarence sleeps in a hutch in Katie's bedroom.

Extra activity

Write the *Key Words* on the left of the board and simple definitions on the right of the board in random order. Students look back at the text to see the words in context and match the words to the definitions. Check answers as a class.

Listening

Exercise 1 (Track 2.9)

- Tell students that Anna has got a special dog and elicit suggestions of what its special ability could be.
- Play the recording for students to check their ideas.

Answer

Dickens is a special dog because he is an actor.

Audioscript:
See Teacher's Book page 225

Exercise 2 (Track 2.9)

- Repeat the recording for students to answer the questions.

Answers

1a climbs 1b jumps 1c swims 1d dances
2 Anna teaches Dickens.
3 He loves learning new things.

Exercise 3 (Track 2.9)

- Repeat the recording for students to peer-correct the answers.
- Check answers as a class.

Further practice:
Workbook page 40

Writing   An animal fact sheet

Revision

First – Write the following prompts on the board:

A you / like / animals?
B no / hate / animals
A why ? / scared ?
B yes / not like / spiders or insects / lot of legs
A know / scared / snakes / love / birds and fish
B really ? / brother / parrot / I / not like

Second – Elicit a conversation line by line from students using the prompts. Do not allow students to write anything down.

Third – Drill the conversation for correct pronunciation. Divide the class in half down the centre. Tell the half on the left that they are going to be A and the half on the right that they are going to be B. Build up the conversation step by step until students can perform it unprompted.
(Complete conversation:
A *Do you like animals?*
B *No, I don't. I hate animals.*
A *Why? Are you scared of them?*
B *Yes, I am. I don't like spiders or insects. They've got a lot of legs!*
A *I know. I'm scared of snakes but I love birds and fish.*
B *Really? My brother's got a parrot but I don't like it.)*

Exercise 1

* Read the Writing File with students.
* Ask students what other common abbreviations they can think of (e.g. months – *Jan*, *Feb*; days – *Mon*, *Tues*; kilogram – *kg*; centimetres – *cm,* etc.).

Exercise 2

* Students cover the Komodo Dragon: fact sheet and look only at the article.
* They find the most important information in the article then uncover the fact sheet and compare their notes about the key information.

Possible Answers

Komodo dragons – very big, 3 m, 90 kg, brown or grey, small head, long tail, short legs. From Indonesia – deserts, tropical regions. Eat birds, mammals, reptiles. Run fast, climb trees. Dig holes. Sleep in hole because cool.
Yes, the information is the same.

Exercise 3

* Read through the example with students.
* Individually, students rewrite the sentences as notes.

Possible Answers

2 Spiders eat insects; catch in webs
3 Snakes can't run/walk; can swim

Exercise 4

* Students read the fact sheet again and answer the questions.
* They check in pairs before you check answers as a class.
* Check answers by asking pairs of students to read questions and answers.

Answers

2 They are brown or grey.
3 They come from Indonesia.
4 They eat birds, mammals and reptiles.
5 They sleep in holes.

Extra activity

Students choose an unusual or endangered animal and find a picture of it on the internet. They label the picture using the vocabulary for parts of the body seen on Students' Book page 47.

Exercise 5

* Remind students that further information on these animals is available by searching the internet.
* Explain that students should only make brief notes of the facts at this point.

Answers

Students' own answers

Exercise 6

* Read through the 'My unusual animal' writing guide. Show students how the example text in Exercise 2 is organised into *Appearance*, *Habitat*, *Diet* and *Other Facts*.
* Tell them that they should organise their text in the same way.
* Draw students' attention to the 'Remember!' checklist.

Answers

Students' own answers

Extra activity

Add an extra 10–15 vocabulary items from this unit to the collection of Word Cards.
Revise all the vocabulary by playing a word clues game. Tell students that they are going to have an informal vocabulary 'test'. Choose one of the vocabulary cards and choose five 'clue words' to help students guess what it is. For example, if you have the word *parrot* the five clue words might be *wings*, *colours*, *talk*, *pet* and *beak*. The words should neither be too obvious nor too obscure. Students write down what they think the word is. On the count of three, everybody calls out the word they have written down. Those who guess correctly win one point. Repeat the procedure, either choosing words yourself or allowing stronger groups or individual students to give the clue words themselves. The winner is the student with the most points.

Further practice:
Workbook page 41

Writing An animal fact sheet

1 **Read the Writing File.**

> **Writing File** **Making notes**
>
> When we write notes we …
> * use abbreviations:
>   *for example* → *e.g.*
>   *very* → *v*
> * include only the key information:
>   *Emperor penguins are 122 cm tall and they weigh 45 kilos. They can't fly.* →
>   *Emperor penguins: 122 cm tall, weigh 45 kilos. Can't fly.*

2 **Find the key information in this article. Is the same information in the fact sheet?**

Komodo Dragons

Appearance

Komodo dragons are very big lizards. They grow to 3 metres and weigh 90 kilos. They are usually brown or grey in colour and they have a small head, a long tail and four short legs.

Habitat

Komodo dragons are from Indonesia. They live in deserts and in tropical regions.

Diet

Komodo dragons like eating birds, mammals, for example, goats and deer, or other reptiles.

Other Facts

Komodo dragons can run fast and they can climb trees. They dig holes in the ground and sleep in them because they can stay cool there.

Komodo Dragon: fact sheet

Colour:	brown or grey
Length:	3 metres
Weight:	90 kilos
Country:	Indonesia
Habitat:	deserts and tropical regions
Diet:	birds, mammals, e.g. goats, deer, reptiles
Other facts:	can run fast & climb trees; dig holes & sleep in them – stay cool

3 **Copy the sentences. Rewrite them as notes.**

1 Komodo dragons have got very strong legs and they can climb trees.

Komodo dragons v strong legs; can climb trees

2 Spiders eat insects. They catch them in their webs.

3 Snakes can't run or walk but they can swim.

4 **Read the fact sheet again. Answer the questions.**

1 How heavy are Komodo dragons?

They weigh 90 kilos.

2 What colour are they?
3 What country do they come from?
4 What do they eat?
5 Where do they sleep?

5 **Think of an unusual animal and make notes to complete the fact sheet.**

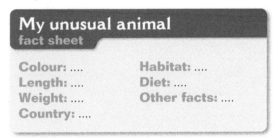

My unusual animal fact sheet

Colour: ….   Habitat: ….
Length: ….   Diet: ….
Weight: ….   Other facts: ….
Country: ….

6 **Write a short article about your animal. Use the model from Exercise 2 and your notes from Exercise 5.**

My unusual animal

1 Appearance
   They are … . (colour / length / weight)
2 Habitat
   They live in … . (place / country)
3 Diet
   They eat … . (animals / plants)
4 Other facts
   They can … . (run / fly / swim / climb / jump)

Remember!
* Include the key information from your notes.
* Use the vocabulary in this unit.
* Check your grammar, spelling, and punctuation.

51

Refresh Your Memory!

Grammar Review

1 Copy and complete the frequency line with these adverbs.

always	hardly ever	~~never~~	often

0%	→	50%	→	100%
never	....	sometimes	....	usually	....

2 Put the words in order to make sentences.

1 the / I / to / music / at / never / weekend / listen
I never listen to music at the weekend.
2 o'clock / up / usually / get / at / You / seven
3 ever / We / grandparents / hardly / our / visit
4 talk / I / always / my / parrot / to
5 cycle / often / school / We / to
6 under / My / usually / the / sleeps / cat / bed

3 Read the answers. Complete the questions.

1 *Where* does your friend live?
She lives in Paris.
2 .... do you take your dog to the beach?
Because he loves swimming in the sea.
3 .... do you cycle to school?
Never. I haven't got a bike.
4 .... is your favourite possession?
My mobile phone.
5 .... is your English teacher?
My teacher is Mrs Clarkson.
6 .... do you have piano lessons?
After school on Thursdays.

4 Complete the Pet Advice sheet with *You must* or *You mustn't*.

1 *You must feed your dog twice a day.*

Pet Advice: Dogs

1	✓	feed your dog twice a day
2	✓	take your dog for a walk every day
3	✓	give your dog a place to sleep
4	✗	give your dog unhealthy food, for example, chocolate
5	✗	shout at your dog
6	✓	keep your dog on a lead

Vocabulary Review

5 Complete these unusual animal words with *a, e, i, o* and *u*.

1 h*i*ss*i*ng c*o*ckr*oa*ch
2 t_r_nt_l_
3 pygmy g_ _t
4 g_ _nt r_bb_t
5 fr_g
6 p_r_nh_
7 pyth_n
8 p_rr_t
9 l_z_rd
10 st_ck _ns_ct

6 Look at the animals from Exercise 5 again. Find …

1 four animals with four legs. *pygmy goat, ...*
2 three animals with a tail.
3 two animals with six legs.
4 two animals with no legs.
5 one animal with two legs.
6 one animal with eight legs.

7 Complete the sentences with these words.

arms	beak	fingers	neck
paws	tail	toes	~~wings~~

1 My parrot can fly because she's got *wings*. She eats her food with her .... .
2 My dog is black and white. He's got four white .... and a black .... .
3 I've got ten .... on my feet and ten .... on my hands.
4 Chimpanzees have got two legs and two .... .
5 Giraffes have got four long legs and a long .... .

Speaking Review

8 ◖◗ 2.10 Make sentences. Then listen and check.

Jim you / like / play / football?
Do you like playing football?

Mike No, I don't. I like / watch / football on TV. you / like / watch / TV?

Jim No. I love / listen / to music and read / books, but I hate / watch TV.

Dictation

9 ◖◗ 2.11 Listen and write in your notebook.

✓ **My assessment profile:** Workbook page 130

Refresh Your Memory!

Exercise 1

Answers

From left to right: *never*, hardly ever, *sometimes*, often, *usually*, always

Exercise 2

Answers

2 You usually get up at seven o'clock.
3 We hardly ever visit our grandparents.
4 I always talk to my parrot.
5 We often cycle to school.
6 My cat usually sleeps under the bed.

Exercise 3

Answers

2 Why   3 How often   4 What   5 Who   6 When

Exercise 4

Answers

2 You must take your dog for a walk every day.
3 You must give your dog a place to sleep.
4 You mustn't give your dog unhealthy food, for example, chocolate.
5 You mustn't shout at your dog.
6 You must keep your dog on a lead.

Exercise 5

Answers

2 tarantula   5 frog   8 parrot
3 pygmy goat   6 piranha   9 lizard
4 giant rabbit   7 python   10 stick insect

Exercise 6

Answers

1 *pygmy goat*, giant rabbit, frog, lizard   4 piranha, python
2 pygmy goat, giant rabbit, lizard   5 parrot
3 hissing cockroach, stick insect   6 tarantula

Exercise 7

Answers

1 *wings*, beak   2 paws, tail   3 toes, fingers   4 arms
5 neck

Exercise 8 (Track 2.10)

Answers and Audioscript

Jim   *Do you like playing football?*
Mike No, I don't. I like watching football on TV. Do you like watching TV?
Jim   No, I love listening to music and reading books, but I hate watching TV.

Exercise 9 (Track 2.11)

Answers and Audioscript

My pet is a hissing cockroach. It's got six legs but it hasn't got any wings. I like holding my pet and feeding it. You must feed hissing cockroaches two or three times a week. They never bite and they are very good pets.

My assessment profile:
Workbook page 130

Extra activity

Revise vocabulary connected with animals and basic verb forms:
– Draw the fantasy animal on the board and write its name *pyranharoach* underneath. Explain that it is a combination of three animals. Students identify the three animals (*python*, *piranha* and *cockroach*).
– Write the sentence prompts around the animal on the board. In pairs, students use their imagination to complete the other sentence prompts. Take feedback as a class.
– In pairs, students invent their own fantasy animal. They draw a picture and invent an appropriate name. Students write sentences about it using the sentence prompts on the board. Monitor and help with vocabulary and feed in ideas if necessary.
– Delete the *pyranharoach* from the board. Pairs take turns drawing their fantasy animals on the board and telling the class about them. Monitor but do not interrupt students' fluency.
– Make a note of any mistakes related to the content of this unit to go over with the class afterwards but make sure these mistakes remain anonymous during the correction stage.

Culture 2 – Education in the UK:
See Teacher's Book page 220 and Students' Book page 122 (for extra reading, discussion and writing work).

Real World Profiles

- *Chennai*, formerly known as Madras, is one of the oldest and largest cities in India. With a population of nearly 5 million, its main businesses are car manufacturing and software exporting. The Arignar Anna Zoo is 19 miles from the centre of Chennai and was the first zoo open to the public in India. It is in fact more like a safari park than a zoo, with very large enclosures surrounded by moats, giving the impression that the animals all inhabit the same space.
- *Mahout* is the term for a person who rides an elephant. Traditionally this would be a boy who is paired with an elephant as a young child and then remains with that elephant for the rest of its life. Since 2008 the elephants at Arignar Anna Zoo have been used to offer elephant safari rides around the zoo. Further information about both Chennai and the Arignar Anna Zoo is available on the internet.
- *Lavindya* is a real person and more information about her and her unusual friendship with orphaned elephant Giri is available by searching the internet.

Exercise 1

- Draw attention to the photos and ask students what they can see.
- Students read the profile and decide if the sentences are true or false.
- When checking answers, ask students to correct the false sentences.
- If you have a world map available, ask students where India and Chennai are.

Answers

1 False (She lives in India.)
2 False (She is six years old.)
3 True

Exercise 2 (Track 2.12)

- Students read the text again and answer the questions.
- If you wish, play the recording for students to listen and read.
- Students check in pairs before you check answers as a class.
- Elicit from stronger students or explain yourself the meaning of any new vocabulary.

Answers

2 Because her father is a 'mahout' and works at the zoo. He is a special keeper for the baby elephants.
3 She rides an elephant to school.
4 In the afternoon she plays football with the elephants.
5 She lies down next to them and pats their trunks.

Extend the work on India and ask students to investigate and find out five facts about the country and express these as sentences. Give students two or three sentences as examples, e.g.
1 The capital of India is New Delhi.
2 The Indian flag is orange, white and green with a small blue circle, etc.
Ask some students to say their sentences for the class.

Class discussion

- Read through the questions with students.
- They then work in pairs or small groups talking about the questions.
- Monitor but do not interrupt fluency.
- Take feedback as a class.
- Ideally the class discussion activity should be completed in English but you may want to support weaker students with some L1.

Ask students additional questions related to the topic of the text, e.g.
1 What other things do you know about India?
2 Do you think it's a good part of the world to live in? Why/Why not?
3 What countries are near India?
4 Is Lavindya's daily routine similar to yours?
5 Do you think Lavindya is lucky to live in the zoo? Why/Why not?

In this unit have you …
… used Grammar and Vocabulary worksheet?
… used Reading and Listening worksheet?
… used Writing worksheet?
… used Speaking worksheet?
… used Unit test?

With the exception of the Writing worksheets, all the Teacher's Resources are at two levels of difficulty:
*   For students who need extra help and support
** For students who require an additional challenge

Real World Profiles

✳ Lavindya's Profile

👤 **Age:**
6

Home country:
India

City:
Chennai

Reading

1 **Read Lavindya's profile. Are the sentences true (T) or false (F)?**

1 Lavindya lives in the USA.
2 She is ten years old.
3 She lives in Chennai.

2 🔊 **2.12** **Read about Lavindya and her family. Answer the questions.**

1 Where does Lavindya have a bath?
In a small pool outside.

2 Why does she live at Arignar Anna Zoo?
3 How does she go to school?
4 What does she do in the afternoon?
5 What does she do when the elephants are tired?

Lavindya's Best Friend

It is seven o'clock in the morning in Chennai, southern India. Lavindya always has her morning bath before school. But she doesn't have a bath at home. She has a bath in a small pool outside with her best friend, a baby elephant!

Lavindya lives at Arignar Anna Zoo with her parents, brothers and sisters. Her father is a 'mahout' – he works at the zoo and he is a special keeper for the baby elephants. Lavindya is only six years old, but she can control the elephants and she has a very special friendship with them.

At eight o'clock in the morning, Lavindya goes to school, but she doesn't travel on a school bus. She rides an elephant to school. The elephant carries her backpack with its trunk. After school, Lavindya plays football with the elephants.

Now it is the evening, and the baby elephants are tired. Lavindya lies down next to them and pats their trunks. Sometimes they all sleep together – friends together in the day and friends together at night.

Class discussion

- Can you see elephants in your local zoo?
- How do you go to school in the morning?
- Think of three reasons why it's good to have a friendship with an animal.

◀ 53 ▶

5 Out and About!

Grammar	Present continuous; Present simple and Present continuous
Vocabulary	Activities; Weather and seasons
Speaking	Expressing surprise
Writing	A blog

Vocabulary Activities

1 🔊 2.13 **Match the photos to these words. Then listen, check and repeat.**

bowling	climbing
dancing	gymnastics
hiking	ice-skating
kayaking	mountain biking
painting	playing an instrument
pony trekking	rollerblading
singing	surfing *1*

Word list page 77   **Workbook** page 108

2 **Read the clues. Guess the name of the activity from Exercise 1.**

1 You do these two activities on water. *surfing, …*
2 You need a pony for this activity.
3 You need a bicycle for this activity.
4 You use a ball in this activity.
5 You walk a lot in this activity.
6 You make music in these two activities.

3 🔊 2.14 **Listen. Copy and complete the activities Joe and Lisa do at the Holiday Camp.**

	morning	afternoon
Joe	*mountain biking*	
Lisa		

4 **Write three sentences about activities you like and don't like.**

I like rollerblading but I don't like kayaking.

Brain Trainer Activity 3
Go to page 116

54

Unit contents

Vocabulary
→ Activities – *bowling, climbing, dancing, gymnastics, hiking, ice-skating, kayaking, mountain biking, painting, playing an instrument, pony trekking, rollerblading, singing, surfing*
→ Weather – *cloudy, cold, foggy, hot, raining, snowing, sunny, warm, windy*
→ Seasons – *spring, summer, autumn, winter*

Grammar
→ Present continuous – affirmative, negative, questions and short answers
→ Present simple and Present continuous

Communication
→ Expressing surprise
→ Writing a blog – My blog; Word order

Pronunciation
→ *-ing* endings

Culture 3 – British Food

Key competences
→ Linguistic competence
→ Competence in knowledge and interaction with the physical world
→ Data processing and digital competence
→ Interpersonal, social and civic competence
→ Cultural and artistic competences
→ Learning-to-learn
→ Autonomy and personal initiative

Vocabulary   Activities

Cultural notes
- *hiking* refers to a strenuous walk, often in hilly or rough terrain. A common excursion in hills or mountains, it is usually a long, tiring activity.
- *kayaking* is carried out in a type of small canoe with a double paddle. Popular on rivers, rapids and the ocean but can be dangerous.
- *pony trekking* involves riding out into the countryside. It can take an hour or two, or even a whole day. It is for older children and adults.

Exercise 1 (Track 2.13)
- Individually, students match the words and the pictures.
- Play the recording for students to listen and check.
- Repeat the recording. Pause after each word to check students' pronunciation.

Answers
2 rollerblading
3 pony trekking
4 hiking
5 gymnastics
6 mountain biking
7 ice-skating
8 kayaking
9 climbing
10 dancing
11 playing an instrument
12 painting
13 singing
14 bowling

Exercise 2
- Individually, students identify the activities.
- They then check in pairs before you check answers as a class.

Answers
1 *surfing*, kayaking
2 pony trekking
3 mountain biking
4 bowling
5 hiking
6 playing an instrument, singing

Extra activity
Reinforce vocabulary and spelling by doing a group mime activity at this point. Ask one student to come to the front of the class and turn his or her back to the board. Write one of the activities on the board. On the count of three, everybody else in the class mimes the activity for the student to guess. After the student has guessed the word, ask him or her to spell it for you. Repeat the process until you have revised all 14 items.

Exercise 3 (Track 2.14)
- Play the recording for students to complete the table.
- Check answers by drawing the table on the board and asking individual students to complete the missing information.

Answers

	morning	afternoon
Joe	*mountain biking*	rollerblading
Lisa	surfing	mountain biking

Exercise 4
- Students work individually, writing their sentences.
- Monitor and point out errors for students to self-correct.
- Ask some students to say their sentences for the class to hear.

Answers
- Students' own answers

Further practice:
Workbook pages 42 and 108

Brain Trainer Activity 3
See Teacher's Book page 214 and Students' Book page 116

Reading

Revision

First – Revise the activities seen on the previous Vocabulary page by miming them for your students (*bowling*, *climbing*, *dancing*, *gymnastics*, *hiking*, *ice-skating*, *kayaking*, *mountain biking*, *painting*, *playing an instrument*, *pony trekking*, *rollerblading*, *singing*, *surfing*). Drill for pronunciation and word stress.

Second – Read the following clues and ask students to identify the activities:

1 You use different colours to make pictures in this activity. (Answer: *painting*)
2 You need a big animal to do this activity. It isn't for small children. (Answer: *pony trekking*)
3 You usually do this activity in the mountains. You use your hands and your feet. (Answer: *climbing*)
4 You do this activity in the sea on a board. It's very popular in Brazil. (Answer: *surfing*)
5 You make a noise in this activity but you don't need a musical instrument. (Answer: *singing*)
6 This is usually a winter activity but you can do it in the summer in a special place. (Answer: *ice-skating*)

Third – Check answers and spelling by asking individual students to write answers on the board.

Cultural notes

- *Corcovado Mountain* lies within the city limits of Rio de Janeiro. Its name in Portuguese means 'hunchback'. The statue of Christ the Redeemer stands on the top of the mountain.
- *Copacabana beach*, in the southern part of Rio de Janeiro, is one of the most famous beaches in the world. It's renowned for its excellent surfing conditions.

Extra activity

Books closed. Write the following word skeleton on the board:
C _ _ _ _ _ _ _ _ _ (Answer: *Copacabana*)
Pick individual students, asking them to say a letter. If the letter they choose is in the word, write it in the correct position. If it is not, write it in a column on one side of the board. When students think they know what the word is, they put their hands up.
Repeat the process with:
C _ _ _ _ _ _ _ _ (Answer: *Corcovado*)
Ask students if they know where these places are and what they know about them.
If you have a world map available, show students where Rio de Janeiro is.

Exercise 1

- Draw attention to the photos and ask students what they can see.
- Individually, students match the photos to the paragraphs.

Exercise 2

- Make sure students understand not to read in detail at this point.
- Students scan the text quickly to check their answers.

Answers

1 B   2 A   3 D   4 C

Exercise 3 (Track 2.15)

- Students choose the correct options.
- If you wish, play the recording for students to listen and read.
- Check answers by asking individual students to read the sentences.
- Elicit from stronger students or explain yourself the meaning of any new vocabulary.

Answers

2 mountain biking   3 doesn't like   4 afternoon   5 like
6 surfing

Exercise 4 (Track 2.16)

- Ask students what they think Ricky's job could be.
- Collate suggestions on the board.
- Play the recording for students to listen and check.

Answer

Ricky is a stuntman.

Exercise 5

- Ask two students to read aloud the example question and answer.
- Check the pronunciation of the questions before students work in pairs.
- In pairs, students ask and answer the questions.
- Monitor and help with vocabulary but do not interrupt fluency.

Extra activity

Take feedback as a class on the questions in Exercise 5. Ask students to tell you about any sports or activities which are typical of their country. Find out how much consensus there is amongst the group regarding favourite sports and free time activities.

Further practice:
Workbook page 43

Reading

1   Read the text quickly. Match photos (1–4) to the correct paragraph (A–D).

2   Read the text and check your answer to Exercise 1.

3   🎧 2.15   Read the text again. Choose the correct options.
  1 Ricardo *is / isn't* at university today.
  2 The first thing Ricky does is *mountain biking / climbing*.
  3 The reporter, Amanda, *likes / doesn't like* hiking up Corcovado Mountain.
  4 Ricky and Amanda are on Copacabana beach in the *morning / afternoon*.
  5 Lots of people in Brazil *like / don't like* surfing.
  6 Ricky is very good at *swimming / surfing*.

4   🎧 2.16   Guess the job. Then listen to Ricky and check.

5   **What about you?** In pairs, ask and answer.
  1 What sports/activities are popular in your country?
  2 What sports do you like?
  3 What activities do you usually do in your free time?

> What sports are popular in your country?

> Lots of people like rollerblading.

Guess the job!

Reporter Amanda Moreno is spending the day with nineteen-year-old Ricardo Dos Santos. He's a university student from Brazil.

A It's 6.00 a.m. and I'm having breakfast with Ricardo – nickname Ricky – on Corcovado Mountain in Rio de Janeiro. It's December, so the weather is great at the moment. The students aren't studying – they're on holiday. Today, I'm taking photos of Ricky for our **Guess the job!** competition.

B Ricky's first activity today is mountain biking. He isn't riding down the road – he's riding up the road. It isn't easy!

C It's 11.00 a.m. Now we're hiking up the mountain for Ricky's next activities. I'm not enjoying it, but Ricky likes walking and climbing. Now we're at the top. Ricky is rollerblading and skateboarding. He's having fun!

D Now it's 4.00 p.m. We aren't on the mountain, we're on Copacabana beach. Ricky is swimming and surfing. Surfing is a popular sport here and Ricky is very good at it. But why is he doing all these activities? Can you **guess the job?**

Is Ricky ...
a a professional sportsperson?
b a stuntman in a film?
c a holiday camp instructor?

Email your answers to:
guessthejob@smart.com

55

Grammar Present continuous

Affirmative	
I	'm (am) singing.
He/She/It	's (is) singing.
You/We/They	're (are) singing.
Negative	
I	'm (am) not singing.
He/She/It	isn't (is not) singing.
You/We/They	aren't (are not) singing.

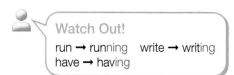

Watch Out!

run → running   write → writing
have → having

1 Study the grammar tables. Choose the correct options to complete the rules.

> **1** The verb *to do* / *to be* goes before the main verb in the Present continuous.
> **2** We add *-ing* / *-es* to the end of the main verb.
> **3** The verb *to be* goes *before* / *after* the main verb in the question form of the Present continuous.

2 Write the *-ing* forms of the verbs.

1 go *going*	**3** do	**5** swim	**7** play
2 watch	**4** have	**6** walk	**8** run

Pronunciation *-ing* endings

3a 🔊 **2.17** Listen to the verbs and *-ing* endings from Exercise 2.

b 🔊 **2.17** What sound does the *i* make? Say *-ing* out loud.

c 🔊 **2.17** Listen again and repeat.

4 Make sentences.

1 Juan (not get up / sleep).
Juan isn't getting up. He's sleeping.
2 Enrique and Erica (not ice-skate / bowl).
3 Mr Chapman (not surf / sing).
4 Adriana and I (not study / dance).
5 I (not skateboard / paint my room).
6 Miss Green (not swim / run).

Questions and short answers	
Am I singing?	Yes, I am. No, I'm not.
Is he/she/it singing?	Yes, he/she/it is. No, he/she/it isn't.
Are you/we/they singing?	Yes, you/we/they are. No, you/we/they aren't.

Grammar reference Workbook page 94

5 🔊 **2.18** Complete the text with the verbs. Use the Present continuous. Listen and check.

The dance act you [1] *are watching* (watch) now is the *Hot Street Crew*! Look at this! Kayla [2] .... (not dance), she [3] .... (do) gymnastics here! Now Leroy and Des [4] .... (jump)! They [5] .... (have) fun! In the studio the audience [6] .... (not sit) in their seats. They're standing and clapping. What a great dance!

6 Look at the picture and answer the questions.

It's 9.00 p.m. in Cancún, Mexico.
1 Are the Morales family sitting in the living room?
Yes, they are.
2 Is Elena watching TV?
3 Is her mum writing a letter?
4 Is the dog having dinner?

7 Make questions. Ask and answer for Elena.

1 your dog / sleep?
2 your parents / read?
3 you / sit / next to your mum?
4 you and your parents / eat / pizza?

8 What about you? Imagine it's 6.00 p.m. on Saturday. What are you doing now?

> *I'm listening to my favourite band on my MP3 player.*

56

Grammar   Present continuous

Language notes

This unit introduces the Present continuous for actions happening at the moment of speaking. Remember to grade your language appropriately throughout the unit and not inadvertently use the Present continuous to refer to the future.

We form the Present continuous by adding *-ing* to the infinitive of the verb. However there are three exceptions to this rule:

- If the infinitive ends with a consonant + stressed vowel + consonant, we double the consonant, e.g. *stop*, *run* and *begin* which become *stopping*, *running* and *beginning*.
- If the infinitive ends with a vowel + consonant + *-e*, we omit the *-e*, e.g. *write*, *have* and *come* which become *writing*, *having* and *becoming*.
- If the infinitive ends in *-ie*, the *-ie* changes to *-y*, e.g. *lie* and *die* which become *lying* and *dying*.

Exercise 1

- Read the grammar tables with students.
- Students work individually, completing the rules and referring back to the grammar tables where necessary.

Answers

1 to be   **2** *-ing*   **3** before

Exercise 2

- Read the 'Watch Out!' section in the grammar tables with students.
- If you have a stronger group, elicit from the class the spelling rules for the Present continuous.
- Ask individual students to write answers on the board to check spelling.

Answers

2 watching   **3** doing   **4** having   **5** swimming
6 walking   **7** playing   **8** running

Pronunciation   *-ing* endings

Language notes

In most parts of the UK the final *-g* of the *-ing* form is a very soft sound and is often almost unpronounced. Only when an *-ing* form is followed by another vowel, e.g. *Are you speaking English?* does it become slightly stronger.

Exercise 3a (Track 2.17)

- Play the recording for students to listen to the *-ing* forms from Exercise 2.

Exercise 3b (Track 2.17)

- Ask students to listen carefully to the sound of the 'i'.

Answer

/ɪ/

Exercise 3c (Track 2.17)

- Play the recording for students to listen and repeat. Pause as appropriate to check students' pronunciation.

Further practice:
Workbook page 123

Exercise 4

- Individually, students make the sentences.
- Check answers as a class. Ask students to give you the full forms of the contractions.

Answers

2 Enrique and Erica aren't ice-skating. They're bowling.
3 Mr Chapman isn't surfing. He's singing.
4 Adriana and I aren't studying. We're dancing.
5 I'm not skateboarding. I'm painting my room.
6 Miss Green isn't swimming. She's running.

Exercise 5 (Track 2.18)

- Students work individually to complete the text.
- Play the recording for students to listen and check.
- Ask individual students to write answers on the board to check spelling. Ask students to give you the full forms of the contractions in items 2 and 6 and the contracted forms of the other items.

Answers

2 isn't dancing   **3** 's doing   **4** are jumping   **5** 're having
6 aren't sitting

Exercise 6

- Check answers by asking pairs of students to read questions and answers.

Answers

2 No, she isn't/is not. She's/is listening to her MP3 player.
3 Yes, she is.
4 No, it isn't/is not. It's/is sleeping.

Exercise 7

- Students make questions for Elena and answer them.

Answers

1 Is your dog sleeping? Yes, it is.
2 Are your parents reading? No, they aren't/are not.
3 Are you sitting next to your mum? Yes, I am.
4 Are you and your parents eating pizza? Yes, we are.

Exercise 8

- Monitor and point out errors for students to self-correct.

Further practice:
Workbook pages 44 and 94–95

Brain Trainer Activity 2
See Teacher's Book page 214 and Students' Book page 116

Vocabulary   Weather and seasons

Revision

First – Draw a table on the board with three columns marked *regular*, *no -e* and *double consonant*. Students copy the table into their notebooks.

Second – Tell students you are going to read ten verbs and that they must write them in the correct column according to the correct spelling of the *-ing* form. They will get one point for each correct answer. Use *paint* as an example of a word in the first column.

Third – Read the following items and then check answers by asking individual students to write the words on the board. *dance, do, go, have, play, run, skate, swim, trek, watch* (Answers: *regular* – *doing, going, playing, watching*; *no -e* – *dancing, having, skating*; *double consonant* – *running, swimming, trekking*)

Extra activity

Books closed. Revise the months and pre-teach the seasons and weather words. Draw a line on the board representing the year and elicit the 12 months. Write these under the line, from January to December. Check spelling by asking students to spell the words to you. Point to March, April and May and ask students *'What season is this?'* to elicit *spring* in the northern hemisphere or *autumn* in the southern hemisphere. Repeat the procedure to elicit the other seasons.
Use the sentence *'In my country in spring it's …'* to elicit typical weather for that season. Drill the vocabulary for pronunciation and word stress. Do not allow students to write anything down.
Repeat the procedure to elicit the weather for the other seasons.

Exercise 1 (Track 2.19)

- In pairs, students match the words in the box with the pictures.
- Check answers as a class.

Answers

2 sunny	8 warm
3 snowing	9 hot
4 windy	10 spring
5 cloudy	11 summer
6 foggy	12 autumn
7 cold	13 winter

Exercise 2 (Track 2.20)

- Students look at the weather map.
- Individually, students complete the sentences.
- Play the recording for students to listen, check and repeat. Pause as appropriate to check students' pronunciation.

Answers

2 warm   3 cloudy   4 raining   5 cold   6 snowing
7 sunny   8 windy   9 foggy

Exercise 3 (Track 2.21)

- Play the recording for students to choose the correct options.
- Repeat the recording, pausing after each section to check students' answers.

Answers

1 b   2 c   3 a   4 c

Exercise 4

- Ask two students to read aloud the example question and answer.
- Elicit a second question from the class.
- Students work in pairs, asking and answering questions about the weather map.
- Monitor but do not interrupt fluency unless they make mistakes with the weather vocabulary.

Extra activity

Stronger groups or fast finishers use the weather map and report in Exercise 2 as a model to prepare their own weather report for another region of the world. Tell students to decide on a region of the world, decide what season it is and to prepare a weather map and report accordingly. Students work in groups of three to prepare and then present their report to the class. Their classmates have to guess what season it is based on the information in the report.

Further practice:
Workbook pages 45 and 108

Brain Trainer Activity 4
See Teacher's Book page 214 and Students' Book page 116

Vocabulary Weather and seasons

1 🔊 2.19 **Match the pictures to these words. Then listen, check and repeat.**

autumn	cloudy	cold	foggy
hot	raining *1*	snowing	spring
summer	sunny	warm	windy
winter			

Word list page 77 **Workbook** page 108

2 🔊 2.20 **Look at the picture. Complete the sentences with the weather words from Exercise 1. Then listen, check and repeat.**

What's the weather like today?

Let's look at the weather in Western Europe. In Portugal the weather is ¹ *hot* right now.

In Spain, it's a lovely ² .... day. But it's ³ .... in France. It's ⁴ .... there, too.

Switzerland is very ⁵ .... and it's ⁶ .... at the moment, as well.

In Italy, they've got nice ⁷ .... weather, but it's ⁸ ...., too.

And in the UK the weather isn't cold, but it is ⁹ .... .

3 🔊 2.21 **Listen. Choose the correct weather.**

1 **a** it's raining **b** it's cold **c** it's foggy
2 **a** it's sunny **b** it's snowing **c** it's cloudy
3 **a** it's windy **b** it's cloudy **c** it's sunny
4 **a** it's cold **b** it's warm **c** it's hot

4 **Look at the map in Exercise 2. In pairs, ask and answer.**

Is it foggy in Spain? *No, it isn't.*

Brain Trainer Activity 4 Go to page 116

57

Chatroom — Expressing surprise

Speaking and Listening

1 **Look at the photos. Which of these things can you see?**

1 a dog   4 a rat
2 a farm   5 a river
3 an otter   6 a bridge

2 🔊 **2.22** **Listen and read the conversation. Answer the questions.**

1 Where are the children?
    They are at Willow End.
2 What does Monica often do in summer?
3 Is Nick taking a photo of Sunny?
4 What animals are in the water?
5 What are these animals doing?
6 What does Julia tell Nick to do?

3 **Act out the conversation in groups of three.**

Monica	Here we are! This is Willow End. It's my favourite place. It's nice in summer – I often swim in the river here.
Julia	But not today! Brrr! The water's very cold.
Nick	Wow! This is an amazing place!
Monica	Look at the bridge.
Julia	Great! I love it!
Monica	Are you taking a photo of Sunny, Nick?
Nick	No. I'm looking at that animal in the water.
Julia	Yuk! Is it a rat?
Monica	No, it's an otter. I sometimes see them here.
Nick	Really? There aren't many otters. They're very rare. Look! Two otters! They're swimming.
Julia	How amazing! Take a photo, Nick.

Say it in your language …
Here we are!
Yuk!

58

Chatroom Expressing surprise

Revision

First – Tell students what five members of your family are doing at the moment. This can be real or fictional. Students listen to your sentences and decide if they are true or false. For example:

1 My mother's working.
2 My father's tidying the house.
3 My sister's studying.
4 My brother's watching TV.
5 My dog's having breakfast.

Second – Individually, students write five sentences. Monitor and point out errors for students to self-correct.

Third – Students work in pairs, reading their sentences and deciding which are true or false.

Speaking and Listening

Extra activity

Divide the class into two groups and assign each group a character (*Monica* or *Nick*). Within their group students work in pairs, writing down everything they have learnt about their character up to this point. Collate feedback about each character on the board.
(Answers: *Monica – gets up early every day because the bus leaves her village at 7.15, lives on a farm, hates getting up early, etc.; Nick – has got a dog called Sunny, has got a games console, loves farms, etc.*)

Exercise 1

- Draw attention to the photos and ask students what they can see.
- Check answers as a class.

Answers

1 a dog **3** an otter **5** a river **6** a bridge

Extra activity

Stronger groups or individual students try to describe what is happening in the photos. Encourage them to use the Present continuous to talk about the actions in progress. Check students are clear about the names of the characters before they start work in pairs describing what they can see. Monitor and help with grammar and vocabulary but do not interrupt fluency.

Brain Trainer Activity 1
See Teacher's Book page 214 and Students' Book page 116

Exercise 2 (Track 2.22)

- Play the recording for students to listen and read.
- Individually, students answer the questions.
- They then check in pairs before you check answers as a class.

Answers

2 She often swims in the river.
3 No, he's looking at an animal in the water/river.
4 (There are) two otters.
5 They're swimming.
6 She tells Nick to take a photo.

Exercise 3

- Divide the class into groups of three.
- Groups act out the conversation.
- Monitor and correct students' pronunciation as appropriate.
- Nominate one group to perform the conversation for the class.

Say it in your language ...

Ask students to find the phrases in the conversation and look at them in context to try to deduce the meaning.

Here we are! – a common expression used to get people's attention when we have arrived at our destination after a journey. Can be used in many informal contexts and with all means of transport.

Yuk! – an exclamation used to express distaste or revulsion. Can be used in many contexts, often to refer to smells or tastes. Should be used with caution however as people could be offended or interpret it as rude if they feel they are responsible for the reaction.

Exercise 4

- Students refer back to the conversation and match the expressions to the objects.
- Check answers as a class.

Answers

1 a   **2** c   **3** b

Exercise 5

- Read through the phrases for expressing surprise with the class.
- Drill the phrases for word stress and intonation.

Exercise 6 (Track 2.23)

- Play the recording for students to listen and repeat. Pause as appropriate to check students' pronunciation.
- In pairs, students act out the conversation.
- Monitor and correct students' pronunciation as appropriate.

Extra activity

Before students act out the conversation in pairs, drill it for correct pronunciation. Divide the class in half down the centre. Tell the half on the left that they are going to be Stella and the half on the right that they are going to be Steve. Build up the conversation step by step until students can perform it unprompted.
Change over the two groups and repeat the procedure so that both groups have practised both parts.
Students then work in pairs, acting out the conversation.

Exercise 7

- Elicit a second conversation from the class using the first set of prompts.
- Students then make their own conversations by replacing the words in purple.

Exercise 8

- Students use their own ideas to make more situations and then act them out.

Further practice:
Workbook pages 46 and 117

Grammar   Present simple and Present continuous

Language notes

Your students' L1 may or may not distinguish between actions taking place at the time of speaking and routine actions. Some languages tend to use a simple form in both cases, leaving a lot to be inferred from the context, and some students may therefore have more problems than others with the distinction between the two aspects. Another common confusion arises with stative verbs (*like*, *love*, *hate*, *want*, etc.) which are rarely found in the continuous form. This distinction is not covered at this point in *Next Move* and the exception posed by these forms is not an issue here.

Exercise 1

- Read the grammar table with students.
- Check answers as a class.

Answers

1 b   **2** a

Exercise 2

- Individually, students decide if the words are usually used with the Present simple or Present continuous.
- They then compare their answers in pairs.

Answers

2 Present simple	**5** Present simple
3 Present simple	**6** Present simple
4 Present continuous	**7** Present continuous

Exercise 3

- When checking answers, ask students to identify which words or expressions helped them identify the Present simple or Present continuous.

Answers

2 Present simple ('every Sunday')
3 Present simple ('usually')
4 Present continuous ('now')
5 Present continuous ('now')
6 Present simple ('on Saturdays')

Exercise 4

- Individually, students choose the correct options.
- They then check in pairs before you check answers as a class.

Answers

2 do   **3** doesn't go   **4** Are they climbing   **5** gets up
6 isn't sleeping

Further practice:
Workbook pages 47 and 94–95

4 Look back at the conversation. Match an expression to each object.

1 Wow!   **a** Willow End
2 Great!   **b** the otters
3 How amazing!   **c** the bridge

5 Read the phrases for expressing surprise.

Something nice surprises you	You are surprised by some information	You are surprised by an event
Wow! Great! How amazing!	Really?	Look!

6 〉〉 2.23 Listen to the conversation. Act out the conversation in pairs.

Stella Hi Steve. It's me, Stella. Guess what I'm doing!

Steve I don't know. ¹ Are you shopping in town?

Stella No, I'm ² having a drink in the Rainforest café.

Steve Really?

Stella And ³ Brad Pitt is standing near me. I'm taking a photo.

Steve Wow! How amazing!

7 Work in pairs. Replace the words in purple in Exercise 6 with these words. Act out the conversation.

1 eating at a pizza restaurant / sitting on a bus / going to a football match

2 watching a football match / waiting for a film premiere / going to a concert

3 actor / singer / sportsperson

8 Act out the conversation again with your own words and ideas.

Grammar   Present simple and Present continuous

Present simple	Present continuous
I **often** swim here.	They're swimming.
I **sometimes** see them.	He's looking at the animals now.

Watch Out!

always, usually, often, sometimes, hardly ever, never → every day / week / month

happening now, at the moment

Grammar reference Workbook page 94

1 Study the grammar table. Match the tenses to the actions.

1 Present simple   **a** action happening now
2 Present continuous   **b** routine

2 Do we use the Present simple or the Present continuous with these words?

1 now   *Present continuous*
2 always   5 usually
3 every week   6 never
4 now   7 at the moment

3 Are these sentences in the Present simple (Ps) or Present continuous (Pc)?

1 They're playing football at the moment. *Pc*
2 My grandma comes for dinner every Sunday.
3 Do you usually get up at 6.00 a.m.?
4 Jim isn't watching TV now.
5 He is studying.
6 We get up late on Saturdays.

4 Choose the correct options.

1 Harry and Lucy *go / are going* on a school trip.
2 I often *do / am doing* my homework in the living room.
3 He *doesn't go / isn't going* ice-skating every day.
4 *Do they climb / Are they climbing* at the moment?
5 Jenny *gets up / is getting up* late on Saturdays.
6 The dog *doesn't sleep / isn't sleeping* now.

59

Reading

1 Look quickly at the texts. What kind of texts do you think they are?

1 articles   **2** emails   **3** poems

The Fog

I like the fog,
It's soft and cool,
It hides everything,
On the way to school.

I can't see a house,
I can't see a tree,
Because the fog
Is playing with me.

The sun comes out,
The fog goes away,
But it shall be back
Another day.

Anon

Weather

Weather is hot,
Weather is cold,
Weather is changing
As the weeks unfold.

Skies are cloudy,
Skies are fair,
Skies are changing
In the air.

It is raining,
It is snowing,
It is windy
With breezes blowing.

Days are foggy,
Days are clear,
Weather is changing
Throughout the year!

Meish Goldish

Autumn wind
The mountain's shadow
is trembling.

Kobayashi Issa

Key Words

soft	to change / changing
breeze	to blow / blowing
shadow	to tremble / trembling

2 Read and check your answer to Exercise 1.

3 Read this definition of a Haiku. Which poem is a Haiku?

A Haiku is a very short Japanese poem. A Haiku usually talks about one of the four seasons.

4))) 2.24 Read the poems again. Answer the questions.

1 Does 'The Fog' poet like fog? *Yes, he does.*
2 Is the 'Weather' poem talking about weather at one time of year?
3 Which season is the Haiku about?
4 Which poem has four verses?
5 Which poem doesn't use rhyme?
6 How many weather words can you find in all the poems?

Listening

1))) 2.25 Listen and match the people (1–3) to the season they are talking about.

1 Blake   **a** spring
2 Yoko   **b** summer
3 Paulo   **c** autumn

2))) 2.25 Listen again. Are the sentences true (T) or false (F)?

1 Blake is from Canada.
2 Blake likes the colour of autumn flowers.
3 Yoko is American.
4 Cherry blossom flowers are pink and white.
5 Paulo likes summer.
6 Argentinian summer is in July.

Reading

Cultural notes

- A *Haiku* is a very short form of poem, Japanese in origin and written vertically. When translated into English, they are usually made up of 17 syllables and printed on three lines. Kobayashi Issa (Japan, 1763–1827) was a poet and a Buddhist priest. He was famous for his haiku poems and is seen as one of the masters of the art of the haiku. Curiously, his pen name *'Issa'* means *'cup of tea'*.
- *Meish Goldish* is an author who specialises in writing books for schools and libraries.

Exercise 1

- Draw attention to the photos and the texts and ask students what they can see.

Exercise 2

- Students read the texts and check their answers to Exercise 1.

Answer

3 poems

Exercise 3

- Read the definition of a Haiku with students.

Answer

Autumn wind …

Key Words

Be prepared to focus on the Key Words, either by pre-teaching them, eliciting their meaning after students have read the text, or through dictionary or definition writing work.

soft – an adjective to describe something which is gentle to the touch and not hard

to change/changing – when something is not the same over a period of time

breeze – a gentle wind, usually used with a positive connotation

to blow/blowing – the movement of a wind or a breeze

shadow – the cool, dark area on the ground behind objects when the sun is shining

to tremble/trembling – to vibrate or move backwards and forwards quickly, often because of cold or fear

Exercise 4 (Track 2.24)

- Students read the poems again and answer the questions.
- If you wish, play the recording for students to listen and read.
- Students check in pairs before checking answers as a class.

Answers

2 No, it isn't.
3 It's about autumn.
4 'Weather' has four verses.
5 The Haiku doesn't use rhyme.
6 There are 14 words: *breezes, clear, cloudy, cold, cool, fair, fog, foggy, hot, raining, snowing, sun, wind, windy*

Listening

Exercise 1 (Track 2.25)

- Play the recording for students to listen and match the speakers and the seasons.
- Check answers as a class.

Answers

1 c   2 a   3 b

Audioscript:
See Teacher's Book page 225

Exercise 2 (Track 2.25)

- Repeat the recording for students to decide if the sentences are true or false.
- When checking answers, ask students to correct the false sentences.

Answers

1 True
2 False (Blake likes the colour of autumn trees.)
3 False (Yoko is Japanese but she lives in America.)
4 True
5 True
6 False (Argentinian summer is in January.)

Extra activity

Write the following sentences on the board. Repeat the recording for students to complete the sentences.
1 Blake is from … in Canada. (*Blake is from <u>Calgary</u> in Canada.*)
2 In autumn the trees in Canada are … . (*In autumn the trees in Canada are <u>orange, red, yellow and gold</u>.*)
3 Yoko … Japan. (*Yoko <u>loves</u> Japan.*)
4 In Japan they have … in spring. (*In Japan they have a <u>special festival</u> in spring.*)
5 Paulo is from … in Argentina. (*Paulo is from <u>Buenos Aires</u> in Argentina.*)
6 In summer, Paulo … with his friends. (*In summer, Paulo <u>goes swimming</u> with his friends.*)
Students compare their ideas before checking answers as a class.

Further practice:
Workbook page 48

Writing   A blog

Revision

First – Write the following sentences on the board:
1 My next activity on Saturdays.
2 In Spain it's a lovely warm day but I don't like dancing.
3 I often do my homework in the afternoon is painting.
4 I usually hiking up the mountain.
5 I like singing but it's cloudy.
6 At the moment we're get up at 7.30 a.m.

Second – Tell students that the sentences have got mixed up. They need to break each sentence into two pieces and reorganise them to make six logical sentences. Students work in pairs, solving the puzzle.

Third – If students find the activity difficult, show them where the break is in each sentence. Check answers as a class. (Answers: *1 My next activity in the afternoon is painting.; 2 In Spain it's a lovely warm day but it's cloudy.; 3 I often do my homework on Saturdays.; 4 I usually get up at 7.30 a.m.; 5 I like singing but I don't like dancing.; 6 At the moment we're hiking up the mountain.*)

Exercise 1

- Read the Writing File with students.

Language note

Basic word order in English is relatively inflexible compared to some other languages. There are languages with much more flexibility regarding the placement of the subject and the verb. Indeed in some languages it is often not even necessary to include the subject pronoun as the conjugation of the verb itself indicates the person.

Exercise 2

- Students read the blog and find the verbs that follow the subjects.
- Collate answers on the board.

Answers

1 get up; 'm getting up, 'm
2 is, lives, loves, goes, is waiting
3 're, use

Exercise 3

- Individually, students order the words.
- Check answers by asking individual students to read the sentences.

Answers

2 We go to school at half past eight.
3 The dog is swimming in the river.
4 They like rollerblading.
5 Nat and Mia are hiking in the mountains.
6 My friends and I often go bowling.

Exercise 4

- Students read the blog again and answer the questions.
- They then check in pairs before you check answers as a class.

Answers

2 It's really cold. It's snowing and foggy.
3 No, it isn't. There are only a couple of hours of light in the day.
4 Erik loves winter sports/kayaking and ice-skating.
5 Erik is waiting for Julio with the snow shoes.

Exercise 5

- Explain that students should only make notes at this point or write short sentences.
- Encourage students to ask you for any vocabulary they need.

Answers

Students' own answers

Exercise 6

- Read through the 'My blog' writing guide. Tell students they must now present their information as a complete text, not as notes or unconnected sentences.
- Make sure students understand that they should answer questions 1 and 2 in the first paragraph, questions 3, 4 and 5 in the second paragraph and questions 6 and 7 in the third paragraph.
- Draw students' attention to the 'Remember!' checklist.

Answers

Students' own answers

Extra activity

Add an extra 10–15 vocabulary items from this unit to the collection of Word Cards.
Revise all the vocabulary by playing a definitions game. Tell students that they are going to work in teams, making definitions for the others to guess. Demonstrate yourself with one of the words. For example, if you have the word *dancing* the definition might be *'It's an activity you do with your body. You move with music.'* Divide the class into five teams and give each team an equal number of vocabulary cards. If you have a few cards left over, give these to the stronger teams or fast finishers. Students work together writing simple definitions for the words. Monitor and point out errors for students to self-correct. Groups take turns to read their definitions and the rest of the class have to guess what the word is. The teams that guess correctly win one point. The winner is the team with the most points.

Further practice:
Workbook page 49

Writing A blog

1 **Read the Writing File.**

 Writing File **Word order**

The **subject** of a sentence comes before the **verb** in English.
I get up at 6.00 a.m.
Sam and Anna are having breakfast.

2 **Read Julio's blog. Find the verbs that follow these subjects.**

1 I   **2** he / Erik   **3** we

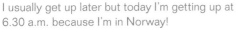

Monday morning

I usually get up later but today I'm getting up at 6.30 a.m. because I'm in Norway!

We're on a school exchange trip to Tromsø, an island in the Arctic Circle. It's really cold here! It's snowing now and it's foggy, too. In winter there are usually only a couple of hours of light in the day.

Erik is my exchange buddy. He lives here and he loves winter sports. He often goes kayaking and ice-skating. Do you know Tromsø is Norway's candidate for the 2018 Winter Olympics?

It's 7.00 a.m. now and Erik is waiting for me with the snow shoes. We use them to go to school – it's cool!

Julio

3 **Put the words in order to make sentences.**

1 writing / her blog / is / Layla
Layla is writing her blog.
2 go to school / We / at half past eight
3 The dog / swimming / in the river / is
4 like / rollerblading / They
5 Nat and Mia / are / in the mountains / hiking
6 go / My friends and I / bowling / often

4 **Read the blog again. Answer the questions.**

1 Why is Julio in Norway?
Because he is on a school exchange trip.
2 What is the weather like in Tromsø?
3 Is it light all day in Tromsø in winter?
4 What activities does Erik like?
5 What is Erik doing now?

5 **Imagine you are on an exchange trip. Answer the questions about your trip.**

1 What time do you usually get up?
2 Are you doing things at different times today?
3 Where are you?
4 What is the weather like in this place?
5 What is the weather like at home?
6 Who is your exchange buddy?
7 What activities does he/she like?

6 **Write a short blog about your exchange trip. Use 'My blog' and your answers from Exercise 5.**

 My blog

Paragraph 1 introducing a topic
I usually ... but today I ... .
Paragraph 2 talking about a place
It's ... in ... . (place)
Paragraph 3 talking about a person
(name) is ... .
He / She lives / likes / often goes ... .

 Remember!
● Check word order for subjects and verbs.
● Use the vocabulary in this unit.
● Check your grammar, spelling and punctuation.

61

Refresh Your Memory!

Grammar Review

1 Complete the postcard with the verbs in the Present continuous.

Hi Tania,

We ¹ 're enjoying (enjoy) our holiday in Portugal. I ² .... (sit) by the swimming pool with my little brother, Jack. I ³ .... (watch) him because my parents ⁴ .... (make) the dinner. Jack ⁵ .... (not swim) at the moment. He ⁶ .... (play) with some cats. The cats ⁷ .... (run) away from my brother – they ⁸ .... (not have) fun!

See you soon,

Nicole

Tania Bexon
7 Manor Road
Stoke Newington
London N15 7LS

2 Make questions with the Present continuous.

1 you / sit / in a classroom?

Are you sitting in a classroom?

2 your teacher / talk / to the class?
3 you / watch / TV?
4 you and your friend / talk?
5 all the students / listen / to the teacher?
6 your friend / write / in his/her notebook?

3 Answer the questions in Exercise 2.

1 *Yes, I am.*

4 Put the verb in the correct tense, Present simple or Present continuous.

1 Georgia (clean) her teeth every morning.

Georgia cleans her teeth every morning.

2 We (have) our breakfast now.
3 It (not rain) at the moment.
4 He often (hike) in the spring.
5 They (rollerblade) in the park now.
6 She never (watch) TV after 10 p.m.
7 He (study) every day.
8 I (visit) my grandma today.

Vocabulary Review

5 Find the odd one out.

1 **a** kayaking
   b *pony trekking*
   c surfing
2 **a** ice-skating
   b singing
   c dancing
3 **a** climbing
   b hiking
   c playing an instrument
4 **a** rollerblading
   b bowling
   c painting
5 **a** singing
   b pony trekking
   c hiking

6 Complete the sentences with a weather word.

1 It isn't sunny today. It's r*aining.*
2 It's warm today, but it's c _ _ _ _ _, too.
3 It's very cold today and it's s _ _ _ _ _ _ now.
4 The weather is w _ _ _ _ and cold today.
5 This morning it's very grey and f _ _ _ _ outside.

Speaking Review

7))) 2.26 **Choose the correct options to complete each conversation. Then listen and check.**

1
Girl *Hey! / Wow!* What are you doing?
Boy I'm taking a photo of you! Smile!

2
Girl Guess what! I've got tickets for the Kings of Leon concert tonight!
Boy *Look! / Really?*

3
Boy Jennifer Lopez is sitting near me.
Girl *How amazing! / Hey!*

Dictation

8))) 2.27 **Listen and write in your notebook.**

✓ **My assessment profile:** Workbook page 131

Refresh Your Memory!

Exercise 1

Answers

2 'm/am sitting
3 'm/am watching
4 are making
5 isn't/is not swimming
6 's/is playing
7 are running
8 aren't/are not having

Exercise 2

Answers

2 Is your teacher talking to the class?
3 Are you watching TV?
4 Are you and your friend talking?
5 Are all the students listening to the teacher?
6 Is your friend writing in his/her notebook?

Exercise 3

Answers

Students' own answers
1 Yes, I am. / No, I'm not.
2 Yes, he/she is. / No, he/she isn't.
3 Yes, I am. / No, I'm not.
4 Yes, we are. / No, we aren't.
5 Yes, they are. / No, they aren't.
6 Yes, he/she is. / No, he/she isn't.

Exercise 4

Answers

2 We're/are having our breakfast now.
3 It isn't/is not raining at the moment.
4 He often hikes in the spring.
5 They're/are rollerblading in the park now.
6 She never watches TV after 10 p.m.
7 He studies every day.
8 I'm/am visiting my grandma today.

Exercise 5

Answers

1 b 2 a 3 c 4 c 5 a

Exercise 6

Answers

2 cloudy 3 snowing 4 windy 5 foggy

Exercise 7 (Track 2.26)

Answers

2 Really? 3 How amazing!

Exercise 8 (Track 2.27)

Answer

I'm writing this letter from Rio in Brazil. I'm on a school exchange trip and I'm having a great time. It's January so it's winter in North America but it's summer here! It's really warm and sunny today but sometimes it's cloudy, too.

My assessment profile:
Workbook page 131

Extra activity

Revise the vocabulary from the unit and the Present simple and continuous:
– Draw the sun symbol on the left side of the board and elicit the adjective *sunny*.
– Continue drawing the symbols yourself and eliciting the words or ask students to draw pictures on the board to represent the weather words studied in this unit.
– Draw the mountain biking symbol on the right side of the board and elicit the activity (*mountain biking*).
– Either you or your students draw up other pictures to represent the activities in this unit.
– Drill all the vocabulary for pronunciation and word stress. Check spelling by asking students to spell the words to you. Do not allow students to write anything down.
– Draw up the first speech bubble and elicit an example sentence using the Present continuous.
– Draw up the second speech bubble. Make sure students understand that *spring* and *January* are only examples and that they can use any season or month. Elicit an example sentence using the Present simple.
– Students work in pairs, making as many sentences as possible. Monitor and correct students' pronunciation as appropriate.
– Make a note of any mistakes related to the content of this unit to go over with the class afterwards but make sure these mistakes remain anonymous during the correction stage.

Culture 3 – British Food:
See Teacher's Book page 221 and Students' Book page 123 (for extra reading, discussion and writing work).

Science File   Why is the sky blue?

Cultural notes

- *Rayleigh scattering* is the technical name for the effect which makes the sky appear blue to us. Light from the sun travels through space in a straight line but when it meets the earth's atmosphere it also meets dust and water particles, which act in the same way as the milk in the experiment. As the light waves bump into these particles they scatter them causing the sky to appear blue, the sun to appear yellow (from space it appears white), and the sunset to appear red and orange.

- *Rainbows* are also an optical effect caused when direct sunlight hits water particles in the atmosphere. A rainbow is not a physical object and therefore you can never reach it. It will always appear to the viewer at a 42° angle opposite the sun. The 'seven' distinct colours seen in the rainbow are an effect of human colour vision and were originally defined by Isaac Newton although the gradations in colour are in fact gradual and imperceptible. There are various ways of making a rainbow artificially, one of which is explained at the end of these notes.

- Further information on Rayleigh scattering, rainbows and ideas for experiments is available on the internet.

Language notes

Be prepared to elicit from stronger students or explain yourself the meaning of the following lexical items which appear in the Reading text: *to switch (it) on, to shine, to break up, light wave, atmosphere, sunset, sunrise*

Exercise 1

- Students scan the text quickly and match the sentences.
- Check answers as a class.

Answers

1 b   2 a

Exercise 2 (Track 2.28)

- Use the pictures to clarify the meaning of any new vocabulary.
- Students read the text and answer the questions.
- If you wish, play the recording for students to listen and read.
- Students check in pairs before you check answers as a class.
- Check answers by asking pairs of students to read questions and answers.

Answers

2 Blue
3 It breaks up into different coloured light waves.
4 It breaks up in the same way as light through the milk and water mixture.

My Science File

Exercise 3

- Divide the class into pairs, wherever possible grouping stronger students with weaker ones.
- Tell them that information is available on the internet explaining the scientific process which causes rainbows.

Exercise 4

- Students use the items to try to make a rainbow indoors.
- Monitor and help where necessary.

Exercise 5

- Draw students' attention to the first part of the 'Why is the sky blue?' text. Tell them that they should write their 'rainbow' experiment in the same way.
- Students also include a diagram to illustrate the experiment.

Answers

How to make a rainbow
This experiment shows us how rainbows form.
You need …
- a torch   • a glass   • a bottle of water
- a sheet of paper

1 Fill the glass with water.
2 Close the curtains and make the room as dark as possible.
3 Put the paper on the floor.
4 Shine the torch through the edge of the glass of water.
5 Move the torch and the paper until you see the rainbow on the paper.

In this unit have you …
… used Grammar and Vocabulary worksheet?
… used Reading and Listening worksheet?
… used Writing worksheet?
… used Speaking worksheet?
… used Unit test?

With the exception of the Writing worksheets, all the Teacher's Resources are at two levels of difficulty:
*   For students who need extra help and support
** For students who require an additional challenge

Science File

Why is the sky blue?

This experiment shows us why the sky is blue.

You need ...

- a torch
- a 1-litre plastic bottle
- some milk
- some water

1 Put 750 ml of water into the bottle.

2 Put the torch under the bottle and switch it on. Look down on it from above. What colour is the light?

3 Add one teaspoon of milk to the water and mix it together. Shine the torch again and look down on the bottle. Now the light in the middle of the bottle is orange, and the light at the sides of the bottle is blue.

Why does this happen?

The light from the torch has lots of different colours. When it passes through the milk and water mixture, it breaks up into different coloured light waves. The blue light wave is short. The orange light wave is long. So the blue light wave is at the side of the bottle and the orange light wave is at the top of the bottle. In the same way, light from the sun breaks up into different colours when it comes into our atmosphere. In the day we see the short blue light waves. At sunset and at sunrise we see the long red and orange light waves.

Reading

1 **Read the text quickly. Match (1–2) to (a–b).**

1 Blue light waves are ...   **a** long.
2 Orange light waves are ...   **b** short.

2)) 2.28 **Read the text again. Answer the questions.**

1 What colour is the light in the middle of the bottle? *Orange*
2 What colour is the light at the sides of the bottle?
3 What happens when the light passes through the water and milk mixture?
4 What happens when light from the sun comes into our atmosphere?

My Science File

3 **Find out about rainbows. Find out ...**
- when rainbows happen.
- why we see rainbows.

4 **In pairs, create an experiment to make a rainbow. Use some of these things:**
- a torch
- a glass
- a bottle of water
- a sheet of paper
- a mirror
- a CD or DVD
- a window

5 **Write your instructions for the experiment in your notebook.**

6 Delicious!

Grammar	Countable and uncountable nouns; *Many/Much/A lot of*; Comparatives
Vocabulary	Food and drink; Adjectives
Speaking	Ordering food
Writing	Instructions

Vocabulary Food and drink

1 🔊 2.29 **Match the items in the photos to these words. Then listen, check and repeat.**

banana	bread	broccoli	cheese
chicken	eggs	ham	juice
pasta	prawns	rice	salmon
sausages	tea	tomatoes	tuna
water	yoghurt *1*		

Word list page 77 **Workbook** page 109

2 **Copy and complete the table with food from Exercise 1.**

Carbohydrates	Fish
bread, ...	*tuna, ...*
Fruit and Vegetables	**Dairy**
banana, ...	*cheese, ...*
Meat	**Drinks**
sausages, ...	*water, ...*

3 **In pairs, ask and answer.**
1 What do you usually have for breakfast/ lunch/dinner?
2 What's your favourite food?
3 What's your favourite drink?

What do you usually have for breakfast?

I usually have bread and cheese.

 Brain Trainer Activity 3
Go to page 117

Unit contents
Vocabulary
→ Food and drink – *banana, bread, broccoli, cheese, chicken, eggs, ham, juice, pasta, prawns, rice, salmon, sausages, tea, tomatoes, tuna, water, yoghurt*
→ Adjectives – *clean, cold, delicious, dirty, disgusting, horrible, hot, large, noisy, quiet, small, wonderful*

Grammar
→ Countable and uncountable nouns with *a/an* and *some*
→ *Many/Much/A lot of*
→ Comparatives

Communication
→ Ordering food
→ Writing – Instructions; Sequence words – *First, Then, Finally*

Pronunciation
→ Word stress

Culture 4 – London Transport

Key competences
→ Linguistic competence
→ Interpersonal, social and civic competence
→ Learning-to-learn
→ Autonomy and personal initiative

Vocabulary   Food and drink

Stronger groups can brainstorm vocabulary they already know before looking at the vocabulary in the Students' Book. Books closed. In pairs or small groups, students list all the food and drink vocabulary they can think of. Students change partners or groups and peer teach the vocabulary they have thought of. Collate suggestions on the board and correct students' spelling and pronunciation as appropriate.

Exercise 1 (Track 2.29)
• Individually, students match the words and the photos.
• Play the recording for students to listen and check.
• Repeat the recording. Pause after each word to check students' pronunciation.

Answers

2 banana	8 prawns	14 tomatoes
3 juice	9 rice	15 ham
4 broccoli	10 eggs	16 bread
5 water	11 tea	17 cheese
6 chicken	12 sausages	18 tuna
7 pasta	13 salmon	

Extra activity

Write the alphabet on the board in three or four columns. Books closed. In pairs, students think of one food or drink for each letter of the alphabet. Tell them that there is no common food or drink for the letters *u* and *x* in English. Monitor and check students' spelling.
Check answers by asking students to write words on the board. Drill the vocabulary for pronunciation and word stress.
(Possible answers: **a**pple, **b**anana, **c**heese, **d**oughnut (AmE donut), **e**ggs, **f**ish, **g**rapes, **h**am, **i**ce-cream, **j**uice, **k**etchup, **l**amb, **m**ilk, **n**ut, **o**range, **p**asta, **q**uiche, **r**ice, **s**almon, **t**ea, **u**–, **v**egetables, **w**ater, **x**–, **y**oghurt, **z**ucchini. Italicised words not part of the active vocabulary of this unit.)

Exercise 2
• In pairs, students complete the table.
• Check answers by drawing the table on the board and asking individual students to complete the missing information.

Answers

Carbohydrates: *bread*, pasta, rice
Fruit and vegetables: *banana*, broccoli, tomatoes
Meat: *sausages*, chicken, ham
Fish: *tuna*, prawns, salmon
Dairy: *cheese*, eggs, yoghurt
Drinks: *water*, juice, tea

Exercise 3
• Ask two students to read aloud the example question and answer.
• Students work in pairs, asking and answering the questions.
• Monitor and help with vocabulary but do not interrupt fluency.

Extra activity

Stronger groups or individual students feed back to the class about their partners' answers in the third person, e.g. *John usually has bread and cheese for breakfast.* Collate answers on the board and find out which are the most popular foods and drinks in the group.

Further practice:
Workbook pages 50 and 109

Brain Trainer Activity 3
See Teacher's Book page 215 and Students' Book page 117

Reading

Revision

First – Revise food and drink vocabulary by drawing on the board a simple picture of a plate with two sausages, two fried eggs and some bread. Alongside draw a simple picture of a yoghurt pot and a spoon, e.g.

Tell students this is your favourite meal and elicit what they can see in the picture.

Second – Individually, students draw a picture of their favourite meal. Remind them to use words from the Vocabulary page where possible.

Third – Each student shows his/her picture to the class. Students say what they can see in the picture. Feed in new vocabulary as necessary.

Exercise 1

- Draw attention to the photos and the text and ask students what they can see.
- They then work in pairs, matching the fridges to the people.

Exercise 2

- Make sure students understand not to read in detail at this point.
- Students scan the text quickly to check their answers.

Answers

1 Chuck   2 Juanita   3 Caitlin

Extra activity

Ask students to name all the food in the fridges without looking back at the previous Vocabulary page. Check answers and spelling by asking individual students to write words on the board. Note that neither *apple* nor *raspberry* have been covered at this point so be prepared to elicit the words from stronger students or teach them yourself. Drill the vocabulary for pronunciation and word stress.

Exercise 3 (Track 2.30)

- Students work individually, deciding if the sentences are true or false.
- If you wish, play the recording for students to listen and read.
- When checking answers, ask students to correct the false sentences.
- Elicit from stronger students or explain yourself the meaning of any new vocabulary and if you have a world map, make sure students know where Patagonia (Argentina) and Wisconsin (USA) are.

Answers

1 *False* (Juanita has got salmon, prawns and tuna.)
2 True
3 False (Caitlin is vegetarian.)
4 False (They drink lots of/a lot of water.)
5 True
6 False (Chuck loves yoghurt.)

Exercise 4

- Ask two students to read aloud the example question and answer.
- Check the pronunciation of the questions before students work in pairs.
- In pairs, students ask and answer the questions.
- Monitor and help with vocabulary but do not interrupt fluency.
- Make a note of any mistakes to go over with the class afterwards.

Extra activity

Books closed. Give your students a ten-item spelling test. Students listen and write the following words:

1 prawns   6 chicken
2 salmon   7 yoghurt
3 biscuits   8 juice
4 broccoli   9 sausages
5 vegetables   10 carbohydrates

Check answers by asking individual students to write words on the board. Students self-correct and give themselves one point for each word they spell correctly.

Further practice:
Workbook page 51

Reading

1 **Look at the photos. Write** *Juanita*, *Caitlin* or *Chuck*.

  1 This person's fridge has got some fruit in it.
  2 This person's fridge has got 24 eggs in it.
  3 This person's fridge has got 10 carrots in it.

2 **Read and check your answers to Exercise 1.**

3 🔊 2.30 **Read the article again. Are the sentences true (T) or false (F)?**

  1 Juanita hasn't got any fish in her fridge. *F*
  2 Juanita likes rice salad.
  3 Caitlin likes meat.
  4 Caitlin's family don't drink much water.
  5 There are a lot of sausages in Chuck's fridge.
  6 Chuck doesn't like yoghurt.

4 **What about you? In pairs, ask and answer.**

  1 What's in your fridge at home?
  2 Are you a vegetarian?
  3 Are you a good cook?
  4 What food don't you like?

> What's in your fridge at home?

> I think we've got some vegetables, cheese, …

Look!
This is our fridge!

Juanita

I live in El Calafate, a small town in Patagonia. Today we're preparing a barbecue, so we've got lots of chicken, sausages and salmon in our fridge. There's a rice salad with prawns and tuna – it's delicious! We've also got twenty-four eggs because my mum loves making cakes.

Caitlin

My family is from Scotland and we're vegetarians, so we haven't got any meat in our fridge. We usually have a lot of vegetables and today we've got some broccoli, ten carrots and a lot of tomatoes. We haven't got any milk and we haven't got much juice, but that's **OK**, because we all drink lots of water.

Chuck

We're from Wisconsin. I've got a big family and a very big fridge! Today we've got some ham, lots of bread and sausages. We haven't got many eggs, but there's a lot of yoghurt, because we all love yoghurt. We've also got lots of fruit because I often make smoothies for breakfast.

65

Grammar

Countable and uncountable nouns

Countable nouns		Uncountable nouns
Singular	Plural	
a banana	some bananas	some bread
an apple	some apples	some rice
an egg	some eggs	some pasta

1 Study the grammar table. Choose the correct options to complete the rule.

We use *much* / *many* with countable nouns and *much* / *many* with uncountable nouns.

2 Are these words countable or uncountable?

1 chicken *uncountable*
2 broccoli
3 vegetable
4 water
5 tomato
6 sausages
7 banana
8 salmon
9 tuna
10 yoghurt

Pronunciation   Word stress

3a))) 2.31 Listen to the words in Exercise 2. Where is the stress?

chicken

b))) 2.31 Listen again. Copy and put the words under the correct heading.

chicken	tomato

c))) 2.31 Listen again and repeat.

Many/Much/A lot of

How many?	How much?
How many eggs have you got?	How much bread have you got?
We haven't got any eggs.	We haven't got any bread.
We haven't got many eggs.	We haven't got much bread.
We've got some/four eggs.	We've got some bread.
We've got a lot of eggs.	We've got a lot of bread.

Grammar reference Workbook page 96

4 Look at the picture. Choose the correct options.

1 How *much* / *many* pasta is on the table?
2 How *much* / *many* eggs are on the table?
3 How *much* / *many* bread is on the table?
4 How *much* / *many* cheese is on the table?
5 How *much* / *many* tomatoes are on the table?

5 Answer the questions in Exercise 4. Use *not much* / *many* or *a lot of*.

1 *There is a lot of pasta.*

6 Complete the conversation with these words.

Not much	much	many	~~some~~	a lot of

Chen What's in your lunchbox, Billy?
Billy I've got ¹*some* ham sandwiches.
Chen How ² .... sandwiches have you got?
Billy Four.
Chen That's ³ .... sandwiches! And how ⁴ .... water have you got?
Billy ⁵ .... . My water bottle is very small.

7 What about you? **What's in your favourite sandwich? In pairs, ask and answer.**

What have you got in your sandwich?

I've got a lot of chicken and some tomatoes.

Grammar   Countable and uncountable nouns

- Students are introduced here to countable and uncountable nouns with *a/some/any*, *(How) much/many* and *a lot of*. Students may also be familiar with the expression *lots of*, which is frequently used in place of *a lot of*. Both *lots of* and *a lot of* can be used with both countable and uncountable nouns and are therefore unlikely to cause students problems.
- Some words, including *chicken*, *salmon* and *tuna*, can be either countable or uncountable depending on the context. In the case of animals, they are countable when referring to the living animal and uncountable when referring to the food.

Exercise 1

- Read the grammar table with students.
- Students work individually, completing the rule and referring back to the grammar table where necessary.
- Remind students of the use of *some* in affirmative sentences and *any* in negatives and questions only.

Answers

We use *many* with countable nouns and *much* with uncountable nouns.

Exercise 2

- Students classify the words as countable or uncountable.
- Check answers by drawing two columns on the board, one for countable and one for uncountable, and asking individual students to classify the vocabulary.

Answers

2 uncountable	5 countable	8 uncountable
3 countable	6 countable	9 uncountable
4 uncountable	7 countable	10 uncountable

Pronunciation   Word stress

Exercise 3a (Track 2.31)

- Write *chicken* on the board and play the recording for students to identify the stress.
- Play the recording for students to identify the stress in the other words.

Answers

2 **broc**coli	5 to**ma**to	8 **sal**mon
3 **vege**table	6 **saus**ages	9 **tu**na
4 **wa**ter	7 ba**na**na	10 **yogh**urt

Exercise 3b (Track 2.31)

- Draw students' attention to the two possibilities.
- Make sure they understand how the two columns relate to the word stress.
- Repeat the recording for students to classify the other words.

- Check answers as a class.

Answers

chicken, **broc**coli, **vege**table, **wa**ter, **saus**ages, **sal**mon, **tu**na, **yogh**urt
to**ma**to, ba**na**na

Exercise 3c (Track 2.31)

- Play the recording for students to listen and repeat.

Further practice:
Workbook page 124

Many/Much/A lot of

Exercise 4

- Students choose the correct options.
- Check answers by asking individual students to read the questions.

Answers

2 many   3 much   4 much   5 many

Exercise 5

- Individually, students answer the questions.
- Check answers by asking pairs of students to read questions and answers.

Answers

2 There aren't many eggs.	4 There isn't much cheese.
3 There is a lot of bread.	5 There are a lot of tomatoes.

Exercise 6

- Students check in pairs before you check answers as a class.
- After checking answers, pairs act out the conversation.
- Monitor and correct students' pronunciation as appropriate.
- Nominate one group to perform the conversation for the class.

Answers

2 many   3 a lot of   4 much   5 Not much

Exercise 7

- Students work in pairs, talking about their favourite sandwich.
- Ask pairs of students to think of funny or unusual combinations for their sandwiches, e.g. *banana and cheese, egg and pasta*, etc.
- Take feedback as a class and find out how much consensus there is in the group about the most popular and least popular sandwiches.

Further practice:
Workbook pages 52 and 96–97

Brain Trainer Activity 2
See Teacher's Book page 215 and Students' Book page 117

Vocabulary   Adjectives

Revision

First – Revise food and drink vocabulary and countable and uncountable nouns by playing 'In my fridge there's …' with the class. Demonstrate the activity by saying 'In my fridge there's some juice.' Elicit a second sentence from a stronger student, e.g. 'In my fridge there's some juice and three eggs.' Nominate a third student to repeat the sentence and add one more item. Check students understand the game before continuing.

Second – Students play the game in groups of three to five. Do not allow students to write anything down. Monitor and correct students' pronunciation as appropriate.

Third – Play the game as a class two or three times, seeing how many items students can remember in total.

Extra activity

Write the word *OPPOSITE* vertically down the centre of the board. Add three dashes before the first *O* of *OPPOSITE* and five dashes after to indicate letters. Pick individual students, asking them to say a letter. If the letter they choose is in the word, write it in the correct position. If it is not, write it in a column on one side of the board. When students think they know what the word is, they put their hands up. (Answer: *unpopular*)
Add two dashes before the first *P* of *OPPOSITE* and four dashes after. Repeat the procedure. (Answer: *popular*).
Continue working down the puzzle until students have completed all the words and the board looks as follows.

```
U N P O P U L A R
  P O P U L A R
  E X P E N S I V E
    B O R I N G
      S M A L L
    B I G
    I N T E R E S T I N G
  C H E A P
```

Ask students to match the pairs of opposite words. (Answers: *big–small*, *boring–interesting*, *cheap–expensive*, *popular–unpopular*)

Exercise 1 (Track 2.32)

- Make sure students understand that they should choose the correct option according to the point of view of the speaker. The person who says 1–6 likes the restaurant. The person who says 7–12 doesn't!
- Play the recording for students to listen and check.
- Repeat the recording, pausing after each sentence to check students' pronunciation.

Answers

2 hot	6 clean	10 small
3 delicious	7 horrible	11 noisy
4 large	8 cold	12 dirty
5 quiet	9 disgusting	

Exercise 2

- In pairs, students say the opposites of the adjectives.
- Check answers by asking individual students to say pairs of words.

Answers

2 large   3 dirty   4 cold   5 disgusting   6 wonderful

Exercise 3

- Individually, students choose the correct option.
- Check answers by asking individual students to read the sentences.
- Drill the sentences for pronunciation and intonation.

Answers

2 quiet   3 cold   4 large   5 wonderful   6 dirty

Exercise 4 (Track 2.33)

- Students work individually, completing the text.
- Play the recording for students to listen and check.

Answers

2 large   3 quiet   4 clean   5 wonderful   6 delicious

Extra activity

Help students memorise the vocabulary by playing 'opposites tennis'. Demonstrate with a stronger student, explaining that you are going to say an adjective and they must respond with the opposite. The student then says a new adjective and you respond with the opposite, e.g.
Teacher quiet
Student noisy – clean
Teacher dirty – horrible
Student wonderful, etc.
Explain that, like real tennis, the rhythm is very important. The speed is not important but the person who breaks the rhythm loses and the other player wins a point. Stronger groups or pairs can use both the opposite adjectives covered in Unit 1 and those taught on this page to make the game more challenging.

Further practice:
Workbook pages 53 and 109

Brain Trainer Activity 4
See Teacher's Book page 215 and Students' Book page 117

Vocabulary   Adjectives

1 🔊 2.32 **Look at the pictures and choose the correct options to complete the sentences. Then listen, check and repeat.**

clean	cold	delicious	dirty	disgusting	horrible
hot	large	noisy	quiet	small	~~wonderful~~

Word list page 77   **Workbook** page 109

1 Fernando's is a *wonderful / horrible* restaurant!
2 The coffee is *hot / cold*.
3 The food is *disgusting / delicious*!
4 We've got *small / large* tables.
5 The music is *quiet / noisy*.
6 The kitchen is very *clean / dirty*.

7 Fernando's is a *wonderful / horrible* restaurant!
8 The coffee is *hot / cold*.
9 The food is *disgusting / delicious*!
10 We've got *small / large* tables.
11 The music is *quiet / noisy*.
12 The kitchen is very *clean / dirty*.

2 **Say the opposites.**
1 quiet *noisy*
2 small
3 clean
4 hot
5 delicious
6 horrible

3 **Choose the correct options.**
1 Don't eat this food! It's *clean / delicious / disgusting*.
2 I can't hear the radio. It's very *small / cold / quiet*.
3 I don't want this tea. It's *large / noisy / cold*.
4 There are 2,000 students in this school. It's a *quiet / large / delicious* school.
5 I like this book. It's *horrible / wonderful / quiet*.
6 Don't sit there. The table is *noisy / dirty / wonderful*.

4 🔊 2.33 **Complete the text with these words. Then listen and check.**

clean	delicious	large
quiet	~~small~~	wonderful

I love visiting my aunt. She lives in a very ¹ *small* house in the country with only two rooms, but the garden is ² .... – it's nearly 30 metres long! It's always ³ .... at my aunt's house because there aren't any cars or people near her. My aunt hates dirt, so her house is always very ⁴ .... . My favourite time of day at my aunt's house is teatime. My aunt is a ⁵ .... cook and she makes ⁶ .... cakes. I love eating them!

 Brain Trainer Activity 4 Go to page 117

 67

Chatroom Ordering food

Speaking and Listening

1 Look at the photo. Answer the question.

1 Where are Monica, Julia, Nick and Leo?

2 **2.34 Listen and read the conversation. Answer the questions.**

1 Why are the children at the restaurant?
It's Nick's birthday.

2 Do they sit at the small table or the large table?
3 What does Julia order?
4 Who orders the pasta with chicken?
5 Who orders some garlic bread?
6 Who doesn't want a drink?
7 Does Monica like her pizza?

3 Act out the conversation in groups of five.

Julia	Hi everyone! Happy birthday, Nick! Is this table OK?
Nick	It's very small. That table's better. It's larger.
Monica	Yes, but it's much noisier. Let's stay here.
Julia	OK. Here's the menu.
Waiter	Are you ready to order?
Julia	Yes. I'd like the ham and cheese pizza, please.
Monica	Me too!
Nick	I'll have the pasta with chicken, please. And some garlic bread. Yum!
Leo	Spaghetti with tomato sauce for me, please.
Waiter	And would you like anything to drink?
Monica	No, I'm OK, thanks.
Nick	Can we have some water, please?
Waiter	Yes, of course.
***	
Waiter	How is your food?
Monica	It's delicious, thanks.

Say it in your language ...
Yum!
Yes, of course.

68

Chatroom   Ordering food

Revision

First – Write the following words on the board randomly: *clean, cold, delicious, dirty, disgusting, horrible, hot, large, noisy, quiet, small, wonderful*

Second – Tell students to match the words to form pairs of opposites.

Third – Check answers by asking individual students to say pairs of words.
(Answers: *clean – dirty*; *cold – hot*; *delicious – disgusting*; *horrible – wonderful*; *large – small*; *quiet – noisy*)

Speaking and Listening

Extra activity

In pairs, students brainstorm ideas for a birthday party menu. They agree on six food and drink items which they think are essential to a good party. Take feedback as a class and collate suggestions on the board. Encourage students to use *have got* and *some/a lot of* in their answers, e.g. *'On our party menu we've got some sausages and a lot of chocolate biscuits.'* Drill the vocabulary for pronunciation and word stress.

Exercise 1

- Students look at the photo and answer the questions.
- They compare their ideas in pairs before checking answers as a class.

Answer

They are at a restaurant.

Brain Trainer Activity 1
See Teacher's Book page 215 and Students' Book page 117

Exercise 2 (Track 2.34)

- Play the recording for students to listen and read.
- Individually, students answer the questions.
- They then check in pairs before checking answers as a class.

Answers

2 They sit at the small table.
3 Julia orders the ham and cheese pizza.
4 Nick orders the pasta with chicken.
5 Nick orders some garlic bread.
6 Monica doesn't want a drink.
7 Yes, she does. It's delicious.

Exercise 3

- Divide the class into groups of four. One student takes the role of both Leo and the waiter.
- Groups act out the conversation.
- Monitor and correct students' pronunciation as appropriate.
- Nominate one group to perform the conversation for the class.

Say it in your language …

Ask students to find the phrases in the conversation and look at them in context to try to deduce the meaning.

Yum! – exclamation commonly used to show that we like the food or drink we have just tasted. The opposite, 'Yuk!', was seen in Unit 5. As 'Yum!' has a strongly positive connotation there is no danger of sounding rude.

Yes, of course. – short response to respond positively to a request. Used with polite, musical intonation to indicate that the request is well within the limits of what is normal or acceptable and therefore there is no problem. You might use it in class if a student asks you, for example, if they can use their dictionary to help them with an exercise, or if they make any other sort of reasonable, polite request.

Extra activity

Elicit a conversation from the students between a waiter and a customer. Tell the class that they are going to be the customer and that you are going to be the waiter. Do not allow students to write anything down. Start the conversation yourself by saying *'Good afternoon. Are you ready to order?'* and eliciting an appropriate response from the class, e.g. *'Yes, I'd like the salmon with rice, please.'* Drill the students' sentence for correct pronunciation then ask a further question yourself. Elicit a second response from the students and drill again. Build up the conversation step by step until students can perform it unprompted.

Exercise 4

- Students read the conversation again and find the phrases.
- Check answers as a class.
- Drill the phrases for pronunciation and intonation.

Answers

Waiter   *Are you ready to order?*; *Would you like anything to drink?*; *How is your food?*

Children Yes. *I'd like … ; I'll have … ; … for me, please.* No, I'm OK, thanks.; *Can we have … ; It's delicious, thanks.*

Exercise 5

- Read through the phrases for ordering food in a restaurant with the class.
- Point out that *Would you … ?* and *I'd like …* are both commonly used to be polite.

Exercise 6 (Track 2.35)

- Play the recording for students to listen to the conversation.
- In groups of four, students act out the conversation.
- Monitor and correct students' pronunciation as appropriate.

Exercise 7

- Elicit a second conversation from the class using the first set of prompts.
- Students then make their own conversations by replacing the words in purple.
- Stronger groups or fast finishers can use their own ideas to make more situations.

Further practice:
Workbook pages 54–55 and 118

Grammar   Comparatives

Language notes

- Students are introduced here to comparative forms and are presented with the spelling rules. When reading through the grammar table, draw students' attention to the double consonant in *hotter*. The doubling of a final consonant is a relatively common feature of English when the base ends in consonant–vowel–consonant. This also happens with both the formation of the present participle (*stop–stopping*) and the Past simple (*stop–stopped*). The only exception to this rule is words ending in *-w* or *-y* where the consonant is not doubled, e.g. *slow–slower* (not *slowwer*) and *play–playing/played* (not *playying* or *playyed*).
- In American English further exceptions are also made to this rule, e.g. *travel–traveled* (AmE)/*travelled* (UK).
- Note that *long adjectives* is used to refer to adjectives of two or more syllables. There are however a few exceptions when an adjective has a very weak second syllable, the most common of which are *quiet–quieter* (not *more quiet*) and *clever–cleverer* (not *more clever*).

Exercise 1

- Read the grammar table with students.
- Students work individually, completing the rules and referring back to the grammar table where necessary.
- Read the 'Watch Out!' section in the grammar table with students.

Answers

1 *-er*   **2** more

Extra activity

Students brainstorm all the adjectives they already know. Write them on the board. Students then classify the words according to the formation of the comparative. (Possible answers: short adjectives – *small, old, big, cheap, clean, cold, hot, new, old, quiet*; short adjectives ending in *-e* – *nice, large*; adjectives ending in *-y* – *dirty, noisy*; long adjectives – *interesting, boring, delicious, disgusting, expensive, horrible, popular, unpopular, wonderful*; irregular adjectives – *bad, good*)

Exercise 2

- Individually, students complete the sentences.
- They then check in pairs before you check answers as a class.
- Check answers by asking individual students to read the sentences.
- Point out the use of *than* in all the sentences.

Answers

2 noisier   **3** more disgusting   **4** cheaper   **5** newer
6 more expensive

Exercise 3

- In pairs, students write sentences.
- Monitor and help with grammar and vocabulary if necessary.
- Ask some pairs to say their sentences for the class to hear.

Answers

Students' own answers

Extra activity

Write on the board: *Mondays* and *Saturdays*. Elicit sentences from the class comparing Mondays and Saturdays, e.g. *'Saturdays are better than Mondays.'*, *'Mondays are more boring than Saturdays.'* Tell students to work in pairs comparing any two things of their choice: actors, cars, cities, school subjects, etc. When they can't think of any more sentences they change the two things and continue making sentences. Monitor and point out errors for students to self-correct. Ask the pairs to say some of their sentences for the class to hear.

Further practice:
Workbook pages 55 and 96–97

4 Look back at the conversation. What questions does the waiter ask? How do the children reply?

Waiter … *Are you ready to order?*

Children …

5 Read the phrases for ordering food in a restaurant.

Waiter/Waitress	Customer
Are you ready to order? Would you like anything to drink? Yes, of course. How is your food?	I'd like the ham and cheese pizza, please. I'll have the pasta with chicken, please. Spaghetti with tomato sauce for me, please. No, I'm OK, thanks. Can we have some water, please? It's delicious, thanks.

6 🔊 2.35 Listen to the conversation. Act out the conversation in groups of four.

Waiter Are you ready to order?
Nick Yes, I'll have the ¹ cheese sandwich, please.
Monica I'd like the ² salmon with broccoli, please.
Julia I'll have the ³ prawn salad, please.
Waiter Would you like anything to drink?
Nick No, I'm OK, thanks.
Monica Me too!
Julia Can I have a glass of ⁴ orange juice, please?
Waiter Yes, of course.

7 Work in groups of four. Replace the words in purple in Exercise 6. Use these words and/or your own ideas. Act out the conversations.

Are you ready to order?

Yes, I'll have … .

1 ham sandwich / chicken sandwich / egg sandwich

2 sausages with carrots / tuna with tomatoes / pasta with prawns

3 egg salad / ham salad / tuna salad

4 apple juice / water

Grammar Comparatives

Short adjectives	
small	smaller
clean	cleaner
hot	hotter

Short adjectives ending in -*e*	
large	larger

Adjectives ending in -*y*	
dirty	dirtier

Long adjectives	
wonderful	more wonderful

Irregular adjectives	
bad	worse
good	better

Watch Out!
Her school is smaller than your school.
The pasta is more delicious than the pizza.

Grammar reference Workbook page 96

1 Study the grammar table. Complete the rules.

To make the comparative form, we add ¹…. to the end of a short adjective, and use the word ²…. in front of a long adjective.

2 Complete the sentences with the comparative adjectives.

1 My house is *colder (cold)* than your house.
2 This table is …. *(noisy)* than that table.
3 The chicken is …. *(disgusting)* than the fish.
4 The poster is …. *(cheap)* than the DVD.
5 My watch is …. *(new)* than your watch.
6 Harry's camera is …. *(expensive)* than Sam's camera.

3 Work in pairs. Find five differences between you and your partner. Use these ideas.

1 old / young
2 tall / short
3 long / short hair
4 large / small family
5 light / dark eyes
6 big backpack / small backpack

69

Reading

1 Look at the photos. What are the places?

  a holiday camps
  b restaurants
  c hotels

Three Unusual .....

Every week we find three unusual places around the world. This week we're looking at amazing restaurants from three different countries.

 Ithaa: The Undersea Restaurant

You can watch the fish and listen to the sea in this restaurant. It's in the Maldives and it's five metres below the sea. There is space for fourteen people in the restaurant. The food is expensive – dinner for two people is $150 – but the view is wonderful.

 The Treehouse Restaurant

Do you like being outside? Do you like looking at the trees and the sky? This restaurant is ten metres above the ground in a treehouse in a forest in New Zealand. You can have lunch or dinner, look at the trees and listen to the birds. Bring a jumper because it's cold here in the evenings.

 Dinner in the Sky

The home of this restaurant is Belgium, but it can be in New York, London, Paris or in your home town. It travels around the world on a big lorry. Do you want a view of a city or of the sea? You can choose with 'Dinner in the Sky'. There is one large table with 22 chairs and it is 50 metres above the ground! Don't look down!

Key Words

unusual	below	space
outside	jumper	lorry

2 Read the text and check your answer to Exercise 1.

3 🔊 2.36 Read the text again. Answer the questions.

  1 Is Ithaa a cheap restaurant?
    No, it's an expensive restaurant.
  2 How many people can eat at Ithaa?
  3 Why do you need warm clothes for the Treehouse Restaurant?
  4 What animals can you listen to at the Treehouse Restaurant?
  5 How many people can eat at Dinner in the Sky?
  6 What's special about Dinner in the Sky?

Listening

1 Match the national dishes (1–3) to the countries (a–c).

  1 empanada   **a** England
  2 moussaka   **b** Chile
  3 fish and chips **c** Greece

2 🔊 2.37 Listen and check your answers to Exercise 1.

3 🔊 2.37 Listen again. Are the sentences true (T) or false (F)?

  1 Diego is from Greece.
  2 An empanada has meat or vegetables inside.
  3 There is fish and cheese in moussaka.
  4 Lots of people in England like fish and chips.

Reading

Cultural notes

The three restaurants featured in the text are all real. Further information is available on the internet.

Exercise 1

- Draw attention to the photos and the text and ask students what they can see.
- Individually, students guess what the places are.
- Collate suggestions on the board.

Exercise 2

- Students scan the text quickly and check their answers.
- Ask students if they have ever been to an unusual restaurant.

Answer

b

Key Words

Be prepared to focus on the Key Words, either by pre-teaching them, eliciting their meaning after students have read the text, or through dictionary or definition writing work.

unusual – not ordinary or typical, strange or original in some way

below – a position, the opposite of 'on top of' and a synonym of 'under'

space – the room there is for people or things inside another thing

outside – not in a building, in the open air

jumper – a warm item of clothing, made of wool and worn on the top part of the body, usually over a shirt

lorry – a large vehicle for carrying heavy things

Exercise 3 (Track 2.36)

- Individually, students read the text again and answer the questions.
- If you wish, play the recording for students to listen and read.
- Students check in pairs before you check answers as a class.
- Elicit from stronger students or explain yourself the meaning of any new vocabulary.

Answers

2 Fourteen people can eat at Ithaa.
3 Because it's cold there in the evenings.
4 You can listen to the birds.
5 Twenty-two people can eat at Dinner in the Sky.
6 It travels around the world on a lorry and you can eat dinner in different places.

Extra activity

Stronger groups or individual students invent an unusual restaurant and write a short descriptive text about it, e.g. a restaurant on a tube train, a restaurant where there is only fruit on the menu, etc. They can also draw a picture to illustrate it. Monitor and help with grammar and vocabulary if necessary.

Listening

Exercise 1

- Individually, students guess where the dishes come from.
- Ask students if they have ever eaten any of the dishes.

Exercise 2 (Track 2.37)

- Play the recording for students to check their ideas.
- Elicit the names and basic ingredients for some of the national dishes of your students.

Answers

1 b 2 c 3 a

Audioscript:
See Teacher's Book page 226

Exercise 3 (Track 2.37)

- Repeat the recording for students to decide if the sentences are true or false.
- When checking answers, ask students to correct the false sentences.

Answers

1 False (He's from Chile.)
2 True
3 False (There is meat with vegetables, tomatoes, cheese and a milk sauce in moussaka.)
4 True

Extra activity

Write the following questions on the board. Repeat the recording for students to listen and answer the questions (answers in brackets).

1 What other ingredient has empanada sometimes got? (*prawns*)
2 What adjective does Diego use to describe empanada? (*delicious*)
3 Where is Tony from? (*Greece*)
4 What adjective does the interviewer use to describe moussaka? (*nice*)
5 Where is Katie from? (*England*)
6 Who loves fish and chips? (*everyone*)
Students compare their answers in pairs before you check answers as a class.

Further practice:
Workbook page 56

Writing Instructions

Revision

First – Prepare a *Live Listening* about a special or unusual restaurant that you know. This can be real or fictional. Remember to grade your language appropriately. Include adjectives to describe both the food and the restaurant, comparatives to talk about what it is like compared to other restaurants and countable and uncountable nouns to talk about the menu. Use the following text as an example:

My favourite restaurant is an Italian restaurant next to my house. The food is delicious and cheap so the restaurant is popular and noisy. It's bigger than other restaurants in my area and it's cleaner, in fact it's wonderful. I always eat a pizza with a lot of cheese, tomatoes and ham and I usually have some garlic bread, too. Delicious, delicious, delicious!

Second – Students listen and make notes under two categories – *the food* and *the restaurant*. They also decide if they would like to go to the restaurant or not and note their reasons.

Third – Students compare their answers in pairs. Collate answers on the board. Find out how many students would like to go to the restaurant and why.

Extra activity

Books closed. Pre-teach the new vocabulary in Exercise 2 using mime as if you were on a cookery programme. Explain to students that you are going to tell them how to make something. They have to listen to you and take note of both the ingredients and the process. Weaker students may need to use some L1 to help them complete the task. Write the ingredients on the board and then talk students through the process, demonstrating clearly all the new words through mime, e.g. *chop, blend, pour, freezer*, etc. Students compare their ideas in pairs before looking at the recipe.

Exercise 1

- Read the Writing File with students.
- Draw students' attention to the use of the imperative for giving instructions in recipes.

Exercise 2

- Students read the recipe and find examples of *first*, *then* and *finally*.

Answers

First, chop the banana …	First, pour the drink …
Then, add the raspberries …	Then, put a stick …
Finally, pour the mixture …	Finally, take it out of the freezer …

Exercise 3

- Students put the sentences into the correct order and link them using the sequence words.

Answers

How to make a cup of tea: First, (c) put the teabag into the cup. Then, (a) add hot water. Finally, (b) drink your tea.

Exercise 4

- Individually, students answer the questions.
- They check in pairs before you check answers as a class.
- Check answers by asking pairs of students to read questions and answers.

Answers

2 You need five tablespoons of yoghurt.
3 No, it isn't.
4 You put the paper cups into the freezer.

Exercise 5

- Explain that students should only make notes at this point or write short sentences.
- Encourage students to ask you for any vocabulary they need.

Answers

Students' own answers

Exercise 6

- Read through the 'My milkshake' writing guide. Show students how the recipe is structured with the ingredients and quantities first and then the instructions using sequence words and imperatives.
- Draw students' attention to the 'Remember!' checklist.

Answers

Students' own answers

Extra activity

Add an extra 10–15 vocabulary items from this unit to the collection of Word Cards.
Revise all the vocabulary by playing a questions game. Tell students that they are going to work in groups of three, asking questions to identify words. Demonstrate yourself with one of the words. Students ask you *yes/no* questions to identify what the word is, e.g. *'Is it an adjective?'*, *'Have you got one in your bag?'*, *'Is there one in the classroom?'*, etc. Divide the class into groups of three and give each student the same number of vocabulary cards. If you have a few cards left over, give these to the stronger groups or fast finishers. Students work together, taking turns to ask and answer questions until they have identified all the words. Monitor and point out errors for students to self-correct.
When a group finishes with their vocabulary cards, they change them with another group until all the groups have revised all the cards.

Further practice:
Workbook page 57

Writing Instructions

1 Read the Writing File.

Sequence words

> **First**, open the bag.
> **Then**, take out the crisps.
> **Finally**, eat the crisps.

2 Read the recipe. Find the sequence words, *first, then* and *finally*.

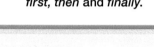

Chop!   Add!   Pour!

Banana and Raspberry Yoghurt Smoothie

Blend!

Ingredients
- 1 banana
- 10–12 raspberries
- 5 tablespoons of raspberry yoghurt
- 3 tablespoons of milk

First, chop the banana. Put the banana into a blender. Then, add the raspberries, the yoghurt and the milk. Blend for thirty seconds. Finally, pour the mixture into a glass and drink it! You can add sugar, but it's better with no sugar.

You can also make frozen smoothies with this recipe. First, pour the drink into small paper cups. Then, put a stick into the cup and put the cup into the freezer. Finally, take it out of the freezer after two hours and enjoy your frozen yoghurt smoothie.

Smoothie

3 Put these sentences into the correct order. Rewrite them using *first, then* and *finally.*

How to make a cup of tea:
a add hot water.
b drink your tea.
c put the teabag into the cup.

4 Read the recipe again. Answer the questions.
1 How many bananas do you need? *one*
2 How much yoghurt do you need?
3 Is the recipe better with some sugar?
4 Where do you put the paper cups?

5 Create your own milkshake recipe. Choose two or three ingredients from the list below.

ice cream
banana
raspberry
strawberry
mango
pineapple
cocoa

6 Write your recipe. Use 'My milkshake' and your ingredients from Exercise 5.

My milkshake
.... and .... milkshake
Ingredients
• *250 ml of milk*
• *1 / 2 / 3 ...*
• *2 / 3 tablespoons of ...*
First, ... / Then, ... / Finally, ...
You can also make ... .
Enjoy your ... .

Remember!
- Use sequence words (*first, then, finally*).
- Use the vocabulary in this unit.
- Check your grammar, spelling and punctuation.

71

Refresh Your Memory!

Grammar Review

1 Are these words countable (C) or uncountable (U).

banana *C*	broccoli	cheese	egg
ham	pasta	prawn	rice
sausages	tomatoes	water	yoghurt

2 Choose the correct options to complete the conversation.

Joe How *much / many* chicken have we got in the fridge?

Freda Not *much / many*.

Joe Oh, OK. What about eggs and bread?

Freda We've got *much / a lot of* eggs but we haven't got *much / many* bread.

Joe How *much / many* sausages have we got?

Freda We've got six sausages, but we haven't got *any / no* ham.

Joe How *much / many* cheese have we got?

Freda We've got *a lot of / much* cheese.

3 Make the comparative form of these adjectives.

1 delicious *more delicious*
2 large
3 dirty
4 small
5 cold
6 noisy
7 wonderful
8 clean

4 Make sentences with comparative adjectives.

1 Lucy's mobile phone / small / Sally's mobile phone

   Lucy's mobile phone is smaller than Sally's mobile phone.

2 My bike / large / your scooter
3 The summer in Spain / hot / in England
4 The Italian restaurant / good / the Chinese restaurant
5 My bedroom / clean / your bedroom
6 Your dog / noisy / my dog
7 Villages / quiet / towns
8 The pizza / delicious / the pasta

Vocabulary Review

5 Complete the food words.

1 c h e e s e
2 t _ _ a _ _ _ s
3 b r _ _ _ _ _ i
4 j _ i _ _
5 _ r _ _ d

6 Complete the sentences with these words.

clean	~~delicious~~	disgusting	large
quiet	small	wonderful	

1 This egg sandwich is *delicious* but it's very .... . I want another sandwich now!
2 You must have .... hands when you cook food.
3 My MP3 player's very ....! I can't hear the music.
4 This yoghurt is very old. It's .... .
5 I love this film. It's ....!
6 My cousin lives in a very .... house. It's got six bedrooms and four bathrooms.

Speaking Review

7 🔊 2.38 **Put these phrases into the correct place in the conversation. Then listen and check.**

I'll have	It's delicious,	~~Are you ready to order?~~	
I'm OK	Would you like		

Waiter ¹ *Are you ready to order?*

Greg Yes. I'd like the pasta with tomato, please.

Bea ² .... the chicken with broccoli, please.

Waiter ³ .... anything to drink?

Greg Yes, please. Can I have a glass of water?

Bea ⁴ ...., thanks.

Waiter How is your food?

Greg ⁵ ...., thank you.

Dictation

8 🔊 2.39 **Listen and write in your notebook.**

✓ **My assessment profile:** Workbook page 132

Refresh Your Memory!

Exercise 1

> ### Answers
>
> **Countable nouns:** *banana*, egg, prawn, sausages, tomatoes
> **Uncountable nouns:** broccoli, cheese, ham, pasta, rice, water, yoghurt

Exercise 2

> ### Answers
>
> **Joe** How *much* chicken have we got in the fridge?
> **Freda** Not <u>much</u>.
> **Joe** Oh, OK. What about eggs and bread?
> **Freda** We've got <u>a lot of</u> eggs but we haven't got <u>much</u> bread.
> **Joe** How <u>many</u> sausages have we got?
> **Freda** We've got six sausages but we haven't got <u>any</u> ham.
> **Joe** How <u>much</u> cheese have we got?
> **Freda** We've got <u>a lot of</u> cheese.

Exercise 3

> ### Answers
>
> **2** larger   **3** dirtier   **4** smaller   **5** colder   **6** noisier
> **7** more wonderful   **8** cleaner

Exercise 4

> ### Answers
>
> **2** My bike is larger than your scooter.
> **3** The summer in Spain is hotter than in England.
> **4** The Italian restaurant is better than the Chinese restaurant.
> **5** My bedroom is cleaner than your bedroom.
> **6** Your dog is noisier than my dog.
> **7** Villages are quieter than towns.
> **8** The pizza is more delicious than the pasta.

Exercise 5

> ### Answers
>
> **2** tomatoes   **3** broccoli   **4** juice   **5** bread

Exercise 6

> ### Answers
>
> **1** *delicious*, small   **2** clean   **3** quiet   **4** disgusting
> **5** wonderful   **6** large

Exercise 7 (Track 2.38)

> ### Answers
>
> **2** I'll have   **3** Would you like   **4** I'm OK   **5** It's delicious

Exercise 8 (Track 2.39)

> ### Answers and Audioscript
>
> **1** My favourite meal is prawns with rice. It's delicious.
> **2** Your desk is bigger than mine.
> **3** How many apples are in your bag?
> **4** I don't have much water in my glass.
> **5** The library is very quiet and clean.
> **6** Her pizza is more expensive than his.

My assessment profile:
Workbook page 132

> ### Extra activity
>
> Revise the vocabulary from the unit and *There is/There are* and *some*, *any* and *a lot of*:
> – Draw a large empty fridge and copy the speech bubbles onto the board.
> – Tell students to copy both the empty fridge and the speech bubbles into their notebooks.
> – Divide the class into pairs, tell half of the students to turn their backs to the board and the other half to sit so they can see the board and be close enough to talk quietly to their partner.
> – Invite some of the students who are looking at the board to come up and draw food items in the fridge until it is full. Make sure the other student in each pair doesn't look at the board.
> – Students then work in pairs, the students with their backs to the board asking questions with *'Is/Are there … ?'* and the other students answering. Those with their backs to the board draw the contents of the fridge. Tell them not to worry about the exact position of the objects in the fridge. Monitor and correct students' pronunciation as appropriate.
> – When they have finished, students compare the contents of their fridge with the one on the board.
> – Rub out the food from the fridge, students change roles and repeat the activity with different items in the fridge.
> – Make a note of any mistakes related to the content of this unit to go over with the class afterwards but make sure these mistakes remain anonymous during the correction stage.

Culture 4 – London Transport:
See Teacher's Book page 222 and Students' Book page 124 (for extra reading, discussion and writing work).

Real World Profiles

Cultural notes

- *Louis Barnett* (UK, born 1991) is a chocolate maker who, at the age of only 13, began supplying two of the UK's largest supermarket chains. After problems with both academic progress and bullying at school, his parents decided to give him a home education and from the age of 11 he focused on practical skills. Encouraged to follow his interests, he began to learn about chocolate production. In 2008 after a meeting with him at the House of Commons, prime minister David Cameron described Louis as 'a most remarkable young man who has the makings of becoming one of the significant entrepreneurs of the next decade'.
- *Chokolit* strives to be an environmentally friendly company, cutting out the use of palm oil and reducing unnecessary packaging. The company was named Chokolit due to Louis's inability to spell the word chocolate correctly because of his dyslexia. Further information is available on the internet.

Exercise 1 (Track 2.40)

- Draw attention to the photo and the text and ask students what they can see.
- Individually, students answer the questions.
- If you wish, play the recording for students to listen and read.
- Students check in pairs before you check answers as a class.
- Elicit from stronger students or explain yourself the meaning of any new vocabulary.
- Note that, as students have not yet studied the Past simple, events in this text are in the Present simple. This use of the Present simple is often referred to as the Historic present.

Answers

2 He makes a special chocolate cake.
3 In 2004.
4 He makes the chocolate bars in his kitchen at home.
5 He makes the chocolate bars in a new building.
6 He makes 65,000 chocolate bars.
7 He travels around the world and talks to young people about his story.
8 His message is: 'Some people have problems at school. But everyone can succeed.'

Extra activity

Extend the work on learning difficulties and ask students to investigate and find out some of the problems people with dyslexia and dyspraxia might have. Tell them also to find the names of three famous people who are dyslexic or dyspraxic.
Possible answers
1 People with dyslexia can have problems spelling words correctly.
2 People with dyspraxia sometimes have problems writing.
Famous people with dyslexia include Orlando Bloom, Tom Cruise, Kiera Knightley, Leonardo da Vinci, Tommy Hilfiger, Albert Einstein, John Lennon and Walt Disney amongst many others.
Dyspraxia is less common, the most famous person to acknowledge having dyspraxia is Daniel Radcliffe.
Collate both the problems and the famous people on the board.

Class discussion

- Read through the questions with students.
- They then work in pairs or small groups talking about the questions.
- Monitor but do not interrupt fluency.
- Take feedback as a class.
- Ideally the class discussion activity should be completed in English but you may want to support weaker students with some L1.

Extra activity

Ask students additional questions related to the topic of the text, e.g.
1 What are the ingredients of chocolate?
2 Do you think it's important to use natural ingredients in food? Why/Why not?
3 Do you think it's a good idea to have a home education?
4 Do you know anyone who has problems learning? Think of three things they are good at.
5 What other people do you know who are very young but very successful?

In this unit have you ...

... used Grammar and Vocabulary worksheet?
... used Reading and Listening worksheet?
... used Writing worksheet?
... used Speaking worksheet?
... used Unit test?

With the exception of the Writing worksheets, all the Teacher's Resources are at two levels of difficulty:
* For students who need extra help and support
** For students who require an additional challenge

Real World Profiles

⊛ Louis Barnett's profile

Age:
20

Home country:
England

City:
Kinver

Reading

1 🔊 **2.40** **Read about Louis and 'Chokolit'. Answer the questions.**

   1 Why does Louis leave school in 2002?

   To have a home education.

   2 What does Louis make for his aunt's birthday in 2003?

   3 When does Louis start his company, 'Chokolit'?

   4 Where does Louis make his chocolate bars in 2004?

   5 Where does Louis make his chocolate bars in 2005?

   6 How many chocolate bars does Louis make in 2005?

   7 What does Louis do in 2012?

   8 What is Louis's message?

Louis and Chokolit

May 2002
Louis Barnett is 11 years old. He has problems at school, because he is dyslexic and dyspraxic, so it's difficult for him to read and write. He leaves school and has a home education. At home he doesn't study academic subjects, but he does lots of practical things.

September 2003
Louis buys a recipe book and makes a special chocolate cake for his aunt's 50th birthday. The cake is delicious! Lots of people ask for his cakes. Louis starts to make cakes for local restaurants and shops.

February 2004
It's 2004, and Louis is 12 years old. He starts his own chocolate company, called 'Chokolit'. He wants to make chocolate from natural ingredients. He makes the chocolate in his kitchen at home.

June 2005
Louis has his first contract from a very big chain of supermarkets. He is producing 65,000 bars of chocolate a year. He can't use his parents' kitchen now, so he moves the chocolate production to a new building.

2012
Louis is 20 years old and his company is very successful. He travels around the world and talks to young people about his story. Louis's message is: 'Some people have problems at school. But everyone can succeed.'

Class discussion

- 'Chokolit' is the wrong spelling for the word 'chocolate'. Why do you think Louis' company is called 'Chokolit'?
- Can you make a cake?
- Imagine you want to start your own company. What do you want to make? What is your company's name?

73

Exercise 1

Mia and Jade hardly ever get up before 7 a.m.
Tom sometimes gets up before 7 a.m.
Zak often gets up before 7 a.m.
Ali never gets up before 7 a.m.
Jo usually gets up before 7 a.m.

Exercise 4

2 He mustn't watch TV today.
3 I must do my Maths homework.
4 She must clean her teeth every day.
5 We mustn't be late for class.
6 You mustn't talk in the library.

Review

Grammar
Adverbs of frequency

1 **Make sentences about the people in the table with these adverbs.**

Ella always gets up before 7 a.m.

| always | hardly ever | never |
| often | sometimes | usually |

I get up before 7 a.m.	Ella	Mia + Jade	Tom	Zak	Ali	Jo
Number of days in a year	365	2	70	150	0	351

2 **Make sentences.**

1 go home / They / at half past three / usually
They usually go home at half past three.
2 often / is / late / She
3 hardly / eat pasta / I / ever
4 We / watch a DVD / on Fridays / always
5 at the café / are / sometimes / They / at 4.15.
6 He / uses / his MP3 player / never

Present simple *wh-* questions

3 **Make *wh-* questions for the answers with these words.**

How often   What   ~~When~~   Where   Who   Why

1 you / play tennis / ?
At 4.30
When do you play tennis?
2 your grandparents / live / ?
In London.
3 your favourite film / ?
Star Wars.
4 he / have PE lessons / ?
Every day.
5 Tom Cruise / ?
He's an actor.
6 you / like / Science / ?
Because it's interesting.

74

Exercise 2

2 She is often late.
3 I hardly ever eat pasta.
4 We always watch a DVD on Fridays.
5 They are sometimes at the café at 4.15.
6 He never uses his MP3 player.

Exercise 3

2 Where do your grandparents live?
3 What is/What's your favourite film?
4 How often does he have PE lessons?
5 Who is/Who's Tom Cruise?
6 Why do you like Science?

Must/Mustn't

4 **Make sentences with *must* or *mustn't*.**

1 they / have / breakfast / before 8 a.m.
They must have breakfast before 8 a.m.
2 he / not / watch / TV / today
3 I / do / my Maths homework
4 she / clean / her teeth / every day
5 we / not / be / late for class
6 you / not / talk / in the library

Present continuous

5 **Complete the sentences with the Present continuous of the verbs.**

1 He's *singing* (sing) his favourite song.
2 We .... (have) lunch at the moment.
3 They .... (not tidy) their bedroom.
4 She .... (run) to school because she's late.
5 You .... (not watch) the TV.
6 I .... (play) football with Penny.

6 **Make questions and answers with the Present continuous.**

1 they / use / the computer / ?   ✗
Are they using the computer? No, they aren't.
2 it / snow / at the moment / ?   ✓
3 he / sleep / in the garden / ?   ✓
4 I / do / the correct exercise / ?   ✓
5 you / cycle / a long way / ?   ✗
6 they / swim / in the sea / ?   ✗

Present simple and Present continuous

7 **Complete the conversation with the Present simple or Present continuous.**

Luke Hi, Leia. What ¹ *are you doing* (you / do) at the train station?
Leia I ² .... (wait) for my friend Saskia. She ³ .... (come) here for a week.
Luke That's nice.
Leia Yes. I ⁴ .... (hardly ever / see) her because she ⁵ .... (swim) in competitions every weekend. What about you? Where ⁶ .... (you / go) now?
Luke To the beach.
Leia But it ⁷ .... (rain) today!
Luke I ⁸ .... (always / go) to the beach in the rain.

Exercise 5

2 're/are having
3 aren't/are not tidying
4 's/is running
5 aren't/are not watching
6 'm/am playing

Exercise 6

2 Is it snowing at the moment? Yes, it is.
3 Is he sleeping in the garden? Yes, he is.
4 Am I doing the correct exercise? Yes, you are.
5 Are you cycling a long way? No, I'm/am/ we're/we are not.
6 Are they swimming in the sea? No, they aren't.

Exercise 7

2 'm/am waiting
3 's/is coming
4 hardly ever see
5 swims
6 are you going
7 's/is raining
8 always go

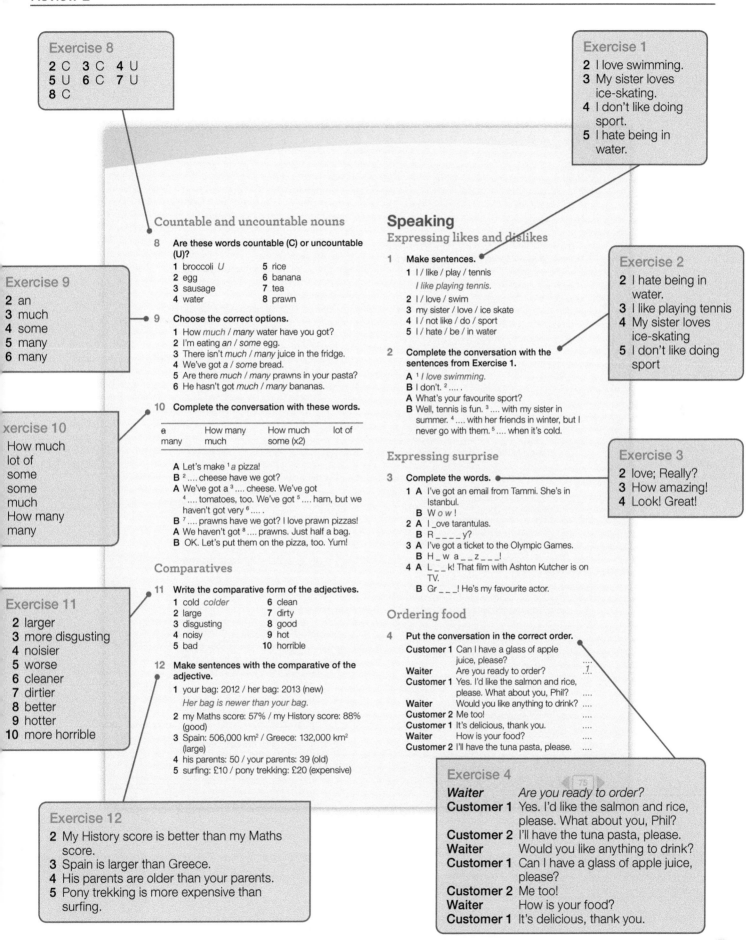

Exercise 8
2 C 3 C 4 U
5 U 6 C 7 U
8 C

Exercise 9
2 an
3 much
4 some
5 many
6 many

Exercise 10
How much
lot of
some
some
much
How many
many

Exercise 11
2 larger
3 more disgusting
4 noisier
5 worse
6 cleaner
7 dirtier
8 better
9 hotter
10 more horrible

Exercise 12
2 My History score is better than my Maths score.
3 Spain is larger than Greece.
4 His parents are older than your parents.
5 Pony trekking is more expensive than surfing.

Countable and uncountable nouns

8 Are these words countable (C) or uncountable (U)?
1 broccoli *U*   5 rice
2 egg   6 banana
3 sausage   7 tea
4 water   8 prawn

9 Choose the correct options.
1 How *much / many* water have you got?
2 I'm eating *an / some* egg.
3 There isn't *much / many* juice in the fridge.
4 We've got *a / some* bread.
5 Are there *much / many* prawns in your pasta?
6 He hasn't got *much / many* bananas.

10 Complete the conversation with these words.

| a | How many | How much | lot of |
| many | much | some (x2) | |

A Let's make ¹ *a* pizza!
B ² .... cheese have we got?
A We've got a ³ .... cheese. We've got ⁴ .... tomatoes, too. We've got ⁵ .... ham, but we haven't got very ⁶ .... .
B ⁷ .... prawns have we got? I love prawn pizzas!
A We haven't got ⁸ .... prawns. Just half a bag.
B OK. Let's put them on the pizza, too. Yum!

Comparatives

11 Write the comparative form of the adjectives.
1 cold *colder*   6 clean
2 large   7 dirty
3 disgusting   8 good
4 noisy   9 hot
5 bad   10 horrible

12 Make sentences with the comparative of the adjective.
1 your bag: 2012 / her bag: 2013 (new)
  Her bag is newer than your bag.
2 my Maths score: 57% / my History score: 88% (good)
3 Spain: 506,000 km² / Greece: 132,000 km² (large)
4 his parents: 50 / your parents: 39 (old)
5 surfing: £10 / pony trekking: £20 (expensive)

Speaking
Expressing likes and dislikes

1 Make sentences.
1 I / like / play / tennis
  I like playing tennis.
2 I / love / swim
3 my sister / love / ice skate
4 I / not like / do / sport
5 I / hate / be / in water

2 Complete the conversation with the sentences from Exercise 1.
A ¹ *I love swimming.*
B I don't. ² .... .
A What's your favourite sport?
B Well, tennis is fun. ³ .... with my sister in summer. ⁴ .... with her friends in winter, but I never go with them. ⁵ .... when it's cold.

Expressing surprise

3 Complete the words.
1 A I've got an email from Tammi. She's in Istanbul.
  B W o w !
2 A I _ove tarantulas.
  B R _ _ _ _ y?
3 A I've got a ticket to the Olympic Games.
  B H _ w a _ _ z _ _ _!
4 A L _ _ k! That film with Ashton Kutcher is on TV.
  B Gr _ _ _! He's my favourite actor.

Ordering food

4 Put the conversation in the correct order.
Customer 1 Can I have a glass of apple juice, please?   ....
Waiter Are you ready to order?   *1*
Customer 1 Yes. I'd like the salmon and rice, please. What about you, Phil?   ....
Waiter Would you like anything to drink?   ....
Customer 2 Me too!   ....
Customer 1 It's delicious, thank you.   ....
Waiter How is your food?   ....
Customer 2 I'll have the tuna pasta, please.   ....

Exercise 1
2 I love swimming.
3 My sister loves ice-skating.
4 I don't like doing sport.
5 I hate being in water.

Exercise 2
2 I hate being in water.
3 I like playing tennis
4 My sister loves ice-skating
5 I don't like doing sport

Exercise 3
2 love; Really?
3 How amazing!
4 Look! Great!

Exercise 4
Waiter Are you ready to order?
Customer 1 Yes. I'd like the salmon and rice, please. What about you, Phil?
Customer 2 I'll have the tuna pasta, please.
Waiter Would you like anything to drink?
Customer 1 Can I have a glass of apple juice, please?
Customer 2 Me too!
Waiter How is your food?
Customer 1 It's delicious, thank you.

Exercise 1

2 tarantula
3 python
4 piranha
5 hissing cockroach
6 parrot
7 stick insect
8 frog
9 giant rabbit
10 lizard

Exercise 4

2 cold
3 snowing
4 spring
5 warm
6 raining
7 Summer
8 hot
9 sunny
10 autumn
11 cloudy
12 foggy
13 windy

2 Review

Vocabulary

Unusual animals

1 Complete the words with the missing letters.

1 p y g _my_ g _o_ a t
2 t _ r _ n t _ _ a
3 p y _ _ o n
4 p i _ _ n _ a
5 h i _ _ i n g c _ _ k r _ _ c h
6 p _ r _ t
7 s _ _ c k i _ s _ _ t
8 f _ _ g
9 g i _ _ t r _ _ b _ t
10 l _ z _ _ d

Parts of the body

2 Complete the sentences with these words.

arms	beak	foot	fingers	~~head~~	legs
neck	paw	tail	toes	wings	

1 A python has got a small _head_ and a long body.
2 A dog's got four .... but a stick insect's got six.
3 A cat's got a long .... .
4 A giraffe's got a long .... .
5 We've got ten .... and ten .... .
6 At the end of my leg, is my .... .
7 At the end of our .... , we've got hands.
8 A .... is the name for a dog's foot.
9 A parrot flies with its .... and eats with its .... .

Activities

3 Match the descriptions to these words.

climbing	hiking
~~kayaking~~	mountain biking
painting	playing an instrument
pony trekking	singing
~~surfing~~	

1 You do this on water. _kayaking, surfing_
2 You do this in Music lessons.
3 You do this in Art lessons.
4 You can do this in a tree.
5 You ride something in this activity.
6 You walk a long way in this activity.

Exercise 2

2 legs
3 tail
4 neck
5 fingers; toes
6 foot
7 arms
8 paw
9 wings; beak

Exercise 3

2 playing an instrument, singing
3 painting
4 climbing
5 mountain biking, pony trekking
6 hiking

Weather and seasons

4 Read Meiko's diary. Complete the words.

- **January 10th**
  I love [1] win _ter_ in Japan. It's very [2] c _ _ _.
  Today it's [3] s _ _ _ ing. I can go skiing soon!

- **April 7th**
  In [4] sp _ _ _ _ we have hanami. We look at the pretty pink flowers on the trees. It's nice and [5] w _ _ m at this time of year.

- **June 15th**
  It's [6] r _ _ n _ _ _ today. I don't like this weather!

- **July 27th**
  [7] S _ _ _ er is here! It's very [8] h _ _ and [9] su _ _ _.

- **October 2nd**
  It's [10] au _ _ _ _. There are red leaves on the trees. It's [11] cl _ _ d _ and [12] f _ _ _ y today. It's very [13] w _ _ d _, too.

Food and drink

5 Put the words in the correct categories.

bananas	bread	broccoli	~~cheese~~
chicken	eggs	ham	juice
pasta	prawns	rice	salmon
sausages	tea	tomatoes	tuna
water	yoghurt		

1 Dairy _cheese_   4 Fruit and Vegetables
2 Fish   5 Drinks
3 Meat   6 Carbohydrates

Adjectives

6 Complete the sentences with these words.

clean	~~delicious~~	dirty	disgusting
large	noisy	quiet	wonderful

1 I love this food. It's _delicious_.
2 Giant rabbits are very .... .
3 Be .... . Your brother's sleeping.
4 I hate cockroaches. They're .... .
5 I'm nice and .... after my shower.
6 I'm always .... after playing football.
7 That parrot talks a lot. It's very .... .
8 We're having a .... holiday. I love it here!

Exercise 5

1 Dairy: _cheese_, eggs, yoghurt
2 Fish: prawns, salmon, tuna
3 Meat: chicken, ham, sausages
4 Fruit and Vegetables: bananas, brocco tomatoes
5 Drinks: juice, tea water
6 Carbohydrates: bread, pasta, ric

Exercise 6

2 large
3 quiet
4 disgusting
5 clean
6 dirty
7 noisy
8 wonderful

Word list

Unit 4   Animal Magic

Unusual animals

frog	/frɒg/
giant rabbit	/ˈdʒaɪənt ˈræbɪt/
hissing cockroach	/ˈhɪsɪŋ ˈkɒkrəʊtʃ/
lizard	/ˈlɪzəd/
parrot	/ˈpærət/
piranha	/pɪˈrɑːnə/
pygmy goat	/ˈpɪgmi ˈgəʊt/
python	/ˈpaɪθən/
stick insect	/ˈstɪk ˈɪnsekt/
tarantula	/təˈræntjʊlə/

Parts of the body

arm	/ɑːm/
beak	/biːk/
fin	/fɪn/
finger	/ˈfɪŋgə/
foot	/fʊt/
hand	/hænd/
head	/hed/
leg	/leg/
neck	/nek/
paw	/pɔː/
tail	/teɪl/
toe	/təʊ/
wing	/wɪŋ/

Unit 5   Out and About!

Activities

bowling	/ˈbəʊlɪŋ/
climbing	/ˈklaɪmɪŋ/
dancing	/ˈdɑːnsɪŋ/
gymnastics	/dʒɪmˈnæstɪks/
hiking	/ˈhaɪkɪŋ/
ice-skating	/aɪs ˈskeɪtɪŋ/
kayaking	/ˈkaɪækɪŋ/
mountain biking	/ˈmaʊntɪn ˈbaɪkɪŋ/
painting	/ˈpeɪntɪŋ/
playing an instrument	/ˈpleɪɪŋ ən ˈɪnstrəmənt/
pony trekking	/ˈpəʊni trekɪŋ/
rollerblading	/ˈrəʊləˌbleɪdɪŋ/
singing	/ˈsɪŋɪŋ/
surfing	/ˈsɜːfɪŋ/

Weather and seasons

autumn	/ˈɔːtəm/
cloudy	/ˈklaʊdi/
cold	/kəʊld/
foggy	/ˈfɒgi/
hot	/hɒt/
raining	/ˈreɪnɪŋ/
snowing	/ˈsnəʊɪŋ/
spring	/sprɪŋ/
summer	/ˈsʌmə/
sunny	/ˈsʌni/
warm	/wɔːm/
windy	/ˈwɪndi/
winter	/ˈwɪntə/

Unit 6   Delicious!

Food and drink

banana	/bəˈnɑːnə/
bread	/bred/
broccoli	/ˈbrɒkəli/
cheese	/tʃiːz/
chicken	/ˈtʃɪkɪn/
eggs	/egz/
ham	/hæm/
juice	/dʒuːs/
pasta	/ˈpæstə/
prawns	/prɔːnz/
rice	/raɪs/
salmon	/ˈsæmən/
sausages	/ˈsɒsɪdʒɪz/
tea	/tiː/
tomatoes	/təˈmɑːtəʊz/
tuna	/ˈtjuːnə/
water	/ˈwɔːtə/
yoghurt	/ˈjɒgət/

Adjectives

clean	/kliːn/
cold	/kəʊld/
delicious	/dɪˈlɪʃəs/
dirty	/ˈdɜːti/
disgusting	/dɪsˈgʌstɪŋ/
horrible	/ˈhɒrɪbəl/
hot	/hɒt/
large	/lɑːdʒ/
noisy	/ˈnɔɪzi/
quiet	/ˈkwaɪət/
small	/smɔːl/
wonderful	/ˈwʌndəfəl/

77

7 Modern History

Grammar	Past simple: *to be*; *There was/There were*; Past simple regular
Vocabulary	Ordinal numbers, years, dates; Regular verbs
Speaking	Talking about the past
Writing	An essay

Vocabulary

Ordinal numbers, years, dates

1 🔊 **3.1** **Listen. Match the numbers you hear to these words. Then listen and repeat.**

fifth	first *1*	fourth	second
third	thirty-first	twentieth	twenty-second

Word list page 111   Workbook page 110

2 **In pairs, ask and answer.**

1 When is your birthday? *The eighteenth of May.*
2 What is the date today?

3 **Match the photos (1–8) to an event (a–h).**

a The Titanic hits an iceberg. *1*
b Russia sends Laika the dog into space.
c Nelson Mandela leaves prison.
d Prince William marries Kate Middleton.
e Howard Carter discovers Tutankhamun's tomb in Egypt.
f The first space vehicle visits Mars.
g In Amsterdam, Anne Frank's family hide because of the war.
h People around the world celebrate the new millennium.

4 🔊 **3.2** **Match each event in Exercise 3 to these years. Then listen and check.**

nineteen forty-two	nineteen twelve *a*
nineteen twenty-two	twenty eleven
two thousand	nineteen fifty-seven
nineteen ninety	two thousand and four

Brain Trainer Activity 3
Go to page 118

78

Unit contents

Vocabulary
→ Ordinal numbers, years, dates
→ Regular verbs – *answer, ask, close, invent, like, listen, phone, stop, study, talk, travel, work*

Grammar
→ Past simple: *to be* – affirmative, negative and questions
→ *There was/There were*
→ Past simple regular: affirmative and negative

Communication
→ Talking about the past
→ Writing an essay; Punctuation 2 – full stops, commas, question marks, exclamation marks

Pronunciation
→ *-ed* endings

Culture 5 – Famous British People

Key competences
→ Linguistic competence
→ Interpersonal, social and civic competence
→ Cultural and artistic competences
→ Learning-to-learn
→ Autonomy and personal initiative

Vocabulary   Ordinal numbers, years, dates

Language notes

- Here students are shown how to talk about dates in a very controlled way. They first cover ordinal numbers in their written form and then look at years before putting them together with the months to form complete dates. At some point you might also wish to explain the commonly used numeric forms of the cardinal numbers, e.g. *1st, 2nd, 3rd*, etc.
- Note also that in years prior to 2000 when the year includes a zero we generally say *'oh'*, e.g. 1805 (*eighteen 'oh' five*), 1909 (*nineteen 'oh' nine*). As dates are rarely written in words rather than numbers this looks relatively unfamiliar when written down.
- When saying the years from 2000 to 2009 we generally say *two thousand, two thousand and one*, etc. For 2010 onwards, we generally split the year into two groups of two digits, e.g. 2010 – *twenty ten*, 2022 – *twenty twenty-two*, etc.
- There are also notable differences between the conventions for writing dates in the UK and the USA. *Next Move* teaches the UK format of *DD/MM/YYYY*. In the USA it is more usual to find dates written starting with the month *MM/DD/YYYY*. Generally this is not problematic but occasionally a date such as *1/12/1999* can cause confusion, as it would be *the first of December nineteen ninety-nine* in the UK but *January the twelfth nineteen ninety-nine* in the USA.

Exercise 1 (Track 3.1)

- Individually, students match the words and the numbers they hear.
- Check answers as a class.
- Repeat the recording. Pause after each word to check students' pronunciation.
- Ask students if they have both cardinal and ordinal numbers in their language.

Answers

first 1   **second** 2   **third** 3   **fourth** 4   **fifth** 5
twentieth 20   **twenty-second** 22   **thirty-first** 31

Exercise 2

- In pairs, students ask and answer the questions.
- Ask each student to tell the class his/her birthday.
- Correct students' pronunciation as appropriate.

Answers

Students' own answers

Exercise 3

- Students match the photos and the events.
- Check answers as a class.

Answers

b 8   **c** 4   **d** 7   **e** 6   **f** 2   **g** 3   **h** 5

Exercise 4 (Track 3.2)

- In pairs or individually, students match the events in Exercise 3 with the years.
- Play the recording for students to listen and check.
- Repeat the recording, pausing after each year to check students' pronunciation.

Answers

b nineteen fifty-seven/1957
c nineteen ninety/1990
d twenty eleven/2011
e nineteen twenty-two/1922
f two thousand and four/2004
g nineteen forty-two/1942
h two thousand/2000

Further practice:
Workbook pages 60 and 110

Brain Trainer Activity 3
See Teacher's Book page 216 and Students' Book page 118

Reading

Revision

First – Write *'My birthday is on the 23rd July.'* on the right of the board. Draw a question mark to the left of the board and point at it to elicit the question *'When's your birthday?'* Drill the question and answer for pronunciation and intonation. Delete *23rd July* from the board and leave a blank space.

Second –Tell students they need to ask all their classmates the question and try to remember the answers. Students move around the classroom and ask and answer the question.

Third – Students form a line with the person whose birthday is first in the year on the left and the person whose is last on the right. In turn each student then tells you his or her birthday.

Exercise 1

- Draw attention to the photo and the text and ask students what they can see.
- Individually, students answer the question.

Answer

the 1960s

Extra activity

Use the three main paragraphs of the text as a running dictation. Divide the class into groups of three. Write the question headers for each paragraph on the board. Students take turns being the runner and dictating to the other two students in their group. When students have completed the three texts, they compare their versions with the originals in the Students' Book. Make sure students spell any difficult words using the English alphabet.

Exercise 2

- Individually, students match the photos to the paragraphs.
- Make sure students understand not to read in detail at this point.

Exercise 3

- Check answers as a class.

Answers

1 d   **2** a, b   **3** c, e

Exercise 4 (Track 3.3)

- Individually, students complete the events with the correct year.
- If you wish, play the recording for students to listen and read.
- Check answers as a class.
- Elicit from stronger students or explain yourself the meaning of any new vocabulary.

Answers

2 1966   **3** 1967   **4** 1969   **5** 1969

Exercise 5 (Track 3.3)

- Students read the text again and complete the sentences.
- They then compare their ideas in pairs.
- Check answers by asking individual students to read the sentences.

Answers

2 radio   **3** clothes   **4** Twiggy   **5** colour
6 Neil Armstrong and Buzz Aldrin

Extra activity

Play 'date bingo' with your class. Write the following years on the board:
1888, 1913, 1933, 1964, 1973, 1974, 1989, 1999, 2001, 2002, 2011, 2012, 2013, 2020
Second – Tell students to draw a small bingo grid, two rows by three columns, and to choose six dates from the board and copy one into each space in their grid.
Third – Elicit a chorus from the class of *'What year is it?'* and then respond with *'It's …'* and one of the years on the board. Make a note of the years as you say them but don't cross them off on the board. The winner is the first student to shout 'Bingo!' Do, however double-check the student's bingo grid before proclaiming him or her the winner.

Exercise 6

- Ask two students to read aloud the example question and answer.
- Check the pronunciation of the questions before students work in pairs.
- In pairs, students ask and answer the questions.
- Monitor and help with vocabulary but do not interrupt fluency.
- If students have photos of their parents or grandparents, ask them to bring them to class to talk about. Remind them that they should ask permission first.

Further practice:
Workbook page 61

Reading

1 **Look at the article and the photos. Are the photos from the 1960s, 70s or 80s?**

2 **Read the text. Match the photos (a–e) to paragraphs (1–3).**

3 **Read and check your answers to Exercise 2.**

4 ⏺ 3.3 **Read the text again. Complete the events with the correct year.**

Event 1 The Beatles' first song in the UK *1962*
Event 2 The model Twiggy is very famous
Event 3 TV in colour for the first time
Event 4 Concorde's first flight
Event 5 The first men on the moon

5 ⏺ 3.3 **Read the text again. Complete the sentences.**

1 *Love me Do* was a song by *The Beatles*.
2 In the 1960s people listened to music on the .... or on records.
3 The colours of .... in the 1960s were very bright.
4 The first fashion model in Madame Tussaud's was .... .
5 Some TV programmes were in .... after 1967.
6 The first two men on the moon were .... .

6 **What about you?** In pairs, ask and answer.

1 What singers do your parents like?
2 Do you and your parents like the same music?
3 Have you got any photos of your parents or grandparents when they were young?

What singers do your parents like?

My father likes Pavarotti.

Flower power!

1 What music was popular?

The Beatles were very popular in many countries. Their first song in the UK was *Love Me Do!* on 5th October 1962. There weren't any MP3 players in the 60s. There were radios and records!

2 What clothes were in fashion?

Clothes were very different! My grandparents were teenagers in the 1960s, so I've got some great photos - look at these trousers and shirts! Bright colours and flowers were very popular! Twiggy was a famous fashion model. She was 'The Face of 1966' in the UK and she was also the first model to appear in Madame Tussaud's waxworks.

3 What else?

Well, it was a time of change. Before 1967 TV was boring – it wasn't in colour! 1969 was an exciting year. Concorde's first flight was in April. Then on 20th July Neil Armstrong and Buzz Aldrin were the first men on the moon.

4 Is this an interesting time in history?

Yes, it is! It's fun to learn about different times and find out what people were like.

Grammar   Past simple: *to be*

Affirmative		
I	was	
He/She/It	was	in the café.
You/We/They	were	

Negative		
I	wasn't (was not)	
He/She/It	wasn't (was not)	at home.
You/We/They	weren't (were not)	

Questions		
Was	I	
Was	he/she/it	at school?
Were	you/we/they	

1 Study the grammar table. Copy and complete the table below.

To be:		
	Present	**Past**
1	I am	I was
2	She is	*She was*
3	....	We were
4	They aren't	....
5	....	It wasn't
6	You aren't	....
7	Are you?	....
8	....	Was he?

2 Choose the correct options to complete the sentences.

At half past seven last night …

1 Luke *was / were* at home.
2 Nick *wasn't / weren't* at his grandmother's house.
3 Lucia and Lidia *was / were* at the cinema.
4 Luke's parents *wasn't / weren't* at a pizza restaurant.
5 Lidia's dog *was / were* in the garden.
6 Lucia's friends *wasn't / weren't* in the park.

There was/There were

Affirmative	
There was a radio/some music.	
There were some children.	

Negative	
There wasn't a TV/any music.	
There weren't any computers.	

Questions and short answers	
Was there a phone/any music?	
Were there any phones?	
Yes, there was. / No, there wasn't.	
Yes, there were. / No, there weren't.	

> **Grammar reference** Workbook page 98

3 Study the grammar table. Complete the rules.

> **1** We use … and … with singular nouns, e.g. *a radio*, to talk about the past.
> **2** We use … and … with plural nouns, e.g. *some computers*, to talk about the past.

4 Complete the questions and write the answers.

1 *Were* there any MP3 players forty years ago? ✗
   No, there weren't.
2 *Was* there colour TV 20 years ago?   ✓
   Yes, there was.
3 .... there any mobile phones 50 years ago?   ✗
4 .... there a man on the moon in 1967?   ✗
5 .... there any DVDs ten years ago?   ✓
6 .... there internet five years ago?   ✓
7 .... there email 30 years ago?   ✗
8 .... there flowers on clothes in the 1960s   ✓

5 What about you? Make sentences about things in your house five years ago. Use these words and/or your own ideas.

There wasn't a guitar in my house five years ago.

DVDs	games console	guitar	laptop
parrot	rabbit	skateboard	

Grammar Past simple: *to be*

Exercise 1

- Read the Past simple of *to be* grammar table with students.
- Students work individually, completing the past and present verb forms and referring back to the grammar table where necessary.
- Check answers by asking individual students to write words on the board.

Answers

1 I am	I was
2 She is	*She was*
3 We are	We were
4 They aren't	They weren't
5 It isn't	It wasn't
6 You aren't	You weren't
7 Are you?	Were you?
8 Is he?	Was he?

Language notes

Students may have problems with the weak pronunciation of *was* (/wəz/) and *were* (/wə/) used in affirmative sentences. Their tendency is to replace it with the stronger pronunciation (/wɒz/ and /wɜː/) generally found only in questions and short answers. After checking answers to Exercises 2 and 4, drill all the sentences and questions to help students practise the pronunciation as part of a stream of connected speech.

Exercise 2

- Individually, students choose the correct options.
- Check answers by asking individual students to read the sentences.
- Drill the questions and answers for pronunciation and intonation (see Language notes above).

Answers

2 wasn't **3** were **4** weren't **5** was **6** weren't

Extra activity

Books closed. Quickly revise *There is/There are* by asking students to talk to each other about what they can see in the classroom, e.g. *'Is there a television in the classroom?' 'No, there isn't, but there's a CD player.'* Monitor and point out errors for students to self-correct.

There was/There were

Exercise 3

- Read the *There was/There were* grammar table with students.
- Students work individually, completing the rules and referring back to the grammar table where necessary.

Answers

1 There was, There wasn't
2 There were, There weren't

Exercise 4

- Students complete the questions and short answers.
- They then check in pairs before you check answers as a class.
- Check answers by asking pairs of students to read questions and answers.
- Drill the questions and answers for pronunciation and intonation (see Language notes above).

Answers

3 Were; No, there weren't.
4 Was; No, there wasn't.
5 Were; Yes, there were.
6 Was; Yes, there was.
7 Was; No, there wasn't.
8 Were; Yes, there were.

Exercise 5

- Monitor and point out errors for students to self-correct.
- Encourage students to ask you for any vocabulary they need.
- Ask some students to say their sentences for the class to hear.

Answers

Students' own answers

Extra activity

Stronger students or individual students prepare a short text about their parents' generation. They use the Reading text on Students' Book page 79 as a model and illustrate their text with pictures from the appropriate decade. After correcting the texts you could display them on the classroom walls or use them as the basis for further comprehension work with your class.

Further practice:
Workbook pages 62 and 98–99

Brain Trainer Activity 2
See Teacher's Book page 216 and Students' Book page 118

Vocabulary   Regular verbs

Revision

First – Before the class, remove five objects from your classroom which are typically on view, e.g. take down a poster from the wall, remove some books from a shelf. Also bring in five things which aren't usually in your classroom, e.g. a plant, an extra desk and chair.

Second – Tell students that you have changed ten things from the classroom since last class. In pairs they should write down the ten things that have changed using *'Last class, there was/were/wasn't/weren't …'* Monitor and help with grammar if necessary.

Third – Check answers as a class by asking individual students to write sentences on the board.

Exercise 1 (Track 3.4)

• In pairs, students match the words in the box with the pictures.
• Play the recording for students to listen, check and repeat.

Answers

2 invent – invented	8 stop – stopped
3 ask – asked	9 like – liked
4 answer – answered	10 study – studied
5 talk – talked	11 close – closed
6 listen – listened	12 work – worked
7 phone – phoned	

Exercise 2

• Individually, students make the spelling rules.
• Check answers as a class.

Answers

2 b 3 a 4 c

Exercise 3

• Students classify the other verbs according to the spelling rules.
• Check answers by drawing four columns on the board, one for each of the rules, and asking individual students to classify the vocabulary.

Answers

1 *answer, ask,* invent, listen, talk, work
2 *like,* close, phone   3 *study*   4 *stop,* travel

Pronunciation   -ed endings

Language notes

Past simple verbs are pronounced with /t/ at the end when the infinitive ends with an unvoiced consonant and with /d/ at the end when the infinitive ends with a voiced consonant. Only when the infinitive ends with the sounds /t/ or /d/, do we add the complete extra syllable /ɪd/.

Note that a very common error is for students to add the extra syllable /ɪd/ to all Past simple verb forms.

Exercise 4a (Track 3.5)

• Play the recording for students to listen to the three endings.

Exercise 4b (Track 3.6)

• Play the recording for students to classify the verbs according to the endings.
• Check answers as a class.

Answers

1 started /ɪd/	4 asked /t/	7 worked /t/
2 watched /t/	5 studied /d/	8 liked /t/
3 opened /d/	6 wanted /ɪd/	9 phoned /d/

Exercise 4c (Track 3.6)

• Repeat the recording, pausing after each item to check students' pronunciation.

Further practice:
Workbook page 124

Exercise 5 (Track 3.7)

• Individually, students complete the text.
• Play the recording for students to listen and check.

Answers

2 studied	5 talked	8 answered
3 worked	6 listened	9 travelled
4 phoned	7 asked	10 liked

Exercise 6

• Individually, students complete the sentences.
• They then check in pairs before you check their answers as a class.

Answers

2 close   3 answer   4 like

Exercise 7

• Individually, students write three sentences.
• Monitor and point out errors for students to self-correct.
• Ask some students to say their sentences for the class to hear.

Answers

Students' own answers

Further practice:
Workbook pages 63 and 110

Brain Trainer Activity 4
See Teacher's Book page 216 and Students' Book page 118

Vocabulary   Regular verbs

1 ◗)) 3.4 **Match the pictures to these words. Then listen, check and repeat.**

answer – answered	ask – asked	close – closed
invent – invented	like – liked	listen – listened
phone – phoned	stop – stopped	study – studied
talk – talked	travel – travelled *1*	work – worked

Word list page 111   **Workbook** page 110

2 **Match the phrases (1–4) to make spelling rules for regular verbs (a-d).**

1 Most verbs (e.g. *ask*) *d*
2 Final *e* (e.g. *like*)
3 Final consonant + *y* (e.g. *study*)
4 Short vowel + consonant (e.g. *stop*)

a Change *y* to *i*, then add -*ed*
b Add -*d*
c Double consonant, add -*ed*
d Add -*ed*

3 **Match the other verbs in Exercise 1 to the spelling rules (1–4).**

answer - 1

Pronunciation   -*ed* endings

4a ◗)) 3.5 **Listen to the –*ed* endings of these three regular verbs.**

1 /d/ listened   2 /ɪd/ invented   3 /t/ talked

b ◗)) 3.6 **Listen to these Past simple regular verbs. Which ending does each verb have, /d/, /ɪd/ or /t/?**

1 started   3 opened   5 studied   7 worked   9 phoned
2 watched   4 asked   6 wanted   8 liked

c ◗)) 3.6 **Listen again. Check your answers.**

5 ◗)) 3.7 **Complete the text with these words in the past. Then listen and check.**

answer	ask	~~invent~~
like	listen	study
talk	travel	phone
work		

Alexander Graham Bell
[1] *invented* the telephone in the 1870s. First, he [2].... inventions from other inventors. Then, he [3].... with his friend, Mr Watson. On 2nd June, 1872, Bell [4].... Mr Watson and [5].... to him. Mr Watson [6].... and Bell [7]...., 'Do you understand what I say?' 'Yes,' [8].... Mr Watson. Bell's words [9].... ten miles. It was the first 'long distance' phone call. People [10].... Bell's idea. The phone changed their lives.

6 **Complete the sentences with verbs from Exercise 1.**

1 Can I *ask* you a question?
2 Please can you .... the door.
3 I can't .... the question.
4 Do you .... your new camera?

7 **Write three sentences about yesterday. Use verbs from Exercise 1.**

> *I phoned Irina yesterday.*

 Brain Trainer Activity 4
Go to page 118

Chatroom Talking about the past

Speaking and Listening

1 Look at the photo. What things has Julia's gran got?

2 🔊 3.8 Listen and read the conversation. Are the sentences true (T) or false (F)?

1 Julia's gran is reading a book. *F*
2 Julia's gran stayed in Poland for a year after her husband moved to England.
3 Julia's grandad posted lots of letters.
4 Julia's grandad often phoned her Gran.
5 It was cheap to make a phone call.
6 The phone box wasn't near the house.
7 Julia's grandparents moved to England two years ago.
8 Julia's grandparents watched TV every evening.
9 They liked pop music.

3 Act out the conversation in groups of three.

Julia	Hello, Gran! Sorry I didn't visit you last weekend. What are you doing?
Gran	I'm reading some old letters from your grandad. You know, I stayed in Poland for two years after he moved to England. He posted a letter to me every day … but he didn't phone me very often.
Julia	Why not?
Grandad	Because it was expensive!
Gran	And the phone was in a phone box two miles away!
Julia	What a pain!
Gran	Then I moved here in the 1960s. That was about fifty years ago.
Grandad	I remember. In those days, we listened to the radio every evening.
Julia	Really? What was your favourite music?
Gran	We loved rock and roll.

Say it in your language …

What a pain!

82

Chatroom   Talking about the past

Revision

First – Write the following infinitives on the board:
answer, clean, climb, close, cycle, dance, juggle, like, live, look, play, stop, travel, use, walk

Second – Students write the Past simple form of the verbs and decide if the endings are pronounced with /d/ or /t/.

Third – Check spelling and pronunciation by asking individual students to write answers on the board and say them correctly.
(Answers: /d/ – *answered, cleaned, climbed, closed, cycled, juggled, lived, played, travelled, used*; /t/ – *danced, liked, looked, stopped, walked*)

Speaking and Listening

Exercise 1

- Draw attention to the photo and ask students what they can see.
- Students look in more detail and answer the question.
- Check the answer as a class.

Possible Answer

Julia's gran has got some letters and some photos.

Brain Trainer Activity 1

See Teacher's Book page 216 and Students' Book page 118

Exercise 2 (Track 3.8)

- Play the recording for students to decide if the sentences are true or false.
- They then check in pairs before you check answers as a class.
- When checking answers, ask students to correct the false sentences.

Answers

1 *False* (She's reading some old letters from Julia's grandad.)
2 False (She stayed for two years.)
3 True
4 False (He didn't phone her very often.)
5 False (It was expensive to make a phone call.)
6 True
7 False (They moved to England in the 1960s/about 50 years ago.)
8 False (They listened to the radio every evening.)
9 False (They liked rock and roll.)

Exercise 3

- Divide the class into groups of three.
- Groups act out the conversation.
- Monitor and correct students' pronunciation as appropriate.
- Nominate one group to perform the conversation for the class.

Say it in your language ...

 Ask students to find the phrase in the conversation and look at it in context to try to deduce the meaning.

What a pain! – exclamation used when we find something irritating or to show sympathy with others in a difficult situation. Not usually used for major problems, it is normally reserved for relatively minor inconveniences, e.g. *'There weren't any buses because of the snow.' 'What a pain!'*

Extra activity

Stronger groups or fast finishers talk about what life was like for their grandparents. Encourage them to use the Past simple of the verb *to be*, *There was/There were* and the affirmative forms of the regular verbs on the previous Vocabulary page, e.g. *'There weren't any MP3 players and there wasn't internet so they listened to music on the radio.'* Monitor and point out errors for students to self-correct.

Exercise 4

- Students read the conversation again and find the phrases.
- Check answers as a class.

Answers

2 Gran   3 Gran   4 Gran   5 Grandad

Exercise 5

- Read through the phrases for talking about past time with the class.

Exercise 6 (Track 3.9)

- Play the recording for students to listen to the conversations.
- In pairs, students act out the conversations.
- Monitor and correct students' pronunciation as appropriate.

Exercise 7

- Students make their own conversations by replacing the words in purple.

Exercise 8

- Students act out their conversations.
- Monitor but do not interrupt fluency unless students make mistakes with the expressions for past time.

Further practice:
Workbook pages 64–65 and 119

Grammar Past simple regular: affirmative and negative

Extra activity

Write the following as a word snake on the board:
closeanswerasktalklikeworkphonestoptravelinvent
Ask students to find the words in the snake and then write the Past simple form. Check answers and spelling by asking individual students to write words on the board.
(Answers: *closed, answered, asked, talked, liked, worked, phoned, stopped, travelled, invented*)

Exercise 1

- Read the grammar table with students.
- Students work individually, answering the questions and referring back to the grammar table where necessary.

Answers

1 No, it isn't.
2 We use *didn't/did not*.

Exercise 2

- Remind students of the Past simple spelling rules presented in Vocabulary on Students' Book page 81.
- Individually, students complete the sentences.
- Check answers and spelling by asking individual students to write answers on the board.

Answers

1 tidied   2 carried   3 danced   4 jumped   5 walked
6 watched   7 stopped

Exercise 3

- Students change the sentences from affirmative to negative.
- Monitor and help with grammar if necessary.
- Check answers by asking individual students to read the sentences.

Answers

2 We didn't carry the computer to the classroom.
3 The actors didn't dance in that film.
4 Our dog didn't jump in the car this morning.
5 My friends and I didn't walk to school last week.
6 We didn't watch a DVD last night.
7 The bus didn't stop near the museum.

Exercise 4

- Individually, students complete the text.
- They check in pairs before you check answers as a class.

Answers

2 tidied	6 wanted
3 didn't/did not help	7 didn't/did not watch
4 played	8 arrived
5 didn't/did not like	

Extra activity

Prepare six sentences about your weekend. Remember to grade your language appropriately. Include both affirmative and negative Past simple verb forms. Some of the sentences should be true and some false.
Read the sentences for students to decide if they think they are true or false. Do not allow students to write anything down apart from the words *true* or *false*. In pairs, students compare their answers.
Tell students to listen again and write down the sentences, but tell them they must change the sentences which they think are false to make them true.
Check answers as a class and confirm which of your sentences were true and which were false.

Further practice:
Workbook pages 65 and 98–99

4 **Look back at the conversation. Who says what?**

1 I didn't visit you last weekend. *Julia*
2 I stayed in Poland for two years.
3 I moved here in the 1960s.
4 That was fifty years ago.
5 In those days, we listened to the radio.

5 **Read the words and phrases for talking about the past.**

Past time expressions
last weekend
for two years
in the 1960s
fifty years ago
in those days

6 🔊 3.9 **Listen to the conversations. Act out the conversations in pairs.**

Stefan Where were you ¹ last weekend? Were you at home?
Nina No, I wasn't. I was ² at my grandparents' house.

Jason I wasn't at school ¹ yesterday morning.
Sonia Really? Why not?
Jason Because I was ² ill.

7 **Work in pairs. Replace the words in purple in Exercise 6 with these words. Act out the conversations.**

Where were you yesterday?
I was at a friend's house.

1 last night / last week / last Friday
2 at the cinema / in Egypt / at school

1 yesterday afternoon / last Thursday / three days ago
2 at the doctor's / at the dentist's / at home in bed

8 **Act out the conversation again with your own words and ideas.**

Grammar Past simple regular: affirmative and negative

Affirmative	
I/You/He/She/It/We/They	listened. danced. studied. travelled.

Negative	
I/You/He/She/It/We/They	didn't (did not) listen. didn't (did not) dance. didn't (did not) study. didn't (did not) travel.

Grammar reference Workbook page 98

1 **Study the grammar table. Answer the questions to complete the rules.**

1 Is the third person (He/She/It) different in the Past simple?
2 How do we make the Past simple negative?

2 **Complete the sentences with the Past simple affirmative.**

1 Yesterday she .... (tidy) her room.
2 We .... (carry) the computer to the classroom.
3 The actors .... (dance) in that film.
4 Our dog .... (jump) in the car this morning.
5 My friends and I .... (walk) to school last week.
6 We .... (watch) a DVD last night.
7 The bus .... (stop) near the museum.

3 **Put the sentences in Exercise 2 in the negative form.**

1 *Yesterday, she didn't tidy her room.*

4 **Complete the text with these verbs in the Past simple.**

arrive	not help	not like	not watch
play	~~stay~~	tidy	want

Last night my parents were out so I ¹ *stayed* at home with my brother, Harry. I ² .... the living room, but Harry ³ .... me. Next, I ⁴ .... games with him, but he ⁵ .... the games. Then, he ⁶ .... to watch *Jaws*, a scary film about a shark. We ⁷ .... it for long. When Mum and Dad ⁸ .... home, my brother and I were behind the sofa!

◀ 83 ▶

Reading

1 **Look at the names (1–6). Can you match them to the photos (a–f)?**

1 Jaws   4 ET
2 Grease   5 Andy Warhol
3 ABBA   6 Kylie

Travel back in time!

Welcome to the Time Tunnels at **The Max Museum of Modern Culture!**

In the first Time Tunnel you can re-live the culture of the 70s. This was a time of freedom for women and young people in America and Western Europe. Andy Warhol was a famous pop artist. He started in the 60s, but he was very popular in the 70s because his work was fresh and modern.

At the cinema, people watched exciting films like *Jaws*, *Star Wars* and *Grease*. In the evening people liked disco music. They danced to ABBA, the European superstars from Sweden. Some film posters and record covers from this time are pieces of art now.

In the second Time Tunnel you can visit the 80s. American culture was 'cool'; many people liked fast food and Hollywood 'blockbuster' films like *ET* and *Wall Street*. People worked long hours and some young people wanted lots of money, but others didn't like this culture of 'Me, me, me'. Graffiti art was one way to show they were angry.

In the 80s people enjoyed some great pop music – for example Kylie Minogue, Madonna and Michael Jackson. Their videos and stage shows were also a type of art.

Key Words		
tunnel	culture	freedom
fresh	blockbuster	angry

2 **Read and check your answers to Exercise 1.**

3 🔊 **3.10** **Read the text quickly. Are these things from the 70s or 80s Time Tunnel?**

a Graffiti art   *80s Time Tunnel*
b Andy Warhol
c *Wall Street*
d Michael Jackson
e *Star Wars*
f ABBA

4 🔊 **3.10** **Read the text again. Answer the questions.**

1 What type of museum is it?
   It is a museum of modern culture.
2 Who was Andy Warhol?
3 Which Swedish band was famous for disco music?
4 What were two examples of American culture?
5 Why was graffiti art popular in the 80s?

Listening

1 🔊 **3.11** **Listen to three people from The Max Museum. Match each speaker to the things they do.**

Speaker 1
Speaker 2
Speaker 3

a take photographs
b sell tickets
c work in the gift shop

2 🔊 **3.11** **Listen again and find these things.**

1 names of two famous people
2 three colours
3 a number

3 **What about you? Imagine you are in the year 2030. In pairs, say what the year 2012 was like.**

84

Reading

Cultural notes

The Max Museum of Modern Culture in the Reading text is not a real place. The things which the Time Tunnels contain, however, are all real, including these from Exercise 2.

- *Graffiti art* – graffiti goes back to the time of Ancient Greece although it was not until the 1980s that it was first classified as art and exhibited as such.
- *Andy Warhol* (USA, 1928–1987) was one of the leading figures of the Pop Art movement. He was famous as both a painter and printmaker with his iconic images.
- *Wall Street* is a drama film, first released in 1987. It stars Charlie Sheen and Michael Douglas as brokers on the financial markets. Douglas won an Oscar for his performance.
- *Michael Jackson* (USA 1958–2009) is often referred to as 'The King of Pop'. According to the Guinness World Records, he was the most successful entertainer of all time.
- *Star Wars* is a science-fiction fantasy film, first released in 1977. It was part of one of the highest grossing film series in cinema history.
- *ABBA* was a Swedish pop group who shot to fame after winning the 1974 Eurovision Song Contest with *Waterloo*. Their songs remain famous today.

Exercise 1

- Draw attention to the photos and the text and ask students what they can see.
- In pairs, students match the photos to the names.

Key Words

Be prepared to focus on the Key Words, either by pre-teaching them, eliciting their meaning after students have read the text, or through dictionary or definition writing work.

tunnel – a long hole, usually through a mountain or underground, that cars can drive through or people can walk through

culture – a general, abstract word to refer to all different artistic areas together

freedom – being able to do anything you want with no restrictions or limitations

fresh – something very new and original, that no one has seen before

blockbuster – a very successful film

angry – an extreme adjective to describe when a person is very unhappy about something

Exercise 2

- Make sure students understand not to read in detail at this point.
- Students scan the text quickly and check their answers to Exercise 1.

Answers

1 e   **2** b   **3** c   **4** f   **5** d   **6** a

Exercise 3 (Track 3.10)

- If you wish, play the recording for students to listen and read.
- Check answers as a class.

Answers

b 70s   **c** 80s   **d** 80s   **e** 70s   **f** 70s

Exercise 4 (Track 3.10)

- Individually, students answer the questions.
- Check answers as a class.
- Elicit from stronger students or explain yourself the meaning of any new vocabulary.

Answers

2 He was a famous pop artist.
3 Abba was famous for disco music.
4 Fast food and Hollywood 'blockbuster' films were two examples of American culture.
5 Because people were angry.

Listening

Exercise 1 (Track 3.11)

- Play the recording for students to listen and match the people and the things they do.
- Check answers as a class.

Answers

1 c   **2** a   **3** b

Audioscript:
See Teacher's Book page 226

Exercise 2 (Track 3.11)

- Repeat the recording for students to find the things.
- They then check in pairs before you check answers as a class.

Answers

1 Andy Warhol, Marilyn Monroe
2 pink, black, grey   **3** five hundred

Exercise 3

- In pairs, students talk about what the year 2012 was like.
- Discuss as a class.

Further practice:
Workbook page 66

Writing   An essay

Revision

First – Revise dates by talking about some historical events with your class. Write the following dates in numbers on the board: *23/4/1616; 14/7/1789; 24/11/1859; 1/1/2000; 11/11/1918; 26/7/1952; 8/12/1980; 31/8/1997*

Second – In pairs, students practise saying the dates. Monitor and point out errors for students to self-correct.

Third – Tell students that something important happened on each of these dates. Students work in pairs, working out what happened on each date. Check answers as a class. Depending on your teaching context, change some or all of these dates to make them more relevant to your students. (Answers: *23/4/1616 – Shakespeare and Cervantes died; 14/7/1789 – French Revolution started; 24/11/1859 – Darwin published 'Origin of Species'; 1/1/2000 – the New Millennium started; 11/11/1918 – First World War ended; 26/7/1952 – Eva Perón died; 8/12/1980 – murder of John Lennon; 31/8/1997 – Princess Diana died*)

Extra activity

Revise the punctuation rules taught in the Writing section of Unit 1. Write the following sentences on the board:
1 ive got a minibus with 15 seats
2 my grandparents favourite group is abba
3 michael jacksons pet was a chimpanzee called bubbles
4 i didnt want to watch the film
5 my brother and i lived in Poland for two years
6 my favourite film is twilight its wonderful
Students add capital letters, full stops and apostrophes to the sentences. Check answers by asking individual students to write sentences on the board.
(Answers: *1 I've got a minibus with 15 seats. 2 My grandparents' favourite group is Abba. 3 Michael Jackson's pet was a chimpanzee called Bubbles. 4 I didn't want to watch the film. 5 My brother and I lived in Poland for two years. 6 My favourite film is Twilight. It's wonderful.*)

Exercise 1

- Read the Writing File with students.
- Ask students if the punctuation rules are the same in their L1 or different.

Exercise 2

- Students add appropriate punctuation to the essay.
- Check answers as a class.

Answers

2 ! **3** , **4** ? **5** ,

Exercise 3

- Individually, students answer the questions.
- They then compare their answers in pairs.
- Check answers by asking pairs of students to read questions and answers.

Answers

2 It was from Japan.   **3** Yes, he was.
4 His favourite character was Ron Weasley.
5 He liked Linkin Park.
6 He likes My Chemical Romance and The Wanted.

Exercise 4

- Individually, students rewrite the sentences with appropriate punctuation.
- Monitor and point out errors for students to self-correct.
- Check answers by asking individual students to write answers on the board.

Answers

2 Who was in the Harry Potter films?
3 How old were you in 2010?
4 We watched TV yesterday afternoon.
5 I liked *Pokemon*, but I didn't like *Yu-Gi-Oh*.

Exercise 5

- Explain that students should only make notes at this point or write short sentences.
- Encourage students to ask you for any vocabulary they need.

Answers

Students' own answers

Exercise 6

- Read through the 'My essay' writing guide. Tell students they must now present their information as a complete text, not as notes or unconnected sentences.
- Show students how the example text is divided into three paragraphs and tell them that they should now organise their notes in the same way.
- Draw students' attention to the 'Remember!' checklist.

Answers

Students' own answers

Extra activity

Add an extra 10–15 vocabulary items from this unit to the collection of Word Cards.
Revise all the vocabulary by playing a <u>missing word game</u>. Choose three words as examples and prepare an example sentence for each one, e.g. *'I … a film last night, but it wasn't very good.'* (Answer: *watched*). Read the three sentences with the class, replacing the '…' with a 'beep' sound. Students have to write down what they think the missing words are. Check answers as a class. Divide the class into pairs and give each pair an equal number of vocabulary cards. Students work together writing simple sentences for the words. Monitor and point out errors for students to self-correct. Groups take turns to read their sentences with a beep in place of the word and the rest of the class have to guess what the word is.

Further practice:
Workbook page 67

Writing   An essay

1   Read the Writing File.

> **Writing File   Punctuation 2**
>
> - We use **full stops (.)** at the end of a sentence.
> - We use **commas (,)** to make a pause in the middle of a sentence, e.g. before *but*.
> - We use **question marks (?)** at the end of a question. Be careful! We don't use question marks at the beginning of a sentence.
> - We use **exclamation marks (!)** to express surprise.

2   Read Jason's essay. What punctuation (1–5) is missing?

When I was young

The 'noughties' (2000–2009) was a good time to be young [1] [.] There were some great TV programmes for kids, like the Japanese cartoon *Yu-Gi-Oh*. *Yu-Gi-Oh* was about Yugi, a high school student with a Pharaoh's spirit. I loved it!
There were also some good films a few years ago. The Harry Potter films were very popular and I was a big fan. I didn't watch them at the cinema, but I watched them on DVD lots of times [2] [...] My favourite character was Ron Weasley [3] [...] but I didn't like Lord Voldemort.
Was there any good music in the noughties [4] [...] I think so. I liked *Linkin Park* [5] [...] but music in the twenty-tens is better. *My Chemical Romance* and *The Wanted* are amazing!
Jason, Australia

3   Read the essay again. Answer the questions.

1 When were the 'noughties'?
   The noughties were from 2000 to 2009.
2 Which country was the programme *Yu-Gi-Oh* from?
3 Was Jason a Harry Potter fan?
4 Who was his favourite character?
5 Which was his favourite band in the 'noughties'?
6 What bands does Jason like now?

4   Rewrite these sentences with commas (if necessary) and a full stop or a question mark.

1 The song was old but it was very popular
   The song was old, but it was very popular.
2 Who was in the Harry Potter films
3 How old were you in 2010
4 We watched TV yesterday afternoon
5 I liked *Pokemon* but I didn't like *Yu-Gi-Oh*

5   Think about when you were young. Make notes about these things. Give reasons.
1 TV programmes you liked – and why
2 films you liked – and why
3 singers and bands you liked – and why

6   Write an essay: 'When I was young'. Use 'My essay' and your notes from Exercise 5.

> **My essay**
>
> **Paragraph 1**
> 1   Say what time you are writing about.
> 2   Say what programmes you liked.
> **Paragraph 2**
> 3   Say what films you liked.
> **Paragraph 3**
> 4   Say what music you liked.
> 5   Compare with music you like now.

Remember!
- Use punctuation correctly.
- Use the vocabulary in this unit.
- Check your grammar, spelling and punctuation.

 85

Refresh Your Memory!

Grammar Review

1 **Complete the text with *was / wasn't* or *were / weren't*.**

• Which countries [1] *were* in the 'Space-Race'?

In the 1950s and 60s Russia and America [2] .... in a 'Space Race'. The first man in space [3] .... Yuri Gagarin from Russia.

• Which country [4] .... first on the moon?

The first rocket on the moon [5] .... American. It was the Russian Luna 2 in 1959, but there weren't any people in this rocket. The first men on the moon [6] .... from Russia. They were from America. The date [7] .... 21st July, 1969. Buzz Aldrin and Neil Armstrong [8] .... on the moon for 21 hours.

2 **Make sentences with *There was / were* or *There wasn't / weren't*.**

1 an MP3 player on the table

There was an MP3 player on the table.

2 not any songs on the MP3 player
3 some DVDs next to a laptop
4 not a car in the garage
5 a mobile phone on the chair
6 some text messages on the phone

3 **Make sentences with the Past simple.**

1 Jake / visit / his friend in hospital yesterday

Jake visited his friend in hospital yesterday.

2 Angelina / play / football with her brother
3 We / phone / our grandparents last night
4 Sam and Sara / study / for their Maths test
5 The students / answer / the teacher's questions
6 The car / stop / near the park

4 **Correct the sentences.**

1 Howard Carter discovered Tutankhamun's tomb in Greece. (Egypt)

He didn't discover Tutankhamun's tomb in Greece, he discovered it in Egypt.

2 The first space vehicle visited Mars in 2012. (2004)
3 People celebrated the millennium in 1998. (2000)
4 Alexander Graham Bell invented the MP3 player. (telephone)
5 For his first 'long distance' call, Bell phoned his mum. (his friend)
6 Anne Frank's family lived in Paris. (Amsterdam)

Vocabulary Review

5 **Write the dates in full in your notebook.**

1 20 / 04 / 1982

The twentieth of April nineteen eighty-two.

2 10 / 03 / 2030
3 3 / 08 / 1861
4 21 / 01 / 2018
5 2 / 10 / 2003
6 1 / 08 / 1999

6 **Match the verbs to the correct Past simple spelling rule.**

1 dance / love
2 travel / drop
3 play / clean
4 tidy / hurry

a add -ed
b change -y to -i, add -ed
c double the consonant, add -ed
d add -d

Speaking Review

7 ◗)) **3.12** **Complete the conversations with a past time word. Then listen and check.**

last	ago	yesterday

Esra Where's Mum?
Eren I don't know. She was here half an hour [1] .... .

Ivan Where were you [2] .... night? Were you at the sports club?
Eva No, I wasn't. I was at home.

Dina Why didn't you go to school [3] .... ?
Paulo Because I was at the doctor's.

Dictation

8 ◗)) **3.13** **Listen and write in your notebook.**

✓ **My assessment profile:** Workbook page 133

Refresh Your Memory!

Exercise 1

Answers

2 were   **3** was   **4** was   **5** wasn't   **6** weren't   **7** was
8 were

Exercise 2

Answers

2 There weren't any songs on the MP3 player.
3 There were some DVDs next to a laptop.
4 There wasn't a car in the garage.
5 There was a mobile phone on the chair.
6 There were some text messages on the phone.

Exercise 3

Answers

2 Angelina played football with her brother.
3 We phoned our grandparents last night.
4 Sam and Sara studied for their Maths test.
5 The students answered the teacher's questions.
6 The car stopped near the park.

Exercise 4

Possible Answers

2 It didn't visit Mars in 2012, it visited Mars in 2004.
3 They didn't celebrate the millennium in 1998, they celebrated it in 2000.
4 He didn't invent the MP3 player, he invented the telephone.
5 He didn't phone his mum, he phoned his friend.
6 They didn't live in Paris, they lived in Amsterdam.

Exercise 5

Answers

2 The tenth of March twenty thirty.
3 The third of August eighteen sixty-one.
4 The twenty-first of January twenty eighteen.
5 The second of October two thousand and three.
6 The first of August nineteen ninety-nine.

Exercise 6

Answers

1 d   **2** c   **3** a   **4** b

Exercise 7 (Track 3.12)

Answers

1 ago   **2** last   **3** yesterday

Exercise 8 (Track 3.13)

Answers and Audioscript

In the 1980s there were computers and mobile phones, but they were big and expensive. There weren't any games consoles and people didn't listen to music on MP3 players. People liked Michael Jackson's music and they watched the first music videos.

My assessment profile:
See Workbook page 133

Extra activity

Revise saying years and talking about historical events using a timeline:
– Draw the timeline in the centre of the board and mark the beginning *1900* and the end *2020* and draw up the word clouds on the left and right of the board.
– Copy the picture of Tutankhamun and the pyramids at the beginning of the timeline but do not write the year. Ask students *'What year was this?'* Elicit the answer (*It was 1922.*) and write the year up on the board, next to the picture. Ask *'What happened in 1922?'* and elicit a sentence using one of the subjects in the cloud on the left and the Past simple of one of the verbs in the cloud on the right, e.g. *'(In 1922) Howard Carter discovered Tutankhamun's tomb in Egypt.'*
– Draw up the speech bubbles and elicit the two questions you asked. Drill the questions for correct pronunciation and intonation.
– Draw up the other events on the timeline but do not include the years. Students then work in pairs asking and answering the questions.
– Monitor and help with vocabulary but do not interrupt fluency.
(Answers: *1922 – Howard Carter discovered Tutankhamun's tomb in Egypt.; 1926 – John Logie Baird invented the television.; 1962 – The Beatles recorded 'Love Me Do!'.; 1967 – People watched colour television for the first time.; 1969 – Neil Armstrong walked on the Moon.; 2000 – Everybody celebrated the Millennium.; 2004 – A space vehicle landed on Mars.; 2011 – Prince William married Kate Middleton.*)

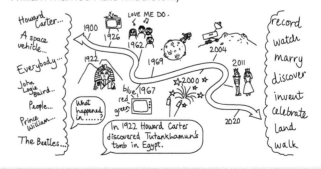

Culture 5 – Famous British People:
See Teacher's Book page 223 and Students' Book page 125 (for extra reading, discussion and writing work).

History File   24 hours in the life of a Roman child

Cultural notes

Ancient Rome was one of the largest empires of antiquity. According to popular myth, Rome was founded in 753 BC by Romulus and Remus, who had been abandoned as babies and saved by a wolf and a family of shepherds. The history of Ancient Rome divides principally into two major periods:
- The *Roman Republic*, established around 509 BC, was governed through a system of annually elected officials. The murder of Julius Caesar in 44 BC is commonly seen as marking the beginning of the transition from Republic to Empire.
- The *Roman Empire* began after the fall of the Republic. It was governed by an autocratic emperor, the first of whom was Augustus. The Empire in the West fell in 476 AD, although the Eastern Roman Empire lasted another millennium until the fall of Constantinople in 1453.

The Romans were vitally important in the development of the Western World, adapting Ancient Greek models and providing the basis for many languages, arts, political systems and religions.

They similarly adopted and adapted Greek educational systems and so influenced the development of educational systems throughout the Western world. Further information on both Ancient Rome and Ancient Egypt and their education systems is available on the internet.

Language notes

Be prepared to elicit from stronger students or explain yourself the meaning of the following lexical items which appear in the Reading text: *honey, wine, slave, to serve, sunrise, tutor, stone, wax tablet, to scratch, pointed stick, public speaking, to fight, hoop, kite, stilts*

Exercise 1
- Draw attention to the pictures and the text and ask students what they can see.
- Make sure students understand not to read in detail at this point.
- They then scan the text quickly to find out what it is about.

Answer
1 b

Exercise 2 (Track 3.14)
- Students read the text and answer the questions.
- If you wish, play the recording for students to listen and read.
- Students check in pairs before you check answers as a class.
- Check answers by asking pairs of students to read questions and answers.

Answers
2 Slaves prepared the food.
3 Schools were very small.
4 They studied Reading, Writing and Maths.
5 The family slaves taught children at home.
6 They played with toys: dolls, hoops, kites and stilts.

My History File

Exercise 3
- Tell students that information is available on the internet about daily life in Ancient Egypt.
- Explain that students should only make notes at this point or write short sentences.

Exercise 4
- Individually, students write their text. Tell them they must now present their information as a complete text, not as notes or unconnected sentences.
- Monitor and help with grammar and vocabulary and feed in ideas if necessary.
- Point out errors for students to self-correct.

In this unit have you …
… used Grammar and Vocabulary worksheet?
… used Reading and Listening worksheet?
… used Writing worksheet?
… used Speaking worksheet?
… used Unit test?

With the exception of the Writing worksheets, all the Teacher's Resources are at two levels of difficulty:
* For students who need extra help and support
** For students who require an additional challenge

History File

24 hours in the life of a Roman child

The day started with breakfast. For rich Romans, there was bread, fish, meat, fruit and honey. Slaves prepared and served the food. For poor Romans breakfast was different. They had bread with water.

Then it was time to go to school. School started very early – before sunrise – and it finished late! Schools were very small. There was usually one tutor and a small group of children. At school, children studied Reading, Writing and Maths. They used small stones to do Maths problems. They practised writing on wax tablets – they scratched the words onto the wax with a pointed stick.

Most children finished school when they were 10 or 11, but some children continued to a 'Grammar school'. Here they studied Latin, Greek, Grammar and Literature. They also practised public speaking. Some children studied at home. Their teachers were the family's slaves. The slaves were often very clever and well-educated and they were good teachers.

After school, the children played with toys at home. The boys often played war games and practised fighting. Some Roman toys are very similar to modern toys. Roman children played with dolls, hoops, kites and stilts.

Reading

1 **Read the text quickly. What do you think it is about?**

a Roman food
b Roman daily life
c Education in Rome today

2 **((•)) 3.14 Read the text again. Answer the questions.**

1 What did rich people have for breakfast?
People had bread, fish, meat, fruit and honey.
2 Who prepared the food for rich people?
3 Were schools big or small?
4 What did children study at school?
5 Who taught children at home?
6 What did children play with at home?

My History File

3 **Do some research into daily life for a child from Ancient Egypt. Find the answers to these questions:**

• When did they get up?
• When did they go to bed?
• What did they eat?
• What did they do?

4 **Write a short paragraph about daily life for an Ancient Egyptian child in your notebook. Use your notes from Exercise 3 to help you.**

87

8 Journeys

Grammar Past simple irregular: affirmative and negative; Past simple: questions
Vocabulary Means of transport; Clothes
Speaking Talking on the phone
Writing A travel diary

Vocabulary Means of transport

1 🔊 **3.15** **Match the vehicles in the picture to these words. Then listen, check and repeat.**

bike	boat	bus	canoe	car *1*
coach	helicopter	lorry	motorbike	plane
scooter	train	tube	van	

> **Word list** page 111   **Workbook** page 111

2 🔊 **3.16** **Which vehicles from Exercise 1 can you hear? Listen and say.**

1 *It's a boat.*

3 **Where do you usually use each type of transport? Complete the list.**

1 on land: **2 at sea**:   **3 in the air**:
car, … .   *boat, … .*   *plane, … .*

4 **Match the verbs to the nouns.**

1 take   **a** a plane
2 sail   **b** a train
3 drive   **c** a bike, a motorbike
4 fly   **d** a boat
5 ride   **e** a car

5 **In pairs, make up an unusual route from your home to another country. You must use at least five different forms of transport.**

> *First, we ride our bikes to the bus stop. Then, we take a bus to the river. Then, we …*

Brain Trainer Activity 4
Go to page 119

88

Unit contents

Vocabulary
→ Means of transport – *bike, boat, bus, canoe, car, coach, helicopter, lorry, motorbike, plane, scooter, train, tube, van*

→ Clothes – *boots, coat, dress, hat, jeans, jumper, pyjamas, sandals, scarf, shoes, shorts, skirt, T-shirt, trainers, trousers*

Grammar
→ Past simple irregular: affirmative and negative
→ Past simple: questions

Communication
→ Talking on the phone
→ Writing a travel diary; Paragraphs

Pronunciation
→ Sounding polite

Culture 6 – British Festivals and Customs

Key competences
→ Linguistic competence
→ Interpersonal, social and civic competence
→ Cultural and artistic competences
→ Learning-to-learn
→ Autonomy and personal initiative

Vocabulary   Means of transport

Language notes

This Vocabulary section introduces a variety of transport words and it is worth bearing in mind the following points:
- A *coach* is more comfortable than a *bus* and is generally used for transport between cities rather than in a city.
- A *scooter* is a much less powerful vehicle than a *motorbike* and is very common for getting around in countries with a warm climate.
- A *van* is much smaller than a *lorry* and is not generally used to transport goods over large distances.

Note that the article *a* is normally used with these means of transport with the exception of *tube* which is referred to as *the tube*.

Exercise 4 introduces various verbs which collocate with the forms of transport. Some of these refer to operating the vehicle (*drive a car, fly a plane*) and some of these refer to being a passenger (*take a train*). This difference in meaning is not covered actively in the Students' Book but is covered in the Revision activity on the next page of the Teacher's Book.

))) Exercise 1 (Track 3.15)
- Individually, students match the words and vehicles in the picture.
- Play the recording for students to listen and check.
- Repeat the recording. Pause after each word to check students' pronunciation.

Answers
2 scooter **3** plane **4** helicopter **5** coach **6** lorry
7 boat **8** train **9** bus **10** canoe **11** tube
12 motorbike **13** van **14** bike

))) Exercise 2 (Track 3.16)
- Play the recording for students to identify the vehicles from the sound effects.
- Students compare their ideas in pairs before you check answers as a class.

Answers
2 It's a plane. **5** It's a motorbike. **7** It's a helicopter.
3 It's a bike. **6** It's a bus. **8** It's a canoe.
4 It's a train

Exercise 3
- Students copy and complete the lists.
- Collate answers on the board.

Answers
1 on land: *car*, bike, bus, coach, lorry, motorbike, scooter, train, tube, van
2 at sea: *boat*, canoe **3 in the air:** *plane*, helicopter

Exercise 4
- In pairs, students match the verbs to the nouns.
- Make sure students understand that there are various possible answers for each verb but that there is only one combination which uses each verb once.
- Check answers as a class.

Answers
1 b **2** *d* **3** e **4** a **5** c

Extra activity

Stronger groups or fast finishers write example sentences using the verb and noun collocations. Monitor and point out errors for students to self-correct. Ask some students to write their sentences on the board, leaving a blank in place of the verb. The rest of the class have to guess what the word is.

Exercise 5
- Read through the example with students.
- Students work in pairs, inventing their route.
- Monitor and help with vocabulary and feed in ideas if necessary.
- Ask some of the pairs to say their routes for the class.

Further practice:
Workbook pages 68 and 111

Brain Trainer Activity 4
See Teacher's Book page 217 and Students' Book page 119

Reading

Revision

First – Revise transport collocations by creating a Venn diagram with students. Copy the five circles onto the board and elicit from students the five verbs from the previous Vocabulary section. Write the verbs within the circles in small clouds.

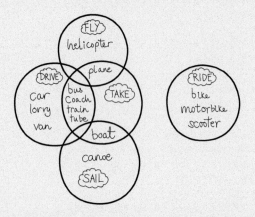

Second – Use the word *bus* as an example. Elicit from students where to put the word on the diagram and ask what the difference is between *drive a bus* (Answer: *It's your job.*) and *take a bus* (*You are a passenger.*). In pairs, students classify the other means of transport from the previous Vocabulary page.

Third – Check answers as a class by asking individual students to write words on the board. Ask what *boat*, *bus*, *coach*, *plane*, *train* and *tube* all have in common (Answer: *You can buy a ticket for them.*).

Cultural notes

Around the World in Eighty Days is a novel by Jules Verne (1828–1905), first published in 1873. It is one of Verne's most popular books and tells the story of Phileas Fogg's attempt to circumnavigate the globe in 80 days in order to win a bet for £20,000 (the equivalent of over £1,000,000 today). Fogg arrives back in London believing he is five minutes too late to win the bet. Passepartout later finds out that they in fact gained a day by crossing the international date line and so Fogg wins his bet. The novel is now in the public domain and can be legally downloaded free on the internet.

Exercise 1

- Draw attention to the picture and the text and ask students what they can see.
- Individually, students guess what the text is about.

Exercise 2

- Individually, students read the text and check their answer to Exercise 1.
- Students scan the text quickly to check their answer to Exercise 1.

Answer

b

Exercise 3 (Track 3.17)

- Individually, students order the events.
- If you wish, play the recording for students to listen and read.
- Check answers as a class.

Answers

a 3   **b** 2   **c** 1   **d** 7   **e** 6   **f** 5   **g** 4

Exercise 4 (Track 3.17)

- Students read the text again and answer the questions.
- They then check in pairs before you check answers as a class.
- Elicit from stronger students or explain yourself the meaning of any new vocabulary.

Answers

2 He lives in Savile Row.
3 He asks for a small bag and his coat.
4 He puts a lot of money and a railway and ship timetable inside the bag.
5 They are at the train station.
6 They leave at 8.45.

Exercise 5

- In pairs, students ask and answer questions about travelling.
- Monitor and help with vocabulary but do not interrupt fluency.
- Make a note of any mistakes to go over with the class afterwards.

Extra activity

Use the story of *Around the World in Eighty Days* as the basis for a *Live Listening*. Plot summaries of the novel are widely available on the internet for you to prepare from. Remember to grade your language appropriately and simplify the story as much as possible. Write the following six events from the story on the board and tell students to put them in order as they listen to you retelling the story.
a Fogg takes a boat to Bombay.
b Fogg travels to Hong Kong and then to San Francisco.
c Fogg sails a small boat home, marries Aouda and completes his journey in 80 days.
d Fogg travels to Egypt by boat and train.
e Fogg takes a train to New York.
f Fogg meets a beautiful princess called Aouda.
(Answers: *1d*; *2a*; *3f*; *4b*; *5e*; *6c*)

Further practice:
Workbook page 69

Reading

1 Look at the extracts (a–c) from *Around the World in Eighty Days* by Jules Verne. Guess. What is it about?

a Phileas Fogg can't find his bag. Is it in France? Is it in China? He travels to 80 countries. But where is his bag?

b It is 1872. Phileas Fogg's friends say, 'No one can travel around the world in 80 days.' 'I can!' says Phileas Fogg. And his adventure begins.

c Phileas Fogg works at a train station. He meets many people from different countries. He hears 80 stories from 80 places around the world, but he never travels.

2 Read and check your ideas to Exercise 1.

3 🔊 **3.17** Read the text quickly. Put the events in the correct order.

a Passepartout gets a bag for Phileas Fogg.
b Phileas Fogg goes into his house.
c Phileas Fogg leaves the Club. *1*
d Phileas Fogg and Passepartout get on a train.
e Phileas Fogg says goodbye to his friends.
f Phileas Fogg sees his friends at the station.
g Phileas Fogg gives his bag to Passepartout.

4 🔊 **3.17** Read the text again. Answer the questions.

1 Where are Phileas Fogg's friends at the beginning of the extract? *They are at the Club.*
2 Where does Phileas Fogg live?
3 Phileas Fogg asks Passepartout for two things. What are they?
4 What does Phileas Fogg put inside the bag?
5 Where are Phileas Fogg's friends at the end of the extract?
6 What time do Phileas Fogg and Passepartout leave Charing Cross Station?

5 What about you? **In pairs, ask and answer.**

1 Do you like travelling?
2 Imagine you are travelling around the world in 80 days. What do you want to put in your suitcase?

Around the World in 80 Days

At 7.25, Phileas Fogg said good night to his friends and left the Club. At 7.50, he opened the door of his house in Savile Row and went in.

'Mr Fogg? Is that you?' said Passepartout.

'We must go to Charing Cross Station immediately. I want to make a journey round the world.'

Passepartout didn't understand him.

'Round the world?' he asked.

'In eighty days,' said Phileas Fogg. 'We must go now. Now!'

'But your bags?'

'I need one small bag. Bring my coat. Wear strong shoes. Move!'

At 8 o'clock, Passepartout was ready with a small bag. 'A quiet life,' he thought. 'Where is my quiet life?'

Phileas Fogg didn't have a lot of things for the journey. He took the bag from Passepartout and put a lot of money and a railway and ship timetable into it. Then he gave the bag to Passepartout.

At the station, Phileas Fogg saw his five friends from the Club.

'You're here to say goodbye? That's kind,' he said.

At 8.40, Phileas Fogg and Passepartout got on the train, and at 8.45 the train started.

89 ▶

Grammar Past simple irregular: affirmative and negative

Base	Affirmative	Negative
buy	bought	didn't (did not) buy
do	did	didn't (did not) do
get	got	didn't (did not) get
give	gave	didn't (did not) give
go	went	didn't (did not) go
have	had	didn't (did not) have
put	put	didn't (did not) put
take	took	didn't (did not) take
think	thought	didn't (did not) think
understand	understood	didn't (did not) understand

Watch Out!

They went to Paris last month.
You didn't go to London last month.
BUT:
I was in London yesterday.
We were in Rome yesterday.

He wasn't in Rome yesterday
They weren't in London yesterday.

Go to page 127 for a full list of irregular Past simple verbs

Grammar reference Workbook page 100

1 Study the grammar table. Complete the rule.

For the Past simple negative form, we put the word .... before the base verb.

2 Are these Past simple verbs regular (R) or irregular (I)?

buy – bought **I**	drink – drank	give – gave
live – lived	say – said	see – saw
study – studied	visit – visited	work – worked

3 Complete the text below with the Past simple.

I ¹ *went* (go) to Birmingham with my friend Ella last weekend. We ² .... (see) a great film at the cinema. After the film, we ³ .... (go) shopping. I ⁴ .... (buy) a new game for my games console. My friend ⁵ .... (get) a book about computers. Then we ⁶ .... (eat) some pizza at a café. At 7 o'clock, we ⁷ .... (take) the bus home. We ⁸ .... (have) a great day.

4 Rewrite the verbs from Exercise 3 in the Past simple negative.

1 *I didn't go.*

5 Complete the article.

True Stories: I changed my life

Jane Fletcher before   Jane Fletcher now

Jane Fletcher is healthier and happier today. Why? She changed her life.

Now she ¹ *walks* (walk) to work every day, but two years ago she ² *didn't walk* (not walk) to work, she ³ *went* (go) by car. Now she ⁴ .... (have) cereal for breakfast, but two years ago she ⁵ .... (not have) cereal for breakfast, she ⁶ .... (have) cake. Now she ⁷ .... (go to bed) at ten o'clock, but two years ago she ⁸ .... (not go to bed) at ten o'clock, she ⁹ .... (go to bed) at midnight. Now she ¹⁰ .... (ride) her bike in the park at the weekend, but two years ago, she ¹¹ .... (not ride) her bike, she drove her car to the city at the weekend.

6 What about you? Write three true sentences about something you changed in your life.

90

Grammar   Past simple irregular: affirmative and negative

Language notes

Note that the 'Watch Out!' box highlights the difference between *go to* for the movement towards a place and *be in* for permanence in a place. Make sure students understand this difference, if necessary, by comparing it with their L1.

Exercise 1

- Read the grammar table with students.
- Students work individually, completing the rule and referring back to the grammar table where necessary.
- Make sure students understand that they need to memorise the irregular verb forms.
- Draw students' attention to the list of irregular verbs on page 127 of the Students' Book.

Answer

didn't

Exercise 2

- In pairs, students classify the words as regular or irregular.
- Check answers by drawing two columns on the board, one for regular and one for irregular, and asking individual students to classify the vocabulary.

Answers

regular: live – lived, study – studied, visit – visited, work – worked
irregular: *buy – bought*, drink – drank, give – gave, say – said, see – saw

Extra activity

Stronger groups do some additional work on pronunciation and the past verb forms. Write the following headers on the board:

A   E   I   O   U
/eɪ/   /iː/   /aɪ/   /əʊ/   /uː/

Make sure students understand how the pronunciation of the vowel sounds relates to the phonetic symbols. Write these words in a column down one side of the board:
buy, climb, do, drove, fly, gave, go, play, ride, say, see, take
Students classify the verbs according to the vowel sound. They then compare their answers in pairs. Check answers by asking individual students to write words under the correct symbol on the board. Ask them to tell you the past form of the present verbs and vice-versa. (Answers: /eɪ/ *gave, play, say, take;* /iː/ *see;* /aɪ/ *buy, climb, fly, ride;* /əʊ/ *drove, go;* /uː/ *do*)

Exercise 3

- Individually, students complete the text.
- They then check in pairs before you check answers as a class.
- Check spelling by asking students to spell the words to you.

Answers

2 saw   **3** went   **4** bought   **5** got   **6** ate   **7** took
8 had

Exercise 4

- Students change the verbs from affirmative to negative.
- Check answers by asking individual students to write the negatives on the board.

Answers

2 We didn't see   **6** we didn't eat
3 we didn't go   **7** we didn't take
4 I didn't buy   **8** We didn't have
5 My friend didn't get

Exercise 5

- Students work individually, completing the text.
- Make sure students understand that they need to use both Past simple and Present simple verbs in the text.
- Check answers as a class.

Answers

4 has   **8** didn't go to bed
5 didn't have   **9** went to bed
6 had   **10** rides
7 goes to bed   **11** didn't ride

Exercise 6

- Students write three sentences about things that changed their lives using the Past simple.
- Monitor and point out errors for students to self-correct.

Answers

Students' own answers.

Extra activity

Students write an additional two false sentences about things that changed their lives. They then work in pairs, reading their sentences from Exercise 6 and including their false sentences and deciding if each other's sentences are true or false. Monitor but do not interrupt fluency unless they make mistakes with the Past simple verb forms. Ask some students to say their sentences for the class to hear. The class tries to identify the false sentences.

Further practice:
Workbook pages 70 and 100–101

Brain Trainer Activity 2
See Teacher's Book page 217 and Students' Book page 119

Vocabulary   Clothes

Revision

First – Books closed. Give your students a ten-item spelling test. Students listen and write the following words:
1 take   **2** went   **3** work   **4** drank   **5** bought   **6** travel   **7** understood   **8** studied   **9** answer   **10** thought

Second – Check answers by asking individual students to write words on the board. Students self-correct and give themselves one point for each word they spell correctly. Drill the vocabulary for pronunciation and word stress.

Third – In pairs, students decide if the verbs are base verbs or Past simple and if they are regular or irregular. They then write the Past simple forms for the base verbs and vice-versa. Check answers as a class.
(Answers: regular base verbs – *work/worked*, *travel/travelled*, *answer/answered*; irregular base verbs – *take/took*; regular Past simple – *studied/study*; irregular Past simple – *went/go*, *drank/drink*, *bought/buy*, *understood/understand*, *thought/think*)

Exercise 1 (Track 3.18)

- In pairs, students match the words in the box with the pictures.
- Play the recording for students to listen, check and repeat.
- Repeat the recording. Pause after each word to check students' pronunciation.

Answers

2 jumper   **3** shoes   **4** T-shirt   **5** trousers   **6** boots   **7** coat   **8** scarf   **9** hat   **10** skirt   **11** shorts   **12** jeans   **13** pyjamas   **14** trainers   **15** sandals

Exercise 2 (Track 3.19)

- Students classify the clothes words according to the category.
- Play the recording for students to listen and check.

Answers

a *coat*, jumper, T-shirt
b jeans, shorts, skirt, trousers
c dress, pyjamas
d boots, sandals, shoes, trainers
e hat, scarf

Exercise 3

- Students choose the correct options.
- Check answers by asking individual students to read sentences from the text.

Answers

2 jumper   **3** boots   **4** coat   **5** scarf   **6** dress   **7** pyjamas

Exercise 4 (Track 3.20)

- Play the recording for students to listen and identify Ben's sister.

Answer

b Molly

Exercise 5

- Remind students of the use of the Present continuous to talk about actions happening now.
- Students work in pairs, choosing one person in the class and describing what they are wearing.
- Monitor but do not interrupt fluency unless they make mistakes with the clothes vocabulary or the Present continuous.

Extra activity

Stronger groups or fast finishers brainstorm all the clothes vocabulary which they already know. Students peer teach the vocabulary they have thought of. They then classify it in the same way as in Exercise 2, specifying the part of the body on which it is worn. Collate answers on the board along with the other vocabulary from the lesson by drawing a stick figure on the board and dividing it up as follows:

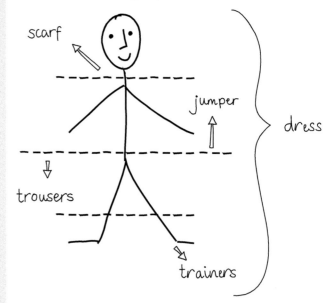

Include the five example words to help students place the vocabulary correctly on the diagram.

Further practice:
Workbook pages 71 and 111

Brain Trainer Activity 5
See Teacher's Book page 217 and Students' Book page 119

Vocabulary Clothes

1))) 3.18 **Match the pictures to these words. Then listen, check and repeat.**

boots	coat	dress *1*	hat	jeans
jumper	pyjamas	sandals	scarf	shoes
shorts	skirt	T-shirt	trainers	trousers

Word list page 111 **Workbook** page 111

2))) 3.19 **Copy and put the clothes words in Exercise 1 into the correct category. Then listen, check and repeat.**

a top half of body
   coat, …. , ….
b bottom half of body
   …. , …. , …. , ….
c whole body
   …. , ….
d feet
   …. , …. , …. , ….
e head and neck
   …. , ….

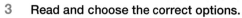

3 **Read and choose the correct options.**

In winter, I usually wear [1] *jeans / shorts*, a [2] *T-shirt / jumper* and [3] *sandals / boots*. When I go outside, I always wear a [4] *skirt / coat* and sometimes I have a [5] *hat / scarf* around my neck, as well. Today, it's very hot and sunny, so I'm wearing a summer [6] *jumper / dress*. My sister isn't feeling well so she's still in bed and she's wearing [7] *trainers / pyjamas*.

4))) 3.20 **Listen. Who is Ben's sister?**

   a Polly   **b** Molly   **c** Holly

5 **In pairs, choose one person in the class. Describe his/her clothes to your partner. Can he/she guess who it is?**

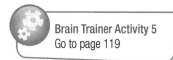
Brain Trainer Activity 5
Go to page 119

Chatroom Talking on the phone

Speaking and Listening

1 Look at the photo. Answer the questions.

   1 Is Julia happy or sad?
   2 What is Nick doing?

2))) **3.21** Listen and read the conversation. Answer the questions.

   1 Who is Mr Davies? *Nick's dad*
   2 Who does Julia want to speak to?
   3 Where is Julia?
   4 What does Julia want to do on Saturday?
   5 Where did Julia wear her scarf yesterday?
   6 What does Julia want to do this evening?

3 Act out the conversation in groups of three.

Mr Davies	Hello?
Julia	Hi, is that Nick?
Mr Davies	No, it isn't. This is his dad. Who's that?
Julia	Hi, Mr Davies, it's Julia. Can I speak to Nick, please?
Mr Davies	Hello, Julia! Hold on ... Nick! Just a minute ... here he is.
Nick	Hi, Julia, where are you?
Julia	I'm at home. Listen, I can't find my favourite purple scarf and I want to wear it on Saturday. Did I leave it at your house?
Nick	I don't know. Did you wear it at school yesterday?
Julia	Yes, I did. But it's not there. I checked this morning. Can I come to your house this evening? I want to look for it.
Nick	OK, see you later. Bye!
Julia	Bye!

Say it in your language ...
Just a minute.
Listen, ...

92

Chatroom   Talking on the phone

Revision

First – Revise clothes vocabulary with students. Say the word 'Vocabulary' and then use a 'silent approach' for the rest of this activity. Mime 'zipping' your mouth closed to make it clear that you are not going to speak. Pick up one student's notebook and look at the class then pick up the pen and pretend to write something down. Then point at the class to indicate that they must write things down.

Second – Hold up one finger to the class to indicate item number one then point clearly at one student's shoes. Point at the class and pretend to write something down. Monitor and check students understand the game before continuing.

Third – Continue holding up your fingers and pointing at clothes until you complete ten items. The items will vary depending on the season and what students are wearing. Limit the vocabulary to that covered on the previous Vocabulary page. 'Unzip' your mouth and check answers. Ask individual students to write answers on the board to check spelling. Students may also have used descriptive adjectives or even written complete sentences. Praise students for this, but do not give students who haven't written sentences the impression that they have done something wrong.

Speaking and Listening

Exercise 1

- Students look at the photos and answer the questions.
- They compare their ideas in pairs before checking answers as a class.

Answers

1 Julia is sad.
2 Nick is talking on the phone.

Brain Trainer Activity 1
See Teacher's Book page 217 and Students' Book page 119

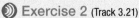 Exercise 2 (Track 3.21)

- Play the recording for students to listen and read.
- Individually, students answer the questions.
- They then check in pairs before you check answers as a class.

Answers

2 She wants to speak to Nick.
3 Julia is at home.
4 She wants to wear her favourite purple scarf.
5 She wore it at school.
6 She wants to go to Nick's house and look for her scarf.

Drill the conversation for correct pronunciation. Divide the class in three blocks, one to your left, one in the centre and one to your right. Tell the group on the left that they are going to be Mr Davies, the group in the centre that they are going to be Julia and the group on the right that they are going to be Nick. Build up the conversation step by step until students can perform it unprompted.
Change over the three groups and repeat the procedure twice so that all three groups have practised all three parts.

Exercise 3

- Divide the class into groups of three.
- Groups act out the conversation.
- Monitor and correct students' pronunciation as appropriate.
- Nominate one group to perform the conversation for the class.

Say it in your language ...

 Ask students to find the phrases in the conversation and look at them in context to try to deduce the meaning.

Just a minute. – informal phrase frequently used both on the phone and in other contexts to ask a person to wait for a moment. Care must be taken with the intonation in order not to appear irritated. You might use it in class if two students are asking for your attention at the same time, or a student might use it if you are starting to check an exercise and they haven't quite finished.

Listen, ... – phrase used to focus attention on something we are going to say which we consider to be important. Often used after the pleasantries at the beginning of a conversation to indicate that we are coming to the reason for the conversation. Often followed by a short pause to further emphasise what comes next.

Exercise 4

- Students refer back to the conversation to find the phrases.
- Check answers as a class.
- Drill the phrases for pronunciation and intonation.

Answers

Can I speak to Nick, please?
Hold on …

Exercise 5

- Read through the phrases for talking on the phone with the class.
- Drill the phrases for word stress and intonation.
- Students read the conversation again and find the phrases.

Pronunciation   Sounding polite

Language notes

This Pronunciation section highlights the importance of intonation. Students of many nationalities have problems sounding interested and polite in English due to the unintentional transfer of the intonation patterns of their own language to English. It is important therefore throughout the course to drill not only discrete items of vocabulary and grammar but also phrases and conversations so that students start to assimilate the intonation patterns of connected speech.

Exercise 6a (Track 3.22)

- Play the recording for students to listen and decide who is more polite.

Answer

Felicity

Exercise 6b (Track 3.22)

- Repeat the recording. Pause after each sentence to check students' pronunciation.

Extra activity

Drill the two conversations, with students changing roles so that they all play Henry, Gemma and Felicity. Exaggerate the intonation patterns with students so that they really note the difference between being polite and being rude.

Further practice:
Workbook page 124

Exercise 7 (Track 3.23)

- Play the recording for students to listen to the conversations.
- In pairs, students act out the conversations.
- Monitor and correct students' pronunciation as appropriate.

Further practice:
Workbook pages 72 and 120

Grammar   Past simple: questions

Language notes

Students may have problems with the pronunciation of the auxiliary *did* in question forms, particularly when it combines with subject pronouns. Their tendency is to pronounce them as two discrete items, when they are usually pronounced as one phonetic unit, e.g.
Did you … ? (/dɪdʒə/); Did he … ? (/dɪdɪ/).

Exercise 1

- Read the grammar table with students.
- Students work individually, completing the rule and referring back to the grammar table where necessary.

Answer

Did

Exercise 2 (Track 3.24)

- Students read the answers and complete the questions.
- Monitor and help with grammar if necessary.
- Play the recording for students to listen and check the questions.
- Drill the questions and the answers for pronunciation and intonation.

Answers

2 did you get   **3** did you do   **4** did you leave
5 Did you fly   **6** did you come

Exercise 3

- Read through the example with students.
- Individually, students write questions and answers.
- They then check in pairs before you check answers as a class.

Answers

B *Yes, I did, I had lunch with her. Then*, we went to the cinema.
A What film did you see?
B We saw the new Kristen Stewart film.
A Did you enjoy it?
B I didn't like it. I thought it was very boring.

Exercise 4

- Individually, students write questions about holidays using the ideas in the box.
- Check students' questions before they work in pairs, asking and answering questions about their favourite holidays.
- Monitor but do not interrupt fluency unless they make mistakes with the Past simple verb forms.

Further practice:
Workbook pages 73 and 100–101

Brain Trainer Activity 3
See Teacher's Book page 217 and Students' Book page 119

4 Look back at the conversation. How does Julia ask to speak to Nick? How does Mr Davies ask Julia to wait?

5 Read the phrases for talking on the phone.

> **Talking on the phone**
>
> Hi / Hello, is that …?
> Who's that?
> It's … .
> Can I speak to …, please?
> Hold on.
> Just a minute.
> Here he is.
> See you later.
> Bye!

Pronunciation   Sounding polite

6a))) 3.22 Listen. Who is more polite, Gemma or Felicity?

Henry	Hello.
Gemma	Hello, is that Frank?
Henry	No, it's Henry.
Gemma	Hi, Henry, it's Gemma. Can I speak to Frank, please?
Henry	Hello.
Felicity	Hello, Henry, it's Felicity.
Henry	Hi, Felicity.
Felicity	Can I speak to Frank, please?

b))) 3.22 Listen again and repeat.

7))) 3.23 Listen to the conversations. Act out the conversations in pairs.

Nick	Hello.
Leo	Hi, Nick, it's Leo. Can I speak to Ted, please?
Nick	Hold on.
Mrs Green	Hello.
Monica	Hello, is that Rebecca?
Mrs Green	No, it isn't. This is her mother.
Monica	Oh, sorry. Can I speak to Rebecca, please?
Mrs Green	Yes. Here she is.

Grammar   Past simple: questions

> **Questions and short answers**
>
> Did I/you/he/she/it/we/they **read** the book?
> Yes, I/you/he/she/it/we/they did.
> No, I/you/he/she/it/we/they didn't.

> ***Wh-* questions**
>
> Where did I/you/he/she/it/we/they **go** yesterday?
> I **went** to the cinema.

Grammar reference Workbook page 100

1 Study the grammar table. Complete the rule.

> We make Past simple questions with …. + *I / you / he / she / it / we / they* + verb.

2))) 3.24 Read Jamie's answers and complete the questions. Then listen and check.

1. Where *did you go* (go) last weekend?
   I went to Paris.
2. How …. there? (get)
   I flew there.
3. What …. in Paris? (do)
   I climbed the Eiffel Tower.
4. When …. ? (leave)
   I left on Sunday evening.
5. …. home? (fly)
   No, I didn't. I came home by coach.
6. Why …. home by coach? (come)
   Because I lost my plane ticket!

3 Make questions and answers.

A you / meet / Jane / yesterday?
B I / have / lunch with her. Then / we / go / to the cinema
A Did you meet Jane yesterday?
B Yes, I did. I had lunch with her. Then, …
A What / film / you / see?
B We / see / the new Kristen Stewart film
A you / enjoy it?
B I / not like / it. I / think / it / be / very boring

4 In pairs, find out about your partner's favourite holiday. Use these ideas.

do some painting	go kayaking
go rollerblading	go to museums
listen to music	meet up with friends
play football	stay in a hotel

93

Reading

1 Look at the photo. Where do you think these people live?

a in a village   b in a tent   c in a big city

AZAB'S JOURNEY

Azab is thirteen years old. He lives in Niger, in West Africa, but he doesn't live in a village or a town, and his family doesn't have a house. Azab is a Wodaabe nomad. There are more than 40,000 Wodaabe people in Niger. They live in simple tents and they travel every two or three days. They follow the rain and move to places with water and grass for their cattle. The cows are very important for the Wodaabe people because cows' milk is their main food. They make yoghurt and butter with the milk and when they are near a village, they sell the milk and buy other food.

Azab can't read or write, and he doesn't go to school. But last month he did an essential job for his family. 'I managed my family's herd,' said Azab. 'I walked with the cows every day. I watched them and I helped them when they were sick.'

Last year, Azab's family travelled more than 3,000 kilometres around West Africa. 'There was no rain,' said Azab. 'We went from one place to another place. We didn't find food and we were very hungry. It was a very difficult time.'

> **Key Words**
>
> | nomad | to follow | cattle |
> | essential | to manage | herd |

2 Read and check your answer to Exercise 1.

3 🔊 3.25   Read the text quickly. Choose the correct description.

Wodaabe nomads …
a live in villages in Niger and sell cows.
b travel around West Africa and don't have houses.
c move to different places because they don't have cows.

4 🔊 3.25   Read the text again. Answer the questions.

1 How old is Azab? *Azab is thirteen years old.*
2 How many Wodaabe people live in Niger?
3 Why do they move to different places?
4 What do they usually eat?
5 What did Azab do last month?
6 Why was life difficult for Azab's family last year?

Listening

1 🔊 3.26   Listen to Rose's conversation with Erik. Answer the questions.

1 Did she have a good day or a bad day?
2 Where is she now?

2 🔊 3.26   Listen again. Are the sentences true (T) or false (F)?

1 Rose got up late because she didn't hear her alarm clock.
2 Rose took the bus to school.
3 Rose liked her journey to school today.
4 Rose got to school late.
5 Rose's teacher was angry because she didn't have her homework.
6 Rose is doing her homework now.

◀ 94 ▶

Reading

The *Wodaabe nomads* described in the text are real people. Their annual journey from south to north takes place during the wet season from May to September. The character of Azab, whose name means 'wandering' in Arabic, is fictional.
Further information is available by searching the internet.

Exercise 1
- Draw attention to the photo and the text and ask students what they can see.
- Individually, students guess where the people live.

Exercise 2
- Make sure students understand not to read in detail at this point.
- Students scan the text quickly and check their answer to Exercise 1.

Answer

b

Key Words

Be prepared to focus on the Key Words, either by pre-teaching them, eliciting their meaning after students have read the text, or through dictionary or definition writing work.

nomad – a person who doesn't live in one place, but moves from place to place during the year

to follow – to go behind and on the same route

cattle – a general word referring to cows and similar animals

essential – something absolutely necessary

to manage – to be able to do something, often something quite difficult

herd – a group of cows together is referred to as a herd

Exercise 3 (Track 3.25)
- Students choose the correct description.
- If you wish, play the recording for students to listen and read.
- Check the answer as a class.

Answer

b

Exercise 4 (Track 3.25)
- Students read the text again and answer the questions.
- Check answers by asking pairs of students to read questions and answers.
- Elicit from stronger students or explain yourself the meaning of any new vocabulary.

Answers

2 More than 40,000 Wodaabe people live in Niger.
3 They follow the rain and move to places with water and grass for their cattle.
4 They usually eat cow's milk, yoghurt and butter.
5 He managed the family's herd/walked with the cows every day.
6 Because there was no rain and they didn't find food.

Extra activity

Give students the following definition as an example and ask them which of the Key Words it is:
This person moves from one place to another place. He or she doesn't have a permanent home. (Answer: *nomad*)
Individually or in pairs, students write definitions for the other words in the box. Monitor and help with vocabulary and grammar if necessary.
(Possible answers: *to follow – This is an action. To go after a thing or a person.*; *cattle – This is a general word. It means cow but it's uncountable.*; *essential – This describes something very, very important. You can't live if you don't have this thing.*; *to manage – This is an action. It is to control something.*; *herd – This is a group of cows altogether.*)

Listening

Exercise 1 (Track 3.26)
- Play the recording for students to listen and answer the gist questions.
- Check answers as a class.

Answers

1 She had a bad day.   2 She's at home.

Audioscript:
See Teacher's Book page 226

Exercise 2 (Track 3.26)
- Repeat the recording for students to decide if the sentences are true or false.
- They then compare their answers in pairs.
- Ask students to correct the false sentences.

Answers

1 True
2 False (She rode her bike.)
3 False (It rained and she arrived at school really wet and cold.)
4 True
5 False (Her teacher was angry because she was late.)
6 False (She left her homework at school.)

Further practice:
Workbook page 74

Writing   A travel diary

Revision

First – Write the following items from the unit on the board and ask students to unscramble them (answers in brackets): *ryrol* (lorry), *premuj* (jumper), *costore* (scooter), *rainrest* (trainers), *danlass* (sandals), *ajamspy* (pyjamas), *cheerpilot* (helicopter), *boretimok* (motorbike)

Second – Check answers and spelling by asking individual students to write words on the board.

Third – In pairs, students make their own scrambled words using vocabulary from the Students' Book. They change their words with another pair and try to unscramble them.

Cultural notes

- *New Delhi* is the capital of India. It has a population of nearly 300,000 and is growing fast. It is within the larger administrative region of Delhi, which has a population of nearly 17 million.
- *Lodi Gardens* is a vast park complex in Delhi which contains numerous tombs and various other historically important buildings.
- *Dilli Haat* market in Delhi sells both foods and handicrafts and has sections for each state of India showcasing everything the country has to offer.
- *Agra* has a population of over 1.5 million. The Taj Mahal, its most famous monument, gets over three million visitors a year.
- *The Taj Mahal* was started in 1632 by emperor Shah Jahan in memory of his wife, Mumtaz Mahal. The mausoleum complex with its gardens and reflective pools was finished in 1653. It is one of the most famous buildings in the world.

Exercise 1

- Read the Writing File with students.

Exercise 2

- Students read the travel diary and match the paragraphs to the descriptions.
- Check answers as a class.

Answers

1 C   2 B   3 A

Exercise 3

- Individually, students answer the questions.
- They then compare their answers in pairs.
- If you have a world map available, ask students where Delhi and Agra are.

Answers

2 Yes, he did.
3 They listened to the guide and walked around the building.
4 No, they didn't.

Exercise 4

- Students work individually, dividing the text into three paragraphs.
- They then compare their ideas in pairs before you check answers as a class.

Answer

Tuesday

We got up early today and walked to the Dilli Haat market. The market is very close to our hotel. Dilli Haat market is very interesting. You can buy lots of different things there. I loved the clothes and my sister liked the food!

We took a bus from the market to Lodi Gardens. They are very beautiful. We had a picnic and watched the birds.

I really liked the shopping in the morning and the gardens were amazing.

Exercise 5

- If your students have not travelled very extensively, brainstorm information about students' home town(s) on the board and encourage them to write from the point of view of a tourist visiting their city.
- Explain that students should only make notes at this point or write short sentences.
- Encourage students to ask you for any vocabulary they need.

Answers

Students' own answers

Exercise 6

- Read through the 'My diary' writing guide. Tell students that they should now organise their notes into clear paragraphs.
- Draw students' attention to the 'Remember!' checklist.

Answers

Students' own answers.

Extra activity

Add an extra 10–15 vocabulary items from this unit to the collection of Word cards.

Revise all the vocabulary by organising a peer test. Give each student in the class two or three cards. They can look at the cards but must not show them to anyone else. Write the following questions on the board:
How do you say ... in English?
How do you spell it?
Demonstrate with one or two vocabulary cards, using students' L1 in the first question. Students move around the classroom, ask the questions and find out how many of their classmates can remember the words and spell them correctly. Take feedback as a class and identify any words students have particular problems remembering.

Further practice:
Workbook page 75

Writing   A travel diary

1   Read the Writing File.

2   Read the travel diary. Match the paragraphs (A–C) to the descriptions (1–3).

1   Summary of the day
2   Description of the Taj Mahal
3   Description of the journey to Agra

My Indian Diary by Jamie Weller
Monday

A   Today we travelled 200 kilometres from Delhi to the Taj Mahal in Agra. We went by bus and the journey took three hours. It was very hot and there were a lot of people, but we enjoyed the trip.

B   When we arrived at the Taj Mahal, we were amazed. It looks beautiful in photographs, but it's more beautiful in real life! Our guide talked about the history of the building and then we walked around it.

C   We returned to Delhi in the evening. We were very tired when we got back to our hotel, but it was a fantastic day. The Taj Mahal is awesome!

3   Read the diary again. Answer the questions.

1   How far is Agra from Delhi? *It is 200 kilometres.*
2   Did Jamie like travelling on the bus?
3   What did they do when they arrived at the Taj Mahal?
4   Did they stay in Agra on Monday night?

4   Read the text and divide it into paragraphs.

paragraph 1 Description of the market
paragraph 2 Description of the Lodi Gardens
paragraph 3 Summary of the day

Tuesday

We got up early today and walked to the Dilli Haat market. The market is very close to our hotel. Dilli Haat market is very interesting. You can buy lots of different things there. I loved the clothes and my sister liked the food! We took a bus from the market to Lodi Gardens. They are very beautiful. We had a picnic and watched the birds. I really liked the shopping in the morning and the gardens were amazing.

5   Imagine you are on holiday. Answer the questions.

1   What did you see?
2   What did you buy?
3   Did you enjoy the experience? Why?/Why not?

Places to visit
museums / interesting buildings / the seaside / an amusement park / a palace / a park / gardens
Adjectives
Positive: interesting / amazing / great
Negative: noisy / horrible / dirty
Things to do
buy souvenirs / swim in the sea / visit museums

6   Write your travel diary. Use 'My diary' and your notes from Exercise 5.

My diary

paragraph 1
Yesterday / Last summer / Last weekend I went to … .
We went by bus / train / plane.
We saw … .
paragraph 2
I / My sister / My mother bought … .
paragraph 3
It was interesting / great / terrible … .

 Remember!
● Divide your writing into paragraphs.
● Use the vocabulary in this unit.
● Check your grammar, spelling and punctuation.

Refresh Your Memory!

Grammar Review

1 **Choose the correct options.**

1 I *didn't understand* / *not understood* the homework, so I *didn't do* / *not did* it.
2 Mary *speak* / *spoke* to Jason yesterday.
3 We *saw* / *see* your cousin on his motorbike this morning.
4 He *go* / *went* to Rome by plane.
5 My friends *didn't* / *don't* take the bus to school yesterday, they *take* / *took* the train.

2 **Complete the text with the Past simple form of the verbs.**

Last Saturday I ¹ *had* (have) a picnic with my uncle and my cousins. We ² .... (drink) fruit smoothies and we ³ .... (have) some delicious sandwiches. After the food, we all ⁴ .... (sing) songs together. It ⁵ .... (be) a wonderful day.

3 **Put the words in order to make questions.**

1 my message / Did / you / to Tom / give / ?
   Did you give my message to Tom?
2 you / at the supermarket / did / What / buy / ?
3 your friends / at midnight / leave / the party / Did / ?
4 books / How many / read / last year / you / did / ?
5 Sarah / in the Maths test / get / 100% / Did / ?
6 last summer / Where / go / did / on holiday / you / ?

4 **Make questions and answers.**

1 you / go to the park / yesterday?
   No. I / go to the sports centre
   Did you go to the park yesterday?
   No, I didn't. I went to the sports centre.
2 you / play tennis with Peter / at the sports centre?
   No. we / go swimming
3 you and Peter / have lunch / at the café?
   No. we / have lunch / at Peter's house
4 you / take the bus home / after lunch?
   No. I / walk / home
5 you / do your homework / in the afternoon?
   No. I / listen / to music
6 you / send an email to your friend / in the evening?
   No. I / phone my friend

Vocabulary Review

5 **Complete the transport sentences with the missing letters.**

1 *Cars*, l _ _ _ _ _ _ and v _ _ _ d _ _ _ _ on land.
2 B _ _ _ _ s _ _ _ at sea.
3 P _ _ _ _ _ and h _ _ _ _ _ _ _ _ _ _ f _ _ in the air.

6 **Read and match.**

1 You wear these on your feet when you play sport.   **a** dress
2 You wear these on your feet in the summer.   **b** sandals
3 You wear this on the top half of your body.   **c** scarf
4 You wear them in bed.   **d** trainers
5 Girls wear this.
6 You wear this on your head.   **e** jumper
7 You wear this round your neck.   **f** trousers
8 You wear them on your legs.   **g** hat
                                                          h pyjamas

Speaking Review

7 🔊 3.27 **Complete the phone conversation with these words. Then listen and check.**

Bye	Can I speak	hold on
~~is that~~	See you later	Who's speaking

Tina Hello.
James Hello, ¹ *is that* Maddy?
Tina No, it's Tina. ² .... , please?
James Hi Tina, it's James. ³ .... to Maddy, please?
Tina Yes, ⁴ .... . Here she is.
Maddy Hi James.
James Hi Maddy, I'm bored. Can I come round to your house this afternoon?
Maddy Yes, of course.
James OK, then. ⁵ .... . Bye.
Maddy ⁶ .... .

Dictation

8 🔊 3.28 **Listen and write in your notebook.**

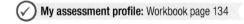 **My assessment profile:** Workbook page 134

 96

Refresh Your Memory!

Exercise 1

> **Answers**
>
> **2** spoke   **3** saw   **4** went   **5** didn't, took

Exercise 2

> **Answers**
>
> **2** drank   **3** had   **4** sang   **5** was

Exercise 3

> **Answers**
>
> **2** What did you buy at the supermarket?
> **3** Did your friends leave the party at midnight?
> **4** How many books did you read last year?
> **5** Did Sarah get 100% in the Maths test?
> **6** Where did you go on holiday last summer?

Exercise 4

> **Answers**
>
> **2** Did you play tennis with Peter at the sports centre?
>   No, I didn't. We went swimming.
> **3** Did you and Peter have lunch at the café?
>   No, we didn't. We had lunch at Peter's house.
> **4** Did you take the bus home after lunch?
>   No, I didn't. I walked home.
> **5** Did you do your homework in the afternoon?
>   No, I didn't. I listened to music.
> **6** Did you send an email to your friend in the evening?
>   No, I didn't. I phoned my friend.

Exercise 5

> **Answers**
>
> **1** *Cars*, lorries and vans drive on land.
> **2** Boats sail at sea.   **3** Planes and helicopters fly in the air.

Exercise 6

> **Answers**
>
> **2** b   **3** e   **4** h   **5** a   **6** g   **7** c   **8** f

Exercise 7 (Track 3.27)

> **Answers**
>
> **2** Who's speaking   **3** Can I speak   **4** hold on
> **5** See you later   **6** Bye

Exercise 8 (Track 3.28)

> **Answers and Audioscript**
>
> Yesterday, I took a bus to the shopping centre. I bought a new jumper and a scarf. Then, I had lunch with a friend. After lunch I went home and wrote a letter to my uncle. What did you do yesterday? Did you go out or did you stay at home?

My assessment profile:
Workbook page 134

Extra activity

Revise the topic of journeys and the Past simple:
– Draw the holiday diary up but without the pictures. Tell students this is the story of your last holiday.
– Complete Monday with the plane, the Eiffel Tower the French flag and the frogs' legs and ask students to make questions, e.g. *'Did you go to Paris?'*, *'What did you eat?'*, *'What did you see?'*, etc. Answer the questions yourself. Remember to grade your language appropriately.
– Fill in Tuesday and encourage students to ask you more questions, e.g. *'Did you take a train to Rome?'*, *'What did you do?'*, etc.
– Complete the other days of the week. Students work in pairs, asking about the destinations and using their imagination where necessary. Monitor but do not interrupt fluency. Encourage students to be as inventive as possible.
– Write up the speech bubbles underneath the diary. As a class, nominate one student to start talking about the holiday in the first person. Explain that you are going to click your fingers and say a name and then the next student will have to continue the narration. Students should therefore listen very carefully to their classmates.
– Start the activity, clicking your fingers to change speaker. Ask questions if students cannot think of things to say. Keep changing speakers until all students have spoken at least once.
(Answers: *Monday–Paris*; *Tuesday–Rome*; *Wednesday–Greece*; *Thursday–New York*; *Friday–Mexico*; *Saturday–London*; *Sunday–home*).

Culture 6 – British Festivals and Customs:
See Teacher's Book page 224 and Students' Book page 126 (for extra reading, discussion and writing work).

Real World Profiles

Cultural notes

- *The Republic of Uganda* is a country in the east of Africa, on the Equator. It is landlocked, although the southern part of the country includes a significant part of Lake Victoria, the largest tropical lake in the world. Despite substantial natural resources, including untapped natural oil and gas, it remains one of the world's poorest countries due to poor economic policies and instability. In recent years the economy has improved slightly but the benefits have yet to be felt by the majority of the population.
- *Phiona Mutesi* (Uganda) is actually not sure when she was born, although the World Chess Federation has estimated it to be 1993. After both her father and older sister died, she left school as her family could no longer afford to pay for her to study. Thanks to the Sports Outreach Institute she learnt how to play chess and they continue to support her. Chess in Uganda is usually limited to those who have attended only the most elite schools so her success is exceptional and inspiring given the poverty of her family compared to the players she usually beats.

Exercise 1 (Track 3.29)

- Draw attention to the photos and the text and ask students what they can see.
- Students read the text and answer the questions. If you have a world map available, show students where Kampala in Uganda and Juba in Southern Sudan are.
- If you wish, play the recording for students to listen and read.
- Elicit from stronger students or explain yourself the meaning of any new vocabulary.

Answers

2 She learnt to play chess at her church.
3 She practised every evening at home with her brothers.
4 Some people laughed at her because her clothes were simple and she was poor.
5 Yes, she did.
6 She went to Juba in 2009, when she was 13 years old.
7 They came from 17 countries (16 other countries plus Uganda.).

Extra activity

Extend the work on inspiring people and ask students to investigate and write five sentences about a famous person (or a person they know) who has become successful despite personal difficulty or coming from a disadvantaged background. Examples include J.K. Rowling, Jim Carrey, Shania Twain and Hillary Swank.

Class discussion

- Read through the questions with students.
- They then work in pairs or small groups talking about the questions.
- Monitor but do not interrupt fluency.
- Take feedback as a class.
- Ideally the class discussion activity should be completed in English but you may want to support weaker students with some L1.

Extra activity

Ask students additional questions related to the topic of the text, e.g.
1 What other things do you know about Uganda?
2 Do you think it's a good part of the world to live in? Why/Why not?
3 Can you play chess? Do you play well? Are any of your friends good chess players?
4 Do you think sport can help change people's lives? Why/Why not?
5 Imagine you go to Uganda. What things are new or unusual for you?

In this unit have you ...

... used Grammar and Vocabulary worksheet?
... used Reading and Listening worksheet?
... used Writing worksheet?
... used Speaking worksheet?
... used Unit test?

With the exception of the Writing worksheets, all the Teacher's Resources are at two levels of difficulty:
*   For students who need extra help and support
** For students who require an additional challenge

Real World Profiles

Phiona Mutesi's profile

Age:
17

Home country:
Uganda

City:
Kampala

Reading

1 **3.29 Read about Phiona. Answer the questions.**

1 When did Phiona leave school?
When she was 8 years old.

2 Where did she learn to play chess?

3 How did she become good at the game?

4 Why did some people laugh at Phiona?

5 Did Phiona win the chess competition in 2007?

6 When did she go to Juba?

7 How many countries did the children at the competition come from?

Phiona's Journey

Phiona Mutesi is from a very poor part of Uganda and she left school when she was 8 years old. The following year, when she was 9, she joined a chess club at her church. Her brothers went there and she followed them. At first, she didn't know what chess was, but she liked the chess pieces! She practised every evening at home with her brothers and she soon became very good at the game.

In 2007, Phiona entered her first competition. She was 11 years old, and she played chess against people aged 18, 19 and 20. Some people laughed at her because her clothes were simple and she was poor. But she won the competition and people stopped laughing.

In 2009, when she was 13 years old, Phiona Mutesi made her first journey to another country. She travelled on a plane from her home, in Uganda, to Juba in Southern Sudan, to play chess in an international competition with children from 16 other countries. She won all her games and she won the girls' title.

Now she is the number 2 chess player in Uganda. Her teacher, Robert Katende, says, 'In chess, it does not matter where you come from. Only where you put the pieces.'

Class discussion

- Is there a chess club in your town or school?

- What do you like to do after school?

- Imagine Phiona's journey to Juba. What things were new or unusual for her?

9 Technology Time

Grammar	*Be going to;* Present continuous for future arrangements
Vocabulary	Technology; Technology phrases
Speaking	Asking for information
Writing	A story

Vocabulary Technology

1)) 3.30 **Match the objects in the photos to these words. Then listen, check and repeat.**

blog	broadband
digital radio	ebook *1*
IM (instant messaging)	interactive whiteboard
memory stick	netbook
screen	smartphone
social networking site	WiFi

Word list page 111   **Workbook** page 112

2 Complete the sentences with words from Exercise 1.

1 I did my homework on my home computer, then I took it to school on a m*emory stick*.
2 I don't use a laptop, I use a n .... because it's smaller.
3 You can talk to lots of friends and share photos on a s .... .
4 It's faster to go on the internet with b .... .
5 The s .... on a mobile phone is very small.
6 You can use a W .... internet connection in many different places.
7 My dad always listens to the sports news on his d .... .

3 Read the definition and say the word.

1 Teachers sometimes write on this in the classroom. *Interactive whiteboard*
2 This is a fast way to send short messages.
3 This is a mobile phone which has email and an MP3 player.
4 This isn't a paper book. It's electronic.
5 This is an online diary.

4 In pairs, ask and answer about technology.

Do you use IM?   *Yes, I sometimes / often use it.*

No, I never use it.

Brain Trainer Activity 3
Go to page 120

98

Unit contents

Vocabulary
→ Technology – *blog, broadband, digital radio, ebook, IM (instant messaging), interactive whiteboard, memory stick, netbook, screen, smartphone, social networking site, WiFi*
→ Technology phrases – *charge your mobile phone, chat online, download videos/music/films, go online, send a text, send emails, use a search engine, use the internet, use WiFi, write a blog*

Grammar
→ *Be going to* – affirmative, negative, questions and short answers
→ Present continuous for future arrangements

Communication
→ Asking for information
→ Writing a story – Review

Pronunciation
→ Weak form of *to*

Key competences
→ Linguistic competence
→ Data processing and digital competence
→ Interpersonal, social and civic competence
→ Learning-to-learn
→ Autonomy and personal initiative

Vocabulary   Technology

))) Exercise 1 (Track 3.30)
- Individually, students match the words and the pictures.
- Play the recording for students to listen and check.
- Repeat the recording. Pause after each word to check students' pronunciation.

Answers
2 netbook   8 smartphone
3 digital radio   9 WiFi
4 IM (instant messaging)   10 interactive whiteboard
5 memory stick   11 broadband
6 social networking site   12 screen
7 blog

Exercise 2
- Individually, students complete the sentences.
- They then check in pairs before you check answers as a class.
- Check answers by asking individual students to read the sentences.

Answers
2 netbook   5 screen
3 social networking site   6 WiFi
4 broadband   7 digital radio

Exercise 3
- In pairs, students match the definitions with words from Exercise 1.
- Check answers as a class.

Answers
2 IM (instant messaging)   3 smartphone   4 ebook
5 blog

Extra activity
Stronger groups or fast finishers work on definition writing technique. Individually or in pairs, students write definitions for the other seven words in the box in Exercise 1. Monitor and help with vocabulary and grammar if necessary. They swap their definitions with another pair and try to identify each other's words.

Exercise 4
- Ask two students to read aloud the example question and answers.
- Students work in pairs, asking and answering questions about technology.
- Monitor and help with vocabulary but do not interrupt fluency.

Extra activity
Set up a 'class survey'. Students prepare a table in their notebooks as follows:

	Yes	No
Question 1		
Question 2		
Question 3		

Use the question *'Have you got an ebook?'* as an example of a *yes/no* question about technology. Students think of three of their own *yes/no* questions using vocabulary from this lesson. They then ask all the students in the class their questions. Tell them they need only record the number of students who answer *yes* and *no*, not the names. When students finish, they prepare simple graphs to display the results and present these to the class.

Further practice:
Workbook pages 76 and 112

Brain Trainer Activity 3
See Teacher's Book page 218 and Students' Book page 120

Reading

Revision

First – Write the following word snake on the board:
wimemoryenetinteractivebroadsmartdigital

Second – Write a second word snake on the board:
bookstickradiobandwhiteboardbookfiphone

Third – Students match the word parts from the first word snake with the word parts from the second to make technology vocabulary. Check answers by asking individual students to write the words on the board. Make sure students are clear about whether the items are written as one or two words.
(Answers: *WiFi, memory stick, ebook, netbook, interactive whiteboard, broadband, smartphone, digital radio*)

Extra activity

Write the word *CLASSICS* vertically down the centre of the board. Add four dashes and a space before the first *C* of *CLASSICS* and eight dashes followed by a space and another eight dashes after to indicate letters. Pick individual students, asking them to say a letter. If the letter they choose is in the name, write it in the correct position. If it is not, write it in a column on one side of the board. When students think they know what the word is, they put their hands up. (Answer: *Hans Christian Andersen*)
Add two dashes followed by a space and another three dashes before the *L* of *CLASSICS* and three dashes after. Repeat the procedure. (Answer: *J K Rowling*). Continue working down the puzzle until students have completed all the names and the board looks as follows.

```
      HANS CHRISTIAN ANDERSEN
   JK ROWLING
            AA MILNE
            CS LEWIS
      CHARLES DICKENS
   JRR TOLKIEN
         LEWIS CARROLL
  WILLIAM SHAKESPEARE
```

Tell students that all these writers have written famous books and created famous characters. In pairs, students write down the names of some of the books they have written and/or the characters they have created. Take feedback as a class and ask students which of the books they have read. Ask if they read them in paper or ebook format.
(Possible answers: *Hans Christian Andersen – The Ugly Duckling, The Little Mermaid*; *J K Rowling – Harry Potter*; *A A Milne – Winnie the Pooh*; *C S Lewis – The Chronicles of Narnia*; *Charles Dickens – Oliver Twist, A Christmas Carol*; *J R R Tolkien – The Hobbit, The Lord of the Rings*; *Lewis Carroll – Alice's Adventures in Wonderland*; *William Shakespeare – Romeo and Juliet, Hamlet*)

Exercise 1

- Draw attention to the photo and the text and ask students what they can see.
- Individually, students answer the question.

Exercise 2

- Make sure students understand not to read in detail at this point.
- Students scan the text quickly to check their answer.

Answer

c

Exercise 3 (Track 3.31)

- Students read the text and add the sentences to the paragraphs.
- If you wish, play the recording for students to listen and read.
- Check answers as a class.

Answers

1 c   **2** b   **3** a

Exercise 4 (Track 3.31)

- Individually, students complete the sentences.
- Students check in pairs before you check answers as a class.
- Elicit from stronger students or explain yourself the meaning of any new vocabulary.

Answers

2 change   **3** soft   **4** pictures   **5** Japan
6 mobile phone   **7** short

Exercise 5

- Ask two students to read aloud the example question and answer.
- Check the pronunciation of the questions before students work in pairs.
- In pairs, students ask and answer the questions.
- Monitor and help with vocabulary but do not interrupt fluency.
- Take feedback as a class and find out how much consensus there is in the group about reading.

Extra activity

Stronger groups or fast finishers brainstorm ideas for a short 'ten-sentence' novel. They then write the beginning of a story in three sentences and give their story to another student. The other student adds the middle of the story in four more sentences and passes it to another student, who concludes the story in three sentences. Return each story to the student who started it for them to read.

Further practice:
Workbook page 77

Reading

1 Look at the text and the photos. What do you think the text is about?

  a The future of novels

  b Ebooks vs mobile phones

  c The future of reading

2 Read the text and check your answer to Exercise 1.

3 🔊 3.31 Read the text. Add sentences (a–c) to paragraphs (1–3).

  a Why don't you write one today?

  b They're going to be waterproof, too, so we can read them in the bath!

  c phone texts, instant messages and short messages on social networking sites.

4 🔊 3.31 Read the text again. Complete the sentences with one word from the text.

  1 These days people often read text on a *screen*.

  2 Soon, ebooks are going to ..... .

  3 Ebooks with flexible screens are ..... .

  4 In the future, ebooks can have 3D ..... .

  5 'Keitai' are popular in ..... .

  6 You read 'keitai' novels on a ..... .

  7 Twitter novels are very ..... .

5 What about you? In pairs, ask and answer.

  1 Do you read paper books or ebooks?

  2 Which is better, an ebook or a paper book?

  3 Can you write a Twitter novel?

> *Do you read paper books, ebooks or no books?*

> *I read paper books. I love reading!*

---

e-reading!

← → C ⌂

e - reading!

1 We use computers all the time and we read text on a screen every day – [1].... Many people use their mobile phone to read and some have ebooks. What do you use? What are you going to use in the future?

2 Ebooks are going to change in the future. We know that makers of ebooks are going to give them flexible screens so they're soft and easy to carry. [2].... But what are we going to see after that? Imagine a new generation of ebooks that can read you a story, books that can change colour, books with 3D pictures. All of them are going to be possible.

3 What about books for mobile phones? In Japan, 'keitai' are popular. These are very short novels for people to read on their mobile phones. Teenagers can become writers of 'keitai' novels. They also like the new fashion for Twitter novels. They're only 140 characters long – that's shorter than this paragraph! [3]....

◀ 99 ▶

Grammar *Be going to*

Affirmative		
I	'm (am)	going to read an ebook at the weekend.
You/We/They	're (are)	
He/She/It	's (is)	

Negative		
I	'm not (am not)	going to use IM this evening.
You/We/They	aren't (are not)	
He/She/It	isn't (is not)	

Questions and short answers		
Am	I	going to buy a laptop tomorrow?
Are	you/we/they	
Is	he/she/it	

Yes, I am. / No, I'm not.
Yes, you/we/they are. / No, you/we/they aren't.
Yes, he/she/it is. / No, he/she/it isn't.

Watch Out!

Use *be going to* with these expressions:
tomorrow / next week / next month / next year / soon

Grammar reference Workbook page 102

1 Study the grammar table. Complete the rules.

> 1 Before *going to* we use the verb ..... .
> 2 To make the negative, we add .... before *going to*.
> 3 In the question form, the first words are .... .

2 Complete the sentences with the affirmative of *be going to*.

> 1 I *'m going to stay* (stay) with my grandparents this summer.
> 2 Ella .... (climb) Sydney Harbour Bridge next month.
> 3 Nina's family .... (fly) to Rio de Janeiro at the weekend.
> 4 Omar and his mum .... (visit) the Leaning Tower of Pisa tomorrow.
> 5 My dad .... (run) a marathon next week.

3 The sentences in Exercise 2 are false. Rewrite them in the negative.

> 1 *I'm not going to stay with my grandparents this summer.*

4 You are going to interview people at a technology exhibition. Make questions.

> 1 you and your friends / look at / the new social networking site?
>
> *Are you and your friends going to look at the new social networking site?*
>
> 2 your dad / use / IM?
> 3 teacher / buy / an interactive whiteboard?
> 4 you / read / a blog?
> 5 your mum / change / her old mobile phone for a smartphone?
> 6 you / watch / a film on a big screen?

Pronunciation Weak form of *to*

5a))) 3.32 Listen to the word *to* in these questions.

> 1 Are you going to play on this new games console?
> 2 Is your dad going to buy a netbook?
> 3 Is your mum going to ask about broadband?
> 4 Are you going to listen to this digital radio?

b))) 3.32 Listen again and repeat.

6 In pairs, ask and answer the questions in Exercise 4.

7 What about you? In pairs, talk about three pieces of technology you're going to use this week.

> *I'm going to go on Facebook this evening. It's my favourite social networking site.*

> *I'm going to write a blog on the internet about my school.*

Grammar *Be going to*

Language notes

This unit introduces both *be going to* to talk about
intentions and future plans and the Present continuous
to talk about future arrangements. Students are often
not clear about the difference. In the unit students are
never actively required to distinguish between the two
forms in any one exercise as each is covered in isolation.
However, you might need to help students understand
that by *intentions and future plans* we mean actions
that we want to do but which are not concrete, i.e. they
don't involve buying tickets, planning with other people
or confirmation of any type. By *future arrangements* we
mean activities which have in some way been confirmed,
either by making a specific arrangement about the day
and the time with another person, or by buying tickets or
by formally confirming that we will do something.

Exercise 1

* Read the grammar table with students.
* Students work individually, completing the rules and
referring back to the grammar table where necessary.

Answers

1 be (am/is/are) 2 not 3 Am/Are/Is

Exercise 2

* Individually, students complete the sentences.
* Check answers by asking individual students to write
answers on the board.

Answers

2 's/is going to climb
3 is/are going to fly
4 are going to visit
5 's/is going to run

Exercise 3

* Students change the sentences from affirmative to
negative.
* Monitor and help with grammar if necessary.
* Check answers by asking individual students to read
the sentences.

Answers

2 Ella isn't/is not going to climb Sydney Harbour Bridge
next month.
3 Nina's family isn't/is not/aren't/are not going to fly to
Rio de Janeiro at the weekend.
4 Omar and his mum aren't/are not going to visit the
Leaning Tower of Pisa tomorrow.
5 My dad isn't/is not going to run a marathon next week.

Exercise 4

* Students make the questions.
* Check answers as a class.

Answers

2 Is your dad going to use IM?
3 Is your teacher going to buy an interactive whiteboard?
4 Are you going to read a blog?
5 Is your mum going to change her old mobile phone for a
smartphone?
6 Are you going to watch a film on a big screen?

Pronunciation   Weak form of *to*

Language notes

For students, one of the many barriers to fully
understanding native speakers is the pronunciation of the
numerous weak forms involving the schwa (/ə/), e.g. *of*
/əv/, *for* /fə/, *a* /ə/, *an* /ən/, *the* /ðə/, etc. It is important
therefore throughout the course to drill not only discrete
items of vocabulary and grammar but also phrases and
conversations so that students start to assimilate how
these words are pronounced as part of a stream of
connected speech.

Exercise 5a (Track 3.32)

* Play the recording for students to listen to
pronunciation of the word *to*.
* Write /tə/ on the board and drill it, making sure that
students understand that in the questions it is
unstressed.

Exercise 5b (Track 3.32)

* Repeat the recording for students to listen and
repeat. Pause after each sentence to check students'
pronunciation.

Further practice:
Workbook page 124

Exercise 6

* Drill the questions in Exercise 4 for pronunciation and
intonation, paying particular attention to the weak form
of *to*.
* In pairs, students ask and answer the questions.

Exercise 7

* Ask two students to read aloud the example question
and answer.
* Students work in pairs, asking and answering questions
about technology.
* Monitor but do not interrupt fluency unless students
make mistakes with the pronunciation of the questions
or *going to*.

Further practice:
Workbook pages 78 and 102–103

Brain Trainer Activity 2
See Teacher's Book page 218 and Students' Book page 120

Vocabulary   Technology phrases

Revision

First – Write the following sentences from the Reading text on the board:

1 Many people use their mobile phone <u>to</u> read.   /tə/
2 We read text on <u>a</u> screen every day.   /ə/
3 These are very short novels <u>for</u> people to read on their mobile phones.   /fə/
4 We use computers all <u>the</u> time.   /ðə/
5 All <u>of</u> them are going to be possible.   /əv/
6 That's shorter <u>than</u> this paragraph.   /ðən/
7 Teenagers <u>can</u> become writers of keitai novels.   /kən/
8 What <u>are</u> we going to see after that?   /ə/

In pairs, students read the sentences and try to agree how the underlined words are pronounced.

Second – Read the sentences for students to listen and repeat. Make sure you pronounce the underlined weak forms correctly. Ask students to identify what sound is common to all eight words.

Third – Write the phonetic symbols for the weak forms in a column next to each sentence and write the schwa symbol (/ə/) in large letters to the right. Explain that this is the most common sound in spoken English. Drill the sentences for pronunciation and sentence stress.

Exercise 1 (Track 3.33)
• Students look at the pictures and complete the technology phrases.
• Play the recording for students to listen and check.
• Repeat the recording. Pause after each sentence to check students' pronunciation.

Answers

2 use 3 use 4 send 5 send 6 chat 7 write
8 download 9 use 10 charge

Extra activity

Stronger groups or fast finishers write out the vocabulary in two columns (the verbs on the left and the nouns on the right), e.g.
go   online
use   WiFi
use   the internet
etc.
They memorise it for one minute. Students then test themselves or their partner by covering first the column of verbs and then the column of nouns and seeing how many technology phrases they can remember.

Exercise 2
• In pairs, students choose words from Exercise 1 to complete the sentences.
• Check answers as a class.

Answers

1 *email*, a text
2 videos, music, films
3 blog/email/text
4 online
5 WiFi, search engine, internet
6 mobile phone

Exercise 3
• Read through the example with students.
• Remind them of the use of *going to* to talk about intentions.
• Monitor and check students' spelling and grammar.
• Students take turns telling the class their sentences.

Answers

Students' own answers

Extra activity

In pairs, students make a wordsearch using words from both Vocabulary pages in the unit. They draw a grid, ten squares by ten squares and include ten items from the unit. They then complete the remaining squares with random letters. They swap their puzzles with another pair and try to find each other's words.

Further practice:
Workbook pages 79 and 112

Brain Trainer Activity 4
See Teacher's Book page 218 and Students' Book page 120

Vocabulary Technology phrases

1 🔊 **3.33** Complete the technology phrases with these verbs. Then listen, check and repeat.

| charge | chat | download | ~~go~~ | send (x2) | use (x3) | write |

> **Word list** page 111 **Workbook** page 112

1 *Go* **online** today – buy a ticket for the technology fair.

2 You can .... **WiFi** to play the latest games. They're really exciting!

3 You can .... **the internet** on a super-fast broadband connection.

4 You can .... **emails** to our technology experts and ask your technology questions.

5 You can .... **a text** to our technology competition – the prize is a netbook!

6 You can .... **online** to a sports star, a pop star and an actor! Ask them a question!

7 You can .... **a blog** about your day – take some photos, too.

8 You can .... **videos, music and films** – it's all free today!

9 You can learn how to .... a new **search engine**.

10 You can .... **your mobile phone** with a solar-powered charger – it uses energy from the sun!

2 Choose words from Exercise 1 to complete each sentence.

1 People can send information by *email* or .... .
2 You can download .... , ... or .... from the internet.
3 You can write a .... .
4 You can chat .... to a pop star.
5 You can use .... , a .... or the .... .
6 You charge your .... with a solar-powered charger.

3 **What about you? Imagine you are at a technology fair. Choose some activities to do. Make a list. Tell the class.**

Morning   *use WiFi to play games, … .*
Afternoon   *download films, … .*
Evening   *write, … .*

> *In the morning, I'm going to use WiFi to play games.*

 **Brain Trainer Activity 4**
Go to page 120

101 ▶

Chatroom Asking for information

Speaking and Listening

1 **Look at the photo. Where are Monica, Julia and Nick?**
   a at the Wildlife Club
   b at a radio station
   c at school

2))) **3.34** **Listen and read the conversation. Are the sentences true (T) or false (F)?**
   1 The Wildlife Club helped some animals last week. *F*
   2 The council wanted to build a road in Willow End.
   3 The club sent photos to a newspaper.
   4 The council decided not to build at Willow End.
   5 There are five people in the club.
   6 The club isn't looking for new members.

3 **Act out the conversation in groups of four.**

DJ	Welcome to Radio X! I'm talking to a Wildlife Club today. Hi guys! Now, last month your Wildlife Club helped some animals. Can you tell us more?
Julia	Yes, we found rare otters in Willow End, but the council wanted to build a new neighbourhood there.
DJ	What happened?
Nick	We took photos of the otters to the newspaper and the council aren't building it now.
DJ	That's brilliant! Now, tell me about your club.
Monica	Well, it's small – four people … and a dog!
DJ	And what are you planning?
Julia	Well, this summer we're making a nature reserve for the otters, so we're looking for more members.
DJ	OK, we're helping the club to find more members, so phone in now!
Nick	Thank you.

Say it in your language …
That's brilliant!
Well, …

102

Chatroom   Asking for information

Revision

First – Quickly review the pronunciation of the alphabet with the class, paying particular attention to any letters which habitually cause problems to your learners. Then write the word *ebook* on the board. Ask students to spell it for you chorally. Draw an arrow under the word pointing from the end to the beginning and ask students to spell it again backwards.

Give your students a ten-item backward spelling test. Check students understand the game before continuing. Spell the following words starting at the end:

1 blog   (g o l b)
2 screen   (n e e r c s)
3 netbook   (k o o b t e n)
4 go online   (e n i l n o   o g)
5 download   (d a o l n w o d)
6 broadband   (d n a b d a o r b)
7 smartphone   (e n o h p t r a m s)
8 digital radio   (o i d a r   l a t i g i d)
9 memory stick   (k c i t s   y r o m e m)
10 search engine   (e n i g n e   h c r a e s)

Second – Check answers by asking individual students to write words on the board. Students self-correct and give themselves one point for each word they spell correctly. Drill the vocabulary for pronunciation and word stress.

Third – In pairs, students spell other words from the course backwards. Monitor and help with the pronunciation of the alphabet if necessary.

Speaking and Listening

Exercise 1

- Draw attention to the photo and ask students what they can see.
- Check the answer as a class.

Answer

b

Brain Trainer Activity 1
See Teacher's Book page 218 and Students' Book page 120

 ### Exercise 2 (Track 3.34)

- Before playing the recording, check students understand the meaning of *council* and *neighbourhood*.
- Individually, students decide if the sentences are true or false.
- They then check in pairs before you check answers as a class. When checking answers, ask students to correct the false sentences.

Answers

1 *False* (The Wildlife Club helped some animals last month.)
2 False (The council wanted to build a new neighbourhood in Willow End.)
3 False (The Club took photos to a newspaper.)
4 True
5 False (There are four people and a dog.)
6 False (The club is looking for new members.)

Exercise 3

- Divide the class into groups of four.
- Groups act out the conversation.
- Monitor and correct students' pronunciation as appropriate.
- Nominate one group to perform the conversation for the class.

Say it in your language …

Ask students to find the phrases in the conversation and look at them in context to try to deduce the meaning.

That's brilliant! – used to respond to a piece of good news or something positive which someone has done. You might use it in class while monitoring students' work if a student has done something particularly well. Shouldn't be overused in order not to undermine its value.

Well, … – common hesitation device, giving the speaker a moment to formulate what he or she is going to say. Sounds better than 'Ummm …' and 'Errr …' which convey a sense of the speaker having no idea what to say next.

Extra activity

Stronger groups work in pairs or threes and prepare a radio interview about a club which they are part of. This can be real or fictional. They then perform their conversations for the class.

Exercise 4

- Students read the conversation again and find the phrases.
- Check answers as a class.

Answers

2 DJ   **3** DJ   **4** DJ   **5** Monica   **6** DJ   **7** Julia

Exercise 5

- Students refer back to the conversation and find the phrases.
- Drill the phrases for pronunciation and intonation.

Answers

1 Can you tell us more?; Tell me about your club.
2 What are you planning?

Exercise 6

- Read the phrases for asking for information with the class.

Exercise 7 (Track 3.35)

- Play the recording for students to listen to the conversations.
- In pairs, students act out the conversations.
- Monitor and correct students' pronunciation as appropriate.

Exercise 8

- Students make their own conversations by replacing the words in purple.
- Monitor but do not interrupt fluency unless students make mistakes with the phrases for asking for information.
- Stronger groups or fast finishers can use their own ideas to make more situations.
- Nominate two or three pairs to perform some of their conversations for the class.

Further practice:
Workbook pages 80 and 121

Grammar   Present continuous for future arrangements

Exercise 1

- Read the grammar table with students.

Exercise 2

- Students read the conversations and complete them with the Present continuous affirmative or negative.
- They then compare their answers in pairs.
- Check answers by asking pairs of students to read the conversations.

Answers

A Are *you wearing* fancy dress to Oscar's party next week?
B No, I'm not going in fancy dress.
A I'm staying at home tonight. What about you? Are you going out?
B Yes, I am. I'm helping the Wildlife Club.
A Emma isn't coming to school tomorrow.
B Why not?
A Because she's flying to Milan with her parents.

Exercise 3

- Individually, students write sentences about the people.
- Monitor and help with grammar if necessary.

Answers

Students' own answers

Exercise 4

- Ask two students to read aloud the example question and answer.
- Make sure students understand how to form the other questions.
- They then work in pairs, asking and answering the questions.
- Monitor but do not interrupt fluency unless they make mistakes with the Present continuous.

Extra activity

Choose a famous person who is known to your students and prepare six phrases about his or her future arrangements, e.g.
David Beckham
1 I'm going to my house in Beverly Hills on Tuesday.
2 I'm going shopping with Victoria on Saturday.
3 I'm playing football on Sunday.
Read the sentences to the class. Students guess who you are talking about. In pairs, students choose another famous person and prepare six sentences about him or her.
Monitor and point out errors for students to self-correct.
Ask pairs to say their sentences for the class to hear. Students guess who their classmates are talking about.

Further practice:
Workbook pages 81 and 102–103

4 **Look back at the conversation. Who says what?**

1 Can you tell us more? *DJ*
2 What happened?
3 That's brilliant!
4 Tell me about your club.
5 Well, it's small.
6 What are you planning?
7 Well, this summer we're making a nature reserve.

5 **Look back at the conversation again. What phrases does the DJ use to ask about these things?**

1 the club
2 the club's plans for the summer

6 **Read the phrases for asking for information.**

Past	Present	Future
What happened?	Can you tell us more? Tell me about …	What are you planning?

7 🔊 **3.35** **Listen to the conversations. Act out the conversations in pairs.**

Kenji I'm not going on holiday this summer.
May Oh, what are you planning?
Kenjl I'm ¹ seeing my friends every day.

Tom I got a really bad mark for my ² Maths homework.
Olivia Why? What happened?
Tom Oh, I didn't understand the question.

Erin I started a brilliant blog last week.
Luke Really? Tell me about it.
Erin Well, it's about ³ social networking sites.

8 **Work in pairs. Replace the words in purple in Exercise 7. Use these words and/or your own ideas. Act out the conversations.**

What are you planning this summer?

I'm travelling to the mountains.

1 writing a blog / chatting online / going to the swimming pool

2 English homework / Science test / History essay

3 the internet / downloading music / using a search engine

Grammar   Present continuous for future arrangements

Affirmative		
I	'm (am)	
You/We/They	're (are)	going to a party tonight.
He/She/It	's (is)	
Negative		
I	'm not (am not)	
You/We/They	aren't (are not)	playing basketball tomorrow.
He/She/It	isn't (is not)	
Questions and short answers		
Are	you/we/they	watching a film tonight?
Is	he/she/it	
Yes, I am. / No, I'm not.		
Yes, you/we/they are. / No, you/we/they aren't.		
Yes, he/she/it is. / No, he/she/it isn't.		

▶ **Grammar reference** Workbook page 102

1 **Study the grammar table.**

2 **Complete the conversations with the Present continuous affirmative or negative.**

A Are *you wearing* (you / wear) fancy dress to Oscar's party next week?
B No, …. (I / not / go) in fancy dress.

A I …. (stay / at home) tonight. What about you? Are …. (you / go) out?
B Yes, I am. I …. (help) the Wildlife Club.

A Emma …. (not / come) to school tomorrow.
B Why not?
A Because …. (she / fly) to Milan with her parents.

3 **What are these people doing this week and at the weekend?**

1 You
2 Your friend
3 You and your friends
4 Your teacher

4 **In pairs, ask and answer the questions in Exercise 3.**

What are you doing this weekend?

I'm going to a new dance class.

◀ 103 ▶

Reading

1 **Look at the text. What is it?**
   a a phone conversation
   b an interview
   c a chatroom discussion

Technology-free week!

Remember, next week is the last week of term and the school is having an official 'technology-free' week – so the chatroom is going offline. How are YOU going to live without technology? Tell us your plans for 'technology-free' week here!

Comments ▼

Why are you doing this to us? I think it's crazy. In fact, it's not possible! I'm going to go mad! I can't live without my MP3 player. It's going to be soooo difficult. I'm going to sing songs all week.
Skaterboy

Last year I went on holiday to a farm. There wasn't any TV and we didn't have a computer. I can live without these things, but it isn't fun! I'm going to do lots of sport next week.
Anya12

I'm going to read ... and eat. In the evenings my friends and I are going to have parties. We're going to play music on the radio – is that OK? Is that technology?
Madmax

In my opinion technology is a problem. We sit around all day and we don't do sport. We don't talk. We can't hear because we have earphones in our ears all day. Technology-free week is a great idea! I think it's fun, too. Are you going to film us?
Smiley

Key Words		
technology-free	offline	live without
crazy	mad	earphones

2 **Read and check your answer to Exercise 1.**

3 🔊 3.36 **Read the text. Are the sentences true (T) or false (F)?**
   1 Skaterboy likes the idea of 'technology-free' week. *F*
   2 Skaterboy is going to study all week.
   3 Anya12 thinks life without technology is great.
   4 Anya12 is going to go to a farm.
   5 Madmax is going to have lots of parties.
   6 Smiley agrees with 'technology-free' week.

4 🔊 3.36 **Read the text again. Answer the questions.**
   1 What is a technology-free week?
      A week where you can't use technology.
   2 Is Skaterboy happy with the idea?
   3 What is Anya12 going to do?
   4 What is Madmax going to play music on?
   5 Why does Smiley think that technology is a problem?

Listening

1 🔊 3.37 **Listen to the interview. Which words do you hear?**

chat	download	email	novel
online	search engine	WiFi	

2 🔊 3.37 **Listen again. Answer the questions.**
   1 Speaker A is going to:
      a learn to use a computer.
      b work for his dad.
      c help his grandad.
   2 Speaker B is going to:
      a go online every day.
      b teach her friends tennis.
      c go to the beach.
   3 Speaker C is going to:
      a write a short story.
      b read a 'keitai' novel.
      c write a 'Twitter' novel.

104

Reading

Exercise 1

- Draw attention to the pictures and the text and ask students what they can see.
- Individually, students decide what they think the text is.

Exercise 2

- Students scan the text quickly and check their answers.

Answer

c

Key Words

Be prepared to focus on the Key Words, either by pre-teaching them, eliciting their meaning after students have read the text, or through dictionary or definition writing work.

technology-free – without technology, the suffix '-free' used in this position always means 'without'

offline – not connected to the internet, the opposite of 'online'

live without – expression used to say something is not strictly necessary for us to survive (the opposite, *can't live without*, is a non-literal expression used to say that something is very, very important to us)

crazy – something or someone very strange, unusual or ridiculous

mad – a synonym of 'crazy', something or someone very strange, unusual or ridiculous

earphones – small objects which we put in our ears to listen to music privately

---

Exercise 3 (Track 3.36)

- Individually, students decide if the sentences are true or false.
- If you wish, play the recording for students to listen and read.
- Students check in pairs before you check answers as a class. When checking answers, ask students to correct the false sentences.

Answers

1 *False* (Skaterboy thinks it's not possible.)
2 False (He's going to sing songs all week.)
3 False (She says life without technology isn't fun.)
4 False (She's going to do lots of sport.)
5 True
6 True

Exercise 4 (Track 3.36)

- Students read the text again and answer the questions.
- Check answers as a class.
- Ask students how they would feel about living for a week without technology.

Answers

2 No, he isn't.
3 She's going to do lots of sport.
4 Madmax is going to play music on the radio.
5 Because we sit around all day, we don't do sport, we don't talk and we can't hear because we have earphones in our ears all day.

Listening

Exercise 1 (Track 3.37)

- Make sure students understand that not all the words are included in the recording.
- Play the recording for students to note down which words they hear.
- Check answers by playing the recording again and telling students to shout *Stop!* whenever they hear a word from the list.

Answers

email, novel, online, search engine

Audioscript:

See Teacher's Book page 226

Exercise 2 (Track 3.37)

- Give students time to read the multiple-choice questions.
- Repeat the recording for students to choose the correct options.
- Check answers as a class.

Answers

1 c   2 c   3 a

Extra activity

Write the following sentences on the board. Repeat the recording for students to decide if they are true or false (answers in brackets).
1 In the interviews the children talk about winter.
 (False – *They talk about summer.*)
2 The first boy's grandad hasn't got a computer.
 (False – *He's got a computer.*)
3 His grandad is going to pay him.   (True)
4 The girl isn't going to do any sport.
 (False – *She's having tennis lessons.*)
5 The girl is going online for one hour every day.
 (False – *She isn't going online at all.*)
6 The second boy wants to be a writer.   (True)
They then compare their answers in pairs. When checking answers, ask students to correct the false sentences.

Further practice:

Workbook page 82

Writing   A story

Revision

First – Revise all the grammar of the level by playing a simple 'Guess Who'-type question game. Choose a famous person, living or dead, but don't tell students who you are thinking of. Students have to guess who it is by asking you questions but you can only reply 'Yes', 'No' or 'I don't know'.

Second – In turn, students ask you questions, e.g. 'Are you a man?', 'Can you sing?', 'Have you got any brothers or sisters?', 'Are you American?', etc. Students can ask a maximum of ten questions. They then write down who they think it is.

Third – Students play the game in small groups, choosing their own famous people. Monitor but do not interrupt fluency unless they make mistakes with the question forms.

Extra activity

Books closed. In pairs, students try to remember the eight Writing File sections they have studied and the content of each. Collate suggestions on the board. Students then look back through the book quickly to find out how much they remembered correctly.
[See Teacher's Book: *Unit 1 – Punctuation: capital letters, full stops and apostrophes* (page 32); *Unit 2 – Linking words: and, or, but* (page 52); *Unit 3 – Time phrases: on + day, in + the morning/the afternoon, at + time* (page 72); *Unit 4 – Making notes: abbreviations and key information* (page 96); *Unit 5 – Word order: subject before verb* (page 116); *Unit 6 – Sequence words: First, Then, Finally* (page 136); *Unit 7 – Punctuation: full stops, commas, question marks, exclamation marks* (page 160); *Unit 8 – Paragraphs* (page 180)]

Exercise 1

• Read the Writing File with students.

Exercise 2

• Check students understand the task before they start.
• Students scan the text quickly and find examples.
• Collate examples of writing skills on the board.

Answers

My friend, the Professor, has got a Time Machine. It's amazing, but it's a secret! This evening we're going to travel to the future. I want to see my town in 2050!
The Time Machine is small and black. There's a big screen and lots of computers. In fact you can get WiFi and download videos!
We're travelling very fast now … BANG! What was that? We're in another time, but when?
I'm going to open the door … We're walking out into the street. There are people in long white clothes. Oh no! We aren't in the future. We're in Rome, 2,000 years ago. It's exciting, but we're going home soon – it's late!

Exercise 3

• Students read the text again and answer the questions.
• They then check in pairs before you check answers as a class.

Answers

2 No, it isn't. It's small.
3 You can travel to the past or the future.
4 Yes, they do.
5 It was 2,000 years ago.
6 Because it's late.

Exercise 4

• Students choose the correct options.
• Check answers by asking individual students to write sentences on the board.

Answers

2 ?   3 .   4 but   5 because   6 and

Exercise 5

• Explain that students should only make notes at this point or write short sentences.
• Encourage students to ask you for any vocabulary they need.

Answers

Students' own answers

Exercise 6

• Read through the 'My story' writing guide. Show students how the example text is divided into three paragraphs and tell them that they must now present their information as a complete text, not as notes or unconnected sentences.
• Draw students' attention to the 'Remember!' checklist.

Answers

Students' own answers

Extra activity

Add an extra 10–15 vocabulary items from this unit to the collection of Word Cards.
Revise all the vocabulary by dividing the class into seven groups and giving each group an equal number of vocabulary cards. If you have a few cards left over, give these to the stronger groups or fast finishers. Quickly remind students of the seven different activities they have done during the course to revise the vocabulary and how to play each [See Teacher's Book: *Unit 2 – Drawing game* (page 52); *Unit 3 – Mime game* (page 72); *Unit 4 – Word clues game* (page 96); *Unit 5 – Definitions game* (page 116); *Unit 6 – Questions game* (page 136); *Unit 7 – Missing word game* (page 160); *Unit 8 – Peer test* (page 180)].
Assign a different game to each group and tell them to play for three minutes. Change each group's cards and game and repeat until each group has played all seven games and used all seven sets of cards.

Further practice:
Workbook page 83

Writing   A story

1   Read the Writing File.

Writing File   **Review**

Remember to use all your writing skills!

a   Check your punctuation
Have you got full stops, capital letters, commas, question marks and exclamation marks?

b   Use linking words
Use *and*, *but* or *because* to join phrases in a sentence.

c   Write in paragraphs
Is information in a group?

2   Read the story and find more examples of each writing skill.

The time machine
A short story by
Olivia Da Silva, age 12

My friend, the Professor, has got a Time Machine. It's amazing, but it's a secret! This evening we're going to travel to the future. I want to see my town in 2050!

The Time Machine is small and black. There's a big screen and lots of computers. In fact you can get WiFi and download videos!

We're travelling very fast now ... BANG! What was that? We're in another time, but when?
I'm going to open the door ... We're walking out into the street. There are people in long white clothes. Oh no! We aren't in the future. We're in Rome, 2,000 years ago. It's exciting, but we're going home soon – it's late!

3   Read the story again. Answer the questions.

1   What is Olivia's friend's name?   *The Professor*
2   Is the Time Machine big?
3   What can you do in the Time Machine?
4   Do they travel to the past?
5   How many years ago was it?
6   Why is Olivia going home?

4   Choose the correct options to make sentences.

1   Joanna's travelling in time , / . but I'm not.
2   Are you going to fly , / ?
3   They aren't going to the past . / ?
4   I haven't got an ebook, *and / but* my dad has.
5   William's using a search engine *but / because* he's doing his homework.
6   We're going to download music *and / but* videos this evening.

5   Choose your transport and place. Make notes about your journey.

Transport   time machine / space rocket
Place   space / the moon / a new planet

6   Write a story. Use 'My story' and your notes from Exercise 5.

My story

Title
Think of a title for your story.

Paragraph 1
Who is your friend?
Do you want to visit the past or the future?
What do you want to see there?

Paragraph 2
Describe your time machine or space rocket.

Paragraph 3
Describe the place and things (and people) you can see.
What place (and time) are you in?

Remember!
● Use punctuation, linking words and paragraphs.
● Use the vocabulary in this unit.
● Check your grammar and spelling.

105

201

Refresh Your Memory!

Grammar Review

1 Complete the text with the correct form of *be going to*.

We ¹ *'re going to go* (go) on holiday to Portugal next week. We ² .... (take) lots of things! My mum ³ .... (read) some ebooks and my dad ⁴ .... (send) emails on his smartphone in the evenings. I ⁵ .... (listen) to lots of new songs on my MP3 player and my two sisters ⁶ .... (do) their homework on their laptop.

2 Make the questions for the holiday questionnaire.

1 *Are you going to watch TV in your room?*

Holiday questionnaire

		Bella	Jessica	Freddie
1	watch TV in your room?	✗	✓	✗
2	eat pizza every week?	✓	✗	✓
3	go swimming every day?	✓	✓	✗
4	see all your friends?	✓	✓	✓
5	play basketball?	✗	✗	✓
6	do any homework?	✗	✗	✗

3 Make six sentences about the three children in Exercise 2.

1 *Jessica is going to watch TV in her room, but Bella and Freddie aren't going to watch TV in their rooms.*

4 Make sentences about arrangements for tomorrow with the Present continuous.

1 Ollie / get up / 11 a.m.

Ollie is getting up at 11 a.m.

2 I / study / online in the morning
3 Isabella and Carlos / not go / to the cinema
4 My brother / clean / Dad's car
5 Fiona / not tidy / her room
6 We / have / chicken and chips for dinner

Vocabulary Review

5 Match five technology words.

1 *digital radio*

~~digital~~	instant	interactive
memory	messaging	networking
~~radio~~	site	social
stick	whiteboard	

6 Choose the correct options.

1 How often do you *use / send / go* online?
2 Can you *use / write / read* WiFi at school?
3 We often *charge / use / chat* the internet for homework.
4 Mum *uses / chats / sends* emails to all her friends at Christmas.
5 Do you *use / charge / send* many texts?
6 I often *chat / send / charge* online to my cousins in Australia.
7 I'm going to *read / charge / go* my mobile phone before I go on holiday.
8 She doesn't often *chat / use / download* music.

Speaking Review

7 🔊 3.38 Match the questions (a–c) to the answers (1–3). Then listen and check.

a What are your plans for the summer?
b What happened?
c Can you tell me more?

1 I passed my exam!
2 Yes, we're doing a radio programme soon.
3 I'm going to go surfing.

Dictation

8 🔊 3.39 Listen and write in your notebook.

 My assessment profile: Workbook page 135

Refresh Your Memory!

Exercise 1

Answers

2 're/are going to take
3 's/is going to read
4 's/is going to send
5 'm/am going to listen
6 are going to do

Exercise 2

Answers

2 Are you going to eat pizza every week?
3 Are you going to go swimming every day?
4 Are you going to see all your friends?
5 Are you going to play basketball?
6 Are you going to do any homework?

Exercise 3

Answers

2 Bella and Freddie are going to eat pizza every week, but Jessica isn't/is not going to eat pizza every week.
3 Bella and Jessica are going to go swimming every day, but Freddie isn't/is not going to go swimming every day.
4 Bella, Jessica and Freddie are going to see all their friends.
5 Freddie 's/is going to play basketball, but Bella and Jessica aren't/are not going to play basketball.
6 Bella, Jessica and Freddie aren't/are not going to do any homework.

Exercise 4

Answers

2 I'm/am studying online in the morning.
3 Isabella and Carlos aren't/are not going to the cinema.
4 My brother 's/is cleaning Dad's car.
5 Fiona isn't/is not tidying her room.
6 We're/are having chicken and chips for dinner.

Exercise 5

Answers

instant messaging, interactive whiteboard, memory stick, social networking site

Exercise 6

Answers

2 use 3 use 4 sends 5 send 6 chat 7 charge
8 download

Exercise 7 (Track 3.38)

Answers

a 3 b 1 c 2

Exercise 8 (Track 3.39)

Answers and Audioscript

Reading is my favourite hobby and I've got lots of books. I sometimes read on my mobile phone on the bus but the screen is very small. My friend Lisa has got an ebook but I'm not going to get one because I think paper books are better. I'm getting a new book tomorrow!

My assessment profile:
Workbook page 135

Extra activity

Revise the use of *be going to* to talk about intentions and future plans and the Present continuous to talk about future arrangements:
– Tell students that as term is nearly over you now have time to make lots of exciting plans. Draw the electronic planner up on the board and explain that you always use your netbook to plan your busy life and this is what your weekend looks like.
– Explain that the items on the left part of the planner are things you have organised for the weekend. Add that the things on the right are the things that you still need to do. Elicit the most appropriate form to talk about each section. (Answer: *timetabled part of the planner – Present continuous*; *'to do' list – be going to*)
– Elicit sentences from students using these forms, e.g. *'You're having lunch and going shopping with Lady Gaga on Friday at one o'clock.', 'You're going to buy a plane ticket to New York.'* In pairs, students make sentences for all of the items on the planner. Check answers by asking individual students to say sentences. Drill the sentences for pronunciation and sentence stress.
– Students work individually, making their own fictional planner for the weekend ahead. They then work in pairs, making sentences in the first person, e.g. *'I'm meeting Kristen Stewart for dinner on Friday at nine o'clock.'*
– Monitor and help with vocabulary but do not interrupt fluency. Ask students to say some of their plans and arrangements for the class to hear.

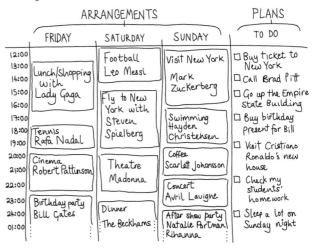

Citizenship File   The Youth Mayors of England

Cultural notes

- *Youth Mayors* are becoming increasingly common in the UK. The objective of such schemes is to give young people a voice in the community and the responsibility and resources to create new projects and services. The system also acts as a point of contact between the local level of government and the young people of the area. Youth Mayors usually serve a 12-month term and any young person from 11–19 living, working or studying in the area can stand as a candidate or register as a voter. Local youth organisations can make applications for funding by presenting their projects or plans to the elected Youth Parliament for evaluation.
- *David Oyedele* was Youth Mayor for Lambeth from April 2011 to April 2012. Like many candidates, he made extensive use of social networking media, including Facebook and Twitter, as part of his campaign and mandate.

Language notes

Be prepared to elicit from stronger students or explain yourself the meaning of the following lexical items which appear in the Reading text: *representative*, *election*, *to vote*, *candidate*, *manifesto*, *area*, *budget*, *crime*, *poverty*.

Exercise 1

- Draw attention to the photos and the text and ask students what they can see.
- Students scan the text quickly and find out why David Oyedele is an important person.

Answer

Because he is the Youth Mayor of Lambeth, London, and represents young people in the area.

Exercise 2 (Track 3.40)

- Students read the text and answer the questions.
- If you wish, play the recording for students to listen and read.
- Students check in pairs before you check answers as a class.
- Elicit from stronger students or explain yourself the meaning of any new vocabulary.

Answers

2 The elections for Youth Mayors are at schools in England.
3 He is sixteen years old.
4 More than 10,000 people voted in the Lambeth Youth Mayor elections.
5 He wrote a rap about Lambeth.
6 His budget is £25,000.
7 He wants to improve school exam results and provide more social and physical activities for young people in Lambeth.

My Citizenship File

Exercise 3

- In pairs, students brainstorm ideas.
- Collate suggestions on the board.
- Remind students of the use of *going to* to talk about intentions and elicit an example sentence using one of the ideas on the board.

Exercise 4

- Students work individually, writing sentences for their manifestos.
- Monitor and help with grammar and vocabulary and feed in ideas if necessary.
- Point out errors for students to self-correct.
- Ask some students to say their sentences for the class.

In this unit have you …

… used Grammar and Vocabulary worksheet?
… used Reading and Listening worksheet?
… used Writing worksheet?
… used Speaking worksheet?
… used Unit test?

With the exception of the Writing worksheets, all the Teacher's Resources are at two levels of difficulty:
*   For students who need extra help and support
** For students who require an additional challenge

Citizenship File

The Youth Mayors of England

David, John, Keiza and Ali are ordinary school children in London. But they are also important people. They are all Youth Mayors. There are more than ten Youth Mayors in England. A Youth Mayor is a representative for young people. There are elections at schools in the area and young people vote for their favourite candidate.

David Oyedele is 16 years old and he is the Youth Mayor of Lambeth, London. More than 10,000 young people, aged between 11 and 19, voted in the Lambeth Youth Mayor elections.

Candidates for the job of Youth Mayor write a manifesto. They describe what they want to do for the area and how they're going to spend their budget. They also record a short video clip. Some candidates use songs, poems or jokes in their video clips. Other candidates are very serious. David wrote a rap about Lambeth for his video.

David won the election and now he has got a budget of £25,000 to spend on the community in Lambeth. There are some problems in this area with crime and poverty, but David has got lots of ideas. He wants to improve school exam results and he wants to provide more social and physical activities for young people in Lambeth.

Reading

1 Read the text quickly. Why is David Oyedele an important person?

2 ◖ 3.40 Read the text again. Answer the questions.
  1 What is a Youth Mayor?
    A representative for young people.
  2 Where are the elections for Youth Mayors?
  3 How old is David Oyedele?
  4 How many people voted in the Lambeth Youth Mayor elections?
  5 What did David do for his election video?
  6 What is David's budget?
  7 What does David want to do for Lambeth?

My Citizenship File

3 You want to be a Youth Mayor. Think about your manifesto.
  • What are the problems in your area?
  • What are your ideas?
  • How are you going to spend your budget?

4 Write five sentences for your manifesto in your notebook.

◀ 107 ▶

③ Review

Grammar

Past simple *to be*

1 Change the sentences into the Past simple.

1 I'm in Mexico. *I was in Mexico.*
2 He isn't a teacher.
3 Are you in town?
4 Is it cold?
5 Am I late?
6 Olivia's happy.
7 They aren't very big.

There was/There were

2 Complete the conversation with the correct form of *there was / there were*.

A ¹ *Was there* a party on Saturday night?
B Yes, ² .... . It was at Sam's house.
A ³ .... lots of people at the party?
B No, ⁴ .... . It was small but it was fun!
A ⁵ .... any good music?
B Yes, the music was fantastic. ⁶ .... a lot of dancing, too. Yasmin's dancing was amazing! ⁷ .... any food, but ⁸ .... some delicious drinks.

Past simple

3 Complete the sentences with the Past simple.

1 I *stopped* (stop) at the station at 7.15 a.m.
2 He .... (study) Japanese in Tokyo for two years. Then .... (work) for a Japanese bank.
3 I .... (phone) Katie's mobile phone this morning but she .... (not answer).
4 They .... (talk) to their mum about the problem, but their mum .... (not listen).
5 We .... (travel) around Britain last summer but we .... (not like) the weather!

4 Complete the text with the Past simple form of these verbs.

cook	hate	play	rain	~~start~~	stay	stop	tidy

The rain ¹ *started* at 7 a.m. yesterday and it ² .... (not). It ³ .... all day. I ⁴ .... (not) football because of the weather. I ⁵ .... at home, and my sister and I ⁶ .... our bedrooms. Mum ⁷ .... pasta for dinner but I ⁸ .... the vegetables with it. Yuk! What a terrible day!

[108]▶

5 What did Brandon do on Saturday? What didn't he do? Make sentences.

1 *He got up early.*
2 *He didn't have a healthy breakfast.*

- get up early ✓
- have a healthy breakfast ✗
- go to town ✓
- buy a present for Cara ✗
- have lunch with Dom ✓
- do his Maths homework ✓
- give Cara her present ✗

6 Complete the text with the Past simple.

'How many seconds are there in a minute?' the teacher ¹ *asked* (ask) the children when they ² .... (come) into the classroom. The question ³ .... (not be) difficult. '60,' they ⁴ .... (answer). 'Good. And how many seconds in a year?' the teacher ⁵ .... (continue). The children ⁶ .... (think) for a moment, but they ⁷ .... (not know). Only James ⁸ .... (put) his hand up. '12,' he ⁹ .... (say). 'There's 2nd January, 2nd February, 2nd March …' .

7 Make questions and answers with the Past simple.

1 when / they / leave / ? (at half past six)
   When did they leave?
   They left at half past six.
2 I / say / the wrong thing / ? (yes)
3 what / he / give / his mum / ? (a book)
4 you / understand / the question / ? (no)
5 how many / glasses of juice / we / drink / ? (nine)
6 they / help / Matt / ? (yes)

8 Complete the conversation in the Past simple.

A Where ¹ *did you go* (go) on holiday this year?
B We ² .... (travel) across Europe by train.
A Cool! How many days ³ .... (the journey, take)?
B It ⁴ .... (take) two weeks.
A ⁵ .... (you, visit) any interesting cities?
B Yes, we ⁶ .... . We ⁷ .... (see) the Eiffel Tower in Paris, and we ⁸ .... (go) to Vienna, Budapest and Athens, too.
A ⁹ .... (you, come) home by train?
B No, we ¹⁰ .... . We ¹¹ .... (fly).

Exercise 9

2 They're/are going to walk to town on Saturday.
3 Samina and I aren't/are not going to tidy our room tonight.
4 A new shop is going to open in the shopping centre soon.
5 She isn't/is not going to come with us tomorrow.
6 I'm/am going to be a doctor.

Exercise 1

2 We heard about it last month.
3 We bought the tickets three weeks ago.
4 I sent her an email yesterday afternoon.
5 I phoned her last night.
6 The match started this morning.
7 She arrived an hour ago.
8 I saw her twenty minutes ago.

Exercise 10

2 'm/am not
3 'm/am going to visit
4 Are your brothers going to go
5 are
6 Is your mum going to drive
7 isn't/is not
8 're/are going to take
9 Are you going to read
10 am
11 aren't/are not going to do
12 're/are going to play

Be going to

9 Make sentences about future plans with *be going to*.
 1 I / see a film / this weekend
   I'm going to see a film this weekend.
 2 they / walk / to town / on Saturday
 3 Samina and I / not tidy / our room / tonight
 4 a new shop / open / in the shopping centre / soon
 5 she / not come / with us / tomorrow
 6 I / be / a doctor

10 Complete the conversation with the correct form of *be going to*.
 A What are your plans for the weekend?
   ¹ *Are you going to be* (be) at home?
 B No, I ² .... . I ³ .... (visit) my grandparents.
 A ⁴ .... (your brothers, go) with you?
 B Yes, they ⁵ .... .
 A ⁶ .... (your mum, drive) you there?
 B No, she ⁷ .... . We ⁸ .... (take) the coach.
 A ⁹ .... (you, read) a book on the coach?
 B Yes, I ¹⁰ .... , but my brothers ¹¹ .... (not do) that. They ¹² .... (play) on their games consoles.

Present continuous for future arrangements

11 Read this family's diary. Make sentences about their arrangements.
 1 *At five o'clock on Monday, Lily's playing tennis with Josh.*

Monday	Lily: 5 p.m., play tennis with Josh
Tuesday	Sam: 6 p.m., see "Tarantula" at the cinema
Wednesday	Mum: buy food for Dad's birthday meal Lily and Sam: cook the meal
Thursday	Lily and Sam: do gymnastics after school
Friday	Mum and Dad: 8 p.m., have dinner at the Red Café Lily: stay at Tasha's house

Speaking
Talking about the past

1 Rewrite the sentences. Use a word or phrase from each box.

ago (x 3)	last (x 3)	this	yesterday
afternoon	an hour	month	
morning	night	~~summer~~	
three weeks	twenty minutes		

It's now 8 p.m. on Saturday 23rd June.
 1 They arranged the concert in August.
   They arranged the concert last summer.
 2 We heard about it in May.
 3 We bought the tickets on 2nd June.
 4 I sent her an email on Friday at 3 p.m.
 5 I phoned her on Friday at 9 p.m.
 6 The match started today at 11 a.m.
 7 She arrived today at 7 p.m.
 8 I saw her today at 7.40 p.m.

Talking on the phone

2 Put the conversation in the correct order.

Poppy	Hi, Edward. Is the band going to meet tonight?	....
Bill	Hello.	.1.
Poppy	Oh, good. Thanks. See you later!	....
Bill	No, it's Bill.	....
Poppy	Hi. Is that Edward?	.2.
Edward	Bye!	
Poppy	Oh, hi, Bill. It's Poppy. Can I speak to Edward, please?	....
Edward	Yes, it is. At half past six.	....
Bill	OK. Hold on. Here he is.	....

Asking for information

3 Make questions.
 1 you / me / tell / Can / more / ?
 2 plans / are / What / your / ?
 3 happened / What / ?

Exercise 11

At six o'clock on Tuesday, Sam's/is seeing 'Tarantula' at the cinema.
On Wednesday, Mum's/is buying food for Dad's birthday meal and Lily and Sam are cooking the meal.
On Thursday, Lily and Sam are doing gymnastics after school.
At eight o'clock on Friday, Mum and Dad are having dinner at the Red Café. On Friday, Lily is staying at Tasha's house.

Exercise 3

1 Can you tell me more?
2 What are your plans?
3 What happened?

Exercise 2

Bill	Hello.
Poppy	Hi. Is that Edward?
Bill	No, it's Bill.
Poppy	Oh, hi, Bill. It's Poppy. Can I speak to Edward, please?
Bill	OK. Hold on. Here he is.
Poppy	Hi, Edward. Is the band going to meet tonight?
Edward	Yes, it is. At half past six.
Poppy	Oh, good. Thanks. See you later!
Edward	Bye!

Exercise 1

2 the thirty-first of January, two thousand and seven
3 the twenty-second of August, twenty fourteen
4 the fifteenth of February, nineteen ninety-five
5 the third of March, two thousand and nine
6 the eighth of September, twenty eleven

Exercise 4

on your feet	in bed	on your legs	for cold weather	other
trainers boots sandals shoes	pyjamas	jeans shorts skirt trousers	coat hat jumper scarf	dress T-shirt

Exercise 2

2 invented; travelled
3 studied; asked; answered
4 worked; liked; stopped
5 phoned; talked; listened

Exercise 5

2 ebooks
3 digital radio
4 memory stick
5 blog
6 broadband; WiFi
7 interactive whiteboard
8 screen
9 social networking sites; instant messaging

Exercise 3

1 *coach, plane,* train
2 bus, tube
3 lorry, van
4 boat, canoe

Exercise 6

2 use
3 write
4 read
5 chat
6 charge
7 go
8 send
9 get

3 Review

Vocabulary

Ordinal numbers, years, dates

1 Write these dates in full.
1 4 Nov 1989
the fourth of November, nineteen eighty-nine
2 31 Jan 2007
3 22 Aug 2014
4 15 Feb 1995
5 3 Mar 2009
6 8 Sept 2011

Regular verbs

2 Complete the sentences with the correct Past simple form of these verbs.

answer ask ~~close~~ invent like listen phone stop study talk travel work

1 I didn't buy any food because the shop *closed* early.
2 In 1885, Karl Benz .... the first car. His wife Bertha .... 100 kilometres in it in one day.
3 We .... the Romans in History last week. Jimmy .... some questions about Roman gladiators. Our teacher .... some of his questions, but she didn't know all the answers.
4 Five years ago, my dad .... at a hospital. He .... his job. He was sad when he .... working there.
5 I .... my gran last night. We .... for a long time and she .... to all my problems.

Means of transport

3 Complete the sentences with some of these words.

bike boat bus canoe car ~~coach~~ helicopter lorry motorbike ~~plane~~ scooter train tube van

1 Forty people are going from Madrid to Paris. They can go by *coach, plane* or .... .
2 A family of six people are travelling three kilometres in London and they haven't got bikes. They can go by .... or .... .
3 You are taking 10,000 sausages to different shops in the city. You can use a .... or a .... .
4 You want to travel on water. You can use a .... or a .... .

Clothes

4 Put these clothes into the correct categories.

boots coat dress hat jeans jumper pyjamas sandals scarf shoes shorts skirt T-shirt ~~trainers~~ trousers

on your feet	in bed	on your legs	for cold weather	other
trainers, ...				

Technology

5 Complete the words with the missing letters.
1 I often do my homework on my n e t b o o k.
2 I like reading e _ _ _ k s.
3 We're listening to our d _ _ i t _ _ r _ _ _ o.
4 What's on that m _ m _ _ _ s t _ _ _?
5 He writes an interesting b _ _ _ about his life.
6 We've got b _ _ _ d b _ _ d but we haven't got W _ F _.
7 We've got an i n t _ _ a c _ _ _ _ w _ _ t _ b _ _ _ d in our classroom.
8 Your computer's got a big s _ _ _ _ n!
9 He often goes on s _ c _ _ l n _ _ w _ _ k _ _ _ s _ t _ s but he never uses i _ _ t _ _ t m _ _ s _ _ _ _ g.

6 Complete the text with these words.

chat charge ~~download~~ get go read send use write

I love technology. I ¹ *download* a lot of music and videos, and I often ² .... search engines for my homework. My life is very boring so I don't ³ .... a blog about it. But my sister is travelling in Asia and I ⁴ .... her blog every day. My friends and I often ⁵ .... online after school, about teachers, homework, everything! I ⁶ .... my mobile phone every night, so it's always got power for the next day. I can't ⁷ .... online with it because it isn't a smartphone. But I ⁸ .... a lot of texts to my friends and I ⁹ .... a lot of texts from them too.

110

Word list

Unit 7 Modern History

Ordinal numbers, years, dates

fifth	/fɪfθ/
first	/ˈfɜːst/
fourth	/fɔːθ/
second	/ˈsekənd/
third	/θɜːd/
thirty-first	/ˈθɜːti ˈfɜːst/
twentieth	/ˈtwentiəθ/
twenty-second	/ˈtwenti ˈsekənd/
nineteen fifty-seven	/naɪnˈtiːn ˈfɪfti ˈsevən/
nineteen forty-two	/naɪnˈtiːn ˈfɔːrtʃ ˈtuː/
nineteen ninety	/naɪnˈtiːn ˈnaɪnti/
nineteen twelve	/naɪnˈtiːn ˈtwelv/
nineteen twenty-two	/naɪnˈtiːn twenti ˈtuː/
twenty eleven	/ˈtwenti ɪˈlevən/
two thousand	/tuː ˈθaʊzənd/
two thousand and four	/tuː ˈθaʊzənd ənd fɔːr/

Regular verbs

answer	/ˈɑːnsə/	answered	/ˈɑːnsərd/
ask	/ɑːsk/	asked	/ˈɑːskt/
close	/kləuz/	closed	/kləuzd/
invent	/ɪnˈvent/	invented	/ɪnˈventɪd/
like	/laɪk/	liked	/ˈlaɪkt/
listen	/lɪsən/	listened	/ˈlɪsənd/
phone	/fəun/	phoned	/fəund/
stop	/stɒp/	stopped	/stɒpt/
study	/ˈstʌdi/	studied	/ˈstʌdɪd/
talk	/tɔːk/	talked	/tɔːkt/
travel	/ˈtrævəl/	travelled	/ˈtrævəld/
work	/wɜːk/	worked	/wɜːkt/

Unit 8 Journeys

Means of transport

bike	/baɪk/
boat	/bəut/
bus	/bʌs/
canoe	/kəˈnuː/
car	/kɑː/
coach	/kəutʃ/
helicopter	/ˈhelɪkɒptə/
lorry	/ˈlɒri/
motorbike	/ˈməutəbaɪk/
plane	/pleɪn/
scooter	/ˈskuːtə/
train	/treɪn/
tube	/tjuːb/
van	/væn/

Clothes

boots	/buːts/
coat	/kəut/
dress	/dres/
hat	/hæt/
jeans	/dʒiːnz/
jumper	/ˈdʒʌmpə/
pyjamas	/pɪˈdʒɑːməz/
sandals	/ˈsændəlz/
scarf	/skɑːf/
shoes	/ʃuːz/
shorts	/ʃɔːts/
skirt	/skɜːt/
T-shirt	/ˈtiːʃɜːt/
trainers	/ˈtreɪnəz/
trousers	/ˈtrauzəz/

Unit 9 Technology Time

Technology

blog	/blɒg/
broadband	/ˈbrɔːdbænd/
digital radio	/ˈdɪdʒɪtəl ˈreɪdiəu/
ebook	/ˈiːbuk/
IM (instant messaging)	/aɪ em ˈɪnstənt ˈmesɪdʒɪŋ/
interactive whiteboard	/ɪntəˈræktɪv ˈwaɪtbɔːd/
memory stick	/ˈmeməri ˈstɪk/
netbook	/ˈnetbuk/
screen	/skriːn/
smartphone	/ˈsmɑːtfəun/
social networking site	/ˈsəuʃəl ˈnetwɜːkɪŋ saɪt/
WiFi	/ˈwaɪfaɪ/

Technology phrases

charge your mobile phone	/tʃɑːdʒ jɔːr ˈməubaɪl fəun/
chat online	/tʃæt ɒnˈlaɪn/
download films	/daunˈləud fɪlm/
download music	/daunˈləud ˈmjuːzɪk/
download videos	/daunˈləud ˈvɪdiəuz/
go online	/gəu ˈɒnlaɪn/
send a text	/send ə tekst/
send emails	/send ˈiːmeɪl/
use a search engine	/juːz ə sɜːtʃ ˈendʒɪn/
use the internet	/juːz ði ˈɪntənet/
use WiFi	/juːz ˈwaɪfaɪ/
write a blog	/raɪt ə blɒg/

Spot the difference

Exercise 1

- Intelligence types: Visual/Spatial, Verbal/Linguistic, Intrapersonal
- Learner types: Visual

Answers

1 Sunny isn't/is not in the room.
2 Leo's/has got a red T-shirt, not a purple T-shirt.
3 There aren't/are not any ice skates on the desk.
4 There isn't/is not a backpack under the desk.

Grammar

Exercise 2

- Intelligence types: Visual/Spatial, Verbal/Linguistic, Interpersonal
- Learner types: Visual, Auditory

Answers

A
2 That's wrong. Anya's/has got a skateboard.
3 That's wrong. Hans's/has got a guitar.
4 That's wrong. Paulo's/has got a wallet.

B
1 That's wrong. Anya and Hans have got a camera.
2 That's wrong. Paulo's/has got a watch.
3 That's wrong. Mike's/has got an MP3 player.
4 That's wrong. Paulo's/has got a backpack.

Vocabulary

Exercise 3

- Intelligence types: Verbal/Linguistic, Intrapersonal, Interpersonal
- Learner types: Visual

Answers

1 poster
2 laptop
3 comics
4 games console
5 wallet
6 guitar
7 DVD
8 skateboard

Exercise 4

- Intelligence types: Visual/Spatial, Verbal/Linguistic, Interpersonal
- Learner types: Visual, Auditory

Answers

1 D old/new
2 A big/small
3 B interesting/boring
4 C easy/difficult
5 E cheap/expensive

Definitions of intelligence types and learner types:
See Teacher's Book pages 8–9

Spot the difference

Exercise 1

- Intelligence types: Visual/Spatial, Verbal/Linguistic, Intrapersonal
- Learner types: Visual

Answers

1 Nick's/has got a cap.
2 Monica's life jacket is blue.
3 There isn't/is not any bread in the backpack.

Grammar

Exercise 2

- Intelligence types: Visual/Spatial, Verbal/Linguistic, Intrapersonal
- Learner types: Visual

Possible answers

In my town there are some shops.
There's a bank.
There isn't a sports centre.
There are (two) cinemas.
There aren't any museums.
There are some cafés.

Vocabulary

Exercise 3

- Intelligence types: Visual/Spatial, Verbal/Linguistic, Logical/Mathematical, Intrapersonal
- Learner types: Visual, Auditory

Answers

3a bank, bus station, café, cinema, *hospital*, library, park, police station, town square, train station
3b b bank
    c cinema
    d bus station
    e park
    f café
    g library
    h town square
    i police station
    j train station

Exercise 4

- Intelligence types: Verbal/Linguistic, Bodily/Kinaesthetic, Interpersonal
- Learner types: Kinaesthetic/Tactile

Definitions of intelligence types and learner types:

See Teacher's Book pages 8–9

Brain Trainer 2

Spot the difference

1 Look at the photo on page 24 for one minute. Now study this photo. What differences can you spot?

Grammar

2 Make true sentences about your town using all the sentence starters below. Write the sentences in your notebook. You've got two minutes!

 In my town there are … .

There's a … .

There isn't a … .

There are (two) … .

There aren't any … .

There are some … .

Vocabulary

3a How many places in town can you remember that have got the letter *a* in them? Think of ten.
   1 Hospital

3b Label the places in the pictures.
   a Hospital

 a f
 b g
 c h
 d i
 e j

4 Work in pairs. Choose six words from the list. Tell your partner what to do. Then change roles.

| climb | cycle | dance | fly | juggle | jump |
| play | run | sing | skate | swim | walk |

 Walk (please) … .
(Now) jump … .

113

Spot the difference

Exercise 1

- Intelligence types: Visual/Spatial, Verbal/Linguistic, Intrapersonal
- Learner types: Visual

Answers

1 Nick hasn't got his ice skates.
2 Monica hasn't got a magazine.
3 Monica isn't wearing a watch.

Grammar

Exercise 2

- Intelligence types: Visual/Spatial, Verbal/Linguistic, Intrapersonal
- Learner types: Visual

Possible answers

She doesn't like Maths.
Sam goes to the cinema on Fridays.
You do homework after school.
They like pizza.

Vocabulary

Exercise 3

- Intelligence types: Verbal/Linguistic, Logical/Mathematical, Musical/Rhythmic, Intrapersonal
- Learner types: Auditory

Answers

3a get dressed
3b watch TV

Exercise 4

- Intelligence types: Visual/Spatial, Verbal/Linguistic, Intrapersonal
- Learner types: Visual

Answers

4a 2 PE
  3 Maths
  4 Geography
  5 History
  6 Science
  7 ICT
  8 French

Possible answers

4b English, Literature, Music, Social Science

Definitions of intelligence types and learner types:
See Teacher's Book pages 8–9

Brain Trainer 3

Spot the difference

1 Look at the photo on page 34 for one minute. Now study this photo. What differences can you spot?

Grammar

2 Make five sentences using all the words from the orange, purple and blue boxes.
1 *I get up at 7 a.m.*

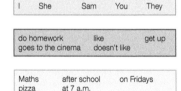

I	She	Sam	You	They

do homework	like	get up
goes to the cinema	doesn't like	

Maths	after school	on Fridays
pizza	at 7 a.m.	

Vocabulary

3a Read the phrases in the box aloud three times. Cover the box. Read the list below. Which phrase is missing?

get up → have a shower → get dressed → have breakfast → start school → have lunch

get up → have a shower → have breakfast → start school → have lunch

3b Now try again.

go home → do homework → meet friends → have dinner → watch TV → go to bed

go home → do homework → meet friends → have dinner → go to bed

4a Look at the books. What are the subjects?
1 *Art*

4b Think of four subjects that are not in the pictures.

114

212

Spot the difference

Exercise 1

- Intelligence types: Visual/Spatial, Verbal/Linguistic, Intrapersonal
- Learner types: Visual

Answers

1 Julia hasn't/has not got a coat.
2 Leo's/has got an apple.
3 Nick's/has got a camera.

Grammar

Exercise 2

- Intelligence types: Verbal/Linguistic, Intrapersonal
- Learner types: Visual

Answers

2 Where 3 How 4 Who 5 What
6 Why

Exercise 3

- Intelligence types: Visual/Spatial, Verbal/Linguistic, Intrapersonal
- Learner types: Visual

Answers

2 She never watches TV.
3 We always play football on Saturday.
4 I usually get up at 7 a.m.
5 He often cycles to school.

Vocabulary

Exercise 4

- Intelligence types: Visual/Spatial, Verbal/Linguistic, Logical/Mathematical, Intrapersonal
- Learner types: Visual, Kinaesthetic/Tactile

Answers

4a PYTHON, LIZARD, PYGMY GOAT, STICK INSECT, GIANT RABBIT, TARANTULA, PIRANHA
4b frog parrot

Exercise 5

- Intelligence types: Verbal/Linguistic, Logical/Mathematical, Intrapersonal
- Learner types: Visual

Answers

2 paws, tail
3 fingers, toes
4 arms, legs
5 heads, necks
6 feet, hands, fins

Definitions of intelligence types and learner types:
See Teacher's Book pages 8–9

Brain Trainer 4

Spot the difference

1 Look at the photo on page 48 for one minute. Now study this photo. What differences can you spot?

Grammar

2 Add the correct *Wh-* word to make questions. You've got one minute!
   1 *When* do you finish school?
   2 .... is my guitar?
   3 .... often do you go to town?
   4 .... is your favourite writer?
   5 .... do you do after school?
   6 .... have you got a camera today?

3 Make sentences with words of the same colour. Then make your own colour puzzle. In pairs, complete your partner's puzzle.
   1 *I sometimes listen to music.*

I	football	usually	7 a.m.	She
to	sometimes	on	often	We
I	cycles	always	never	listen
Saturday	at	to	school	get up
He	watches	play	music	TV

Vocabulary

4a Complete the crossword.

4b There are two animals missing from the puzzle. Can you name them?

5 Unscramble the words to complete the sentences with parts of the body. You've got three minutes!
   1 Parrots have **keabs** and **singw**
      beaks and wings
   2 Our cat has four big **waps** and a long **lait**.
   3 We have ten **nerfsig** and **sote**.
   4 My spider hasn't got **mars**, but it has got eight **gels**.
   5 Deer have small **hades** and long **skenc**.
   6 Snakes haven't got **teef** or **sahnd**. Sea snakes have **nifs**.

115

Spot the difference

Exercise 1

- Intelligence types: Visual/Spatial, Verbal/Linguistic, Intrapersonal
- Learner types: Visual

Answers

1 Julia's/has got the binoculars, not Monica.
2 Nick's/is wearing a cap.
3 Nick's/is taking a photo with his camera not his mobile phone.

Grammar

Exercise 2

- Intelligence types: Visual/Spatial, Verbal/Linguistic, Interpersonal
- Learner types: Visual, Auditory

Answers

1b and 1c She's/is canoeing.
2a He's/is climbing.
2b He's/is playing the guitar.
2c He's/is ice-skating.
3a She's/is pony trekking.
3b She's/is pony trekking.
3c She's/is painting.

Vocabulary

Exercise 3

- Intelligence types: Visual/Spatial, Verbal/Linguistic, Intrapersonal
- Learner types: Visual

Answers

bowling, dancing, hiking, ice-skating, mountain biking, painting, rollerblading, surfing

Exercise 4

- Intelligence types: Visual/Spatial, Verbal/Linguistic, Logical/Mathematical, Intrapersonal
- Learner types: Visual

Definitions of intelligence types and learner types:
See Teacher's Book pages 8–9

Brain Trainer 5

Spot the difference

1 Look at the photo on page 58 for one minute. Now study this photo. What differences can you spot?

Grammar

2 Look at the picture for two minutes, then cover it. Now say a square. Your partner says what the person is doing.

1a – He's climbing.

Vocabulary

3 Look at the picture and find eight activities. You've got two minutes!

4 Read the words in the box aloud three times. Cover the list and write the words in your notebook. Can you remember all the words?

| hot sunny | warm cloudy windy | cold foggy raining snowing |

116

Spot the difference

Exercise 1

- Intelligence types: Visual/Spatial, Verbal/Linguistic, Intrapersonal
- Learner types: Visual

1 Nick and Leo haven't/have not got menus.
2 Leo is wearing a yellow and blue T-shirt, not a blue shirt.
3 There isn't/is not a 'Happy Birthday' balloon.
4 There isn't/is not a photo of the Colosseum/Rome.

Grammar

Exercise 2

- Intelligence types: Verbal/Linguistic, Interpersonal
- Learner types: Auditory

1 *How many*; I've/have got four bananas.
2 How much; We've/have got a lot of pasta.
3 How many; I haven't/have not got any eggs.
4 How much; I haven't/have not got much juice.
5 How much; We've/have got some cheese.
6 How many; I've/have got two ham sandwiches.
7 How many; I've/have got a lot of tomatoes.
8 How much; We haven't/have not got much bread.

Vocabulary

Exercise 3

- Intelligence types: Visual/Spatial, Verbal/Linguistic, Logical/Mathematical, Intrapersonal
- Learner types: Visual

banana, broccoli, ham, pasta, prawns, salmon, tomato, tuna, yoghurt

Exercise 4

- Intelligence types: Visual/Spatial, Verbal/Linguistic, Logical/Mathematical, Intrapersonal
- Learner types: Visual

2 hot
3 large
4 cold
5 delicious
6 noisy
7 quiet
8 disgusting
9 dirty
10 small
11 horrible
12 wonderful

Definitions of intelligence types and learner types:
See Teacher's Book pages 8–9

Spot the difference

Exercise 1

- Intelligence types: Visual/Spatial, Verbal/Linguistic, Intrapersonal
- Learner types: Visual

Answers

1 Julia's grandad isn't/is not wearing a cardigan.
2 Julia's gran is looking at photos.
3 There aren't any flowers.

Brain Trainer 7

Spot the difference

1 Look at the photo on page 82 for one minute. Now study this photo. What differences can you spot?

Grammar

2 Make sentences with words of the same colour. Then make your own colour puzzle. In pairs, complete your partner's puzzle.

1 *She was at the hospital this morning.*

She	any	morning	classroom	at
the	was	the	station	computers
weren't	wasn't	friends	the	hospital
the	I	There	were	brother
ago	in	Lucy's	My	café
fifteen	at	on	in	They
at	the	this	last	minutes
was	were	ago	TV	the
train	an	week	hour	library

 118

Vocabulary

3a Work in pairs. Choose list A or B. Your partner says the dates. Write them down in your notebook. Change roles. Then check your answers.

A	B
1904	1931
1956	1989
2008	2003
2014	2012

3b Now try again.

A	B
17/05/1833	1/12/1899
29/01/1990	7/02/1954
10/04/2000	20/10/2007
6/06/2015	31/08/2020

4a Read the words in the list for one minute. Cover the list and write the words in your notebook. How many can you remember?

asked	liked	talked
closed	phoned	worked

4b Now try again.

answered	listened	studied
invented	stopped	travelled

Grammar

Exercise 2

- Intelligence types: Visual/Spatial, Verbal/Linguistic, Intrapersonal
- Learner types: Visual

Answers

There weren't/were not any computers in the classroom.
Lucy's friends were at the café fifteen minutes ago.
I wasn't/was not at the train station.
My brother was on the TV last week.
They were in the library an hour ago.

Vocabulary

Exercise 3

- Intelligence types: Verbal/Linguistic, Logical/Mathematical, Interpersonal
- Learner types: Auditory

Answers

3a
A nineteen oh four
nineteen fifty-six
two thousand and eight
two thousand and fourteen
B nineteen thirty-one
nineteen eighty-nine
two thousand and three
two thousand and twelve

3b
A the seventeenth of May, eighteen thirty-three
the twenty-ninth of January, nineteen ninety
the tenth of April, two thousand
the sixth of June, twenty fifteen
B the first of December, eighteen ninety-nine
the seventh of February, nineteen fifty-four
the twentieth of October, two thousand and seven
the thirty-first of August, two thousand and twenty

Exercise 4

- Intelligence types: Visual/Spatial, Verbal/Linguistic, Intrapersonal
- Learner types: Visual

Definitions of intelligence types and learner types:
Teacher's Book pages 8–9

Spot the difference

Exercise 1

- Intelligence types: Visual/Spatial, Verbal/Linguistic, Intrapersonal
- Learner types: Visual

Answers

1 Nick's/is wearing a red T-shirt.
2 Julia's/is smiling and happy.
3 Nick's/has got a different mug (striped not spotted).

Brain Trainer 8

Spot the difference

1 Look at the photo on page 92 for one minute. Now study this photo. What differences can you spot?

Grammar

2 Make sentences with words of the same colour. Then make your own colour puzzle. In pairs, complete your partner's puzzle.

1 *I went to London yesterday.*

I	took	a	dinner	yesterday
didn't	bought	went	I	new
to	I	a	I	had
the	London	yesterday	jumper	drink
for	buy	train	pizza	I

3 Work in small groups. Act out something you did last weekend. Your classmates guess what you did. The person who gives the correct answer acts out the next activity.

Did you play football? / No, I didn't.

Vocabulary

4a Find two transport words hidden in the square.

m	o	t	o
c	a	r	r
r	u	l	b
b	e	k	i

4b Now make your own square. Can your partner find the words?

5a Look at the pictures. What are they? You've got three minutes!
1 T-shirt

5b Can you think of five more clothes words? You wear them on your head or your feet.

 119

Grammar

Exercise 2

- Intelligence types: Visual/Spatial, Verbal/Linguistic, Intrapersonal
- Learner types: Visual

Answers

I took the train yesterday.
I didn't buy a drink.
I had pizza for dinner.
I bought a new jumper.

Exercise 3

- Intelligence types: Verbal/Linguistic, Bodily/Kinaesthetic, Interpersonal
- Learner types: Auditory/Kinaesthetic/Tactile

Answers

Students' own answers

Vocabulary

Exercise 4

- Intelligence types: Visual/Spatial, Verbal/Linguistic, Intrapersonal
- Learner types: Visual

Answers

4a car, motorbike
4b Students' own answers

Exercise 5

- Intelligence types: Visual/Spatial, Verbal/Linguistic, Intrapersonal
- Learner types: Visual

Answers

5a 2 skirt
   3 scarf
   4 trousers
   5 jumper
   6 shorts
   7 dress
   8 coat
   9 jeans
   10 pyjamas
5b hat, cap, trainers, shoes, boots

Definitions of intelligence types and learner types:
Teacher's Book pages 8–9

217 ▶

Spot the difference

Exercise 1

- Intelligence types: Visual/Spatial, Verbal/Linguistic, Intrapersonal
- Learner types: Visual

Answers

1 The DJ isn't/is not wearing headphones.
2 Monica's in front of Julia, not behind her.
3 Monica's/is wearing a blue T-shirt, not a pink T-shirt.

Grammar

Exercise 2

- Intelligence types: Visual/Spatial, Verbal/Linguistic, Interpersonal
- Learner types: Visual, Auditory

Answers

1a She's/is going to buy an ebook tomorrow.
1b She's/is going to buy an ebook tomorrow.
1c He isn't/is not going to download a film tomorrow.
2a They aren't/are not going to visit the museum tomorrow.
2b She isn't/is not going to buy a mobile phone tomorrow.
2c He's/is going to do his homework.
3a *They aren't/are not going to visit the museum tomorrow.*
3b They're/are going to write a music blog tomorrow.
3c They're/are going to write a music blog tomorrow.

Vocabulary

Exercise 3

- Intelligence types: Visual/Spatial, Verbal/Linguistic, Intrapersonal
- Learner types: Visual

Answers

broadband, digital radio, ebook, instant messaging, memory stick, netbook, smartphone, social networking site, WiFi

Exercise 4

- Intelligence types: Visual/Spatial, Verbal/Linguistic, Intrapersonal
- Learner types: Visual

Answers

2 Charge your mobile phone
3 Download music
4 Use the internet
5 Send a text
6 Chat online
7 Write a blog

Definitions of intelligence types and learner types:
See Teacher's Book pages 8–9

Brain Trainer 9

Spot the difference

1 Look at the photo on page 102 for one minute. Now study this photo. What differences can you spot?

Grammar

2 Look at the picture for two minutes, then cover it. Now say a name. Your partner says what the people are or aren't going to do tomorrow.

3a – They aren't going to visit the museum tomorrow.

120

Vocabulary

3 Match ten technology words.
1 *interactive whiteboard*

memory ~~whiteboard~~
messaging band stick
net broad phone
smart
digital e book social
networking instant
radio
book site Wi
Fi ~~interactive~~

4 Look at the pictures. What are the mystery phrases?
1 *Send an email*

1 an

  your

  music.

use the

 a

  online.

  a

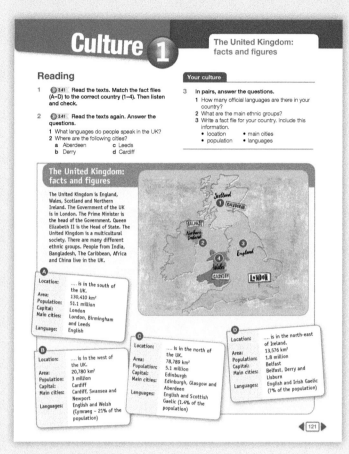

Reading

Exercise 1 (Track 3.41)

- Draw attention to the map, the picture and the texts and ask students what they can see.
- Individually, students match the fact files to the countries.
- If you wish, play the recording for students to listen and read.
- Check answers as a class.

Answers

A England
B Wales
C Scotland
D Northern Ireland

Exercise 2 (Track 3.41)

- Students read the text again and answer the questions.
- They then check in pairs before you check answers as a class.
- Elicit from stronger students or explain yourself the meaning of any new vocabulary, e.g. Government, Prime Minister, Head of State, multicultural, ethnic (group), location, population.

Answers

1 People speak four languages in the UK: English, Welsh, Scottish Gaelic and Irish Gaelic.
2 a Scotland
  b Northern Ireland
  c England
  d Wales

Your culture

Exercise 3

- Read through the questions with the class.
- In pairs, students ask and answer the questions.
- Monitor but do not interrupt fluency.
- Take feedback as a class. After correcting the fact files you could display them on the classroom walls.

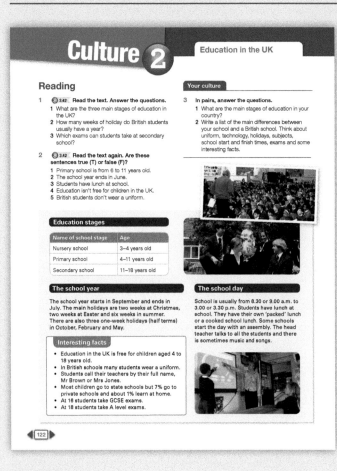

Exercise 2 (Track 3.42)

- When checking answers, ask students to correct the false sentences.
- Elicit from stronger students or explain yourself the meaning of any new vocabulary, e.g. half term, uniform, state school, private school, GCSE exams, A level exams, packed lunch, assembly, head teacher.

Answers

1 False (Primary school is from 4 to 11 years old.)
2 False (The school year ends in July.)
3 True
4 False (Education in the UK is free for children aged 4 to 18 years old.
5 False (In British schools many students wear a uniform.)

Your culture

Exercise 3

- Read through the questions with the class.
- In pairs, students ask and answer the questions.
- Monitor but do not interrupt fluency.
- Take feedback as a class. Collate suggestions for the main differences on the board.

Reading

Extra activity

Books closed. Write *'Secondary school: ___ – ___ years old'* on the board. Ask students what the ages are for secondary education in their country. Write up *'Holiday: ___ weeks a year'* and elicit how many weeks' holiday your students have in total. Finally write up *'Exams: ___ years old and ___ years old'* and elicit the main examination points for your students. Students open their books and skim read the text to find out how similar or different the secondary education system is in the UK.

Exercise 1 (Track 3.42)

- Draw attention to the photos and the text and ask students what they can see.
- Individually, students answer the questions.
- If you wish, play the recording for students to listen and read.
- Students compare their answers in pairs.
- Check answers by asking pairs of students to read questions and answers.

Answers

1 nursery, primary and secondary school
2 thirteen (two weeks at Christmas, two weeks at Easter, six weeks in summer and three half-term holidays)
3 GCSE and A level exams

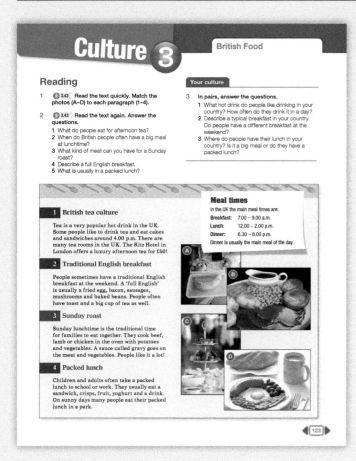

Reading

Books closed. Write the following word snake on the board:

sausagegravyeggcakebaconfruittoastbreadsandwich potatoesteabeef

Ask students to find the words in the snake. Books open. Students match the words with the foods in the photos. Drill the vocabulary for pronunciation and word stress, paying particular attention to the consonant clusters in /ˈsænwɪtʃ/ and the plural form /ˈsɒsɪdʒəz/. (Answers: *bacon*, *beef*, *bread*, *cake*, *egg*, *fruit*, *gravy*, *potatoes*, *sandwich*, *sausage*, *tea*)

Exercise 1 (Track 3.43)

- Draw attention to the photos and the text and ask students what they can see.
- Individually, students match the photos to the paragraphs.
- If you wish, play the recording for students to listen and read.
- Check answers as a class.

Answers

1 C **2** D **3** B **4** A

Exercise 2 (Track 3.43)

- Students read the text again and answer the questions.
- They then check in pairs before you check answers as a class.
- Elicit from stronger students or explain yourself the meaning of any new vocabulary, e.g. *cake*, *sandwich*, *traditional*, *fried (egg)*, *sausage*, *mushroom*, *baked beans*, *toast*, *beef*, *lamb*, *chicken*, *oven*, *potatoes*, *sauce*, *gravy*, *vegetables*, *crisps*, *fruit*, *yoghurt*, *drink*.

Answers

1 People eat cakes and sandwiches for afternoon tea.
2 British people often have a big meal at Sunday lunchtime.
3 You can have beef, lamb or chicken for a Sunday roast.
4 A full English breakfast includes a fried egg, bacon, sausages, mushrooms and baked beans with toast and tea.
5 There is usually a sandwich, crisps, fruit, yoghurt and a drink in a packed lunch.

Your culture

Exercise 3

- Read through the questions with the class.
- In pairs, students ask and answer the questions.
- Monitor but do not interrupt fluency.
- Take feedback as a class. If you have students from a variety of backgrounds, students can find the similarities and differences between their national dishes.

Reading

Exercise 1 (Track 3.44)

- Draw attention to the photos and the text and ask students what they can see.
- Individually, students match the headings to the paragraphs.
- If you wish, play the recording for students to listen and read.
- Check answers as a class.

Answers

1 B   2 E   3 C   4 D   5 A

Exercise 2 (Track 3.44)

- Students read the text again and answer the questions.
- Elicit from stronger students or explain yourself the meaning of any new vocabulary, e.g. *traffic, shape, tunnel, flow, college, level, conductor, street, facing forward/back.*

Answers

1 They use public transport because London is very big and travelling by car is expensive and often slow.
2 The other name for the London Underground is 'the tube'.
3 The River Thames flows through central London. 2,000 people use river boats on the Thames to get to work every day. On a boat from Greenwich to central London you can see the London Eye, the Tower of London and Big Ben.
4 Almost 500,000 people cycle to work or college every day.
5 A 'double-decker' is a red London bus with two levels.
6 Five people (and the driver) can travel in a black cab.

Your culture

Exercise 3

- Read through the questions with the class.
- In pairs, students ask and answer the questions.
- Monitor but do not interrupt fluency.
- Take feedback as a class.

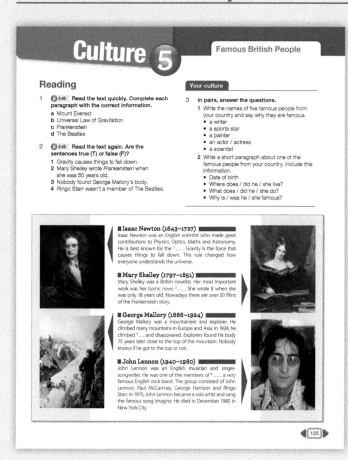

Reading

Books closed. Write *Newton*, *Shelley*, *Mallory* and *Lennon* on the board. Tell students that they are all surnames of famous British people. Ask them if they know what their first names are and why they are famous. If they don't know, don't tell them yet. In pairs, students order the people according to when they think they lived.

Books open. Draw students' attention to the pictures, the names and the dates.

Exercise 1 (Track 3.45)

- Draw attention to the pictures and the text and ask students what they can see.
- Individually, students complete the paragraphs.
- If you wish, play the recording for students to listen and read.
- Check answers as a class.

Answers

1 b   **2** c   **3** a   **4** d

Exercise 2 (Track 3.45)

- Students read the text again and decide if the sentences are true or false.
- When checking answers, ask students to correct the false sentences.
- Elicit from stronger students or explain yourself the meaning of any new vocabulary, e.g. *contribution*, *explorer*, *mountaineer*, *novel*, *nowadays*, *rule*, *singer-songwriter* and *solo artist*.

Answers

1 True
2 False (She wrote it when she was only 18 years old.)
3 False (Explorers found his body 75 years later close to the top of the mountain.)
4 False (Ringo Starr was a member of The Beatles.)

Your culture

Exercise 3

- Read through the questions with the class.
- In pairs, students ask and answer the questions.
- Monitor but do not interrupt fluency.
- Take feedback as a class. Collate suggestions on the board for the famous people and why they are famous before students complete the writing task in Exercise 2.

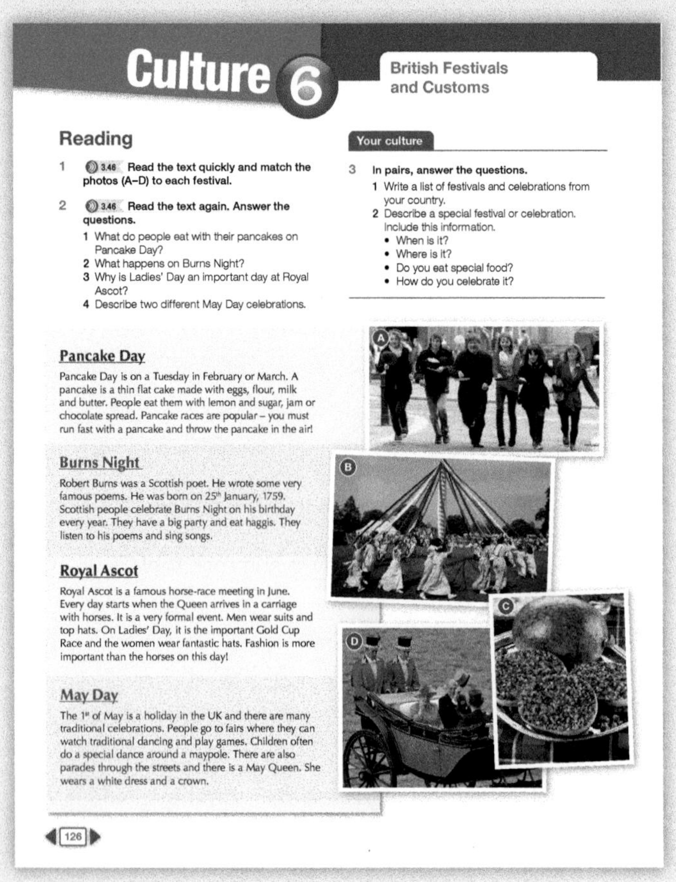

Culture 6 — British Festivals and Customs

Reading

1   **3.46** Read the text quickly and match the photos (A–D) to each festival.

2   **3.46** Read the text again. Answer the questions.
 1 What do people eat with their pancakes on Pancake Day?
 2 What happens on Burns Night?
 3 Why is Ladies' Day an important day at Royal Ascot?
 4 Describe two different May Day celebrations.

Your culture

3   In pairs, answer the questions.
 1 Write a list of festivals and celebrations from your country.
 2 Describe a special festival or celebration. Include this information.
  • When is it?
  • Where is it?
  • Do you eat special food?
  • How do you celebrate it?

Pancake Day
Pancake Day is on a Tuesday in February or March. A pancake is a thin flat cake made with eggs, flour, milk and butter. People eat them with lemon and sugar, jam or chocolate spread. Pancake races are popular – you must run fast with a pancake and throw the pancake in the air!

Burns Night
Robert Burns was a Scottish poet. He wrote some very famous poems. He was born on 25th January, 1759. Scottish people celebrate Burns Night on his birthday every year. They have a big party and eat haggis. They listen to his poems and sing songs.

Royal Ascot
Royal Ascot is a famous horse-race meeting in June. Every day starts when the Queen arrives in a carriage with horses. It is a very formal event. Men wear suits and top hats. On Ladies' Day, it is the important Gold Cup Race and the women wear fantastic hats. Fashion is more important than the horses on this day!

May Day
The 1st of May is a holiday in the UK and there are many traditional celebrations. People go to fairs where they can watch traditional dancing and play games. Children often do a special dance around a maypole. There are also parades through the streets and there is a May Queen. She wears a white dress and a crown.

126

Reading

Extra activity

Books closed. Elicit from the class the months of the year and write them on the board from left to right. Draw an arrow right at the beginning of January and write *New Year*. Draw further arrows relating to festivals in the students' own country and elicit the names for these, e.g. *Easter, Valentine's Day, Halloween.* Drill the vocabulary for pronunciation and word stress.
Books open. Students look at the four British festivals and tell you where to mark them on the calendar.

Cultural note

The 1st of May is a holiday in the UK if it is a Monday. Otherwise the holiday is on the first Monday in May.

)) Exercise 1 (Track 3.46)

• Draw attention to the photos and the text and ask students what they can see.
• Individually, students match the photos to the paragraphs.
• If you wish, play the recording for students to listen and read.
• Check answers as a class.

Answers

Pancake Day A
Burns Night C
Royal Ascot D
May Day B

)) Exercise 2 (Track 3.46)

• Play the recording for students to listen and read and answer the questions.
• Elicit from stronger students or explain yourself the meaning of any new vocabulary, e.g. *pancake, thin, flat, flour, milk, butter, lemon, sugar, jam, poet, haggis, carriage, formal (event), suit, (top) hat, fair, maypole, parade, crown.*

Answers

1 People eat lemon and sugar, jam or chocolate spread with their pancakes.
2 People have a big party, eat haggis, sing songs and listen to the poems of Robert Burns.
3 Because it is the Gold Cup Race and also because the women wear fantastic and fashionable hats.
4 People go to fairs and watch traditional dancing (around a maypole) and play games. There are parades through the streets and there is a May Queen. She wears a white dress and a crown.

Your culture

Exercise 3

• Read through the questions with the class.
• In pairs, students ask and answer the questions.
• Monitor but do not interrupt fluency.
• Take feedback as a class. If you have students from a variety of backgrounds, students can tell each other about some of their festivals and customs.

Students' Book Audioscripts

CD1 Track 17   Unit 1, page 16
Listening Exercises 1 and 2

1

Presenter Is this your collection, Peter?
Boy 1 Yes, this is my *Karate Kid* collection. It's my favourite film and Dre is my favourite character. He's really good! The actor is Jaden Smith. His dad is Will Smith.

2

Presenter Peter's mum is here. Is Peter's collection big?
Mum Well, it's a small collection really. He's got about 20 things, but some of those things are big. Look at the costume. These things are not cheap but they're very popular.

3

Presenter And here's Peter's brother. Are you a *Karate Kid* fan, too?
Boy 2 No! It's boring! My favourite film is *Toy Story*. Buzz is cooool!

CD1 Track 29   Unit 2, page 26
Listening Exercise 1

Interviewer Next please. Hello! What's your name?
Kate My name's Kate. Kate Moore.
Interviewer OK, Kate. Can you swim?
Kate Yes, I can. I can swim and I can run very fast.
Interviewer Excellent. And what about singing and dancing? Can you sing?
Kate Um …
Interviewer Ah. Can you dance?
Kate Yes, I can.
Interviewer Well, thank you Kate. Next please! What's your name?
Latika Hello, I'm Latika Malik. I can climb trees and I can jump up high.
Interviewer Mmm hm. Can you swim?
Latika Oh, no, I can't swim. But I can sing and dance.
Interviewer Right, well thank you, Latika.

CD1 Track 42   Unit 3, page 36
Listening Exercises 1 and 2

Interviewer Jin is with us today. He goes to school in China. Jin, what time does your school day start?
Jin Our day starts at 7.30 a.m. and we finish school at 5.00 p.m.
Interviewer That's a long day! Do you have a lunch break?
Jin Of course. We have a two-hour lunch break.
Interviewer All students at your school wear a uniform: what do you wear?
Jin At school I wear a white shirt and blue trousers. But for PE we wear yellow shirts.
Interviewer When do you have PE lessons?
Jin In our school we do exercise every day! It's fun!
Interviewer That's great. And do you like studying?
Jin Yes, we do. We study in summer, too!

CD2 Track 9   Unit 4, page 50
Listening Exercises 1 and 2

Interviewer Hello, today Anna is in the studio, with her dog, Dickens. Anna, why is your dog special?
Anna Well, Dickens is an actor! He's the star in a film.
Interviewer What does he do in the film?
Anna He climbs a tree, he jumps out of a car and then he swims in the sea. And he dances with a cat!
Interviewer That's amazing. Do you teach Dickens?
Anna Yes, I do. He's a great student. He loves learning new things!
Interviewer Does he like talking on the radio? Can you say 'Hello', Dickens?
Anna Dickens! Say hello!
Dickens Woof.

CD2 Track 25   Unit 5, page 60
Listening Exercises 1 and 2

1

My name's Blake. I'm from Calgary in Canada. My favourite time of year is autumn because the trees here are orange and red and yellow and gold. It's fantastic!

2

My name's Yoko. I'm Japanese but I live in America. I love my country – spring is fantastic in Japan. There is cherry blossom on all the trees – the flowers are small and pink and white; we have a special festival for this time of year.

3

My name's Paulo. I'm from Buenos Aires in Argentina. My favourite time of year is summer. Our summer is in January! It's hot and sunny every day so I go swimming with my friends.

CD2 Track 37   Unit 6, page 70
Listening Exercises 2 and 3

Interviewer	Today I'm talking to three children about their national dishes. Where are you from, Diego?
Diego	I'm from Chile.
Interviewer	Tell me about Chile's national dish.
Diego	Well, we often eat empanada. It's a kind of bread with meat or vegetables inside. Sometimes we have empanada with prawns. It's delicious!
Interviewer	And what about you, Tony?
Tony	I'm from Greece, and our national dish is moussaka. It's meat with vegetables, tomatoes, cheese and a milk sauce.
Interviewer	Very nice. Katie, you're from England.
Katie	That's right.
Interviewer	And what's England's national dish?
Katie	Oh, I think it's fish and chips. Everyone loves fish and chips.
Interviewer	Thank you Diego, Tony and Katie.

CD3 Track 11   Unit 7, page 84
Listening Exercises 1 and 2

1

Speaker 1	My job? I work in the gift shop at the Museum. People can buy copies of paintings there. Andy Warhol paintings are always popular – people often buy that big pink picture of Marilyn Monroe.

2

Speaker 2	I love my job. I take photographs of the art in the exhibitions, so we can put the photos in our brochure. Have you got the new brochure with the black and grey graffiti picture? That's my photo.

3

Speaker 2	Am I an artist? No, I sell tickets here! It's a great place to work – we're very busy because the new 'Time Tunnels' exhibition opened this week. About five hundred people visited yesterday!

CD3 Track 26   Unit 8, page 94
Listening Exercises 1 and 2

Erik	Hi Rose, how are you?
Rose	Not good! Today was a terrible day.
Erik	Why? What happened?
Rose	Well, I got up late because I didn't hear my alarm clock. Then I missed the school bus.
Erik	Oh no! So how did you get to school?
Rose	I rode my bike. But then it started to rain. So when I arrived at school I was really wet and cold.
Erik	Oh dear.
Rose	The teacher was angry because I was late and she gave me extra homework.
Erik	Uh oh!
Rose	And now I'm at home and I've got another problem.
Erik	What's that?
Rose	I left my homework at school!

CD3 Track 37   Unit 9, page 104
Listening Exercises 1 and 2

Interviewer	What are you doing this summer? Have you got any plans?

A

Boy A	I'm teaching my grandad about technology this summer! He's got a computer but he can't send emails or use a search engine! He's going to pay me £2.00 an hour.

B

Girl B	I'm having a technology-free summer! I'm going to see my friends every day and we're going to the beach. I'm having tennis lessons, too. I'm not going online at all!

C

Boy C	My plans? Well, I want to be a writer so I'm going to write a short story. It isn't going to be a 'keitai' novel or a 'Twitter' novel, though. I want to write a real book.

Workbook Audioscripts

Track 5   Unit 1, page 14
Listening Exercises 1–3

Harry Hi Kim. What's in that bag?
Kim It's my new Zac Efron poster. It's for my bedroom. Zac's my favourite actor. I've got all three *High School Musical* DVDs. He's fantastic in them.
Harry Yes, they're really popular films. What other films is Zac in? Is he in *Karate Kid*?
Kim No, he's in *Hairspray*, *17 Again* and *Charlie St Cloud*. I haven't got those DVDs but I've got some of his songs on my MP3 player.
Harry Is he a singer?
Kim Yes, of course he is. The *High School Musical* films have got lots of songs! He's a dancer too.

Track 9   Unit 2, page 22
Listening Exercises 1 and 2

Maddy I'm tired. Where are we? Are we near the cinema now?
Tom I don't know. Have you got the map, Maddy?
Maddy Yes, it's in my backpack with my mobile phone.
Tom Can I have it, please?
Maddy Yes. Here you are, Tom.
Tom Thanks. Let's see. We're next to a police station.
Maddy There's a statue of a king in front of a museum over there. And I can see a train station.
Tom We're here. We're in Green Street. The cinema's in the next street.
Maddy That's great. You've got the tickets, haven't you?
Tom Yes, they're in my bag. Let's go.

Track 13   Unit 3, page 30
Listening Exercises 1 and 2

Interviewer Today we welcome Darren Wentworth. Darren, you're thirteen but you don't go to school. Why not?
Darren My parents are teachers and I study at home with my two sisters. We have lessons with our mum and dad. It's called home schooling.
Interviewer What do you study?
Darren The same subjects as other school children: Maths, English, History, Geography, Art, French, Science …
Interviewer What about Music?
Darren I play the guitar and my sisters have piano lessons. My guitar lesson is on Wednesdays.
Interviewer How do you make friends?
Darren We meet other home-schooled children every week. We go to the swimming pool, a museum or the cinema. We have fun together.

Track 17   Unit 4, page 40
Listening Exercises 1–3

Interviewer Today photographer Ben Jonson's with us. He's Pet Photographer of the Year. Ben, tell us about your work.
Ben Every day's different. Every day I take photos of different animals.
Interviewer Are there people in the photos?
Ben Not usually.
Interviewer You've got a website. Are there any unusual pets on your website?
Ben Yes, there's a photo of a red frog on a twig.
Interviewer Are there any funny photos?
Ben Yes, the photo of a tarantula on a man's head is funny. It looks like his hair.
Interviewer Do the animals bite you?
Ben Hardly ever. Luckily!
Interviewer Finally, what's your favourite photo?
Ben It's a photo of a goat.
Interviewer Thank you, Ben.

Track 20   Unit 5, page 48
Listening Exercises 1 and 2

Fliss Dan, have we got Art next?
Dan No, it's PE now. Hurry up. We're late.
Fliss Where's Helen?
Dan Look. She's playing tennis with George.
Fliss What's Olivia doing?
Dan She's swimming. You can play tennis or go swimming.
Fliss What are you doing?
Dan It's sunny so I'm playing tennis. What about you?
Fliss Well, I haven't got my swimming costume with me, so I can't go swimming.
Dan So you're playing tennis too!
Fliss Yes.
Dan I love PE when the weather's nice. I hate playing football when it's raining.
Fliss I like winter sports. I go ice-skating every week in winter. I usually go skiing with my family in February too.
Dan My favourite sport is surfing. Every summer we go to the beach. It's great!

Track 24   Unit 6, page 56
Listening Exercises 1–3

Interviewer	*Young Masterchef* is the popular TV cooking competition for children between 10 and 12 years old. We have with us this year's winner, 11-year-old George. Congratulations, George. Tell us what happens in the competition.
George	We cook meals for different people. Sometimes for writers, sometimes for pop stars or actors. It's exciting.
Interviewer	Today, George is cooking his winning meal for us. What is it?
George	First, I'm making tomato soup. Then I'm cooking fish with potatoes. Finally, I'm making my favourite dish: strawberry cheesecake.
Interviewer	That sounds delicious. Do you want to be a cook?
George	Yes, I'd like to be a chef with my own restaurant.

Track 29   Unit 7, page 66
Listening Exercises 1 and 2

Interviewer	The start of the new millennium was many years ago now. We asked two people what they remember. Katy, where were you at 12 o'clock on 1st January 2000?
Girl	I was at home in Edinburgh with my family. I was only five years old but we all stayed up until midnight. We watched the celebrations on TV.
Interviewer	What about you, Toby?
Man	I was in London with friends. There were thousands of people in the streets. We listened to Big Ben strike twelve and then we watched the fireworks over the River Thames. It was an amazing night.

Track 34   Unit 8, page 72
Listening Exercises 1–3

Mum	Let's go to Scotland for our holiday this year.
Paul	That's a great idea. How do we get there?
Sally	Let's fly.
Mum	No, that's expensive.
Sally	Dad can drive us there.
Dad	I'm not driving. It's a long way and I don't want to drive for five hours.
Paul	Can we go by train?
Mum	No, we can't, Paul. There are three changes and we always have heavy bags.
Paul	Sally takes too many clothes.
Sally	No, I don't. What about going by coach?
Paul	I don't want to go by coach. Coaches make me sick.
Mum	I've got a better idea. Let's stay at home this summer.
Paul & Sally	But Mum …

Track 37   Unit 9, page 82
Listening Exercises 1 and 2

Teacher	Welcome to the High School Quiz Night. Two teams are going to compete to win tonight. Let's start. Round 1 is Technology. 1 Who invented the television?
Student 1	John Logie Baird.
Teacher	Correct. 2 Our school's going to buy IWBs for every classroom. What's an IWB?
Student 2	Instant messaging.
Teacher	No, that's IM. What's an IWB?
Student 3	An interactive whiteboard.
Teacher	Correct. 3 What technology can you use to read novels?
Student 4	Ebooks.
Teacher	Correct. 4 What does WWW stand for?
Student 3	World Wide Web.
Teacher	Correct. 5 What are MySpace and Facebook?
Student 1	Search engines.
Teacher	No.
Student 4	Social networking sites.
Teacher	Correct. 6 Where does solar power come from?
Student 2	The Sun.
Teacher	Correct. OK. The next round is Music.

Track 41   Speaking and Listening 1, page 113
Listening Exercises 3 and 4

Mum	Joe, you're late and you aren't ready for school.
Joe	I know, Mum. Where are my things? Where's my backpack?
Mum	It's behind the door.
Joe	And my school books?
Mum	They're on your desk.
Joe	Where are my football boots?
Mum	They're under your bed.
Joe	Have you got my MP3 player?
Mum	No, I haven't. Look! It's next to the laptop. Have you got your mobile phone?
Joe	Yes, I have. It's in my backpack!
Mum	Is that everything?
Joe	Yes, it is.
Mum	OK.
Joe	Bye, Mum.
Mum	Bye.

Track 44   Speaking and Listening 2, page 114
Listening Exercises 3 and 4

Teacher Sit down and listen, please. Welcome to the museum. There's lots to see and enjoy but remember there are other people here. Don't run or shout. Please don't touch the objects. You've got an hour to look round. Stay with your group and don't go outside. Come back here at half past twelve, please.
Will Louise, Zak. Let's go!
Louise Look at those boots.
Will They're very small.
Zak What's this?
Will It's an old chair.
Zak Be careful, Louise! There's a dinosaur behind you!
Louise Ha ha! It isn't real!

Track 47   Speaking and Listening 3, page 115
Listening Exercises 3 and 4

Fergal There's a fantastic film on at the cinema tonight. It's about some aliens. Do you want to come?
Maria I'm not sure. I've got a horse-riding lesson at quarter to six.
Fergal When does your riding lesson finish?
Maria It's half an hour. It finishes at quarter past six. What time does the film start?
Fergal It starts at half past seven and it finishes at ten past nine.
Maria That's fine. Yes, I want to see it. What time is it now?
Fergal It's twenty past five.
Maria OK. See you outside the cinema at five past seven.
Fergal Great. See you later.

Track 50   Speaking and Listening 4, page 116
Listening Exercises 3 and 4

Millie Hi George! I'm so happy. *X Factor*'s on TV again tonight. It's my favourite programme.
George I don't like *X Factor*.
Millie Why not?
George I don't like singing competitions!
Millie What do you like watching?
George I like watching sport, especially football.
Millie I hate watching football. It's so boring.
George I'm a Chelsea fan and I love watching the games on TV.
Millie What's your favourite programme?
George It's *Springwatch*.
Millie That isn't a sports programme.
George I know. It's a wildlife programme. I like learning about birds and animals.

Track 53   Speaking and Listening 5, page 117
Listening Exercises 3 and 4

Richard Hello, Aunty Brenda.
Brenda Hello, Richard. Happy Birthday.
Richard Mum, Dad, Aunty Brenda's here.
Dad Really? This is a surprise! How nice to see you, Brenda. Come in.
Brenda I've got a present for you, Richard.
Richard Wow! A skateboard. That's fantastic! Thank you so much.
Brenda There's a book too.
Richard Great! I love it.
Dad Can you stay for dinner?
Brenda I'm sorry I can't. I've got an interview on Radio 5 this evening.
Richard How cool is that! Can I go to the studio with you?
Brenda Maybe next time, but not today. I'm sorry but I must go. Have a lovely birthday, Richard.
Richard Thanks, Aunty Brenda. Bye.
Brenda Bye.

Track 56   Speaking and Listening 6, page 118
Listening Exercises 3 and 4

Waiter Hello.
Elena Hello. Can we sit next to the window, please?
Waiter Yes, of course. Here are the menus.
Elena Thank you.
Hans Are you ready to order?
Olivia Yes. I'd like chicken with tomato sauce, please.
Waiter Would you like anything to drink?
Olivia Yes, I'd like some orange juice, please. What about you, Elena?
Elena I'll have the salmon and broccoli. And can I have a glass of apple juice, please? Hans?
Hans I'd like the ham and cheese pizza and I'll have apple juice too, please.
Waiter Is that everything?
Hans Yes, thank you.
Olivia How is your food?
Elena It's delicious.
Hans Yes, this is an excellent restaurant.

Track 59   Speaking and Listening 7, page 119
Listening Exercises 3 and 4

Interviewer Today we have with us the American actress, Donna Martin. Donna, you arrived here last Sunday. Is this your first visit to the UK?

Donna No! I was here two years ago. In fact, this is my fifth visit. I love England.

Interviewer You're here to talk about your new film *Generation Rox*. Tell us about it.

Donna It's about two girls. They moved from a small town in the USA to London in the summer of 1966. They stayed for two months. This is their story. It's a very funny film. And the music's great. I love music from the 1960s!

Track 62   Speaking and Listening 8, page 120
Listening Exercises 3 and 4

Joel Hello. Joel speaking.

Rob Hello, Joel. Can I speak to Eve, please?

Joel Who is it, please?

Rob It's Rob.

Joel Hold on. [Eve, it's Rob] Here she is.

Eve Hi, Rob.

Rob Hi, Eve, did you go to the Wildlife Club yesterday?

Eve Sorry, I can't hear you. Can you speak up, please?

Rob Did you go to the Wildlife Club yesterday?

Eve Yes, I did. Why?

Rob Did they talk about the trip to the lake?

Eve Yes.

Rob What date is it?

Eve It's on Saturday, 27th July.

Rob That's great. I'm free on that day. I can go.

Eve Me too.

Rob Fantastic. Thanks for the information, Eve.

Eve That's OK. Bye.

Rob Bye.

Track 65   Speaking and Listening 9, page 121
Listening Exercises 3 and 4

Mum Oh no! What happened, Simon?

Simon I fell off my bike.

Mum Tell me about it.

Simon I was with Paul in the park. We were on our bikes and Anna's dog ran in front of me. I stopped, but I fell off.

Mum Was the dog OK?

Simon Yes, I didn't hit the dog. It was fine.

Mum Your leg's dirty. I'm going to clean it. Now, what are you planning for this evening?

Simon I'm going to Paul's house after dinner.

Mum That isn't a good idea. Stay at home and watch TV with me. There's a good film on tonight.

Simon OK, Mum.

Workbook Answer Key

Starter Unit

Vocabulary
Countries and Nationalities

Exercise 1
2 England
3 French
4 Mexican
5 Greek
6 Brazil

Numbers

Exercise 2
2 18; eigtheen
3 35; thirty-five
4 74; seventy-four
5 293; two hundred and ninety-three
6 1,532; one thousand, five hundred and thirty-two

Spelling

Exercise 3
2 thirteen
3 Edinburgh
4 Bonanza
5 Truro, England

Classroom Objects

Exercise 4

Across
2 backpack
4 ruler
6 notebook
7 pencils

Down
1 calculator
3 desk
4 rubber
5 pens

Days of the Week and Months of the Year

Exercise 5
2 Tuesday
3 Friday
4 Thursday
5 Wednesday
6 Saturday
7 Monday

Correct order:
Sunday
Monday
Tuesday
Wednesday
Thursday
Friday
Saturday

Exercise 6
2 February
3 March
4 April
5 May
6 June
7 July
8 August
9 September
10 October
11 November
12 December

Classroom Language

Exercise 7
2 May
3 Tuesday
4 fifteen
5 interactive whiteboard
6 Brazilian

Exercise 8
2 What's the homework?
3 Can you repeat that please?
4 How do you say 'mesa' in English?
5 Open your books!
6 How do you spell 30?

Grammar *To be*

Exercise 1
2 'm
3 'm
4 is
5 isn't
6 is
7 are
8 aren't
9 are

Exercise 2
2 He
3 We
4 It
5 You
6 I'm

Exercise 3
2 He is at the park.
3 We aren't from Brazil.
4 It isn't very tall.
5 You are fourteen.
6 I'm from London.

Exercise 4
2 Is Lucille French? Yes, she is.
3 Is Luisa Brazilian? No, she isn't. She's Portuguese.
4 Are Nick and Theo Italian? No, they aren't. They're Greek.
5 Is Javier Spanish? Yes, he is.
6 Are Rosa and Mercedes Mexican? Yes, they are.

Wh- questions

Exercise 5
2 Who is your favourite teacher? (Students' own answers)
3 What is your favourite animal?
4 Where is your house?
5 When is your birthday?
6 How old are you?

This/That/These/Those

Exercise 6
2 This
3 These
4 That
5 Those
6 That

Unit 1 My World

Vocabulary Objects

Exercise 1
2 mobile phone
3 ice skates
4 MP3 player
5 watch
6 magazine
7 DVD
8 skateboard

G	A	M	E	S	C	O	N	S	O	L	E
I	F	P	D	J	K	I	L	E	A	Z	M
G	B	3	U	M	B	D	L	Q	Z	W	A
A	M	P	W	T	H	V	V	I	W	A	G
T	P	L	F	P	C	D	W	I	A	T	A
S	K	A	T	E	B	O	A	R	D	C	Z
H	J	Y	C	I	N	A	D	I	S	H	I
I	C	E	S	K	A	T	E	S	T	S	N
Q	K	R	H	P	I	X	Q	G	Y	E	E
S	M	O	B	I	L	E	P	H	O	N	E

Exercise 2
2 poster
3 wallet
4 laptop
5 camera
6 guitar

Exercise 3
b 4 c 1 d 2 e 3 f 5

Exercise 4
2 mobile phone
3 ice skates
4 DVD
5 skateboard

Exercise 5
(any order)
2 A comic is a story with superheroes.
3 A poster is a big picture.
4 A skateboard is a board with wheels.
5 A laptop is a computer.
6 A watch is a small clock.

Reading

Exercise 1
2 Megan
3 Jon
4 Jon
5 Megan
6 Jon

Exercise 2
2 c 3 a 4 e 5 b

Exercise 3
2 T 3 F 4 T 5 T 6 F

Exercise 4
2 No, it isn't.
3 There are six.
4 Yes, she has.
5 Yes, they are.
6 No, it isn't.

Grammar *Have got*

Exercise 1
2 hasn't got
3 have got
4 's got
5 haven't got
6 've got

Exercise 2
2 Have
3 Has
4 haven't
5 has
6 hasn't
7 Have

Exercise 3
2 haven't got
3 hasn't got
4 have got
5 has got
6 have got

Exercise 4
2 haven't got my
3 've got my
4 've got my
5 haven't got my

Exercise 5
2 Have they got laptops? No, they haven't.
3 Has she got a watch? Yes, she has.
4 Has it got a ball? No, it hasn't.
5 Has he got a mobile phone? No, he hasn't.
6 Have they got skateboards? No, they haven't.

Vocabulary Adjectives

Exercise 1
2 a 3 b 4 a 5 a

Exercise 2
2 boring
3 unpopular
4 easy
5 bad
6 cheap

Exercise 3
2 expensive
3 difficult
4 new
5 popular
6 good

Exercise 4
2 popular
3 good
4 small
5 easy
6 expensive

Exercise 5
Students' own answers

 **Talking about position**

Speaking and Listening

Exercise 1
in front of
next to
on
under
in
in
in

Exercise 2
2 It's behind Laura's
3 It's in front of Frank's
4 It's on Frank's desk.
5 It's under the chair.
6 They're in his backpack.

Exercise 3
2 on the computer
3 under the table
4 in the backpack
5 in front of the guitar
6 next to the table

Exercise 4
2 next to
3 under
4 behind
5 in

Exercise 5
It's in his backpack.

Exercise 6
Students' own answers

Grammar

Possessive adjectives and Possessive *'s*

Exercise 1
2 Have you got John's magazines?
3 That is my parents' laptop.
4 Those are Amanda's DVDs.
5 When is Ben's mum's birthday?

Exercise 2
2 your
3 His
4 Her
5 Their
6 My

Exercise 3
2 Charlie's
3 Jenny and Ed's
4 her mum's
5 the students'
6 your parents'

Exercise 4
2 your
3 Her
4 His
5 their
6 our
7 its

Exercise 5
2 They're/are Henry and Soraya's backpacks.
3 It's/Is Lily and Bella's bedroom.
4 They're/are Sasha's notebooks.

Reading

Exercise 1
2 d 3 b 4 a

Exercise 2
2 guitar
3 skateboard
4 guitar
5 comics

Exercise 3
2 Yes, it is.
3 No, it isn't.
4 No, they aren't.
5 Yes, they are.
6 No, it isn't
7 No, it hasn't.

Listening

Exercise 1
a

Exercise 2
2 three
3 Hairspray
4 MP3 player
5 singer and dancer

Exercise 3
2 Yes, it is.
3 Yes, they are.
4 No, she hasn't.
5 Yes, they have.

Writing A personal profile

Exercise 1
2 Helen's room's got pink walls.
3 Her room's got a window.
4 She's a Selena Gomez fan.
5 She's got lots of magazines.
6 Helen's family are in the photo.

Exercise 2
False sentence: Helen's room's got pink walls.

Exercise 3
2 Her clothes are in the cupboard.
3 The poster is on the wall.
4 Her MP3 player is on the desk.
5 The photo is on the table.

Exercise 4
Students' own answers

Exercise 5
Students' own answers

Unit 2 Around Town

Vocabulary Places in Town

Exercise 1
2 shopping centre
3 police station
4 museum
5 park
6 cinema
7 train station
8 café
9 library
Hidden place: 10 a hospital
(11 sports centre
12 bus station
13 town square
14 post office)

Exercise 2
1 b (13) 2 d (14) 3 a (12) 4 c (11)

Exercise 3
2 bank
3 train station
4 hospital
5 library
6 cinema

Exercise 4
2 Excuse me, is the bank near here?
3 Is that behind the hospital?
4 Thank you very much.
5 Yes, it's next to the post office.

Exercise 5
2; 1; 3; 5; 4

Reading

Exercise 1
1; 4; 5; 6; 8; 9; 10; 12

Exercise 2
2 the hotel
3 the banks
4 the café
5 the park

Exercise 3
2 F 3 F 4 F 5 T 6 T

Exercise 4
2 No, it isn't.   5 Yes, it is.
3 Yes, it is.   6 Yes, it is.
4 No, it isn't

Grammar
There is/There are; some/any

Exercise 1
a; c; d; e; f; g

Exercise 2
2 Is there; there isn't
3 any
4 some

Exercise 3
2 There aren't
3 There isn't
4 There are
5 There is
6 There aren't

Exercise 4
(Suggested answers)
2 There's a small dog.
3 There are two bikes.
4 There's one guitar.
5 There's a big tree.
6 There are three people.

Exercise 5
2 Is there a cat? No, there isn't.
3 Are there any magazines? Yes, there are.
4 Is there a swimming pool? No, there isn't.
5 Are there any garden chairs? No, there aren't.
6 Is there a house? Yes, there is.

Vocabulary Action verbs

Exercise 1
2 juggle   5 climb
3 dance   6 cycle
4 skate

2 b 3 a 4 a 5 b 6 a

Exercise 2
2 walk   5 play
3 jump   6 fly
4 sing

Exercise 3
2 cycle
3 walk
4 juggle
5 swim
6 sing

Exercise 4
clim(b)
g(u)itar
ta(l)k
(k)now

Exercise 5
2 a kite   5 six oranges
3 a race   6 the guitar
4 a tree
Students' own answers

 **Orders and warnings**

Speaking and Listening

Exercise 1
2 f 3 a 4 c 5 b 6 d

Exercise 2
2 Don't shout!
3 Don't touch it!
4 Don't move!
5 Be quiet!

Exercise 3
2 Look!
3 Don't shout!
4 Don't play with it!
5 Don't stand in front of it.

Exercise 4
Students' own answers

Grammar
Can/Can't for ability

Exercise 1
2 can't skateboard
3 can climb
4 can fly
5 can't walk

Exercise 2
2 I can   5 he can't
3 it can   6 she can
4 they can't

Exercise 3
2 can't   5 She can't
3 She can   6 She can
4 She can't

Exercise 4
(Students' own answers to questions)
2 Can your dad play the guitar?
3 Can your mum sing and dance?
4 Can you and your friends skate?
5 Can you climb a tree or a mountain?
6 Can you juggle with three balls?

Reading

Exercise 1
2

Exercise 2
2 e 3 b 4 a 5 c

Exercise 3
2 Yes, they are.   5 No, there aren't.
3 Yes, they can.   6 Yes, there is.
4 Yes, they can.

Listening

Exercise 1
1; 3; 4; 7

Exercise 2
2 police station
3 museum
4 train station
5 next street

Exercise 3
2 No, he hasn't.
3 No, she hasn't.
4 No, there isn't.
5 They are in Green Street, next to the police station.
6 Yes, he has.

Writing
A description of a town

Exercise 1
2 or   5 or
3 but   6 and
4 but

Exercise 2
2 centre   6 and
3 station   7 can
4 afternoon   8 or
5 interesting   9 cinema

Exercise 3
2 shopping centre   6 café
3 police station   7 restaurant
4 shops   8 cinema
5 museum

Exercise 4
go shopping; skateboard in the park; watch a film at the cinema; play sports; swim in the pool; have dinner in a French restaurant

Exercise 5
Students' own answers

Unit 3 School days

Vocabulary Daily routines

Exercise 1
2 f 3 d 4 e 5 c 6 a

Exercise 2
2 have a shower   5 go home
3 get dressed   6 have dinner
4 have breakfast   7 go to bed

Exercise 3
2 Sam 3 Bill 4 Sam 5 Bill

Exercise 4
go   home; to school
have   a shower; lunch
get   up; dressed

Exercise 5
2 have   6 have
3 get   7 go
4 have   8 have
5 go   9 go

Reading

Exercise 1
1; 2; 3; 4; 6

Exercise 2
2 a 3 f 4 b 5 d 6 e

Exercise 3
2 likes   5 goes
3 doesn't go   6 goes
4 isn't

Exercise 4
2 Yes, she can.   5 Yes, he has
3 No, it isn't.   6 Yes, he is.
4 Yes, it is.

Grammar

Present simple: affirmative and negative

Exercise 1
2 play; plays   5 watch; watches
3 have; has   6 go; goes
4 do; does

Exercise 2
2 don't get up   5 don't play
3 doesn't have   6 doesn't like
4 doesn't read

Exercise 3
2 /z/   5 /s/
3 /ɪz/   6 /ɪz/
4 /z/

Exercise 4
2 tidies   9 play
3 clean   10 don't go
4 gives   11 watch
5 go   12 like
6 cycles   13 doesn't like
7 walk   14 likes
8 meet

Exercise 5
2 The girl doesn't watch TV. She reads books.
3 The boy doesn't go to the park. He plays computer games at home.
4 The friends don't go to the cinema. They have a picnic.
5 He doesn't study French. He studies English.
6 I don't play football. I do a puzzle.

Vocabulary School subjects

Exercise 1
2 b 3 a 4 d 5 c 6 e

Exercise 2
Across
4 Literature
6 ICT
7 Geography
Down
2 Science
3 History
5 English
8 Art

Exercise 3
2 c 3 a 4 f 5 d 6 b

Exercise 4
2 Music   5 Art
3 Literature   6 Science
4 French

Exercise 5
Students' own answers

Chatroom Time

Speaking and Listening

Exercise 1
What time is it?
It's half past one.
What time does your lesson start?
It's at quarter to four.
… what time does it finish?
It finishes at four fifteen.

Exercise 2
2 d 3 b 4 e 5 a

Exercise 3
2 It's half past eight. It's eight thirty.
3 It's ten to five. It's four fifty.
4 It's ten past eight. It's eight ten.
5 It's quarter past eleven. It's eleven fifteen.
6 It's quarter to four. It's three forty-five.

Exercise 4
2 e 3 g 4 c 5 f 6 a 7 h 8 d

Exercise 5
2 It's twenty past six. What's on TV tonight?
3 There's a great film about monsters.
4 What time does it start?
5 It starts at seven o'clock.
6 When does it finish?
7 At eight forty.
8 OK. Let's watch that.

Exercise 6
Students' own answers

Grammar

Present simple: questions and short answers

Exercise 1
2 Does   5 Do
3 Do   6 Does
4 Does

Exercise 2
2 e do   5 c does
3 f doesn't 6 a don't
4 b does

Exercise 3
(Students' own answers to questions)
2 Do
3 Does
4 Do
5 Does

Exercise 4
2 No, he doesn't   5 No, they don't.
3 Yes, they do.   6 No, she doesn't.
4 Yes, he does.

Exercise 5
(Students' own answers to questions)
2 Does your mum get up at 7 a.m.?
3 Do you tidy your room every day?
4 Does your best friend like animals?
5 Do your parents go to the cinema at the weekend?
6 Does your teacher give you homework every day?

Reading

Exercise 1
2

Exercise 2
2 F 3 T 4 F 5 F 6 T

Exercise 3
2 Yes, they are.   5 Yes, they do.
3 Yes, he does.   6 Yes, he does.
4 No, he emails it.

Listening

Exercise 1
1

Exercise 2
2 has
3 studies
4 don't play
5 meet

Exercise 3
2 sisters
3 other school children
4 piano lessons
5 Wednesdays
6 the cinema

Writing An email

Exercise 1
2 in
3 on
4 at
5 On
6 in
7 on
8 on
9 at
10 on

Exercise 2
Tuesday   party / evening
Wednesday   free
Thursday   free
Friday   guitar lesson / 5.20
Students' own answers

Exercise 3
Students' own answers

Exercise 4
Students' own answers

Check Your Progress 1

Grammar

Exercise 1
1 have got; Its
2 's got; Her
3 've got; parents'
4 John's; hasn't got
5 haven't got; Their

Exercise 2
1 There isn't a
2 There's an
3 There aren't any
4 There are some
5 There isn't a

Exercise 3
1 Yes, he can.
2 Yes, he can.
3 No, they can't.
4 Yes, they can.
5 No, she can't.

Exercise 4
1 don't eat; stay
2 don't wear; wear
3 doesn't cycle; walks
4 Does; teach; doesn't
5 Do; finish; do

Vocabulary

Exercise 5
1 Maths e
2 History c
3 Literature d
4 Geography b
5 Music a

Exercise 6
1 café
2 museum
3 hospital
4 library
5 sports centre

Speaking

Exercise 7
1 f under
2 d behind
3 e in front of
4 a next to
5 b in
6 c on

Exercise 8
1 at quarter past nine
2 at quarter to eleven
3 at half past twelve
4 at two o'clock
5 at ten past three

Translation

Exercise 9
Students' own answers

Dictation

Exercise 10
1 On Monday mornings Helen gets up at eight o'clock.
2 She gets dressed and has her breakfast.
3 She rides her mum's bike to school.
4 Her first lesson is English and then she has Science.
5 She finishes school at ten past three.

Unit 4 Animal Magic

Vocabulary

Unusual animals

Exercise 1
2 pygmy goat
3 giant rabbit
4 frog
5 hissing cockroach

Exercise 2
6 stick insect
7 tarantula
8 lizard
9 parrot
10 python

Exercise 3
2 python
3 parrot
4 pygmy goat

Exercise 4
2 bird
3 rabbit; cat
4 reptile; python
5 hissing cockroach; stick insect
6 piranha
7 spider

Exercise 5
2 Parrots
3 Frogs
4 insects
5 Tarantulas
6 mammals

Exercise 6
2 do
3 have
4 lizard
5 reptile
6 amphibian

Reading

Exercise 1
Photo 2 rabbits

Exercise 2
2 T 3 T 4 F 5 T 6 F

Exercise 3
2 donkeys
3 Year 7
4 likes
5 chickens
6 big

Exercise 4
2 There are four goats.
3 They are on Tuesdays.
4 She learns about animals.
5 She goes early to help on the farm.
6 She feeds them, gives them clean water, cleans the enclosure and collects the eggs.

Grammar

Adverbs of frequency

Exercise 1
2 hardly ever
3 sometimes
4 often
5 usually
6 always

Exercise 2
2 Bob 3 Will 4 Bob 5 Will 6 Will

Exercise 3
Students' own answers

Exercise 4
2 She often watches TV on Sunday.
3 She sometimes goes to the cinema.
4 She always talks to her friends on the phone.
5 She is hardly ever bored.
6 Does she usually do her homework?

Exercise 5
2 Visitors are sometimes scared of the spiders.
3 Our dog never goes on my bed.
4 She always feeds the cat.
5 Do you usually clean the rabbit enclosure?
6 We hardly ever go to the zoo.

Grammar

Present simple with wh- questions

Exercise 1
2 How often
3 Who
4 Why
5 When
6 What

Exercise 2
2 What
3 Where
4 When
5 How often

Exercise 3
2 Who is scared of spiders?
3 How often do you take your dog for a walk?
4 Where do pythons come from?
5 When does the zookeeper feed the rabbits?

Exercise 4
2 Who is your English teacher?
3 Where is your school?
4 When is your birthday?
5 How often is your teacher away?

Vocabulary
Parts of the body

Exercise 1
2 a 3 c 4 b

Exercise 2
2 e 3 a 4 b 5 c

Exercise 3
2 fingers; toes
3 fins; tail
4 head; neck
5 legs; paws

Exercise 4
Students' own answers

 **Likes and dislikes**

Speaking and Listening

Exercise 1
3 ✓ 5 ✓

Exercise 2
3 ✓ 5 ✓ 6 ✓

Exercise 3
2 running   5 cooking
3 playing sport   6 eating
4 watching TV

Exercise 4
Students' own answers

Exercise 5
Students' own answers

Grammar *Must/Mustn't*

Exercise 1
1 b
2 d; f
3 a; e

Exercise 2
2 must
3 mustn't
4 mustn't
5 must

Exercise 3
2 He mustn't eat in the classroom.
3 They must wear a uniform.
4 We mustn't use our mobile phones.
5 She must listen to the teacher.
6 At school.

Exercise 4
2 must shut the gates
3 mustn't talk
4 mustn't stand on the desks
5 must tidy my room
6 must buy a tcket

Exercise 5
Students' own answers

Reading

Exercise 1
b

Exercise 2
2 F 3 F 4 T 5 T 6 F

Exercise 3
2 in newspapers/on his website
3 cats, dogs, horses, rabbits, guinea pigs, parrots and fish
4 in his studio, in the animal's home, outside
5 Because animals like being outside.

Listening

Exercise 1
2

Exercise 2
2 frog
3 tarantula
4 bite
5 goat

Exercise 3
2 Are there any unusual pets on your website?
3 Are there any funny photos?
4 Do the animals bite you?
5 What's your favourite photo?

Writing An animal fact sheet

Exercise 1
2 17 cm; 65 g
3 trees
4 plants and leaves
5 hide very well

Exercise 2
2 lives   6 white
3 garden   7 eyes
4 eats   8 sunny
5 apples   9 cats

Exercise 3
2 hutch
3 special guinea pig food; apples
4 brown and white
5 likes: sunny days; dislikes: cats

Exercise 4
Students' own answers

Unit 5 Out and About

Vocabulary Activities

Exercise 1
bowling; climbing; dancing; gymnastics; hiking; kayaking; painting; rollerblading; singing; surfing

Exercise 2
2 climbing   6 gymnastics
3 dancing   7 kayaking
4 surfing   8 hiking
5 bowling   9 singing

Exercise 3
1 ice-skating; c
2 pony trekking; a
3 playing the flute; d
4 mountain biking; b

Exercise 4
Students' own answers

Exercise 5
2 pony trekking
3 kayaking
4 dancing
5 ice-skating
6 painting
7 bowling
8 play an instrument

Exercise 6
Students' own answers

Reading

Exercise 1
2 e 3 a 4 b 5 c

Exercise 2
2 T 3 F 4 F 5 F 6 T

Exercise 3
2 hasn't got
3 hear
4 can't
5 jumps

Exercise 4
3

Grammar
Present continuous

Exercise 1
2 's/is jogging   5 's/is walking
3 are playing   6 's/is singing
4 are watching

Exercise 2
2 isn't/is not running
3 aren't/are not dancing
4 'm/am not taking

Exercise 3
2 isn't/is not swimming. He's/is surfing
3 isn't/is not dancing. She's/is doing gymnastics.
4 aren't/are not taking photos. They're/are painting.

Exercise 4
2 are swimming
3 'm/am not swimming
4 'm/am kayaking
5 's/is checking
6 's/is telling
7 're/are going
8 aren't/are not walking
9 're/are cycling

Present continuous: questions and short answers

Exercise 5
2 Am 3 Is 4 Are 5 Is

Exercise 6
2 d 3 a 4 e 5 c

Exercise 7
2 Are they surfing? Yes, they are.
3 Is she bowling? Yes, she is.
4 Is it running? No, it isn't.

Vocabulary
Weather and seasons

Exercise 1
2 winter
3 spring
4 autumn

Exercise 2
1 cold
2 warm
3 hot

Exercise 3
2 raining   5 windy
3 sunny   6 cloudy
4 snowing

Exercise 4
2 It's autumn. It's windy.
3 It's spring. It's raining.
4 It's summer. It's hot and sunny.

Exercise 5
Students' own answers

 Expressing surprise

Speaking and Listening

Exercise 1
Expresses surprise: 2; 4; 6
Doesn't express surprise: 3; 5

Exercise 2
Frank is surprised.
Wow!
How amazing!
Really?
Look!

Exercise 3
2 mobile phone
3 tennis
4 actress
5 autographs

Exercise 4
2 How amazing! Can you talk to him?
3 Look! There's a man juggling with six balls.
4 Wow! That's brilliant. Thank you so much.

Exercise 5
Students' own answers

Grammar
Present simple and Present continuous

Exercise 1
2 a / k 3 e / l 4 b / j 5 d / g 6 h / i

Exercise 2
Present simple
2 I work in the hospital.
3 I paint pictures of people.
4 I play songs on the radio every morning.
5 I usually work in the theatre.
6 I always get up early to feed the animals.

Present continuous
2 I'm/am looking after a sick baby.
3 I'm/am drawing a girl at the moment.
4 I'm/am interviewing Katy Perry for today's show.
5 I'm/am making a film in Hollywood at the moment.
6 I'm/am cleaning out the animal enclosure snow.

Exercise 3
2 works
3 gets up
4 cycles
5 start
6 's/is teaching
7 aren't/are not playing
8 's/is raining
9 're/are doing

Exercise 4
(Students' own answers to questions)
2 Is it raining at the moment?
3 Do you sometimes get up early?
4 Does your family usually watch TV in the evening?
5 Do you go to the cinema at the weekend?
6 Does your teacher give you homework every week?

Reading

Exercise 1
1 Thursday
2 Monday
3 Friday
4 Tuesday
5 Wednesday

Exercise 2
2 Grandad
3 Grandma
4 Her brothers
5 Mum

Exercise 3
2 He's/is making a shed.
3 Yes, they do.
4 They're/are having lunch next to the lake.
5 Grandad and Holly are sitting on the beach.
6 They're/are watching TV because it's raining.

Listening

Exercise 1
3 PE

Exercise 2
2 F 3 T 4 F 5 F 6 T

Writing A blog

Exercise 1
2 The races start at half past one.
3 Newton doesn't usually win the team competition.
4 Paul's/is not wearing a red shirt.
5 He's/is in the 100 metres race.

Exercise 2
2 F 3 T 4 T 5 F

Exercise 3
2 cloudy
3 six
4 Newton
5 yellow shirts
6 400 metres; high jump

Exercise 4
Students' own answers

Exercise 5
Students' own answers

Unit 6 Delicious

Vocabulary Food and drink

Exercise 1
2 f 3 a 4 b 5 d 6 c

Exercise 2
2 chicken; pasta; broccoli
3 salmon; vegetables; tea
4 sausages; eggs; bread
5 tuna sandwich; banana; juice
6 ham, cheese and tomato sandwich; water

Exercise 3
2 d 3 b 4 f 5 a 6 c

Exercise 4
2 broccoli   6 carbohydrates
3 yoghurt   7 pasta
4 meat   8 water
5 salmon

Exercise 5
Students' own answers

Reading

Exercise 1
2 England
3 Poland
4 England

Exercise 2
2 Polly 3 Ming 4 Ming 5 Aga 6 Polly

Exercise 3
2 On school days Polly drinks a glass of milk.
3 Aga sometimes has sausages for breakfast.
4 Aga is drinking a glass of juice today.
5 Ming always has a cooked breakfast.
6 Ming's favourite breakfast is rice with prawns.

Exercise 4
2 In the fridge.
3 At the supermarket.
4 From Poland.
5 Her mum.
6 Rice with fish or meat and vegetables.
7 Polly and Ming

Grammar
Countable and uncountable nouns

Exercise 1
2 C   3 U   4 U   5 C   6 U

Exercise 2
2 rice
3 fruit
4 music
5 money

Exercise 3
1 chicken, pasta; salmon; sausage; water; yoghurt
2 banana; potato

Exercise 4
2 some cheese
3 some tomatoes
4 a banana
5 an apple
6 some juice

Many/Much/A lot

Exercise 5
2 How much
3 How many
4 How many
5 How much
6 How many

Exercise 6
2 A lot of cheese
3 Not many apples
4 A lot of sandwiches
5 Not much water
6 Not many bananas

Exercise 7
2 He hasn't got much money.
3 She's got a lot of apples.
4 They've got a lot of DVDs.

Vocabulary Adjectives

Exercise 1
2 a   3 b   4 b   5 a   6 b

Exercise 2

```
N O I S Y D X G D Q
K H O R R I B L E D
W O N D E R F U L W
B T G R G T A I I L
N R D S E Y W E C A
T S I M A L Q Y I R
C L E A N H U A O G
O E I L H T I N U E
L N E L C N E R S A
D I S G U S T I N G
```

1b noisy
2a clean   b dirty
3a hot   b cold
4a small   b large
5a horrible   b wonderful
6a delicious   b disgusting

Exercise 3
2 delicious
3 large
4 noisy
5 clean

Exercise 4
2 Our classroom's cold.
3 The food at school is disgusting.
4 We're very quiet at lunchtime.
5 Science is a horrible subject.
6 The windows in our classroom are dirty.

Exercise 5
Students' own answers

Chatroom Ordering food
Speaking and Listening

Exercise 1
2 C   3 C   4 W   5 C

Exercise 2
1 c   2 b   3 a

Exercise 3
2 T   3 T   4 F   5 F   6 T

Exercise 4
2 I'd   5 have
3 OK   6 ice cream
4 drink

Exercise 5
Students' own answers

Grammar Comparatives

Exercise 1
2 cleaner   8 easier
3 hotter   9 funnier
5 larger   11 more delicious
6 whiter   12 more disgusting

Exercise 2
2 noisier   5 cheaper
3 more difficult   6 better
4 younger

Exercise 3
2 is quieter than
3 is easier to understand than
4 is older than
5 is more expensive than
6 are worse than

Exercise 4
2 taller   7 more difficult
3 bigger   8 faster
4 cleaner   9 more popular
5 tidier   10 noisier
6 better

Exercise 5
2 The green bag is smaller than the yellow bag. The yellow bag is larger than the green bag.
3 Sam's bike is newer than Tom's bike. Tom's bike is older than Sam's bike.
4 Jude's phone is noisier than Ella's phone. Ella's phone is quieter than Jude's phone.
5 Sam's T-shirt is dirtier than Dan's T-shirt. Dan's T-shirt is cleaner than Sam's T-shirt.

Reading

Exercise 1
2

Exercise 2
2 F   3 T   4 T   5 T

Exercise 3
2 It helps you to live a long and happy life.
3 *Jamie's Italian* restaurants
4 15
5 Yes, they do.

Listening

Exercise 1
1

Exercise 2
1 a   2 a   3 b   4 b   5 a

Exercise 3
1 10–12 years old
2 writers, pop stars, actors
3 Yes, he is.
4 potatoes
5 a chef

Writing Instructions

Exercise 1
1 2; 3; 1
2 Then, clean your teeth for two minutes.
3 Finally, wash your brush and put it back in the cup.
2 3; 1; 2
First, open a tin of dog food.
Then, put some food in the dog's bowl.
Finally, give the bowl to the dog.

Exercise 2
2 Add
3 Blend
4 Pour
5 Enjoy

Exercise 3
b

Exercise 4
1 three
2 Yes, there is.
3 chicken
4 the chicken
5 crisps

Exercise 5
Students' own answers

Check Your Progress 2

Grammar

Exercise 1
1 You mustn't walk on your own.
2 You must take food and water.
3 You mustn't go in foggy weather.
4 You must take a map.

Exercise 2
1 Are; wearing
2 do; get up
3 does; finish
4 Is; doing
5 aren't/are not playing
6 'm/am watching

Exercise 3
1 aren't many
2 isn't much
3 aren't many
4 is
5 isn't much

Exercise 4
1 never goes climbing
2 always go rollerblading
3 usually plays the guitar
4 hardly ever goes mountain biking
5 sometimes go ice-skating

Vocabulary

Exercise 5
1 tarantula; bird
2 parrot; frog
3 python; lizard
4 piranha; stick insect
5 pygmy goat; giant rabbit

Exercise 6
1 chicken and ham
2 tuna and prawn
3 cheese and tomato
4 salmon and broccoli
5 sausage and egg

Speaking

Exercise 7
1 d 2 f 3 a 4 e 5 b

Exercise 8
1 I'll have
2 I'd like
3 Would you like anything
4 Can I have
5 I'd like

Translation

Exercise 9
Students' own answers

Dictation

Exercise 10
1 I often go to the zoo because I love animals but I haven't got a pet.
2 It's a large zoo and there are a lot of different animals to visit.
3 There's a wonderful parrot in the bird house.
4 It's got a red head, a grey beak and its wings are green.
5 It likes people and it's popular with children because it's very noisy.

Unit 7 Modern History

Vocabulary
Ordinal numbers, years, dates

Exercise 1
2 second
3 third
4 fourth
5 fifth
6 sixth
7 seventh

Exercise 2
2 9th June
3 17th July
4 22nd November
5 3rd March 1932
6 15th October 2010

Exercise 3
2 2nd April 1966
3 29th February 2012
4 10th December 1911
5 4th September 1944
6 25th August 1997

Exercise 4
2 27/9/2011
3 4/2/1916
4 18/10/1984
5 20/4/2001
6 13/1/1957

Exercise 5
2 seventeenth August two thousand and eight
3 twenty-first July nineteen sixty-nine
4 sixth May nineteen ninety-four
5 fourteenth December nineteen eleven
6 ninth March nineteen fifty-nine

Reading

Exercise 1
3

Exercise 2
1 b 2 e 3 d 4 c 5 a

Exercise 3
2 a 3 f 4 c 5 b 6 e

Exercise 4
2 8th September 1940
3 There were 15 planes.
4 Because it was scary.
5 There wasn't any meat and the vegetables were old.
6 Because Alice's dad is coming home.

Grammar Past simple: to be

Exercise 1
2 was
3 were
4 was
5 was
6 were

Exercise 2
2 My mum wasn't at work.
3 Was your dad at home?
4 We weren't in the class.
5 Was your favourite programme on TV?
6 I was at the swimming pool.
7 There wasn't much food in the fridge.
8 Were there any children in the park?

Exercise 3
2 were
3 weren't
4 was
5 was
6 weren't
7 was
8 wasn't
9 was
10 were
11 was

There was/There were

Exercise 4
2 were
3 was
4 wasn't

Exercise 5
2 Was there
3 Were there
4 Were there
5 Was there
(Students' own answers to questions)

Exercise 6
2 There weren't any boys in the café. There were some girls.
3 There wasn't a post office here two years ago. There was a police station.
4 There wasn't a cat in the garden ten minutes ago. There was a dog.

Vocabulary Regular verbs

Exercise 1
2 e 3 b 4 f 5 a 6 d

Exercise 2

C	L	O	S	E	F	G
K	A	L	T	M	N	D
A	S	L	O	I	Z	O
B	K	A	P	N	I	U
X	T	R	A	V	E	L
L	I	S	T	E	N	P
W	R	T	C	N	L	S
G	R	E	W	T	O	E

Exercise 3
2 /t/ 3 /ɪd/ 4 /t/ 5 /d/ 6 /d/

Exercise 4
2 listened
3 travelled
4 closed
5 asked
6 stopped

Exercise 5
2 b   3 a   4 f   5 c   6 e

Exercise 6
2 phoned
3 talk
4 asked
5 answer
6 close
7 listen
8 studying
9 like
10 stop

 **Talking about the past**

Speaking and Listening

Exercise 1
yesterday; in the 1980s; half an hour ago; last week

Exercise 2
2 ET was popular in the 1980s.
3 The film started half an hour ago.
4 The film was on last week.

Exercise 3
2 three weeks
3 for two hours
4 afternoon

Exercise 4
2 f   3 b   4 e   5 a   6 d

Exercise 5
Students' own answers

Grammar

Past simple regular: affirmative and negative

Exercise 1
2 Present simple
3 Present simple
4 Past simple
5 Past simple
6 Past simple

Exercise 2
2 travelled; didn't travel
3 danced; didn't dance
4 jumped; didn't jump
5 started; didn't start
6 tidied; didn't tidy

Exercise 3
2 didn't listen
3 travelled
4 didn't cook
5 played
6 visited

Exercise 4
2 In PE, they played football.
3 In Science, they studied plants.
4 in History, he studied the kings and queens.
5 in Geography, she started a weather project.
6 In Music, they listened to jazz music.

Exercise 5
2 She climbed trees.
3 She didn't study French.
4 She watched cartoons.
5 She didn't travel to Greece.
6 She listened to Madonna.
7 She didn't tidy her room.

Reading

Exercise 1
1 c   2 b   3 a

Exercise 2
1 b/2   2 a/3   3 c/1

Exercise 3
1 c   2 e   3 a   4 f   5 b   6 d

Exercise 4
2 29th May 1953
3 £2.6 million
4 In prison.
5 Westminster Abbey/In London.
6 Thousands.

Listening

Exercise 1
1

Exercise 2
2 She was at home with her family.
3 She was five.
4 Toby was in London.
5 He was with his friends.
6 The fireworks were over the River Thames.

Writing   An essay

Exercise 1
2 I was born on the 14th January, 1999.
3 My grandparents came from Lamia, a small town in Greece.
4 Were your parents at school together?
5 My grandparents, aunts, uncles and cousins all lived in that house.

Exercise 2
2 d   3 e   4 a   5 b

Exercise 3
2 Bonnie's mum was born in London. Her dad was born in Poland.
3 Her mum moved to Oxford.
4 Her parents met at a party.
5 Her mum's family come from the city.
6 Her dad's family is Polish.

Exercise 4
Students' own answers

Exercise 5
Students' own answers

Unit 8   Journeys

Vocabulary
Means of transport

Exercise 1
2 bus   3 tube   4 car   5 bike   6 scooter

Exercise 2
Across
5 motorbike
7 coach

Down
1 lorry
2 plane
4 canoe
6 boat

Exercise 3
1 canoe
2 motorbike; scooter
3 plane; helicopter
4 bus; coach
5 car; van

Exercise 4
2 ride   3 takes   4 sails   5 flies

Exercise 5
2 a   3 a   4 b   5 c   6 b   7 a

Reading

Exercise 1
a3; b1; c2

Exercise 2
2 Mark
3 Sarah
4 Sarah
5 Charlie
6 Mark

Exercise 3
2 T   3 F   4 T   5 F   6 T

Exercise 4
2 194 days and 17 hours.
3 In California.
4 16 years old.
5 17 years old.
6 Win the Le Mans car race.

Grammar

Past simple irregular: affirmative and negative

Exercise 1
2 thought
3 took
4 got
5 bought
6 understood
7 had
8 did

Exercise 2
2 didn't go
3 didn't ride
4 didn't eat
5 didn't drive
6 didn't do

Exercise 3
2 takes; took   5 saw; sees
3 went; go   6 drink; drank
4 have; had

Exercise 4
2 They didn't buy an old white van.
3 My dad didn't give me £5.
4 I didn't think about our visit to London.
5 She didn't eat a pizza for lunch.

Exercise 5
2 I met my friend at the bus stop.
3 My friend gave me her old magazine.
4 Mum bought a new camera.
5 Dad got a new bike last week.
6 They had lunch in a café.

Exercise 6
2 took   9 had
3 didn't get   10 went
4 spent   11 were
5 saw   12 didn't like
6 didn't see   13 thought
7 was   14 bought
8 didn't have   15 had

Vocabulary Clothes

Exercise 1
2 hat   5 skirt
3 pyjamas   6 trousers
4 scarf   7 shoes

Exercise 2
2 d Sam   3 a Robin   4 b Alex

Exercise 3
1 sandals
2 jeans; jumper
3 coat; boots
4 shorts; T-shirt
Students' own answers

Exercise 4
2 coat   3 shoes   4 skirt   5 jeans
6 pyjamas

Exercise 5
Students' own answers

 Talking on the phone

Speaking and Listening

Exercise 1
2 d   3 e   4 a   5 f   6 b

Exercise 2
Missing phrases: Hold on; Who's that?

Exercise 3
2 Frank's dad.
3 Frank
4 She had a piano lesson.
5 Because Mrs Woods gave the books back.
6 To Beth's house.

Exercise 4
2 Sally
3 fine
4 swimming pool
5 two o'clock

Exercise 5
Students' own answers

Grammar
Past simple: questions

Exercise 1
2 she did   5 it didn't
3 he did   6 we did
4 they didn't

Exercise 2
2 did; go   5 did; finish
3 did; see   6 did; get
4 Did; enjoy

Exercise 3
2 Who did he meet?
3 When did they arrive?
4 What did she wear?
5 Where did you go?
6 How did you get there?

Exercise 4
2 did they go on Monday?
3 did they eat in the evening?
4 did they travel to Cordoba?
5 did Ben see at the station?

Exercise 5
2 d   3 e   4 b   5 a

Exercise 6
2 Yes, she did.
3 Did she lose her bag? No, she didn't.
4 What did she buy? She bought clothes.
5 Did it rain? No, it didn't.

Reading

Exercise 1
boat, train, bus, tube, plane, car, motorbike, helicopter, coach

Exercise 2
1 a   2 c   3 b   4 a   5 b   6 c

Exercise 3
Students' own answers

Exercise 4
2 1863
3 From London to Bahrain.
4 More than 30 metres.
5 a motorbike
6 It started in Paris and finished in Istanbul.

Listening

Exercise 1
1

Exercise 2
2 F   3 F   4 T   5 F

Exercise 3
2 It's a long way.
3 It's five hours.
4 There are three changes and they always have heavy bags.
5 Coaches make Paul sick.
6 Stay at home.

Writing A travel diary

Exercise 1
2

Exercise 2
1 B   2 C   3 A

Exercise 3
2 It started today, at half past eight.
3 They travelled by coach.
4 They arrived at half past two.
5 They walked around the lake.
6 They watched a film.
7 Patsy and Rosa are sleeping in the same room as Karen.

Exercise 4
Students' own answers

Exercise 5
Students' own answers

Unit 9 Technology Time

Vocabulary Technology

Exercise 1
2 netbook
3 screen
4 smartphone
5 memory stick
6 interactive whiteboard
7 ebook

Exercise 2
2 memory stick
3 interactive whiteboard
4 ebook
5 screen
6 netbook
7 smartphone

Exercise 3
2 broadband
3 WiFi
4 social networking sites
5 instant messaging

Exercise 4
2 a   3 c   4 b   5 b   6 a

Exercise 5
Students' own answers

Reading

Exercise 1
1 b   2 c   3 a

Exercise 2
1 ebook
2 digital radio
3 netbook

Exercise 3
2 A   3 C   4 C   5 S   6 A

Exercise 4
1 3,500
2 £105
3 25cm
4 £265
5 Next to your bed.
6 three

Grammar *Be going to*

Exercise 1
2 I'm going to
3 going to; he is
4 Are you; I'm not
5 It isn't
6 We're going to phone

Exercise 2
2 'm/am going to buy
3 's/is going to wear
4 's/is not going to play
5 're/are not going to go
6 're/are going to visit

Exercise 3
2 is going to stop
3 aren't going to play
4 isn't going to buy
5 is going to wear

Exercise 4
2 Is; Yes, she is.
3 Are; No, they aren't.
4 Is; No, he isn't.
5 Is; Yes, he is.
6 Is; Yes, it is.

Exercise 5
Students' own answers

Vocabulary

Technology phrases

Exercise 1
2 a phone
3 videos and films
4 a blog
5 online
6 emails
7 WiFi

Exercise 2
2 use a search engine
3 chat online
4 charge a phone
5 write a blog
6 download music

Exercise 3
2 chatting online
3 writing a blog
4 sending a text
5 charging her phone

Exercise 4
2 broadband
3 goes
4 chatting
5 smartphone
6 uses
7 download
8 charging

Exercise 5
2 charge   e
3 send   d
4 downloading   a
5 chat   c

Chatroom — Asking for information

Speaking and Listening

Exercise 1
2 d   3 a   4 c

Exercise 2
2 Why not; What happened?
3 What are you doing this year?
4 Tell me about it.
5 What are you planning for next year?

Exercise 3
2 Miss Laws, the drama teacher was away sick that term.
3 A musical.

Exercise 4
2 What did you do?
3 What happened?
4 What are you planning for the weekend?

Exercise 5
Students' own answers

Grammar

Present continuous for future arrangements

Exercise 1
2 's staying
3 're visiting
4 is he wearing
5 'm not coming
6 Is the train leaving

Exercise 2
2 isn't/is not closing
3 'm/am going
4 're/are flying
5 A Are; wearing
  B 'm/am not
6 're/are not playing
7 'm/am not going shopping
8 A Is; having
  B is

Exercise 3
2 is she meeting Sam
3 is she watching on Wednesday
4 is she going on Thursday
5 is she playing basketball on Friday
6 is she buying a present for on Saturday

Exercise 4
2 She's/is meeting Sam, at 4.30.
3 She's/is watching the school play.
4 She's/is going to the doctor's.
5 She's/is playing basketball at 5.15.
6 She's/is buying a present for Luke.

Exercise 5
2 Nick's/is pony trekking in the mountains.
3 Nick's/is surfing at the beach.
4 Nick's/is visiting a museum in London.
5 Nick's/is going to a concert in the park.

Reading

Exercise 1
3

Exercise 2
2 USA 1973
3 Japan 1979
4 Finland 1993

Exercise 3
2 Because there weren't any networks.
3 85%
4 half – 50%
5 You can watch films, send emails and play games.
6 They're going to get thinner and smarter.

Listening

Exercise 1
2 IWB
3 novels
4 WWW
5 MySpace and Facebook
6 solar power

Exercise 2
2 interactive whiteboard
3 ebooks
4 World Wide Web
5 social networking sites
6 the sun

Writing *A story*

Exercise 1
2 commas
3 because
4 paragraphs
5 group

Exercise 2

Last week I dropped my mobile phone on the way to school. I looked everywhere for it, but I didn't find it. My mum was very angry with me when I got home.

Yesterday a strange thing happened. My friends got a text from Wayne Rooney. He's my favourite football player and he found my phone!

I'm so happy today. I've got my phone back and Wayne sent me two tickets for the next Manchester United match! I'm going to watch them play Arsenal next month with my dad. Can you believe it?

Dilor

Exercise 3
2 T 3 F 4 T 5 T

Exercise 4
2 His mum was angry because he lost his phone.
3 Wayne Rooney sent a text to Dilor's friends.
4 Wayne sent Dilor two tickets.
5 Manchester United are going to play Arsenal next month.

Exercise 5
Students' own answers

Exercise 6
Students' own answers

Check Your Progress 3

Grammar

Exercise 1
1 went	6 had
2 got	7 watched
3 arrived	8 was
4 visited	9 came
5 didn't go	10 didn't go

Exercise 2
1 Did they have lunch outside? Yes, they did.
2 Did they wear coats? No, they didn't.
3 Did Rachel's mum take any photos? Yes, she did.
4 Were there any cars in the park? No, there weren't.
5 Were there many people in the park? Yes, there were.

Exercise 3
1 They aren't going to buy a netbook. They're going to buy a digital radio.
2 I'm not going to travel by train. I'm going to travel by coach.
3 We aren't going to wear sandals. We're going to wear trainers.
4 He isn't going to download music. He's going to download a film.

Exercise 4
1 On Tuesday, he's visiting his grandad after school.
2 On Wednesday he's going to the doctor's.
3 On Thursday, he's having an extra English lesson at lunchtime.
4 On Friday evening, he's watching the World cup at George's house.
5 On Saturday, he's playing in a football match against Charlton.

Vocabulary

Exercise 5
1 scooter 2002	4 lorry 2011
2 car 2004	5 coach 2012
3 van 2007	

Exercise 6
1 blog / c	4 helicopter / b
2 trainers / e	5 second / a
3 sail / d	

Speaking

Exercise 7
1 c 2 b 3 c 4 a 5 b

Translation

Exercise 8
Students' own answers

Dictation

Exercise 9
1 Yesterday I stayed at my friend's house and we had a great time.
2 First, we spent an hour on a social networking site.
3 Then we downloaded a film from the internet.
4 I took lots of chocolate and sweets and we ate them while we watched the film.
5 After the film we brushed our teeth and got ready for bed.

Grammar Reference 1

Have got

Exercise 1
2 She has not got a camera.
3 We have not got a big house.
4 He has got a collection of Bruce Willis posters.
5 They have got a lot of magazines.
6 The classroom has got white walls.

Exercise 2
2 's got	5 's got
3 's got	6 's got
4 've got	

Exercise 3
2 Maria and Julia have got a magazine. They haven't got a book.
3 Mohammed hasn't got a football. He's got a skateboard.
4 Ben and Leo have got drinks. They haven't got food.

Possessive adjectives

Exercise 4
2 Have you got a new CD? Yes, I have.
3 Have the fans got cameras? No, they haven't.
4 Has the girl got an autograph book? Yes, she has.
5 Have we got tickets for the concert? Yes, we have.

Possessive 's

Exercise 5
2 John's 3 cousins' 4 Mr Black's 5 dog's

Grammar Reference 2

There is/There are; some/any

Exercise 1
1 a 2 c 3 d

2 There is	6 there aren't
3 there aren't	7 there are
4 there are	8 There is
5 There are	9 There isn't

Exercise 2
2 books
3 magazines
4 computer
5 interactive whiteboard

Exercise 3
2 No, there isn't.
3 Yes, there are.
4 No, there aren't.

Exercise 4
2 There isn't a museum in my town.
3 There is a library in my school.
4 There aren't any pets in my house.
5 There isn't a desk in my bedroom.

Exercise 5
2 Ben 3 Andrew 4 Charlie

Exercise 6
2 Andrew 3 Charlie 4 Ben 5 cycle

Exercise 7
Students' own answers

Grammar Reference 3

Present simple: affirmative and negative

Exercise 1
2 play tennis
3 does her homework
4 watches TV
5 meet my friends

Exercise 2
2 learn	5 doesn't speak
3 speak	6 don't speak
4 comes	7 speak

Exercise 3
2 He doesn't have breakfast with his dad. He has breakfast with his mum.
3 He doesn't cycle to school. He walks to school.
4 Lessons don't start at ten o'clock. They start at nine o'clock.

Exercise 4
Students' own answers

Present simple: questions and short answers

Exercise 5
2 Do Mimi and Noah meet their friends after school?
3 Do they have Science on Thursdays?
4 Does he tidy his bedroom at the weekend?
5 Does your sister go to bed before you?

Exercise 6
2 Do students study ICT at your school?
3 Does your school day start at 8.00 a.m.?
4 Do you wear a uniform?
(Students' own answers to questions)

Grammar Reference 4

Adverbs of frequency

Exercise 1
2 Will 3 Zoe 4 Luke 5 Will 6 Luke

Exercise 2
2 They often go horse riding.
3 Luke never plays with the cat.
4 Will sometimes cleans out the rabbits.
5 Zoe and Will always take the dog for a walk.

Present simple with *wh-* questions

Exercise 3
Who, Where, When, What, How, Why
Students' own answers

Exercise 4
2 a / does 5 c / are
3 d / do 6 b / is
4 e / isn't

Must/Mustn't

Exercise 5
2 tidy my room; jump on my bed
3 listen to the teacher; eat in class
4 shut the gates; hurt the animals

Exercise 6
2 You must wear warm clothes.
3 You mustn't walk in the mountains.
4 You mustn't stand under a tree.

Grammar Reference 5

Present continuous

Exercise 1

+ -ing	e + -ing	x2 + -ing
drinking	having	getting
going	making	running
jumping	taking	swimming
watching	writing	sitting

Exercise 2
2 's/is taking 5 are eating
3 's/is driving 6 'm/am talking
4 are wearing

Exercise 3
2 'm/am not reading 5 'm/am doing
3 'm/am looking for 6 're/are learning
4 are you doing 7 'm/am writing

Exercise 4
2 is your family going; a
3 are you sitting; e
4 are they opening; c
5 are we arriving; b

Present simple and Present continuous

Exercise 5
2 The children usually go kayaking.
3 She isn't swimming at the Sports Centre at the moment.
4 I'm taking the dog for a walk today.
5 You don't often sing in the bath.

Exercise 6
2 goes 5 Does she swim
3 Is it raining 6 are we waiting
4 don't get up

Grammar Reference 6

Countable and uncountable nouns

Exercise 1
2 U 3 C 4 C 5 U 7 C 8 U
9 U 10 C

Exercise 2
2 How many 5 How many
3 How much 6 How much
4 How many

Exercise 3
Possible answers
2 There aren't many sandwiches.
3 There's a lot of fruit.
4 There are a lot of sausages.
5 There isn't much juice.
6 There's a lot of crisps.

Comparatives

Exercise 4
2 e happier; happy
3 a more interesting; interesting
4 b taller; tall
5 d nicer; nice

Exercise 5
2 is hotter than the cup of coffee in A.
3 is thinner than the woman in A.
4 is bigger than the salad in A.
5 is dirtier than the boy in A.

Grammar Reference 7

Past simple: *to be*

Exercise 1
2 weren't 8 wasn't
3 wasn't 9 Were
4 was 10 weren't
5 was 11 was
6 was 12 were
7 was 13 was

There was/There were

Exercise 2
2 There were some bananas.
3 There wasn't any chocolate.
4 There was a magazine.
5 There was some water.

Exercise 3
2 Were there any DVDs? No, there weren't.
3 Were there any books or magazines? Yes, there were.
4 Was there a game console? No, there wasn't.

Past simple: regular affirmative and negative

Exercise 4

+ -ed	x2 + -ed	+ -d	-y + -ied
cooked	stopped	closed	studied
listened	dropped	danced	carried
started	travelled	liked	tidied

Exercise 5
2 studied; didn't study
3 didn't stop; stopped

Grammar Reference 8

Past simple: irregular affirmative and negative

Exercise 1
2 got up
3 had
4 went
5 drank

Exercise 2
2 took 8 ate
3 put 9 made
4 drove 10 was
5 read 11 were
6 told 12 arrived
7 had

Exercise 3
2 He didn't eat the ice cream.
3 There weren't any boats.
4 They didn't play beach volleyball.
5 The children didn't make sandcastles.

Exercise 4
2 Paul didn't see a dolphin. He saw a big fish.
3 I didn't swim in the swimming pool. I swam in the sea.
4 Martha didn't ride on a pony. She rode on a donkey.
5 The family didn't have fish for dinner. They had pizza.

Past simple: questions

Exercise 5
2 b   3 b   4 b   5 a

Exercise 6
2 How did you travel?
  I travelled by train.
3 When did you arrive?
  We arrived on 17th August.
4 Who did you go with?
  I went with my family.

Grammar Reference 9

Be going to

Exercise 1
2 They're/are going to play computer games.
3 I'm/am going to read my ebook.
4 He's/is going to charge his phone.
5 She's/is going to send.

Exercise 2
2 is going to sing
3 isn't going to start
4 isn't going to be
5 are going to be
6 are going to go
7 is going to take
8 are going to put

Exercise 3
2 Is she going to go to the bank?
3 Are you going to go to the post office?
4 Is he going to go to the train station?
5 Are they going to go to the supermarket?

Present continuous for future arrangements

Exercise 4
3, 4

Exercise 5
2 aren't/are not flying
3 're/are watching
4 isn't/is not playing
5 'm/am meeting
6 's/is staying

Exercise 6
2 's/is he going
3 are they coming back
4 's/is she wearing
5 Are you watching TV
6 are they doing

Vocabulary 1

Exercise 3
2 keys
3 clock
4 hairbrush
5 cycle helmet

Vocabulary 2

Exercise 3
2 theatre
3 restaurant
4 art gallery
5 supermarket

Vocabulary 3

Exercise 3
2 bell
3 textbook
4 pencil case
5 lunch box

Vocabulary 4

Exercise 3
2 eagle   3 turtle   4 ladybird   5 squirrel

Vocabulary 5

Exercise 3
2 flood   3 rainbow   4 lightning   5 ice

Vocabulary 6

Exercise 3
2 carrots   3 peas   4 cherries   5 cauliflower

Vocabulary 7

Exercise 3
2 help   3 wash up   4 sweep   5 opening

Vocabulary 8

Exercise 3
2 slippers   3 socks   4 jacket   5 gloves

Vocabulary 9

Exercise 3
2 mouse mat
3 printer
4 keyboard
5 document

Speaking and Listening 1

Talking about position
Speaking

Exercise 1
2 on
3 next to
4 in
5 under
6 behind
7 in front of

Exercise 2
2 desk
3 next to
4 in
5 isn't
6 hasn't
7 front
8 where

Listening

Exercise 3
2, 5, 6, 8, 9

Exercise 4
2 school books
3 football boots
4 MP3 player
5 mobile phone

Speaking and Listening 2

Orders and warnings
Speaking

Exercise 1
2 Wait for me!
3 Don't touch it!
4 Stop!
5 Be careful!
6 Watch me!

Exercise 2
2 Go
3 don't
4 Let's
5 Phone
6 Have
7 enjoy
8 do

Listening

Exercise 3
2 objects
3 group
4 outside
5 half past twelve
6 boots

Exercise 4
2 F   3 T   4 F   5 T

Speaking and Listening 3

Time
Speaking

Exercise 1
2 ten past three
3 9 o'clock
4 seven thirty; seven forty five

Exercise 2
2 o'clock
3 past
4 I know
5 What
6 twelve
7 time
8 half

Listening

Exercise 3
2 6.15 3 7.30 4 9.10 5 5.20 6 7.05

Exercise 4
2 Yes, it is.
3 No, she hasn't.
4 Thirty minutes.
5 Yes, she does.

Speaking and Listening 4

Likes and dislikes

Speaking

Exercise 1
(correct answers)
2 a 3 a 4 b 5 b

Exercise 2
2 Do
3 watching
4 hate
5 I
6 rabbits
7 likes
8 don't

Listening

Exercise 3
2 F 3 T 4 T 5 F

Exercise 4
2 He doesn't like listening to bad music.
3 No, she doesn't.
4 *Springwatch*
5 He likes learning about birds and animals.

Speaking and Listening 5

Expressing surprise

Speaking

Exercise 1
2 c 3 a 4 d 5 b

Exercise 2
2 Wow!
3 Look!
4 statue
5 Really?
6 cool

Listening

Exercise 3
2 T 3 F 4 F 5 F

Exercise 4
2 It's his birthday.
3 A skateboard and a book.
4 This evening.
5 On Radio 5.

Speaking and Listening 6

Ordering food

Speaking

Exercise 1
2 c 3 a 4 e 5 b

Exercise 2
2 ready
3 I'll
4 anything
5 glass
6 Would
7 OK
8 like

Listening

Exercise 3
2 the menus
3 chicken
4 apple juice
5 a restaurant

Exercise 4
Customer 1: chicken
Customer 2: salmon, apple juice
Customer 3: pizza

Speaking and Listening 7

Talking about the past

Speaking

Exercise 1
2 yesterday
3 morning
4 minutes ago
5 the 1970s
6 seven years

Exercise 2
2 didn't
3 1980s
4 twenty
5 ago
6 yesterday
7 last

Listening

Exercise 3
2 F 3 F 4 T 5 F 6 T

Exercise 4
2 Two years ago.
3 1966
4 For two months.
5 Music from the 1960s.

Speaking and Listening 8

Taking on the phone

Speaking

Exercise 1
2 Who's that?
3 Is Justin there, please?
4 Just a minute.

Exercise 2
2 This is
3 speak
4 Here
5 thanks
6 just
7 later

Listening

Exercise 3
2 Can I speak to Eve, please?
3 Who is it, please?
4 Hold on.
5 Can you speak up, please?

Exercise 4
2 Yes, she did.
3 To the lake.
4 27th July
5 Yes, he can.

Speaking and Listening 9

Asking for information

Speaking

Exercise 1
2 a 3 b 4 e 5 c

Exercise 2
2 saw
3 Tell
4 bank
5 car
6 happened
7 more
8 going

Listening

Exercise 3
2 F 3 F 4 F 5 T

Exercise 4
2 No, it was Ana's dog.
3 No, he didn't.
4 No, it's dirty.
5 He's going to watch TV.

Pronunciation Reference

Unit 1 Short forms

Exercise 2
1 b 2 a 3 a 4 b

Unit 2 Silent letters

Exercise 2
1 walk   4 climb
2 know   5 guitar
3 talk

Unit 3 -s endings

Exercise 2

/s/	/z/	/ɪz/
jumps walks	flies runs	dances washes

Unit 4 Sentence stress

Exercise 2
1 A I can't swim.
  B No, but you can skate. I can't.
2 A Jess likes playing football.
  B Does she? I don't. I like playing basketball.
3 Peter likes watching films. But Derek likes playing computer games.
4 I've got a new watch.
5 A There's a cat in the garden.
  B No, there isn't. That's our dog!
6 I hate studying at the weekend.

Unit 5 -ing endings

Exercise 2
1 skating   4 sing
2 raining   5 cleaning
3 tidy   6 starting

Unit 6 Word stress

Exercise 2
1 yoghurt   6 tomato
2 carrot   7 tuna
3 broccoli   8 banana
4 dairy   9 salmon
5 water   10 pasta

Unit 7 -ed endings

Exercise 2

/d/	/ɪd/	/t/
opened phoned	started wanted	liked watched

Unit 8 Sounding polite

Exercise 1
Conversation 2 sounds more polite.

Exercise 2
1a NP 2a P 3a P 4a NP
1b P 2b NP 3b NP 4b P

Unit 9 Weak form of to

Exercise 2
Sentences 1, 2 ,4 and 6 have the weak form of to.

Pearson Education Limited,
Edinburgh Gate, Harlow
Essex, CM20 2JE, England
and Associated Companies throughout the world

www.pearsonelt.com

Seventh impression 2020

First published 2013
ISBN 978-14479-4356-3
Set in 9.5/11.5pt LTC Helvetica Neue Light
Printed by CPI UK

Teacher's Book illustrated by Katie Frost
Cover image: *Front:* **Corbis:** Mike Powell